Parallel Computing

Methods, Algorithms and Applications

Parallel Computing
Methods, Algorithms and Applications
Proceedings of the International Meeting on Parallel Computing,
Verona, Italy, 28–30 September 1988

Edited by

David J Evans

Loughborough University of Technology, UK

and

C Sutti

University of Verona, Italy

Adam Hilger, Bristol and New York

British Library Cataloguing in Publication Data

International Meeting on Parallel Computing (1988:
 Verona Italy)
 Parallel computing : methods, algorithms and
 applications : proceedings of the International
 Meeting on Parallel Computing, Verona, Italy, Sept.
 28th–30th, 1988.
 1. Computer systems. Parallel programming
 I. Title   II. Evans, D. J. (David John), 1928–
 III. Sutti, C.
 004'.35

 ISBN 0-85274-224-X

Library of Congress Cataloging-in-Publication Data are available

Honorary Editors
        D J Evans and C Sutti

First printed 1989
Reprinted 1990

Published under the Adam Hilger imprint by IOP Publishing Ltd
Techno House, Redcliffe Way, Bristol BS1 6NX, England
335 East 45th Street, New York, NY 10017-3483, USA

Printed in Great Britain by J W Arrowsmith Ltd, Bristol

Contents

Preface   ix

List of Contributors   xi

Chapter 1: Parallel Computation

Parallel algorithm design   1
D J Evans

Parallel computing and special applications   25
U Schendel

Chapter 2: Parallel Programming and Software

Graphics tools for developing high-performance algorithms   39
O Brewer, J Dongarra, D Levine and D Sorensen

Multitasking directives for FORTRAN: a generic alternative to parallel
FORTRAN   51
C Arnold, B Brode and J Blair

Chapter 3: Parallel Algorithms for Linear and Non-linear Equations

Parallel iterative methods for solving large sparse sets of linear equations   61
L C W Dixon

Parallel algorithms for sparse matrix solution   73
I S Duff

Vectorizing the modified Huang algorithm of the ABS class on the
IBM 3090 VF   83
M Bertocchi and E Spedicato

Householder factorization on distributed architectures   91
M Cosnard and E M Daoudi

Vectorized ILU preconditioners for general sparsity patterns   103
S Filippone and G Radicati di Brozolo

Complexity of parallel polynomial computations   115
D Bini

Substructure technique for parallel solution of linear systems in finite
element analyses   127
L Brusa and F Riccio

Chapter 4: Parallel Methods for Ordinary and Partial Differential Equations

The arithmetic mean method for solving large systems of linear
ordinary differential equations on a vector computer   143
I Galligani and V Ruggiero

Parallelism in a highly accurate algorithm for turbulence simulation   157
C Canuto and C Giberti

Vector and parallel implementation of a 2-D fluid-dynamics code for
inertial confinement fusion on an IBM 3090-VF vector multiprocessor   169
S Atzeni

Iteration-by-subdomain algorithms for systems of hyperbolic equations 181
A Quarteroni

A parallel algorithm for a three dimensional inverse acoustic
scattering problem   193
F Aluffi-Pentini, E Caglioti, L Misici and F Zirilli

Chapter 5: Parallel Algorithms for Linear and Non-linear Optimization

Nonlinear optimization codes for real time solution of large scale
problems: a case study on the parallel vector supercomputers
CRAY X-MP and IBM 3090/VF   201
D Conforti and L Grandinetti

Vector and parallel performances of minimization algorithms based on
homogeneous models   213
A Peretti and C Sutti

Vector and parallel processing applications of nonlinear optimization
algorithms: design problems, experimental results   225
G Patrizi and C Spera

Chapter 6: Parallel Computer Applications

Toeplitz matrices, homothety and least squares approximation   237
F Sloboda

Parallel processing of programs coupling symbolic and numerical
computations   249
J S Kowalik

An expert system for numerical optimization: parallel computation   257
J J McKeown

Applications of highly parallel processors   269
H M Liddell

Panel Session

Supercomputing in industry and research institutions: status and
perspectives   281
Chairman: J S Kowalik; Vice-Chairman: C Sutti

Author Index   283

Keyword Index   285

Preface

The International Meeting on Parallel Computing: Methods, Algorithms and Applications was held in Verona, Italy on 28–30 September 1988.

It is our great pleasure to thank the following organizations who were sponsors for the meeting:

Consiglio Nazionale delle Ricerche
Università degli Studi di Verona
Università della Calabria (CS)
Consorzio Universitario Veronese

Alliant Comp.Sys.France SA
Cineca (Italy)
CISE Tecn.Innovative SpA
Control Data Italia SpA
ENEA (Italy)
IBM Italia SpA
Siemens Data SpA (Italy)

Banca Agricola Mantovana
Banca Popolare di Verona
Cassa di Risparmio di Verona, VI, BL
Società Cattolica di Assicurazione

The purpose of the meeting was to focus attention and bring together researchers in the various areas of computer science, mathematics and engineering which contribute to the usage, development and design of supercomputers and parallel computers and their relevant application algorithms.

These proceedings contain all the papers presented at the meeting and are grouped into six chapters: parallel computation, parallel programming and software, parallel algorithms for linear and non-linear equations, parallel methods for ordinary and partial differential equations, parallel algorithms for linear and non-linear optimization and parallel computer applications.

The papers in Chapter 1 contain some of the basic principles of parallel algorithms and their design and their adaptation for, or mapping on, specific parallel architectures.

Since algorithms for parallel and supercomputer software systems are designed for high performance then it is important that appropriate methods and software tools exist for evaluating their performance. This issue is discussed in the papers presented in Chapter 2.

As a large majority of scientific and engineering problems which are solved on computers result in large-scale linear or non-linear systems then it is only appropriate that parallel algorithms for these topics are discussed in detail in Chapter 3.

Chapter 4 discusses another important class of problems which result in differential equations that are compute intensive and which arise in the scientific research now being solved on supercomputers. Hitherto such problems could not be considered seriously or viable due to lack of computing power and computer storage. It is in these areas that the important advancements in science are expected to occur in the future.

Further, it is only fitting that Chapter 5 discusses the new parallel and super-computer algorithms for linear and non-linear optimizations which are the topics for which the university research groups in Verona, Cosenza, Rome and Bergamo have a long and distinguished record.

The final chapter introduces parallel applications to a more wider range of subject areas which are likely to expand rapidly as the usage of parallel computers develops in the future.

Finally, a summary of the vigorous panel discussion session on supercomputing in industry and research institutions completes the proceedings.

The organizers of the meeting:

L C W Dixon, *Hatfield Polytechnic, UK*
D J Evans, *Loughborough University, UK*
I Galligani, *Università di Bologna, Italy*
L Grandinetti, *Università della Calabria, Cosenza, Italy*
A Mathis, *ENEA, Italy*
C Sutti, *Università di Verona, Italy*
G Radicati di Brozolo, *ECSEC IBM, Italy*
R Rossi, *CINECA, Italy*

are to be congratulated for giving up much of their valuable time to make the meeting such a success.

D J Evans and C Sutti
November 1988

List of Contributors

F Aluffi-Pentini, *Roma (Italy)*

C Arnold, *ETA Systems Inc. (USA)*

S Atzeni, *Associazione EURATOM-ENEA SULLA FUSIONE (Italy)*

M Bertocchi, *Bergamo (Italy)*

D Bini, *Roma (Italy)*

J Blair, *ETA Systems Inc. (USA)*

O Brewer, *Argonne National Laboratory (USA)*

B Brode, *ETA Systems Inc. (USA)*

L Brusa, *CISE Tecnologie Innovative SpA (Italy)*

E Caglioti, *Roma (Italy)*

C Canuto, *Parma (Italy)*

D Conforti, *Cosenza (Italy)*

M Cosnard, *Lyon (France)*

E M Daoudi, *Lyon (France)*

L C W Dixon, *Hatfield (UK)*

J Dongarra, *Argonne National Laboratory (USA)*

I S Duff, *Harwell (UK) and CERFACS (France)*

D J Evans, *Loughborough (UK)*

S Filippone, *IBM (Italy)*

I Galligani, *Bologna (Italy)*

C Giberti, *Pavia (Italy)*

L Grandinetti, *Cosenza (Italy)*

J S Kowalik, *Boeing (USA)*

D Levine, *Argonne National Laboratory (USA)*

H M Liddell, *London (UK)*

J J McKeown, *Belfast (UK)*

L Misici, *Camerino (Italy)*

G Patrizi, *Roma (Italy)*

A Peretti, *Verona (Italy)*

A Quarteroni, *Brescia (Italy)*

G Radicati di Brozolo, *IBM (Italy)*

F Riccio, *CISE Tecnologie Innovative SpA (Italy)*

V Ruggiero, *Ferrara (Italy)*

U Schendel, *Berlin (FRG)*

F Sloboda, *Dubravska (Czechoslovakia)*

D Sorensen, *Argonne National Laboratory (USA)*

E Spedicato, *Bergamo (Italy)*

C Spera, *Siena (Italy)*

C Sutti, *Verona (Italy)*

F Zirilli, *Roma (Italy)*

Parallel algorithm design

D.J. Evans

Department of Computer Studies, Loughborough University of Technology, Loughborough, Leicestershire, LE11 3TU, U.K.

ABSTRACT: The increasing interest in parallel processing has greatly encouraged the recent developments in the design of parallel algorithms which are already supplanting the current trend of exploiting the vectorisation of existing FORTRAN programs. This 'vectorisation' phase of activity was deemed necessary because of the financial investment which has been involved in the construction of existing large scale programming packages and the ready availability of vector super-computers such as the CRAY 1, CYBER 205.
However with the recent rapid developments in VLSI technology the current research trends are focussing on:
1. Parallel numerical algorithms with a large granularity of inherent parallelism present which can be exploited on computer systems with a relatively small number of powerful processors (multiprocessors, MIMD systems).
2. Highly parallel computational structures to benefit from the elaborate parallelism involved in compute bound problems, i.e. linear algebra and related fields which is achieved by directly mapping the parallel computational streams onto silicon (VLSI processor arrays, systolic algorithms).
The motivations for these two active research areas is our expectation that parallel processing will provide the potential that a parallel or multiprocessor with p processors will be able to solve a problem with a p-fold speed-up whilst the progress in VLSI will enable the construction of parallel computers with many thousands of processing elements to be technically possible.
However, to achieve these expectations in computing power it will be necessary for a complete re-appraisal of the manner in which problems and algorithms are re-designed into parallel form.

1. INTRODUCTION

It is now almost 20 years since the principal classification of parallel computer architectures i.e. SIMD/MIMD was proposed by Flynn. Since that time it has become evident that the SIMD class are leading to high performance special purpose architectures while the MIMD class employing a large number of micro-processors i.e. multiprocessors are becoming the general purpose parallel computers of the future.

Multiprocessor systems are optimised for multiple job throughput whilst parallel processors, in contrast, focus on the efficient execution of single jobs. Both however, can employ a number of processors to achieve high performance.

Multiprocessor systems can be classified according to the degree of interaction between the processing modules such as:

> Loosely coupled processors
> Tightly coupled processors

In loosely coupled processors the communication and interaction takes place on the basis of information exchange.

Tightly coupled processors share a common memory on a high speed multiplexed bus.

Loosely Coupled System

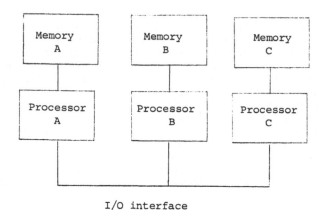

I/O interface

FIGURE 1

Principal architecture characteristics:
1. Disjoint primary memory
2. Communication data link at hardware level
3. Latency of communications
4. Performs concurrent processes asynchronously
5. Distributed processing

Tightly Coupled System

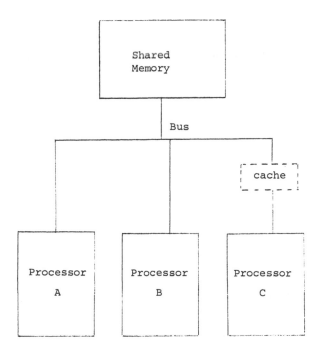

FIGURE 2

Principal architecture characteristics:
1. Shared memory
2. All processors can obtain code in memory and execute it
3. I/O and peripherals (resources) are shared
4. Communication latency in actual memory access time
5. Synchronisation of processors

It was previously well known that there was an upper limit (<6-8) to the
number of CPU's you can put on a single bus before you eventually reach
the bandwidth communication problem. In the past this has been grossly
exaggerated but it has now recently become obvious that this can be
mitigated through the use of a cache memory (Figure 2). Thus with
sophisticated cache techniques using a copy back strategy the number of
bus accesses can be reduced by a factor of 5 allowing the use of up to
30-50 CPUs on many applications and yielding a linear speed-up performance.

The complete parallel processing solution available today allows you to
share your workload with unprecedented power, performance and growth and
reliability, i.e.
   Power from high speed microprocessors
   Performance from running many tasks in parallel
   Growth by adding more processors as and when needed, whilst
       protecting your software investment

<u>Reliability</u> from quality assured components and the resilience of multiple high availability systems.

Thus, the benefits of parallel processing are enormous.

At the present time both the loosely coupled and shared memory computer architectures are the subject of intense competition for a central position in the marketplace. However it is clear that the shared memory architecture has a programming model that is much more closely aligned with the traditional uni-processor approach of recent times making the machine easier to use, adapt existing software systems and re-design algorithms. This suggests that shared memory machines will be more attractive than loosely coupled machines in the near future.

2. DESIGN PRINCIPLES

Parallelism can arise at many different levels in a computational problem which if exposed can be efficiently exploited by parallel computers. Some well known techniques are listed below:

1. *Vectorising existing software*. This is often achieved by changing the order in the evaluation of terms in a complicated expression so that a vector or matrix of components can be handled in one operation.

2. The problem is decomposed into a number of independent subproblems all of which can proceed independently. The solution of these sub-problems are then combined in some way to yield the answer to the original problem. This technique is usually known as a *divide and conquer* or *partitioning* strategy. This results in *load balancing* in which the computation is distributed over several processors.

3. The existence of independent sub-expressions can often be discovered in the calculation when rearranged which can then proceed in parallel instead of sequentially. This is classed as *Implicit Parallelism* and includes examples such as the *recursive decoupling* and *cyclic reduction* algorithms. In such computations the extraction of these sub-expressions can lead to a more balanced decomposition for parallel evaluation.

4. Early methods of solving problems involved the use of simple or explicit methods in which the solution of the L.H.S. was expressed solely in terms of complex functions on the R.H.S. Such methods however suffer from major defects such as instability and divergence and have been replaced in recent times by the more complicated but reliable implicit methods in which it is not easy to exploit or expose the inherent parallelism. Thus, the discovery of new *explicit methods* of solution is important for the development of parallel algorithms.

5. Finally the emergence of 'memoryless' or *systolic algorithms* will result in some fundamental changes in parallel computer architectures. Conventional computers suffer from the problem of the 'Von Neumann' bottleneck where the communication channel between the memory and processor constricts the amount of concurrent computation that can be done. Hence emphasis must be placed on the fact that communication between tasks in a problem is expensive and that computation is cheap, resulting in the need for new computer architectures where the comput-ation is accomplished in a manner as independent of communication costs as possible. Such architectures involve the increased usage of pipe-lines and processor arrays which has recently become possible due to

the revolution in VLSI technology.

3. PARALLEL ALGORITHM RESEARCH

The main aims are as follows:

1. To discover and design alternative solution methods which offer parallelism in one form or another.
2. To study the suitability of each parallel scheme for implementation on different parallel computer systems.
3. To obtain the performance analysis of the implemented procedures.

To date some vectorisation strategies have already been identified in programming techniques. These are as follows:

1. Separate loops into vectorisable/nonvectorisable code
2. Restructure loop so that the innermost loop has the largest range
3. Eliminate data dependency and subscript ambiguity using compiler directives to deal with ambiguous statements.
4. Unroll outer Do loops to avoid memory references.
5. Chain memory store and read operations.
6. Replace If tests by conditional vector merge procedures.

However the primary feature that distinguishes parallel algorithms and systems from the more usual uniprocessor situation is that parallelism entails the use of facilities or resources not present in sequential solutions, i.e. namely:

i)   multiple processors
ii) data communication
iii) synchronisation to determine the state of related processors
     (a special type of communication).

The introduction of these factors into the computation can make significant changes in the algorithm design.

Algorithm Structure

Algorithms can contain parallelism at different levels, which may be:

1. Apparent in the high level problem specification (global parallelism).
2. Arise from the method of solution (algorithm parallelism).
3. Arise in the details of the solution (low level or implicit parallelism).

These 3 categories can often be associated with coarse, medium and fine grain parallelism.

Whilst the transformations of associativity, commutativity and distributivity in arithmetic expressions can yield some low level parallelism gains the most spectacular gains can be derived from the use of *fan-in algorithms*.

Consider the example,

$$S = a_0 + a_1 + a_2 + a_3 + a_4 + a_5 + a_6 + a_7 = \sum_{0}^{n-1} a_i$$

Sequential Form

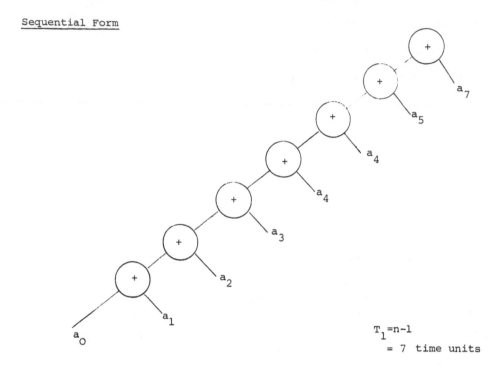

$T_1 = n-1$
$= 7$ time units

FIGURE 3: Narrow highly structured tree

Parallel Form

Fan-in algorithm

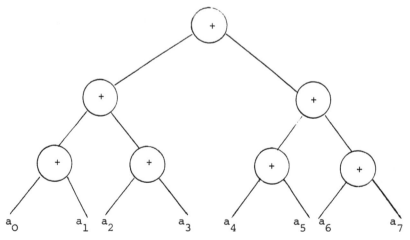

$T_p = \log n$
$= 3$ time
units

FIGURE 4: Broad balanced tree

Then $T_1 = n-1 = 7$ $T_p = \lceil \log n \rceil$ for $p = \left\lfloor \dfrac{n}{2} \right\rfloor$

The gains from the fan-in algorithm are enormous.

Some typical values for T_p and $S_p = T_1/T_p$ are:

$\underline{n}$	$\underline{T_p = n}$	$\underline{S_p = O(n/\log n)}$
4	2	2
16	4	4
256	8	32
1024	10	102
16384	14	1170

Next we show how the application of parallel computers can affect the fundamental way in which the numerical computation of *initial value* or *marching type problems* can be solved.

Consider the linear second order equation $y''+f(x)y'+g(x)y=k(x)$ with boundary conditions given at one end of the range only, i.e. y and y' are known at x=a. Thus, we have 2 initial conditions to start the integration procedure, proceeding to calculate y_i at $x_i=a+hi$, i=1,2,... by a step-by-step process.

The derivatives are replaced by the usual central difference formulae, i.e.

$$y'' \simeq (y_{r+1}-2y_r+y_{r-1})/h^2 \text{ and } y' \simeq (y_{r+1}-y_r)/2h , \qquad (3.1)$$

to yield a 3-term recurrence equation of the form,

$$(1+\tfrac{1}{2}hf_r)y_{r+1}-(2-h^2g_r)y_r+(1-\tfrac{1}{2}hf_r)y_{r-1}+Cy_r = h^2k_r , \qquad (3.2)$$

where C is a difference correction operator involving the higher order derivatives which is neglected for the initial integration of the range [a,b].

Similar methods can be applied to first order equations of the form $y'+f(x)y=k(x)$ to yield the less accurate two term recurrence relation,

$$y_{r+1}(1+\tfrac{1}{2}hf_{r+1})-y_r(1-\tfrac{1}{2}hf_r)+Cy_{r+\frac{1}{2}} = \tfrac{1}{2}h(k_r+k_{r+1}) . \qquad (3.3)$$

For non-linear equations of the form $y''=f(x,y)$, the recurrence relation is also generally nonlinear but some form of linearisation can usually be applied to obtain a linear 3 term equation of the form, i.e.

$$y_{r+1} = b_{r+1}y_r + a_{r+1}y_{r-1} + Cy_r . \qquad (3.4)$$

For the parallel evaluation of the second order recurrence relations

$$y_{r+1} = b_{r+1}y_r + a_{r+1}y_{r-1} , \quad r=1,2,\dots,N, \qquad (3.5)$$

we can rewrite it more simply in first order form as,

$$y_{r+1} = A_{r+1}y_r , \qquad (3.6)$$

where,

$$y_{r+1} = \begin{bmatrix} y_{r+1} \\ y_r \end{bmatrix} , \quad A_{r+1} = \begin{bmatrix} b_{r+1} & a_{r+1} \\ 1 & 0 \end{bmatrix} , \quad r=1,2,\dots,N. \qquad (3.7)$$

Then, the solution to the differential equation can be obtained as,

$$Y_{r+1} = A_{r+1}Y_r = A_{r+1}A_rY_{r-1} = \cdots \prod_{i=1}^{r} A_iY_i \; . \tag{3.8}$$

Finally, the solution by parallel evaluation can be obtained by use of the *fan-in algorithm* which is depicted below as,

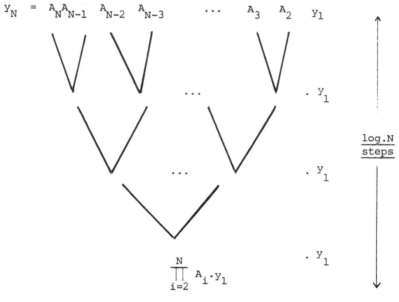

FIGURE 5

Since matrix vector multiplication is associative, y_N can be computed using the *recursive doubling* technique in $O(\log_2 N)$ steps. Naturally, the numerical stability of these computational strategies needs to be investigated further but nevertheless it does illustrate a fundamentally *new strategy* for solving *initial value* or *marching problems*. A comparison of the sequential *'step by step'* procedure with the parallel *'grand leap'* process is given in Figure 6.

Polynomial Evaluation

Sequential form
The Horner scheme is,

$$Q(x) = \sum_{0}^{n} a_ix^i = a_0 + x(a_1 + x(a_2 + \ldots + x(a_{n-1} + xa_n)\ldots)$$

and due to the strict sequential ordering imposed by the brackets it follows that $O(n)$ operations cannot be avoided. Also, it is clear that the availability of more than 1 processor has no power to speed-up the calculation.

However, by load distribution we can obtain a parallel algorithm as follows,

Parallel form

Consider the case when $n = p\log_2 p$ where p is the number of processors availabe and is a power of 2. Then rewriting the polynomial $Q(x)$ in the form,

$$Q(x) = a_0 + Q_1(x) + x^q Q_2(x) + \ldots + x^{(p-1)q} Q_p$$

where

$$Q_i(x) = a_k x + a_{k+1} x^2 + \ldots a_{k+q} x^q$$

with $q = \log_2 p$, $k = (i-1)p + 1$.

The procedure is carried out by distributing the coefficients $a_1, a_2, \ldots, a_q$ to proceddor P_1; $a_{q+1}, a_{q+2}, \ldots, a_{2q}$ to P_2, etc. Then for each i, Q_i can be computed sequentially in P_i simultaneously in a time proportional to the degree $O(q)$. Then, x is distributed to all the processors and $x, x^2, \ldots$ $, x^p$ is formed by the fan-in process. Lastly, the multiplication of $x^i Q_i$ is completed and the p terms $x^i Q_i$ summed by the fan-in process with the final addition of a_0 giving an asymptotic speed-up of p for a p processor system.

For example, for n=8, we have,

Sequential strategy $\quad Q(x) = a_0 + x(a_1 + \ldots x(a_7 + a_8 x) \ldots)$

Parallel strategy $\quad Q(x) = a_0 + (a_1 x + a_2 x^2) + x^2(a_3 x + a_4 x^2) + x^4(a_5 x + a_6 x^2) +$

$$x^2(a_7 x + a_8 x^2)$$

$$= a_0 + Q_1 + x^2 Q_2 + x^4 Q_3 + x^6 Q_4$$

Thus, the computation of the polynomial is distributed across the 4 processors to produce a broad balanced tree. (c.f. Fig.4).

Sequential strategy: Step by Step

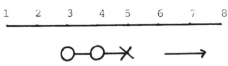

Parallel strategy: Grand Leap

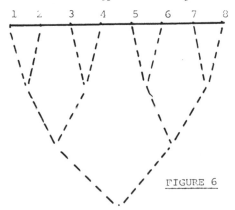

FIGURE 6

4. A NEW EXPLICIT METHOD FOR PARABOLIC EQUATIONS

Consider the following second order parabolic equation,

$$\frac{\partial U}{\partial t} = \frac{\partial^2 U}{\partial x^2} \ , \quad 0 \leqslant x \leqslant 1, \ 0 < t \leqslant T \tag{4.1}$$

subject to the initial-boundary conditions

$$U(x,0) = f(x), \ 0 < x < 1 \ ,$$

$$U(0,t) = g(t), \ 0 < t \leqslant T \ , \tag{4.1a}$$

and $U(1,t) = h(t)$.

A uniformly-spaced network whose mesh points are $x_i = i\Delta x$, $t_j = j\Delta t$ for $i=0,1,\ldots,m,m+1$ and $j=0,1,\ldots,n,n+1$ is used with $\Delta x = 1/(m+1)$, $\Delta t = T/(n+1)$ and $\lambda = \Delta t/(\Delta x)^2$, the mesh ratio.

A weighted approximation to the differential equation (4.1) at the point $(x_i, t_{j+\frac{1}{2}})$ is given by

$$-\lambda\theta u_{i-1,j+1} + (1+2\lambda\theta)u_{i,j+1} - \lambda\theta u_{i+1,j+1} = \lambda(1-\theta)u_{i-1,j} + (1-2\lambda(1-\theta))u_{ij} +$$

$$\lambda(1-\theta)u_{i+1,j} \ , \quad i=1,2,\ldots,m. \tag{4.2}$$

This approximation can be displayed in a more compact matrix form as

$$\begin{pmatrix} a & b & & & & \\ c & a & b & & & \\ & c & a & b & & \\ & & & \ddots & & \\ & & & & c & a & b \\ & & & & & c & a \end{pmatrix}_{(m \times m)} \begin{pmatrix} u_1 \\ u_2 \\ \vdots \\ \vdots \\ u_{m-1} \\ u_m \end{pmatrix}_{j+1} = \begin{pmatrix} f_1 \\ f_2 \\ \vdots \\ \vdots \\ f_{m-1} \\ f_m \end{pmatrix}_j \tag{4.3}$$

i.e.,

$$Au = f \ , \tag{4.4}$$

where,

$$c = -\lambda\theta, \ a = (1+2\lambda\theta), \ b = -\lambda\theta;$$

$$\left. \begin{array}{l} f_1 = \lambda(1-\theta)(u_{0j}+u_{2j})+\lambda\theta u_{0,j+1}+(1-2\lambda(1-\theta))u_{1,j} \ ; \\[4pt] f_i = \lambda(1-\theta)(u_{i-1,j}+u_{i+1,j})+(1-2\lambda(1-\theta))u_{ij}, \ i=2,3,\ldots,m-2,m-1; \\[4pt] f_m = \lambda(1-\theta)(u_{m-1,j}+u_{m+1,j})+(1-2\lambda(1-\theta))u_{mj}+\lambda(1-\theta)u_{m+1,j} + \\[4pt] \qquad \lambda\theta u_{m+1,j+1} \quad \text{and} \\[4pt] u = (u_{1,j+1}, u_{2,j+1}, \ldots, u_{m,j+1})^T \ \text{and} \ f = (f_1, f_2, \ldots, f_m)^T. \end{array} \right\} \tag{4.4a}$$

We note that f is a column vector of order m consisting of the boundary values as well as known u values at time level j while u are the values at time level (j+1) which we seek. We also recall that (4.4) corresponds to the fully implicit, the Crank-Nicolson, the Douglas and the classical explicit methods when θ takes the values $1, \frac{1}{2}, \frac{1}{2}, -1/12\lambda$ and 0 with accuracies of the order $O([\Delta x]^2+\Delta t)$, $O([\Delta x]^2+[\Delta t]^2)$, $O([\Delta x]^4+[\Delta t]^2)$ and $O([\Delta x]^2+\Delta t)$ respectively.

Let us assume that we have an *even number of intervals* (corresponding to an odd number of internal points, i.e. m odd) on the real line $0 \leqslant x \leqslant 1$. A similar analysis holds for m even. We can then perform the following splitting of the coefficient matrix A:

$$A = G_1 + G_2 , \tag{4.5}$$

where,

$$G_1 = \begin{pmatrix} a/2 & & & & & & & \\ & a/2 & b & & & & & \\ & c & a/2 & & & & & \\ & & & a/2 & b & & & \\ & & & c & a/2 & & \bigcirc & \\ & & & & & \ddots & & \\ & & \bigcirc & & & & a/2 & b \\ & & & & & & c & a/2 \end{pmatrix}_{(m \times m)} \tag{4.6}$$

and

$$G_2 = \begin{pmatrix} a/2 & b & & & & & \\ c & a/2 & & & & & \\ & & a/2 & b & & & \\ & & c & a/2 & & \bigcirc & \\ & & & & \ddots & & \\ & & & \bigcirc & & a/2 & b \\ & & & & & c & a/2 \\ & & & & & & a/2 \end{pmatrix}_{(m \times m)} \tag{4.7}$$

It is assumed that the following conditions are satisfied:

(i) $G_1 + rI$ and $G_2 + rI$ are non-singular for any $r > 0$, $\theta \geqslant \frac{1}{2}$.

(ii)   For any vectors f_1 and f_2 and for any $r > 0$, the systems

$$(G_1 + rI)u_1 = f_1$$

and $$(G_2 + rI)u_2 = f_2 \tag{4.8}$$

are more easily solved in explicit form since they consist of only (2×2) subsystems.

Thus, with these conditions, system (4.4) becomes

$$(G_1 + G_2)u = f . \tag{4.9}$$

The **Alternating Group Explicit** (AGE) iteration consists of writing (4.9) as a pair of equations

$$(G_1 + rI)u = (rI - G_2)u + f$$

and $$(G_2 + rI)u = (rI - G_1)u + f . \tag{4.10}$$

The AGE method using *the Peaceman and Rachford variant* for the *stationary case* (r=constant) is given by,

$$(G_1 + rI)u^{(p+\frac{1}{2})} = (rI - G_2)u^{(p)} + f \tag{4.11}$$

and
$$(G_2 + rI)u^{(p+1)} = (rI - G_1)u^{(p+\frac{1}{2})} + f, \quad p \geq 0 ,$$

where $u^{(0)}$ is a starting approximation and r is a positive constant called the iteration parameter whose value is chosen to maximize the rate of convergence.

The convergence of the AGE method can be easily shown (Evans, 1985) whilst the optimum parameter r is given by

$$r = (uv)^{\frac{1}{2}} \tag{4.12}$$

where u and v are the minimum and maximum eigenvalues of the submatrices G_1 and G_2.

Variants of the AGE Scheme and its Computation

Many variants of the basic Peaceman-Rachford scheme can be proposed. For example, we have, on modifying the second stage of (4.11),

$$(G_1 + rI)u^{(p+\frac{1}{2})} = (rI - G_2)u^{(p)} + f \tag{4.13}$$

and
$$(G_2 + rI)u^{(p+1)} = (G_2 - (1-\omega)rI)u^{(p)} + (2-\omega)ru^{(p+\frac{1}{2})}$$

where ω is a parameter. For $\omega = 0$ we have the Peaceman-Rachford scheme (4.11) and for $\omega = 1$, we obtain the scheme due to Douglas and Rachford (1956). For G_1 and G_2 symmetric and positive definite and with a *fixed acceleration parameter* $r > 0$, the resulting *generalised AGE scheme* is convergent for any $0 \leq \omega \leq 2$. As we shall see in a subsequent section, a natural extension of the AGE algorithm is to implement it on higher dimensional boundary value problems using the Douglas-Rachford variant.

For the purpose of computation, we shall now attempt to derive equations that are satisfied at each intermediate (half-time) level. For the *Peaceman-Rachford variant*, in particular and with fixed parameter r, the AGE method can be applied to determine $u^{(p+\frac{1}{2})}$ and $u^{(p+1)}$ implicitly by

$$(G_1 + rI)u^{(p+\frac{1}{2})} = (rI - G_2)u^{(p)} + f$$

and
$$(G_2 + rI)u^{(p+1)} = (rI - G_1)u^{(p+\frac{1}{2})} + f \tag{4.14}$$

or explicitly by,

$$u^{(p+\frac{1}{2})} = (G_1 + rI)^{-1}\{(rI - G_2)u^{(p)} + f\}$$

and
$$u^{(p+1)} = (G_2 + rI)^{-1}\{(rI - G_1)u^{(p+\frac{1}{2})} + f\}. \tag{4.15}$$

If we assume *m to be odd (even number of intervals)* and if we write

$$\hat{G} = \begin{bmatrix} r_2 & b \\ c & r_2 \end{bmatrix} \tag{4.16}$$

where
$$r_2 = r + \frac{a}{2} , \tag{4.17}$$

then from (4.6) and (4.7) we have,

$$(G_1+rI) = \begin{pmatrix} r_2 & & & & & & \\ & \hat{G} & & & & & \\ & & \hat{G} & & & & \\ & & & & \bigcirc & & \\ & & & \bigcirc & & & \\ & & & & & \hat{G} & \end{pmatrix}_{(m \times m)}$$

(4.18)

and

$$(G_2+rI) = \begin{pmatrix} \hat{G} & & & & & \\ & \hat{G} & & & & \\ & & & \bigcirc & & \\ & & \bigcirc & & & \\ & & & & \hat{G} & \\ & & & & & r_2 \end{pmatrix}_{(m \times m)}$$

(4.19)

It is clear that (G_1+rI) and (G_2+rI) are block diagonal matrices. All the diagonal elements except the first (or the last for (G_2+rI)) are (2×2) submatrices. Therefore, (G_1+rI) and (G_2+rI) can be easily inverted by merely inverting their block diagonal entries. Hence,

$$(G_1+rI)^{-1} = \begin{pmatrix} \dfrac{1}{r_2} & & & & & \\ & \hat{G}^{-1} & & & & \\ & & \hat{G}^{-1} & & & \\ & & & & \bigcirc & \\ & & & \bigcirc & & \\ & & & & & \hat{G}^{-1} \end{pmatrix}_{(m \times m)}$$

(4.20)

$$= \frac{1}{\Delta} \begin{pmatrix} \Delta/r_2 & & & & \\ & r_2 & -b & & \\ & -c & r_2 & & \\ & & & \bigcirc & \\ & & \bigcirc & & \\ & & & & r_2 & -b \\ & & & & -c & r_2 \end{pmatrix}_{(m \times m)}$$

(4.21)

where $\Delta = r_2^2 - bc$. $\qquad\qquad\qquad\qquad\qquad\qquad\qquad\qquad$ (4.22)

Similarly, we obtain,

$$(G_2 + rI)^{-1} = \frac{1}{\Delta}
\begin{pmatrix}
r_2 & -b & & & & & & \\
-c & r_2 & & & & & & \\
& & r_2 & -b & & & & \\
& & -c & r_2 & & & \bigcirc & \\
& & & & \ddots & & & \\
& & & & & r_2 & -b & \\
& \bigcirc & & & & -c & r_2 & \\
& & & & & & & \\
& & & & & & & \Delta/r_2
\end{pmatrix}_{(m \times m)} \cdot$$

$\qquad\qquad\qquad\qquad\qquad\qquad\qquad\qquad\qquad\qquad\qquad\qquad\qquad$ (4.23)

From (4.15), $u^{(p+\frac{1}{2})}$ and $u^{(p+1)}$ are given by,

$$\begin{pmatrix}
u_1^{(p+\frac{1}{2})} \\
u_2^{(p+\frac{1}{2})} \\
u_3^{(p+\frac{1}{2})} \\
\vdots \\
\\
\\
u_{m-1}^{(p+\frac{1}{2})} \\
u_m^{(p+\frac{1}{2})}
\end{pmatrix} = \frac{1}{\Delta}
\begin{pmatrix}
\Delta/r_2 & & & & \\
& r_2 & -b & & \\
& -c & r_2 & & \bigcirc \\
& & & \ddots & \\
& & & & \\
& \bigcirc & & r_2 & -b \\
& & & -c & r_2
\end{pmatrix}
\begin{pmatrix}
r_1 u_1^{(p)} - b u_2^{(p)} + f_1 \\
-c u_1^{(p)} + r_1 u_2^{(p)} + f_2 \\
r_1 u_3^{(p)} - b u_4^{(p)} + f_3 \\
-c u_3^{(p)} + r_1 u_4^{(p)} + f_4 \\
\vdots \\
r_1 u_{m-2}^{(p)} - b u_{m-1}^{(p)} + f_{m-2} \\
-c u_{m-2}^{(p)} + r_1 u_{m-1}^{(p)} + f_{m-1} \\
r_1 u_m^{(p)} + f_m
\end{pmatrix}$$

$\qquad\qquad\qquad\qquad\qquad\qquad\qquad\qquad\qquad\qquad\qquad\qquad\qquad$ (4.24)

and

$$\begin{pmatrix}
u_1^{(p+1)} \\
u_2^{(p+1)} \\
u_3^{(p+1)} \\
\vdots \\
\\
\\
u_{m-2}^{(p+1)} \\
u_{m-1}^{(p+1)} \\
u_m^{(p+1)}
\end{pmatrix} = \frac{1}{\Delta}
\begin{pmatrix}
r_2 & -b & & & & \\
-c & r_2 & & & & \\
& & r_2 & -b & & \\
& & -c & r_2 & & \bigcirc \\
& & & & \ddots & \\
& \bigcirc & & & r_2 & -b \\
& & & & -c & r_2 \\
& & & & & \Delta/r_2
\end{pmatrix}
\begin{pmatrix}
r_1 u_1^{(p+\frac{1}{2})} + f_1 \\
r_1 u_2^{(p+\frac{1}{2})} - b u_3^{(p+\frac{1}{2})} + f_2 \\
-c u_2^{(p+\frac{1}{2})} + r_1 u_3^{(p+\frac{1}{2})} + f_3 \\
r_1 u_4^{(p+\frac{1}{2})} - b u_5^{(p+\frac{1}{2})} + f_4 \\
-c u_4^{(p+\frac{1}{2})} + r_1 u_5^{(p+\frac{1}{2})} + f_5 \\
\vdots \\
r_1 u_{m-1}^{(p+\frac{1}{2})} - b u_m^{(p+\frac{1}{2})} + f_{m-1} \\
-c u_{m-1}^{(p+\frac{1}{2})} + r_1 u_m^{(p+\frac{1}{2})} + f_m
\end{pmatrix}$$

$\qquad\qquad\qquad\qquad\qquad\qquad\qquad\qquad\qquad\qquad\qquad\qquad\qquad$ (4.25) where $r_1=r-a/2$, $r_2=r+a/2$ and $\Delta=r_2^2-bc$.   (4.26)

The *alternating implicit* nature of the (2×2) groups in the equations (4.14) is shown in Figure 7 where the implicit/explicit values are given on the forward/backward levels for sweeps on the $(p+\frac{1}{2})$th and $(p+1)$th levels.

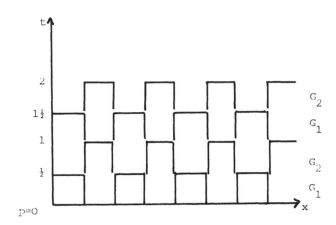

FIGURE 7: The AGE Method (Implicit)

The corresponding explicit expressions for the AGE equations are obtained by carrying out the multiplications in (4.24) and (4.25). Thus we have,

(i)   at level $(p+\frac{1}{2})$

$$u_1^{(p+\frac{1}{2})} = (r_1 u_1^{(p)} - bu_2^{(p)} + f_1)/r_2 ,$$

$$u_i^{(p+\frac{1}{2})} = (Au_{i-1}^{(p)} + Bu_i^{(p)} + Cu_{i+1}^{(p)} + Du_{i+2}^{(p)} + E_i)/\Delta$$

and $$u_{i+1}^{(p+\frac{1}{2})} = (\tilde{A}u_{i-1}^{(p)} + \tilde{B}u_i^{(p)} + \tilde{C}u_{i+1}^{(p)} + \tilde{D}u_{i+2}^{(p)} + \tilde{E}_i)/\Delta$$ $i=2,4,\ldots,m-1$ (4.27)

where,

$$A = -cr_2, \ B = r_1 r_2, \ C = -br_1, \ E_i = r_2 f_i - bf_{i+1}, \ D = \begin{cases} 0 & \text{for } i=m-1 \\ b^2 & \text{otherwise} \end{cases}$$

and $$\tilde{A} = c^2, \ \tilde{B} = -cr_1, \ \tilde{C} = r_1 r_2, \ \tilde{E}_i = r_2 f_{i+1} - cf_i, \ \tilde{D} = \begin{cases} 0 & \text{for } i=m-1 \\ -br_2 & \text{otherwise} \end{cases}$$

(4.27a)

with the following computational molecules (Figure 8),

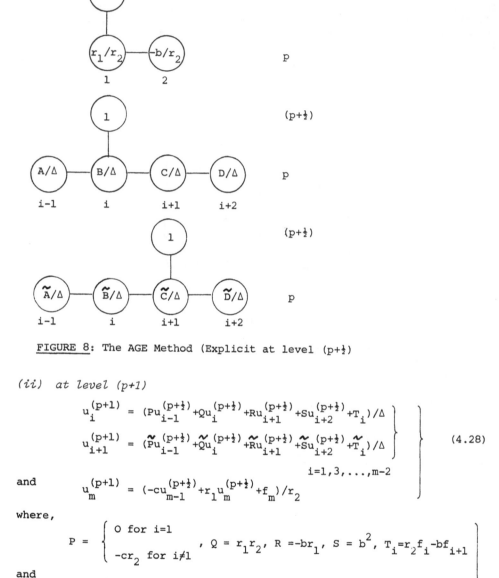

FIGURE 8: The AGE Method (Explicit at level $(p+\frac{1}{2})$

(ii) at level (p+1)

$$u_i^{(p+1)} = (Pu_{i-1}^{(p+\frac{1}{2})} + Qu_i^{(p+\frac{1}{2})} + Ru_{i+1}^{(p+\frac{1}{2})} + Su_{i+2}^{(p+\frac{1}{2})} + T_i)/\Delta$$

$$u_{i+1}^{(p+1)} = (\tilde{P}u_{i-1}^{(p+\frac{1}{2})} + \tilde{Q}u_i^{(p+\frac{1}{2})} + \tilde{R}u_{i+1}^{(p+\frac{1}{2})} + \tilde{S}u_{i+2}^{(p+\frac{1}{2})} + \tilde{T}_i)/\Delta \qquad (4.28)$$

$$i = 1, 3, \ldots, m-2$$

and

$$u_m^{(p+1)} = (-cu_{m-1}^{(p+\frac{1}{2})} + r_1 u_m^{(p+\frac{1}{2})} + f_m)/r_2$$

where,

$$P = \begin{cases} 0 \text{ for } i=1 \\ -cr_2 \text{ for } i \neq 1 \end{cases}, \ Q = r_1 r_2, \ R = -br_1, \ S = b^2, \ T_i = r_2 f_i - bf_{i+1}$$

and

$$\tilde{P} = \begin{cases} 0 \text{ for } i=1 \\ c^2 \text{ for } i \neq 1 \end{cases}, \ \tilde{Q} = -cr_1, \ \tilde{R} = Q = r_1 r_2, \ \tilde{S} = -br_2 ,$$

$$\tilde{T}_i = -cf_i + r_2 f_{i+1}$$

$$(4.28a)$$

with its computational molecules given by Figure 9.

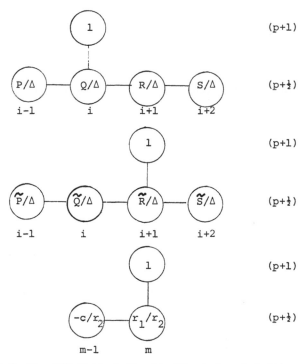

FIGURE 9: The AGE Method (Explicit) at Level (p+1)

Since the equations (4.27) and (4.28) are explicit then their solution on a parallel computer is obvious.

Multidimensional Partial Differential Equations

The AGE method can be readily extended to higher space dimensions. To ensure unconditional stability, the Douglas-Rachford (DR) variant is used instead of the Peaceman-Rachford (PR) formula. In two space dimensions, for example, the specific problem we are considering is the heat equation,

$$\frac{\partial U}{\partial t} = \frac{\partial^2 U}{\partial x^2} + \frac{\partial^2 U}{\partial y^2} + h(x,y,t), \quad (x,y,t) \in R \times (0,T] \qquad (4.29)$$

with the initial condition,

$$U(x,y,0) = F(x,y), \quad (x,y,t) \in R \times \{0\}, \qquad (4.29a)$$

and $U(x,y,t)$ is specified on the boundary of R, ∂R by

$$U(x,y,t) = G(x,y,t), \quad (x,y,t) \in \partial R \times (0,T], \qquad (4.29b)$$

where for simplicity we assume that the region R of the xy-plane is a rectangle.

Consider the two-dimensional heat equation (4.29) with the auxiliary conditions (4.29a) and (4.29b). The region R is a rectangle defined by

$$R = \{(x,y): 0 \leq x \leq L, \ 0 \leq y \leq M\}.$$

at the point $P(x_i, y_j, t_k)$ in the solution domain, the value of $U(x,y,t)$ is denoted by $U_{i,j,k}$, where $x_i = i\Delta x$, $y_j = j\Delta y$ for $0 \leq i \leq (m+1)$, $0 \leq j \leq (n+1)$ and $\Delta x = L/(m+1)$, $\Delta y = M/(n+1)$. The increment in the time t, Δt is chosen such that $t_k = k\Delta t$ for $k = 0, 1, 2, \ldots$ For simplicity of presentation, we assume that m and n are chosen so that $\Delta x = \Delta y$ and consequently the mesh ratio is defined by $\lambda = \Delta t/(\Delta x)^2$. Analogous to the heat equation in one space dimension, a weighted finite-difference approximation to (4.29) at the point $(i,j,k+\frac{1}{2})$ is given by (with $\frac{1}{2} \leq \theta \leq 1$),

$$\frac{\Delta_t u_{i,j,k}}{\Delta t} = \frac{1}{(\Delta x)^2}\{\theta(\delta_x^2 + \delta_y^2)u_{i,j,k+1} + (1-\theta)(\delta_x^2 + \delta_y^2)u_{i,j,k}\} + h_{i,j,k+\frac{1}{2}}$$

(4.30)

which leads to the *five-point formula*,

$$-\lambda\theta u_{i-1,j,k+1} + (1+4\lambda\theta)u_{i,j,k+1} - \lambda\theta u_{i+1,j,k+1} - \lambda\theta u_{i,j-1,k+1} - \lambda\theta u_{i,j+1,k+1}$$

$$= \lambda(1-\theta)u_{i-1,j,k} + (1-4\lambda(1-\theta))u_{i,j,k} + \lambda(1-\theta)u_{i+1,j,k} + \lambda(1-\theta)u_{i,j-1,k} +$$

$$\lambda(1-\theta)u_{i,j+1,k} + \Delta t h_{i,j,k+\frac{1}{2}},$$

$$\text{for } i=1,2,\ldots,m; \quad j=1,2,\ldots,n.$$

(4.31)

We note that when θ takes the values 0, $\frac{1}{2}$ and 1, we obtain the classical explicit, the Crank-Nicolson and the fully implicit schemes whose truncation errors are $O([\Delta x]^2 + \Delta t)$, $O([\Delta x]^2 + [\Delta t]^2)$ and $O([\Delta x]^2 + \Delta t)$ respectively. The explicit scheme is stable only for $\lambda \leq 1/4$ (if $\Delta x \neq \Delta y$, we need $\Delta t/[(\Delta x)^2 + (\Delta y)^2] \leq \frac{1}{8}$). The fully implicit and the Crank-Nicolson schemes are, however, unconditionally stable.

The weighted finite-difference equations (4.31) can be expressed in the more compact matrix form as

$$Au_{(i)}^{[k+1]} = Bu_{(i)}^{[k]} + b + g, \quad i=1,2,\ldots,n.$$

(4.32)

where $u_{(i)}^{[k]}$ are the known u-values at time level k and

$$u_{(i)} = (\underline{u}_1, \underline{u}_2, \ldots, \underline{u}_n)^T \text{ with } \underline{u}_j = (u_{1j}, u_{2j}, \ldots, u_{mj})^T, \quad j=1,2,\ldots,n.$$

Thus, the mn internal mesh points on the rectangular grid system R are ordered *row-wise*.

We observe from (4.32) that the matrix A is of the form,

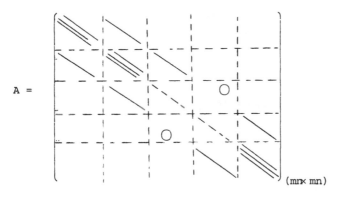

$A =$ $(mn \times mn)$

If we split A into the sum of its constituent symmetric and positive definite matrices G_1, G_2, G_3 and G_4, we have,

$$A = G_1 + G_2 + G_3 + G_4 , \qquad (4.33)$$

where,

$$G_1 + G_2 = \qquad \qquad (4.34)$$

$(mn \times mn)$

with $\mathrm{diag}(G_1 + G_2) = \tfrac{1}{2}\mathrm{diag}(A)$
and

$$G_3 + G_4 = \qquad \qquad (4.35)$$

$(mn \times mn)$

with $\mathrm{diag}(G_3 + G_4) = \tfrac{1}{2}\mathrm{diag}(A)$. However after an appropriate reordering of the grid points (i.e. columnwise) it can be easily shown that $G_3 + G_4$ becomes similar in form to $G_1 + G_2$. Consequently G_1, G_2, G_3 and G_4 are (2×2) block diagonal submatrices.

The Douglas-Rachford formula for the AGE fractional scheme then takes the form,

$$
\left.
\begin{aligned}
(G_1+rI)\underline{u}_{(i)}^{(p+1/4)} &= (rI-G_1-2G_2-2G_3-2G_4)\underline{u}_{(i)}^{(p)}+2\underline{f} \ , \\
(G_2+rI)\underline{u}_{(i)}^{(p+1/2)} &= G_2\underline{u}_{(i)}^{(p)}+r\underline{u}_{(i)}^{(p+1/4)} \ , \\
(G_3+rI)\underline{u}_{(i)}^{(p+3/4)} &= G_3\underline{u}_{(i)}^{(p)}+r\underline{u}_{(i)}^{(p+1/2)} \ , \\
(G_4+rI)\underline{u}_{(i)}^{(p+1)} &= G_4\underline{u}_{(i)}^{(p)}+r\underline{u}_{(i)}^{(p+3/4)} \ .
\end{aligned}
\right\}
\qquad (4.36)
$$

Finally the computational scheme is given in Figure 10.

5. SYSTOLIC ALGORITHMS

Introduction

The importance of fast, computationally intensive matrix arithmetic in signal processing has recently been recognised. In particular, attention has been drawn to the wide variety of digital signal processing comput- ations that are based on the repeated evaluation of the function AX+B for efficient execution. Applications include digital filters, FFT, division and square root operations, polynomial evaluation, recurrence relations, differential equations and matrix computations, etc.

Early work on systolic arrays was aimed at providing special purpose and high performance hardware to eliminate computational and communication bottlenecks in signal processing and later in computing systems. These were illustrated by a variety of arrays of inner product step processors for digital signal processing computations.

A new architectural approach for implementing computationally intensive processing functions in VLSI was considered opportune and necessary incorporating features such as, modularity, regularity, simple short nearest neighbour interconnections, pipelining, parallelism, and a simple control.

The Systolic Approach

Initially identify the computationally intensive parts of a computation, in particular those which requre a basic operation to be computed repeatedly at high speed. The next step is to seek or develop an algorithm that can be implemented on a regular array of identical processing elements. The third step is to map the algorithm onto a systolic architecture and build it as a high performance special purpose processor, based on VLSI technology, or map it onto an existing program- mable array. Various constraints are imposed upon the hardware architecture i.e. nearest neighbour interconnects etc.

Systolic Algorithm

A *systolic algorithm* is an algorithm which possesses the following properties:

1.   The algorithm can be implemented with only a small number of

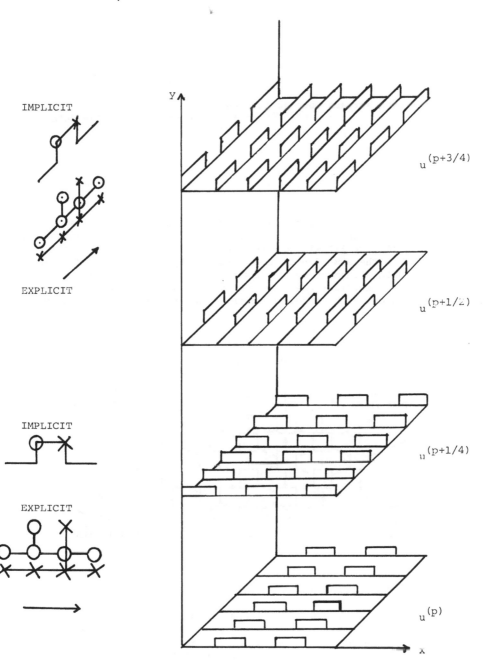

IMPLICIT

EXPLICIT

IMPLICIT

EXPLICIT

$u^{(p+3/4)}$

$u^{(p+1/2)}$

$u^{(p+1/4)}$

$u^{(p)}$

FIGURE 10

different types of logic cells which would be replicated to form a regular structure.

2. Simple and regular data and control flow.
3. Extensive multiprocessing and pipelining is used.
4. The algorithm can be implemented on a regular array of logic cells which are connected together with regular local interconnections.
5. Several data streams move at constant velocities along fixed paths in the network, interacting at cells where they meet. The data paths are highly pipelined and data flow is synchronised by a common clock.

It is also useful to *distinguish between systolic algorithms, which may be mapped onto a systolic or non-systolic machine,* and systolic arrays, which are systolic architectures. (Evans, 1988).

Thus, a systolic array is a regular array of identical functional modules, each of which is connected only to its nearest neighbours for data transfer purposes (Figure 11) with common control and timing so that all the modules perform the same function simultaneously, but on different data items. The data streams move at constant velocities over fixed paths in the network, and interact wherever they meet. High computational throughput without high bandwidth memory links is achieved by multiple use made of each item.

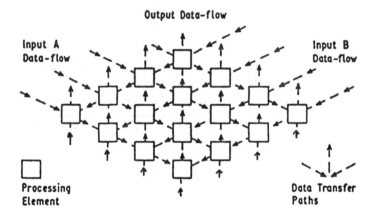

FIGURE 11: Schematic diagram of a systolic array

The precise function of the cells is determined by the class of problems to be solved. Thus, for *pattern matching* applications only very simple processors containing little more than an "AND/OR" gate and a couple of D-type flip-flops are used whilst a basic cell for *picture processing* may contain a few simple logic circuits. For *signal or image processing* arrays the cells will contain a digital adder or multiplier unit.

Further, the connection of the cells and the direction of data flow through the cells will also be application dependent. Common cell interconnections are linearly, orthogonally and hexagonally connected.

Matrix-Vector Multiplication

Many signal processing computations use the inner product step (IPS) cell shown in Figure 12.

Figure 13, for example, shows a linear systolic array suitable for banded matrix-vector multiplication. The data vector stream B moves from right to left through the array, whilst a result stream C moves in the opposite direction. Data values are weighted by the matrix coefficients A, and accumulated into the result stream.

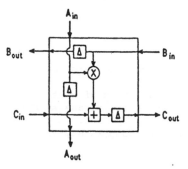

$$A_{out}(t+\Delta) = A_{in}(t)$$

$$B_{out}(t+\Delta) = B_{in}(t)$$

$$C_{out}(t+\Delta) = C_{in}(t) + A_{in}(t) \times B_{in}(t)$$

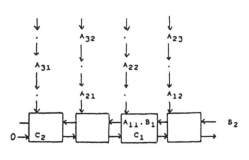

FIGURE 12: Inner-product-step processor

FIGURE 13: Linear array for multiplying a matrix A by a vector B to give a vector C

Similar linear chains may be constructed for numerous other applications. These include polynomial evaluation, digital filtering, correlation/ convolution, recurrence evaluation, discrete Fourier transform, triangular linear system solving, and many other common signal processing functions.

Orthogonally connected arrays of inner product step processors appear to be particularly attractive for 2D image processing functions, whilst orthogonally connected arrays of simpler processors (e.g. full adders and latches) provide fast bit-parallel implementations of some of the linear arrays described above.

Hexagonally connected arrays of inner product step processors provide a particularly powerful hardware for implementing many matrix operations. For example the multiplication of two N×N matrices can be computed in 3N processor cycles. This compares very favourably with the N^3 cycles that would be required with a conventional Von-Neumann processor.

Application Areas

The range of applications for systolic arrays are:

```
Digital filtering
Recurrence evaluation
Matrix-vector and matrix-matrix multiplication
LU decomposition
DFT
FFT
Priority queues
Transitive closure
2-D convolution and tree searching
```

Since then the above applications have been developed further, and many new applications have been identified.

REFERENCES

Evans, D.J., Group Explicit Iterative Methods for Solving Large Linear Systems, Int.Jour.Comp.Math., 19, 1985, 81-108.

Douglas, J. and Rachford, H.H., On the Numerical Solution of Heat Conduction Problems in Two or Three Space Variables, Trans.Am.Math. Soc., 82, 1956, 421-439.

Evans, D.J., Systolic Algorithms, Spec.Iss.Int.Jour.Comp.Math., 25, No. 3 and 4, 1988.

Parallel computing and special applications

Udo Schendel

Freie Universität Berlin
Institut für Mathematik III
Arnimallee 2-6, D-1000 Berlin 33

Abstract: A short overview on Supercomputers will be given. After a characterization of parallel algorithms some basic principles in parallel computing are discussed. Finally a decomposition-method for solving elliptic partial differential equations will be presented.

Keywords: Parallel computer, parallel computation and parallel numerical algorithms, decomposition methods

1 Introductional Remarks

The development of high-speed-computers makes it necessary to reconfigurate well-known methods for solving large and complex systems or to develop new algorithms which are efficient.

The structure of these algorithms and their software are deeply dependent on the architecture of the used computer system and vice versa.

The following figure gives an idea of the importance to respect the adaption of the methods and the architecture of the computer system to the given problem.

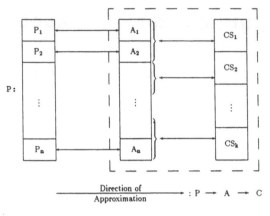

P   : problem
P_i : subproblems
A_i : subalgorithms
CS_k : computer systems

$A := [A_1, A_2, \ldots, A_n]$

$C := [CS_1, \ldots, CS_k]$

Some significant applications are: curve fitting; weather forecast; spin model; simplex optimization; physical field evaluation; evaluation of P/N transitions; solution of linear systems of equations; structure analysis; image processing and others.

2   Characterization of Parallel Computer Architectures

A coarse and famous classification of computer systems is the *classification of Flynn.*

  (i) SISD-Machine: Single-Instruction-Single-Data-Stream-Machine

  (ii) SIMD-Machine: Single-Instruction-Multiple-Data-Stream-Machine

 (iii) MISD-Machine: Multiple-Instruction-Single-Data-Stream-Machine

 (iv) MIMD-Machine: Multiple-Instruction-Multiple-Data-Stream-Machine

Development of new computer architectures with different levels of parallelisms requires a detailed classification which is essential to the comparisons of computers.

Schwartz (1980) made a distinction between Paracomputers and Ultracomputers based on different memory access.

Modern Computers are: CYBER 203/205 (SIMD-Machine), CRAY-1 S, CRAY-X-MP, CRAY-Y-MP, CRAY-2,B, HEP-Denelcor (MIMD-Machine), Hitachi S9/IAP (Integrated Array Processor) (SIMD-Machine), Alliant, FPS (Floating Point System), ETA 10, Sequent, Convex ect.

The different levels of parallelism in parallel computation are shown in the following figure.

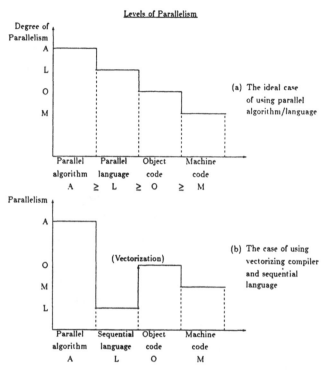

Levels of Parallelism

(a) The ideal case of using parallel algorithm/language

(b) The case of using vectorizing compiler and sequential language

In the terms of Mflops (1 Mflop = 1 million floating point operations per second) *supercomputers* are often defined by performing more than 100 Mflops.

Both pipelined and array supercomputers are designed mainly for vector processing of large arrays of data. Presently, most of the commercially available vector super-computers are pipelined machines owing to their cost-effectiveness. Besides using multiple pipelines in uniprocessor systems, supercomputer manufacturers are also challenging multitasking through the use of multiple processors.

The development of supercomputers is shown in the figure of the space of super-computers.

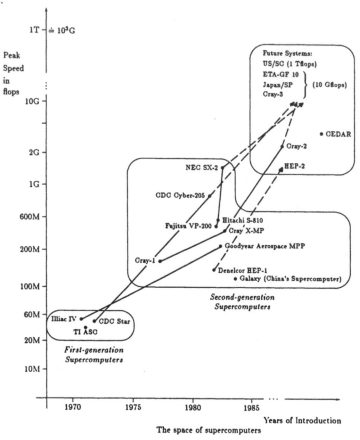

The space of supercomputers

At the highest level **MIMD** computers are classified; they are defined to be control-flow computers capable of processing more than one stream of instructions. The different instruction streams may be processed by seperate instruction processing units as in a multi-microprocessor design or they may timeshare a single instruction processing unit.

Because of the high importance we look a little bit more in detail what physical units make up the **MIMD** computer and how they are interconnected.

The following figures illustrate the *structural taxonomy of MIMD-computer systems*

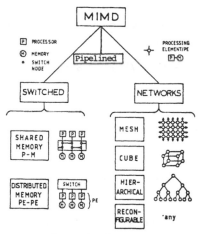

A structural taxonomy of MIMD computer systems.

3   Development of Parallel Numerical Algorithms

In a parallel algorithm, because more than one task module can be executed at a time, concurrency control is needed to ensure the correctness of the concurrent execution. The concurrency control enforces desired interactions among task modules so that the overall execution of the parallel algorithm will be correct. Concurrent control has a great influence on the structure of algorithm.

Characterization of the algorithms

Type	Concurrent Control	Remarks
SIMD-algorithms	central control unit - SIMD -	SIMD machines correspond to synchronous algorithms that require central controls
MIMD-algorithms	asynchronous, shared memory - MIMD -	MIMD machines correspond to asynchronous algorithms with relatively large granularities
Systolic-algorithms	distributed control achieved by simple local control	LSI and VLSI machines for special algorithms

Remarks:

(i) Systolic algorithms are designed for direct hardware implementations.

(ii) MIMD algorithms are designed for executions on general purpose multiprocessors.

(iii) SIMD algorithms are lying between the two other types.

Numerical methods are based on the evaluation of arithmetic expressions. The exploitation on such expressions can be represented by graphs (trees). Application of the laws of the real numbers often leads to "tree-height-reduction" whose possible utilization is dependent on the considered type of computer; that is that an algorithm A is a composition of arithmetic expressions E_k:

$$A = E_1 \circ E_2 \circ \ldots \circ E_n.$$

Given an arbitrary expression A_0 one tries to split this into two smaller expressions A_1 and A_2, which can be calculated simultaneously, each by one processor. For execution on a SIMD-machine the following conditions must be valid:

1. There exists a function f with $A_0 = f(A_1, A_2)$.

2. A_1 and A_2 are computed independent of each other and are of the same complexity.

3. A_1 and A_2 requires the same series of computation.

Further splitting of A_1 and A_2 according to 1. - 3. leads to A_0 by recursive doubling.

Example 1: Recursive doubling [Kogge]
Given
$$S := \{a_1, a_2, \ldots, a_N \mid N = 2^k, k \in \mathbf{N}\} \subset \mathbf{R}$$
and an associative operation $op \in M := \{+, *, max, \ldots\}$ in S.

$$A := a_1 \; op \; a_2 \; op \; \ldots \; op \; a_N$$

shall be calculated.

Associativity gives $\tilde{A} := (a_1 \, op \, a_2) \, op \, (a_3 \, op \, a_4) \, op \, \ldots \, op \, (a_{N-1} \, op \, a_N)$ which can be performed in parallel.

Example 2:

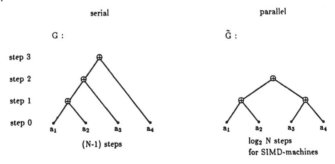

With $N = 2^k$ elements the recursive doubling requires log_2N steps on a SIMD-computer.

Example 3: Mixed expressions
Given

$$A := a_1 + a_2 \star a_3 + a_4$$

by associativity *no* tree-height-reduction is achieved. The tree G for serial exploitation of A is not unique. Communication law for addition transforms A into

$$\tilde{A} := (a_1 + a_4) + a_2 \star a_3$$

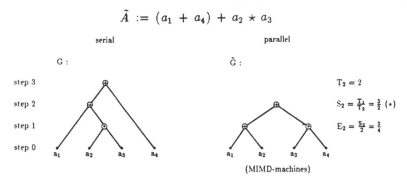

Tree-height-reduction on a **MIMD**-computer is possible.

Among others the following questions arise (s.[Beatty],[Baer],[Bovet],[Kuck], [Murocoka])[6].

1. How many tree-height-reductions can be performed for an arithmetic expression A?

2. Do exist algorithms for tree-height-reduction?

3. How many processors are necessary?

Recurrent relations: Recurrent relations are qualified for the solution of problems which are solved by a sequence $x_1, x_2, \ldots, x_n$, $x_i \in R$ and where each x_i, $i = 1, \ldots, n$ could be dependent on other components x_j $(j < i)$.

Definition: An m-th order linear recurrent system of n equations $R < n, m >$ is defined for $m \leq n - 1$ by

$$R < n, m > := x_n := \begin{cases} 0 & , k \leq 0 \\ c_k + \sum_{j=k-m}^{k-1} a_{kj}\, x_j, & 1 \leq k \leq n \end{cases}$$

If $m = n - 1$ the system is called an ordinary linear recurrent system $R < n >$.

Now we can consider recurrent relations in general.

Definition: A general m-th order recurrent system $R < n, m >$ is defined by

$$R < n, m > := x_k := H[\bar{a}_k; x_{k-1}, x_{k-2}, \ldots, x_{k-m}], \ 1 \leq k \leq n$$

with m initial values $x_{-m+1}, \ldots, x_0$.

H is called the recurrence function and $\bar{a}_k$ is a vector of parameters independent of any of the x_i.

These systems are qualified for SIMD-machines.

Example: For a first order recurrent system we get

$$x_1 := c_1 \qquad \text{initial value}$$
$$x_k := a_k x_{k-1} + c_k, \ 2 \le k \le n$$
$$= H[\bar{a}_k; x_{k-1}]$$

with

$$\bar{a}_k := [a_k, c_k];$$

H is defined by addition and multiplication.

Example: Linear recurrent relations of first order

$$x_1 = b_1$$
$$x_2 = -a_2 x_1 + b_2$$
$$\vdots$$
$$x_k = -a_k x_{k-1} + b_k$$
$$\vdots$$
$$x_n = -a_n x_{n-1} + b_n$$

finally $Lx = b$ with

$$
\left.
\begin{aligned}
l_{ii} &= 1 \quad, i = 1, \ldots, n \\
l_{i,i-1} &= a_i \quad, i = 2, \ldots, n \\
l_{ik} &= 0 \quad else
\end{aligned}
\right\}
\quad L =
\begin{bmatrix}
1 & & & & & 0 \\
a_2 & 1 & & & & \\
 & a_3 & \ddots & & & \\
 & & & \ddots & 1 & \\
0 & & & & a_n & 1
\end{bmatrix}
$$

Solution: $x = L^{-1}b = L_n^{-1}L_{n-1}^{-1} \ldots L_3 L_2^{-1}b.$

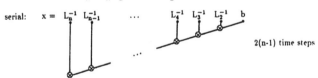

serial: $x = L_n^{-1} L_{n-1}^{-1} \quad \cdots \quad L_4^{-1} L_3^{-1} L_2^{-1} \ b$

2(n-1) time steps

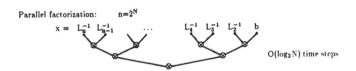

Parallel factorization: $n=2^N$

$x = L_n^{-1} L_{n-1}^{-1} \quad \cdots \quad L_4^{-1} L_3^{-1} L_2^{-1} \ b$

$O(\log_2 N)$ time steps

Remark: look for the inner and global parallelism.

If the given H-function is not associative, there often exist socalled companion functions G with associative properties.

Definition: A function G is called companion function of the recurrence function H if for all x and for all parameter vectors $\bar{a}, \bar{b} \in \mathbb{R}^p$

$$H[\bar{a};\ H[\bar{b}; x]\ ] \ = \ H[G(\bar{a}, \bar{b}); x]$$

with $G : \mathbb{R}^p \times \mathbb{R}^p \rightarrow \mathbb{R}^p$.

All companion functions have the following property:

Theorem: Each companion function G is associative with respect to its recurrent function H; that means: for all x and for all parameter vectors $\bar{a}, \bar{b}, \bar{c} \in \mathbb{R}^p$

$$H[G(\bar{a}, G(\bar{b}, \bar{c})); x] \ = \ H[G(G(\bar{a}, \bar{b}), \bar{c}); x]$$

Conclusion: The existence of G allows the construction of a parallel algorithm by the log-sum-algorithm.

Example: companion-functions in recurrent relations:

$$
\begin{aligned}
x_k \ &:= H[\bar{a}_k; x_{k-1}];\ \bar{a}_k \in \mathbb{R}^p;\ x_0 \text{ initial value}\\
x_2 \ &= H[\bar{a}_2; x_1]\\
&= H(\bar{a}_2; H(\bar{a}_1; x_0)) \ = \ H(G(\bar{a}_2, \bar{a}_1); x_0); \ \ G \text{ companion-function}\\
x_4 \ &= H[\bar{a}_4; x_3]\\
&= H(\bar{a}_4; H(\bar{a}_3; x_2)) \ = \ H(G(\bar{a}_4, \bar{a}_3); x_2)\\
&= H(G(\bar{a}_4, \bar{a}_3); H(G(\bar{a}_2, \bar{a}_1); x_0))\\
&= H(G(G(\bar{a}_4, \bar{a}_3); G(\bar{a}_2, \bar{a}_1)); x_0)\\
x_8 \ &= H[\bar{a}_8; x_7]\\
&= H(\bar{a}_8; H(\bar{a}_7; H(\bar{a}_6; H(\bar{a}_5; x_4))))\\
&= H(G(\bar{a}_8, \bar{a}_7); H(G(\bar{a}_6, \bar{a}_5); x_4))\\
&= H(G(\bar{a}_8, \bar{a}_7); H(G(\bar{a}_6, \bar{a}_5); H(G(G(\bar{a}_4, \bar{a}_3), G(\bar{a}_2, \bar{a}_1); x_0))))\\
&= H(G(G(\bar{a}_8, \bar{a}_7), G(\bar{a}_6, \bar{a}_5)); H(G(G(\bar{a}_4, \bar{a}_3), G(\bar{a}_2, \bar{a}_1); x_0)))\\
&= H(G(G(G(\bar{a}_8, \bar{a}_7), G(\bar{a}_6, \bar{a}_5)), G(G(\bar{a}_4, \bar{a}_3), G(\bar{a}_2, \bar{a}_1))); x_0)
\end{aligned}
$$

Graph for x_{2^k}

Example: Numerical integration; numerical solution of ordinary differential equations; here it is possible to compute the value y_N without knowing explicitly the previous values.

Another concept for solving linear systems, especially tridiagonal system $Ax = b$, is parallelization by permutation. Transformation of A by the permutation matrix P gives a block structured system $\tilde{A}x = \tilde{b}$ where $\tilde{A} = PAP^T$. This can be solved in parallel by the parallel SOR-Method.

In the application area the efficient numerical solution of PDEs is a highly important subject. Besides multigrid methods [2] the domain decomposition methods are very suitable to develop parallel algorithms for PDEs.

4 Domain Decomposition Methods

Another class of techniques that received much attention recently is the class of *domain decomposition techniques* in which the physical domain is divided into *separate subdomains* each handled by a different processor.

Let us consider the numerical solution of the partial differential equation

$$\frac{\partial u}{\partial t} = F(x, u, t, D_x u, D_x^2 u, \dots)$$

where $x \in \Omega \in \mathbb{R}^n$, $0 \leq t \leq \tau$ and $u(x, t) \in \mathbb{R}^m$ satisfies given boundary and initial conditions. Then at t^*,

$$\Omega = \bigcup_{j=1}^{k(t^*)} \Omega_j(t^*)$$

and on each Ω_j

$$\frac{\partial u}{\partial t} = F_j(x, u), \; j = 1, 2, \dots, k(t^*)$$

is defined. Each processor P_j solves one of these partial differential equations over a prespecified time interval.

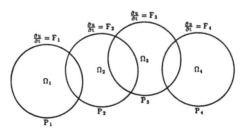

Discretization of the PDE by finite differences or finite elements gives the linear system:

$$
L^h \bar{u} = \begin{bmatrix} A_1 & B_1 & & & & \\ B_1^T & A_2 & B_2 & & & \\ & & \ddots & \ddots & & \\ & & & \ddots & B_{n-1} & \\ & & & B_{n-1}^T & A_n \end{bmatrix} \begin{bmatrix} \bar{u}(1) \\ \bar{u}(2) \\ \vdots \\ \vdots \\ \bar{u}(n) \end{bmatrix} = \begin{bmatrix} \bar{b}(1) \\ \bar{b}(2) \\ \vdots \\ \vdots \\ \bar{b}(n) \end{bmatrix} = \bar{b}
$$

$\bar{u}(i)$ is the numerical approximation to $\bar{u}$ on the points (x_i, y_j), for $j = 1, 2, \ldots, n$. A_i, B_i are (n, n)-tridiagonal matrices with $A_i = A_i^T$.

A solution can be obtained by an iterative process, e.g. SOR-method; preconditioned cg-method; multigrid method; Schwarz algorithm.

The following *Poisson-Equation* will be considered as a special example for solving elliptic PDE's by decomposition methods.

$$
\Delta u = u_{xx} + u_{yy} = f \text{ in } \Omega := \{(0, l) \times (0, 1)\} \subset R_2
$$
$$
u = g \text{ on the boundary } \partial\Omega
$$

with $u \in C^2(\Omega)$, $f \in C^1(\Omega)$, $g \in C^1(\partial\Omega)$.

Discretization on the grid G over Ω,

$$
G := \{(x_i, y_i) \mid x_i = ih, \ y_j = jh; \ i = 1, \ldots, m; \ j = 1, \ldots, n\},
$$

gives the linear system $Lu = b$ as an approximation of the PDE:

$$
L = \begin{bmatrix} A_1 & B_1 & & & & \\ B_1^T & A_2 & B_2 & & 0 & \\ & B_2^T & A_3 & B_3 & & \\ & & \ddots & \ddots & \ddots & \\ 0 & & & B_{m-2}^T & A_{m-1} & B_{m-1} \\ & & & & B_{m-1}^T & A_m \end{bmatrix} \in R^{nm, nm},
$$

with

$$
A_i = \begin{bmatrix} 4 & -1 & & & & \\ -1 & 4 & -1 & & 0 & \\ & -1 & 4 & -1 & & \\ & & \ddots & \ddots & \ddots & \\ & 0 & & -1 & 4 & -1 \\ & & & & -1 & 4 \end{bmatrix} \in R^{n, n}
$$

and $B_i = -I \in R^{n,n}$, $u, b \in R^{nm}$.

Special method: Numerical Schwarz-Algorithms consider a decomposition of Ω into overlapping subdomains Ω_i and Ω_j of Ω:

$$
\Omega = \bigcup_{i-1}^{p}, \ \Omega_i \in R^2 \text{ and } \Omega_i \cap \Omega_j \neq \emptyset.
$$

For $p = 2$ follows for Ω_1 and Ω_2:

$$\Omega_1 = \Omega_{11} \cup \Gamma_{21} \cup \Omega_{12}$$
$$\Omega_2 = \Omega_{21} \cup \Gamma_{12} \cup \Omega_{22} \text{ and}$$
$$\Omega = \Omega_1 \cup \Omega_2$$

After discretization of the Poisson-equation by finite differences we have the following system for the domain Ω:

$$Lu = \begin{bmatrix} K_{11} & K_{12} & 0 & 0 & 0 \\ K_{12}^T & K_{22} & K_{23} & 0 & 0 \\ 0 & K_{23}^T & K_{33} & K_{34} & 0 \\ 0 & 0 & K_{34}^T & K_{44} & K_{45} \\ 0 & 0 & 0 & K_{45}^T & k_{55} \end{bmatrix} \begin{bmatrix} u_1 \\ u_2 \\ u_3 \\ u_4 \\ u_5 \end{bmatrix} = \begin{bmatrix} b_1 \\ b_2 \\ b_3 \\ b_4 \\ b_5 \end{bmatrix} = b$$

The matrix L and the vectors u and b are partitioned according to the decompositon of Ω. The submatrices K_{ij} describe the coupling of the unknown u_i and u_j in the different subdomains. We then have the following systems to be solved in the subdomains Ω_1 and Ω_2 [1]:

$$L_1 v_1 = \begin{bmatrix} K_{11} & K_{12} & 0 \\ K_{12}^T & K_{22} & K_{23} \\ 0 & K_{23}^T & K_{33} \end{bmatrix} \begin{bmatrix} v_{11} \\ v_{12} \\ v_{13} \end{bmatrix} = \begin{bmatrix} e_{11} \\ e_{12} \\ e_{13} \end{bmatrix} = e_1 \text{ with } v_{1i} = u_i, \; i = 1, 2, 3$$

and

$$L_2 v_2 = \begin{bmatrix} K_{33} & K_{34} & 0 \\ K_{34}^T & K_{44} & K_{45} \\ 0 & K_{45}^T & K_{55} \end{bmatrix} \begin{bmatrix} v_{21} \\ v_{22} \\ v_{23} \end{bmatrix} = \begin{bmatrix} e_{21} \\ e_{22} \\ e_{23} \end{bmatrix} = e_2 \text{ with } v_{2i} = u_{2+i}, \; i = 1, 2, 3$$

The right side-vectors e_1 and e_2 are computed by

$$e_1 = \begin{bmatrix} e_{11} \\ e_{12} \\ e_{13} \end{bmatrix} = \begin{bmatrix} b_1 \\ b_2 \\ b_3 - K_{34} u_4 \end{bmatrix} = \begin{bmatrix} b_1 \\ b_2 \\ b_3 \end{bmatrix} - \begin{bmatrix} 0 & 0 & 0 \\ 0 & 0 & 0 \\ 0 & K_{34} & 0 \end{bmatrix} \begin{bmatrix} v_{21} \\ v_{22} \\ v_{23} \end{bmatrix} =: f_1 - G_2 v_1$$

and

$$e_2 = \begin{bmatrix} e_{21} \\ e_{22} \\ e_{23} \end{bmatrix} = \begin{bmatrix} b_3 - K_{23}^T u_2 \\ b_4 \\ b_5 \end{bmatrix} = \begin{bmatrix} b_3 \\ b_4 \\ b_5 \end{bmatrix} - \begin{bmatrix} 0 & K_{23}^T & 0 \\ 0 & 0 & 0 \\ 0 & 0 & 0 \end{bmatrix} \begin{bmatrix} v_{11} \\ v_{12} \\ v_{13} \end{bmatrix} =: f_2 - E_1 v_1$$

Then we have the system

$$Fv := \begin{bmatrix} L_1 & G_2 \\ E_1 & L_2 \end{bmatrix} \begin{bmatrix} v_1 \\ v_2 \end{bmatrix} = \begin{bmatrix} f_1 \\ f_2 \end{bmatrix} =: f$$

which can be solved by the *Block-Jacobi-Method*:

$$\begin{bmatrix} L_1 & 0 \\ 0 & L_2 \end{bmatrix} \begin{bmatrix} v_1^{(K+1)} \\ v_2^{(K+1)} \end{bmatrix} = \begin{bmatrix} f_1 \\ f_2 \end{bmatrix} - \begin{bmatrix} 0 & G_2 \\ E_1 & 0 \end{bmatrix} \begin{bmatrix} v_1^{(K)} \\ v_2^{(K)} \end{bmatrix}$$

This iterative algorithm converges [1] against the solutions v_1^* and v_2^* and it holds for the solution u^* of $Lu = b$:

$$v_1^* = [v_{11}^*, v_{12}^*, v_{13}^*]^T = [u_1^*, u_2^*, u_3^*]^T$$

and

$$v_2^* = [v_{21}^*, v_{22}^*, v_{23}^*]^T = [u_3^*, u_4^*, u_5^*]^T.$$

On a MIMD-system with 2 processors each processor solves a linear system of the kind

$$L_i v_i^{(K)} = e_i^K, \ i = 1, 2, \ \text{with} \ e_1^K = f_1 - G_2 v_2^{(K-1)} \ \text{and} \ e_2^K = f_2 - E_1 v_1^{(K-1)}.$$

Here you have a global and an inner parallelism of the algorithm.

These solutions correspond to the solution of the given PDE on the subdomains Ω_1 respectively Ω_2 with the boundary values $v_2^{(K-1)}$ respectively $v_1^{(K-1)}$ on Γ_{12} respectively Γ_{21}. Convergence results even for the approximation solution on Ω_1 and Ω_2 [7].

An alternative domain decomposition method is the class of *capacity-matrix-methods*. In this case the domain Ω is partitioned into not overlapping subdomains, that is for $\Omega \subset \mathbf{R}^2$:

$$\Omega = \bigcup_{i=1}^{p} \Omega_i, \ \Omega_i \subset \mathbf{R}^2 \ \text{and} \ \Omega_i \cap \Omega_j = \phi.$$

Example:

$$p = 2: \quad \boxed{\Omega_1 \ | \ \Omega_2} \quad \Omega_1 \cap \Omega_2 = \phi, \quad \Omega = \Omega_1 \cup \Omega_2 \cup \Gamma_{12}$$

Discretization of the PDE by the grid G on Ω gives the linear system

$$Lu = \begin{bmatrix} K_{11} & 0 & K_{13} \\ 0 & K_{22} & K_{23} \\ K_{13}^T & K_{23}^T & K_{33} \end{bmatrix} \begin{bmatrix} u_1 \\ u_2 \\ u_3 \end{bmatrix} = \begin{bmatrix} b_1 \\ b_2 \\ b_3 \end{bmatrix} = b.$$

The matrix L and the vectors u and b are partitioned according to the decomposition of Ω [7]. Finally the following *capacity-matrix-system* must be solved:

$$(K_{33} - K_{13}^T K_{11}^{-1} K_{13} - K_{23}^T K_{22}^{-1} K_{23}) u_3 = b_3 - K_{13}^T K_{11}^{-1} b_1 - K_{23}^T K_{22}^{-1} b_2$$
$$\leftrightarrow \qquad C u_3 = e$$

This can be computed by block-Gauss-elimination. Then follows for u_1 respectively u_2 :

$$u_1 = K_{11}^{-1}(b_1 - K_{13} u_3) \ \text{and} \ u_2 = K_{22}^{-1}(b_2 - K_{23} u_3).$$

That is, u_1 and u_2 are solutions of the PDE on the subdomains Ω_1 and Ω_2 with the given boundary values b_1 respectively b_2 on the outer boundaries $\partial\Omega_1$ respectively $\partial\Omega_2$ and the boundary values u_3 on Γ_{12}. For the right side e holds:

$$e = b_1 - K_{11}^{-1} y_1 - K_{22}^{-1} y_2 \ \text{with} \ y_1 = K_{11}^{-1} b_1 \ \text{and} \ y_2 = K_{22}^{-1} b_2.$$

y_1 and y_2 are the solutions of the PDE on Ω_1 and Ω_2 with homogeneous boundary conditions on Γ_{12}. The capacity-matrix-system can be solved by the preconditioned cg-method. The solutions y_1 and y_2 on the subdomains can be solved on a MIMD-system with 2 processors where you have again the inner and outer parallelism. In this case the preconditioners of Dryja [3] and Golub/Mayers [4] have been applied effectively.

References

[1] Bjorstad, P. E. and Widlund, O. B. : Solving elliptic problems on regions partitioned into substructures. In: Birkhoff, G. and Schoenstadt, A. (eds.) : Elliptic Problem Solvers II. Academic Press, New York, 1984.

[2] Dornscheidt, G. and Schendel, U. : Lösung einer elliptischen Randwertaufgabe mit dem Mehrgitterverfahren. Serie A Mathematik, A-88-02, FU Berlin.

[3] Dryja, M. : A finite-element capacitance method for elliptic problems partitioned into subregions. Numer. Math. 44, 153-168, 1984.

[4] Golub, G. H. and Mayers, D. : The use of preconditioning over irregular regions. Lecture at Sixth Int. Conf. on Computing Methods in Applied Sciences and Engineering, Versailles, France, 1983.

[5] Rathmann, S. and Schendel, U. : Über Präkonditionierer bei Dekompositions-methoden. Serie A Mathematik, A-88-13, FU Berlin.

[6] Schendel, U. : Introduction to numerical methods for parallel computers. Ellis Horwood Series, John Wiley and Sons, New York 1984.

[7] Schendel, U. and Schyska, M. : Dekompositionsmethoden zur Lösung elliptischer partieller Differentialgleichungen. Preprint 269/87, Fachbereich Mathematik Serie A, FU Berlin.

[8] Wouk, A. (ed.) : New Computing Environments: Parallel, Vector and Systolic. SIAM, Philadelphia, 1986.

For further references see mentioned titles.

Graphics tools for developing high-performance algorithms*

Orlie Brewer
Jack Dongarra
David Levine
Danny Sorensen

Mathematics and Computer Science Division
Argonne National Laboratory
Argonne, Illinois 60439-4801

Abstract

This paper discusses two tools that aid in the development of parallel algorithms for high-performance computers. We describe the SCHEDULE package which provides an environment for developing and analyzing new parallel algorithms in Fortran that require sophisticated synchronization at a large-grain level. This package provides portability of a user's code and also has a graphics postprocessor for performance analysis and debugging. We also discuss a graphics tool useful for studying memory access patterns of algorithms.

Keywords: parallel algorithms, graphics tools

1. Introduction

For many computational problems, the design and implementation of an efficient parallel algorithm can be a formidable challenge. Efficient parallel programs are more difficult to write than efficient sequential programs, because the behavior of parallel programs is nondeterministic. They are also much less portable, because the structure depends critically on specific architectural features of the underlying hardware (such as the way in which data sharing and process creation are handled).

This paper discusses two tools that aid in the development of parallel algorithms. The SCHEDULE package is a tool to aid in implementing and analyzing a large-grain control flow model of computation. There is a natural graphical interpretation that is useful in designing and implementing parallel algorithms. This graphical interpretation lends itself well to a postprocessing performance analysis by animating the flow of a parallel algorithm's execution. The second tool, the Memory Access Pattern program, is useful in understanding how various algorithms access memory. This tool provides a graphical display of memory access patterns in algorithms. Such patterns can be important in understanding memory bottlenecks in compute-intensive algorithms.

---

*This work was supported by the Applied Mathematical Sciences subprogram of the Office of Energy Research, U.S. Department of Energy, under Contract no. W-31-109-Eng-38.

2. SCHEDULE

The SCHEDULE package provides an environment for the portable implementation of explicitly parallel algorithms in a Fortran setting. Once implemented using SCHEDULE, a user's code is virtually identical for each target machine the application is run on. The package is designed to allow existing Fortran subroutines to be called through SCHEDULE, without modification, thereby permitting users access to a wide body of existing library software in a parallel setting.

The underlying idea in SCHEDULE is that many parallel computations may be represented in a large-grain control flow form and that this is a useful way to think about and construct parallel programs. A parallel program is derived by breaking a problem up into units of computation and control dependencies between them. These dependencies represent assertions made by the user about the order in which computations must occur. This concept is similar to the large-grain data flow ideas [1, 2]. The graph must represent control dependencies, but is not driven by dataflow rules. Moreover, data items are implicitly carried along arcs, but one does not explicitly associate a data item with an arc. This approach greatly reduces the complexity of the graphical representation.

When designing a parallel algorithm using SCHEDULE, one is required to describe the control dependencies, parallel structures, and shared variables involved in the solution. These are then implemented in a Fortran program written in terms of subroutine calls to SCHEDULE. Each pair of SCHEDULE subroutine calls specifies a unit of computation or process that consists of a subroutine name, the subroutine's calling parameters, and the control dependencies necessary to coordinate the parallel execution. The user must take the responsibility of ensuring that the control dependencies specified are valid.

A useful way to think of these units of computation and control dependencies is as a directed acyclic graph. Interpreted graphically, nodes represent units of computation, and arcs represent control dependencies. For each node in the graph, SCHEDULE requires two subroutine calls. One contains information about the user's routine to be called, such as the name of the routine, calling parameters, and a unique tag to identify the process. The second subroutine call defines the dependency in the graph to nodes above and below the one being specified, and specifies the tag to identify the process. These concepts are perhaps more easily grasped through an example.

2.1. Example

A simple example is a parallel algorithm for computing the inner product of two vectors. The intention here is to illustrate the mechanics of using SCHEDULE. This algorithm and the use of SCHEDULE on a problem of such small granularity are not necessarily recommended.

Problem: Given real vectors a and b, each of length n, compute $\sigma = a^T b$.

Parallel Algorithm:

Let $a^T = (a_1^T, a_2^T, ..., a_k^T)$ and $b^T = (b_1^T, b_2^T, ..., b_k^T)$

be a partitioning of the vectors a and b into smaller vectors a_i and b_i.

Compute (in parallel)

$$\sigma_j = a_j^T b_j \,, j = 1, k.$$

When done, compute

$$\sigma = \sigma_1 + \sigma_2 + \cdots + \sigma_k.$$

The first step is to understand the parallel algorithm in terms of schedulable processes and a control dependency graph. The code would consist of a main program to initialize the shared data, a parallel subroutine to compute the inner product by invoking parallel processes to compute σ_j and a subroutine to calculate σ, when all done, by summing the σ_j. The control dependency graph (excluding the main program) is shown in Figure 1

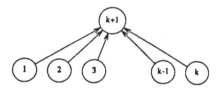

Figure 1.

Dependency Graph for Parallel Inner Product

This graph shows k processes that are not control dependent. Each reads a segment of the shared data a, b, calculates σ_j, and writes the result on its own entry in a temporary array in shared memory. None of these processes needs to read data that another process will write. (This fact is evident in the graphical representation shown in Figure 1, where the processes are *leaves*.) The process labeled $k+1$ which computes $\sigma = \sigma_1 + \sigma_2 + \cdots + \sigma_k$ is control dependent on each of the processes labelled $1, 2, ..., k$. That is, $k+1$ needs to read each entry of the temporary array in order to compute the sum and place it in σ.

From this control dependency graph we may write the parallel program. Each node in the graph is replaced by calls to two SCHEDULE routines to identify both the user subroutine to be executed and the information relating to the dependency graph. The code that will execute in parallel is derived from serial code by replacing calls to the user's subroutines with calls to SCHEDULE routines that invoke these routines. Detailed programming examples may be found in [7].

The mechanism just described allows static scheduling of parallel processes. By this we mean that the number of processes and their control dependencies are known in advance. In many situations, however we will not know the computational graph in advance, and we will need the ability for one process to start or spawn another depending on a computation that has taken place up to a given point in the spawning process. This feature, which we call dynamic spawning, is provided by the SCHEDULE package via routines similar to those for static scheduling.

2.2. Postprocessing Graphics Tools for SCHEDULE

We are interested in an animation of the run-time behavior of our algorithm, visualizing the parallel parts in execution as the application is running. We want to understand what performance issues arise during execution and what bottlenecks develop, and to view where programming errors may cause a parallel program to "hang." Since the control dependency graph has such a natural graphical interpretation, we have developed a postprocessing tool to trace and animate the flow of execution.

To use the graphics facility, the user constructs a SCHEDULE program as previously described, the difference being the user linking to the SCHEDULE graphics library rather than the regular library. The SCHEDULE program is then executed on the parallel processor of interest. While executing, it produces an output file of trace events. The information in the file is a trace of the user specification of the computational graph and the execution of the graph by the computer. The trace file records the definition of the graph along with the execution and completion of the subroutine. When execution has completed, this file is then moved to a workstation where a program to graphically display the information in the trace file has been installed. The current implementation of the graphics facility runs on a Sun workstation under Suntools. We are currently porting the graphics facility to the X Window System. Figure 2 shows an example of a computational graph as it would appear on the screen.

A number of buttons and slide bars help in controlling the information to be viewed. To load a trace file, one first selects the desired trace file and then clicks on the **Load** button; the control dependency graph is then displayed on the screen. The arcs represent the control dependencies between subroutines. There are five states for a static node in the graph: clear, lined, hashed, circled, and black. The *clear* nodes represent subroutines waiting to have their control dependencies satisfied before starting execution. The *lined* nodes represent subroutines whose control dependencies are satisfied, but whose execution has not started. The *hatched* nodes represent subroutines that are currently executing. The *circled* nodes represent subroutines whose execution has been temporarily suspended because they have dynamically spawned other processes. The *black* nodes represent subroutines that have finished execution. The rectangular nodes represent processes that have been spawned dynamically. The numbers associated with each node in the graph represent the *tag* that the user has assigned to each process. The nodes in the dependency graph will change their state as the trace proceeds.

The viewing of events can be stopped or restarted by clicking on the **Stop** or the **Go** button at any time. Execution begins at the bottom of the graph and works its way to the top, with the linear system partitioned by blocks. As the program executed on an Alliant FX/8, an output file was produced which recorded the units of computation as they were defined and executed. The file was then shipped to a Sun workstation where a graphics program interpreted this output, constructed the graph, and played back the execution sequence that was run on the Alliant. In the graph shown in Figure 3, the black nodes show processes that have completed execution, the hatched nodes show executing processes, and the white nodes show processes waiting to execute.

In addition to discovering mistakes in the specification of the graph, this representation is useful in exposing more subtle aspects of the executing program. During execution the bar graph labeled "active processes" at the top tracks the number of processes actually executing. The bar labeled "timing speed" can be adjusted to speed up or slow down the replay. The events will occur in time proportional to execution time. This gives a much better indication of serial bottlenecks and load balancing problems within an executing program. Once load balance anomalies have been discovered, they can be corrected by revising the execution dependencies to force certain processes to complete before others.

2.3. Construction of Dependency Graphs

One way to specify the control dependency graph is for the user to write a Fortran program that calls the SCHEDULE library routines *dep* and *putq* once each for every node in the graph. In addition to specifying the user's subroutine and parameter list, each node must be assigned a unique tag. Since the programming associated with constructing the dependency graph may be tedious and error prone, we have developed a "mouse-driven" graphics input device to use at a workstation.

To use this tool, one clicks on a mouse to create the nodes that will be in the dependency graph. Clicking another button draws the arcs that represent control dependencies between nodes. After constructing the dependency graph in this manner, the user associates his subroutine names and parameter lists with each node via an on-screen menu. With a final mouse click a Fortran program representing the dependency graph is generated automatically.

3. Memory Access Pattern Program

The second tool we discuss, the Memory Access Pattern program, is helpful in understanding how an algorithm uses the memory hierarchy. On modern high-performance computers, memory is organized in a hierarchy according to access time. This hierarchy takes the form of main memory, cache, local memory, and vector registers. The basic objective of this organization is to attempt to match the imbalance between the fast processing speed of the floating-point units and the slow latency time of main memory. In order to be successful, algorithms must effectively utilize the memory hierarchy of the underlying computer architecture on which they are implemented.

The key to using a high-performance computer effectively is to avoid unnecessary memory references. In most computers, data flows from memory into and out of registers and from registers into and out of functional units, which perform the given instructions on the data. Algorithm performance can be dominated by the amount of memory traffic rather than by the number of floating-point operations involved. This situation provides considerable motivation to restructure existing algorithms and to devise new algorithms that minimize data movement.

For computers with memory hierarchy or for true parallel processing computers, it is often preferable to partition the matrices into blocks and to perform the computation by matrix-matrix operations on the blocks. This approach provides for full reuse of data while the block is held in cache or local memory. It avoids excessive movement of data to and from memory and gives a surface-to-volume effect for the ratio of arithmetic operations to data movement, i.e., $O(n^3)$ arithmetic operations to $O(n^2)$ data movement. In addition, on architectures that provide for parallel processing, parallelism can be exploited in two ways: (1) operations on distinct blocks may be performed in parallel; and (2) within the operations on each block, scalar or vector operations may be performed in parallel.

The performance of these block algorithms depends on the dimensions chosen for the blocks. It is important to select the blocking strategy for each of our target machines, and then develop a mechanism whereby the routines can determine good block dimensions automatically.

Since most memory accesses for data in scientific programs are for matrix elements, which are usually stored in two-dimensional arrays (column-major in Fortran), knowing the order of array references is important in determining the amount of memory traffic. We would like to take an arbitrary linear algebra program, have its matrices mapped to a graphics screen, and have a matrix element flash on the screen whenever its corresponding array element was accessed in memory. This type of tool would provide insight into the algorithm's behavior and would enable the programmer to compare the memory access patterns of different algorithms.

3.1. Description of Tools

The MAP tools are intended to provide an "animated" view of the memory activity during execution. These tools allow us to to play back a program's execution to study how an algorithm uses memory, and to experiment with different memory hierarchy schemes and observe their effects on the program's flow of data.

There are two basic aspects to accomplishing our goals: preprocessor instrumentation is accomplished by the Memory Access Pattern Instrumentation (MAPI) program and and postprocessor display graphics, by the Memory Access Pattern Animation (MAPA) program. The MAPI preprocessor analyzes a Fortran module and, for each reference to a matrix element, generates a Fortran statement that calls a MAPI routine that records the reference to the matrix element. In addition, if calls are made to Level 1, 2, or 3 BLAS [8, 5, 4], MAPI translates those calls into calls to MAPI routines that understand the BLAS operations and record the appropriate array references. The replaced routine will record the memory access to be made, as well as the number of floating-point operations to be performed, and then call the Level 1, 2, or 3 BLAS originally intended. The output of MAPI is a Fortran module that, when compiled and linked with a MAPI library, executes the original code and produces a trace file. This trace file is used as input to MAPA in order to display the memory accesses on the arrays in the Fortran code.

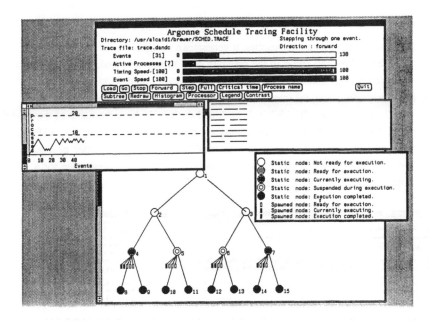

Figure 2: Information on the workstation screen

top node the last thing to execute. The **Full** button is used in conjunction with the **Redraw** button to expand what is displayed on the canvas by a factor of four.

The **Critical time** button is used after execution has completed. It displays the time required to execute the various paths in the graph and can be used to display the critical path of execution (i.e., the path that is taking the most time to execute). The critical path determines the running time of the entire application.

The **Subtree** button is used to display a subtree of the graph. To use this feature, one places the mouse cursor on a node. The node number clicked on will be displayed in bottom right line of the top panel. To see the subtree, one clicks the **Subtree** button. This step can be repeated to zoom in on a particular part of the graph.

The **Step** button is used to single-step through the execution of the trace file. A way to use this is by loading a trace file, starting execution, and stopping execution at the desired point. Then the **Step** button is used to single-step through the execution. The activity can be resumed at normal speeds by clicking the **Go** button. The **Forward** button is used to display the execution either forward or backward in time.

The **Histogram** button will display a histogram of the events run versus the number of processors active.

These tools can influence the design of an algorithm by providing insight into how the program behaves when run in parallel. An example of their use is in the solution of a triangular

3.2. Execution of the Instrumented Program

When the instrumented program executes, it generates a readable ASCII file that contains an encoded description of how the arrays in the program have been referenced. There are basically three types of trace lines generated: array definition, read access, and write access. If a call to one of the BLAS has been made, the trace file may contain the information about a row or column access or both. The name of the BLAS is recorded, and during playback the name of the BLAS executed will be displayed. In addition, the events are time stamped, allowing the MAPA program to merge information with other trace files and have the relative order of operations preserved. We also record the amount of floating-point work that has taken place for a given memory reference. Figure 3 displays the output of MAPA for a view of LU decomposition.

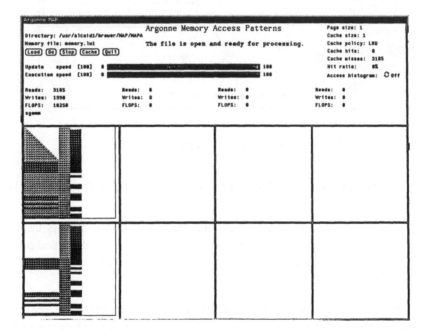

Figure 3. MAPA Output for LU Decompostion

3.3. Cache Modelling

The MAP tools also have a feature to allow statistical analysis and data collection of various cache systems. The cache consists of a simple, single cache memory. The basic cache policy is consecutive linear placement with immediate write-back. The cache placement and replacement algorithms work with pages of cache memory. The size of a cache page is flexible, but is required to be a power of two ranging from 1 to 65536.

There are six cache replacement mechanisms implemented. These are Least Recently Used (LRU), Least Frequently Used (LFU), First-In-First-Out (FIFO), Clock, Last-In-First-Out (LIFO), and Random. The LRU mechanism chooses the page in cache that was used the longest time ago. The LFU mechanism chooses the page that has been used the fewest number of times since it was loaded into the cache. The FIFO mechanism simply keeps track of which order pages were loaded into cache and replaces pages in the same order. The Clock mechanism is an approximation to LRU using FIFO, but as pages are used, a usage bit is set so the page will be skipped over as the FIFO queue is traversed. The LIFO mechanism is similar to the FIFO except that instead of replacing the pages in the order they were loaded, the pages are replaced in reverse order. The Random mechanism simply generates a random page number and replaces that page. When the cache is full and a new page from main memory needs to be loaded into the cache, the current cache replacement mechanism chooses the page in cache to be replaced.

When the MAPA tool executes, an additional box displaying cache activity is shown on the screen. When a cache hit is detected, the corresponding element turns yellow (on a color Sun monitor). When a cache miss is detected, the elements in cache that will be written over turn red.

3.4. MAPA: The Control Panel

The MAPA program maps the arrays to the graphics screen and highlights the elements of the arrays when they are accessed. The program can display up to four different arrays at one time. The top row displays the read accesses to the arrays, and the bottom displays the writes.

The panel subwindow (see Figure 4) is MAPA's main user control interface and contains several features:

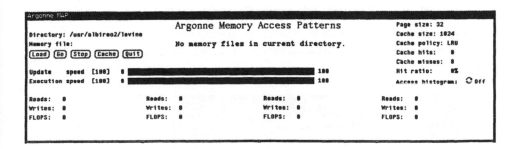

Figure 4. MAPA Control Panel

The **Directory** button allows the user to step through various directories to locate the desired trace file. The **Update speed** slider controls the length of time the memory reference is held on the screen before fading away. The **Execution speed** slider controls the speed at which events are processed when ''GO'' has been chosen. The speed control slider expresses the event display speed as a percentage of the fastest possible speed.

The **Load** button initializes and resets MAPA for another trace file. The **Go** button processes events from the trace file consecutively without stopping. The **Stop** button stops the tracing of events. The **Quit** button exits the MAPA tool.

3.5. Execution of MAPA

The canvas subwindow occupies the lower two-thirds of the window. Graphics information is displayed here. The canvas is divided into two rows of four squares. The first row displays the load activities, and the second row displays the store activity.

Each of the four columns of squares across the canvas can be used to display an array. When the trace file is started, a load of a matrix element is denoted by a blackening of an area of the block used to represent the array. As time evolves and if no further reference is made to that specific matrix element, the area will gradually lighten, until at some time after the original access, it will return to its original color. If a subsequent reference to that element is made, the area representing the element will again darken. In this way a user can observe the locality of reference the program is able to achieve. The same situation is true for store operations. As a store is made, the area representing the element affected darkens and after time the area will return to its original color. If the BLAS have been used, the whole area affected by the operation is changed at once.

3.6. Example

We have been experimenting with three different organizations for the algorithm to factor a matrix in preparation to solving a system of linear equations via Gaussian elimination. Each method performs the same number of floating-point operations; the algorithms differ only in the way in which the data is accessed. The three methods are block jki (a left-looking algorithm), block Crout, and block rank update (a right-looking algorithm). See [6, 3] for more details.

When MAPA displays the trace file produced by merging the trace files from the execution of the instrumented versions of the three different programs, we obtain the picture shown in Figure 5.

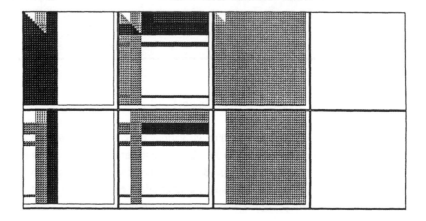

Figure 5. Display of Fortran Execution of a
Matrix of Order 40, Blocksize 5

Table 1 was generated on a matrix of order 100 and a blocksize 64. As can be seen in this case, algorithm 1 (block jki) has fewer store operations over all and slightly more load operations. We would expect this algorithm to perform better than algorithm 3 (block rank update) and marginally faster than algorithm 2 (block Crout).

Table 1. 100 x 100 matrix, blocksize 64

		LU1	LU2	LU3
Random	LOADS	102530	108515	99965
	STORES	33180	37455	90180
Diag.	LOADS	84100	90085	81535
Dominant	STORES	14750	19025	71750

The row marked Diag. Dominant reflects the fact that the matrix is diagonally dominant; thus, no pivoting is performed during the factorization, resulting in fewer memory references. (For these results, it was assumed that the data would be held in the memory hierarchy once it was fetched for the operation (i.e., fetched once for each block operation).

4. Conclusions

We have discussed two tools that aid in the development of parallel algorithms. Both tools rely heavily on the use of post-execution graphical displays to help the programmer understand the behavior of a parallel algorithm

These tools allow users to view trace files generated by executing parallel algorithms. Using such tools provides insight into algorithm behavior and potential bottlenecks.

References

1. R.G. Babb, "Parallel Processing with Large Grain Data Flow Techniques," *IEEE Computer*, vol. 17, 7, pp. 55-61, July 1984.

2. J.C. Browne, "Framework for Formulation and Analysis of Parallel Computation Structures," *Parallel Computing*, vol. 3, pp. 1-9, 1986.

3. J. Demmel, J. Dongarra, J. Du Croz, A. Greenbaum, S. Hammarling, and D. Sorensen, "Prospectus for the Development of a Linear Algebra Library for High-Performance Computers," Argonne National Laboratory Report, ANL-MCS-TM-97, September 1987.

4. J. J. Dongarra, J. DuCroz, I. Duff, and S. Hammarling, "A Set of Level 3 Basic Linear Algebra Subprograms," Argonne National Laboratory Report, ANL-P88-1, September 1988.

5. J. J. Dongarra, J. DuCroz, S. Hammarling, and R. Hanson, "An Extended Set of Fortran Basic Linear Algebra Subprograms," *ACM Trans. Math. Software*, vol. 14, 1, pp. 1-17, March 1988.

6.   J. J. Dongarra, F. Gustavson, and A. Karp, "Implementing Linear Algebra Algorithms for Dense Matrices on a Vector Pipeline Machine," *SIAM Review*, vol. 26, 1, pp. 91-112, January 1984.

7.   J. J. Dongarra and D. Sorensen, "SCHEDULE: Tools for Developing and Analyzing Parallel Fortran Programs," Argonne National Laboratory Report, ANL-MCS-TM-86, November 1986.

8.   C. Lawson, R. Hanson, D. Kincaid, and F. Krogh, "Basic Linear Algebra Subprograms for Fortran Usage," *ACM Transactions on Mathematical Software*, vol. 5, pp. 308-323, 1979.

Multitasking directives for FORTRAN: a generic alternative to parallel FORTRAN

Clifford Arnold

ETA Systems Inc., 1450 Energy Park Dr., St.Paul Mn. 55108

Brian Brode and James Blair

Pacific Sierra Research Corp., 12340 Santa Monica Blvd., Los Angeles, Ca 90025

ABSTRACT: The basic rules and requirements of an operational FORTRAN product strongly conflict with one of the obvious primitives for parallel processing: *Shared variables*. We discuss reasons why FORTRAN can not be formally extended for parallel processing without transforming the language dramatically. We believe such significant changes may be unacceptable to the FORTRAN user community. Then we discuss an alternative for altering FORTRAN for parallel processing without any formal extensions. This is done with a set of a dozen compiler directives. It is our goal to provide a set of directives that are portable and allow efficient code to be generated for a large variety of parallel processing architectures.

1. INTRODUCTION

With the advent of a variety of parallel processing systems, computational investigators are looking for convenient programming models and tools for executing their favorite codes. The first choice of investigators in the physical sciences and engineering appears to be access to parallel processing within FORTRAN. Although this may seem a convenient choice, language designers wishing to provide "Parallel FORTRAN" must understand long–term requirements for the language. We summarize our opinions of these requirements as follows:

- Architectural Independence: Parallel architectures are changing quickly, with many varieties available at any given point in time. A widely used language must not depend on an architectural component unless that component is widely accepted as common to all prevailing systems.

- Shared variables/Local variables: Parallel FORTRAN must manipulate address space that is sharable to multiple Tasks. It must also be able to manipulate address space that is private (local) to an individual Task. In traditional FORTRAN (i.e. ANSI FORTRAN77) with only one Task, the two cases degenerate to one case.

- Parallel Tasks/Synchronization Control Logic: Independent execution streams (Tasks) must be allowed, along with a mechanism for synchronizing among the parallel Tasks. This allows Tasks to be informed when to run and when shared variables have changed their state.

Examples of proposals for parallel FORTRAN environments include FORCE (Jordan 1987), SCHEDULE (Dongarra and Sorensen 1987), the work of Fredrickson, Jones, and Smith (1985), and PCF FORTRAN (Parallel Computing Forum, Leasure et. al. 1988). These efforts have advanced the state of the technology for several reasons (algorithm research, performance analysis and tuning, parallel processing practice) but, by their own admission, all assume a shared memory architecture, and therefore have drawbacks as long term solutions. After all, not all architectures are totally shared memory. Notable exceptions include hypercubes, mesh connected systems, and hierarchical memory systems like Cedar and the ETA10.

There are other alternatives for a Parallel FORTRAN environment. For example, Multitasking Libraries that are callable from FORTRAN require no extensions to the language (e.g. Montry 1985, Snelling 1986, ETA Systems 1988) and can be designed to be architecture independent. With these libraries the user must state at a fairly detailed level what and how to manage the parallelism and data sharing. This can make the use of Multitasking Libraries somewhat cumbersome. Providing formal language extensions allows the compiler to interpret concepts without the user providing all the detailed management issues.

A second alternative is compilation technology that automatically parallelizes the user's program. This technology has been demonstrated independently by Pacific Sierra Research (Alliant 1986), Rice University (Kennedy and Allen 1986, Kennedy 1987), and Kuck and Associates (Leasure and Wolfe 1985). Currently it depends on the context of parallelism being quite small (e.g. within a DO Loop structure). For programs or computer systems that require more macroscopic large grain parallelism (across multiple SUBROUTINE boundaries), the automated parallelism technology is significantly more difficult and not yet available.

2. THE MAJOR DIFFICULTY WITH PARALLEL FORTRAN: MANAGING SHARED DATA

The greatest difficulty with extending FORTRAN for parallel processing is introducing the concept of a SHARED data type. FORTRAN does not provide a strong data typing capability. For example, though a user can declare a variable type, the language does not enforce that type for the lifetime of the variable. This is an attribute of FORTRAN that many of its users know and love. From one Subroutine to the next, a variable can change from a real to an integer to a logical and back again. The lifetime of the variable can be extended via COMMON Blocks or parameter passing, whereas the scope of the data type is *not* carried along. Therefore we see no way to declare variables as SHARED and enforce that state.

On the other hand, FORTRAN does guarantee the variable's location in a linear address space. In architectures with one shared memory, the linear address space is seen identically by all processes. This match is well suited to the language. For this reason, FORTRAN language proposals for multiprocessing on shared memory systems add few if any primitives for data sharing among Tasks. However, on multiple memory architectures (local memory per CPU), FORTRAN's linear address space can be difficult to mimic among multiple Tasks. For example a current version of variable $X(I)$ may not be next to the memory location of $X(I+1)$. "Neighboring" variables may be in entirely separate locations of the memory system. For multi-memory architectures some mechanism must be available to map the non-linear representation of the address space (including multiple copies of the same variable) into the linear (FORTRAN) address space. The most straight-forward primitive moves data among local copies (SEND and RECEIVE), or between local space and shared address space (GET and PUT).

One remaining question is whether all data is assumed shared unless specified as local, or the other way around, or should the user have to declare the Shared vs. Local type for every variable. Unfortunately, the natural choice depends on the architecture. For shared memory architectures the convenient state of variables is SHARED. In such cases, mistakes are made when sharing is inadvertent and the data is trampled by another task. For architectures with local memory, the natural choice for data typing is LOCAL.

The reader should note that we do not resolve the basic issue of how to extend Parallel FORTRAN for data sharing. However, the language-architecture conflict is now apparent: *architectural independence confuses the language strategies for management of data sharing.*

Instead, we have chosen to allude this language issue, and we do so in two ways. First we choose primitives that are independent of the memory architecture. It is generally agreed among language designers that message passing schemes are the most portable among different multiprocessor architectures. Snelling (1986) has demonstrated this in his library design. Its data sharing mechanism is organized around a structure message (3D arrays). His programs are portable among the Cray XMP, ETA10, IBM3090, and FPS T-Series, a demonstration of portability on the widest range of architectures known to this author. Lusk et. al. (1987) have a similar demonstration using Messages in the C programming language. Thus we follow the spirit of messages in our approach. Second, we choose a language syntax with no side effects on traditional FORTRAN.

3. AN ALTERNATIVE APPROACH: MULTITASKING DIRECTIVES

We have developed a programming "language" approach using compiler directives within FORTRAN. The intent is to provide a programming paradigm that is generic across multiprocessor architectures. No modifications to the standard FORTRAN language are needed. The design is oriented to macroscopic parallelism (since compilers can do microscopic parallelism).

There are several other proposals for Multitasking FORTRAN Directives, notably from Cray Research (1986) and Sequent (Osterhaug 1986). The unique aspect of the design described here is the explicit management of shared address space. This has two clear advantages to counterbalance some added programming effort. First, these Directives allow the user to write a program that will operate on a multi–CPU architecture whether its memory structure is local, shared, and a hybrid of the two. They do so by providing the mapping between local and shared address space. Secondly, these directives allow a full tracing of the access history to the shared address space. This can be analyzed after the fact to see if any shared data trampling was done. These two points allow a user to parallel process effectively at a very high level (i.e. macroscopic, or large grain parallel processing) for a variety of systems.

3.1 ETA Systems Multitasking Directives Summary

The current proposal for the ETA Systems Directives is summarized below. The general format for a Directive is:

C#MTL Directive [(argument_1][,argument_2] ...)]

Note throughout Section 3.1 that square brackets "[]" signifies optional information, and ellipsis "..." signifies an optional list.

3.1.1 INITIALIZE ...

The set of directives, INITIALIZE ..., defines multitasking objects necessary to initialize an application's execution for parallel processing under control of the C#MTL Directives. This set of directives should be used at the beginning of the Program's main module.

FORMAT: C#MTL INITIALIZE MAXTASKS (integer constant or PARAMETER)
         C#MTL INITIALIZE SHARED (/common block/][, /common block/...])
         C#MTL INITIALIZE SEMAPHORE (semaphore_1][, semaphore_2...])
         C#MTL INITIALIZE BROADCAST (scalar_1][, scalar_2 ...])

3.1.2 SETTINGS

The Directive, SETTINGS, allows the user to control the program's execution for purposes of tuning and debugging. This directive is optional. It can appear anywhere in the non–parallel portion of the application, and can be reset as the user wishes.

FORMAT: C#MTL SETTINGS (execution_mode_switch,
debug_switch, instrumentation_switch)

3.1.3 BEGIN PARALLEL

The Directive, BEGIN PARALLEL, marks the beginning of a code fragment that is a candidate for parallel processing, and optionally sets the number of virtual tasks assigned to this fragment.

FORMAT: C#MTL BEGIN PARALLEL [(ntasks)]

3.1.4 END PARALLEL

The Directive, END PARALLEL, marks the end of a code fragment as a candidate for parallel processing. It implies a global synchronization of the parallel Tasks running within the excerpt, and returns control back to the serial Master Task.

FORMAT: C#MTL END PARALLEL

BEGIN PARALLEL ... END PARALLEL code fragments that are parallelized are executed by Tasks that are offspring of the "Master" (or root) Task. Such parallelism currently can not be nested. The Master Task, and only the Master Task, executes all the single threaded (non–parallel) portions of the program. Additionally, all the Shared variables are local variables to the Master Task.

The following directives (3.1.5 through 3.1.12) only have meaning when nested inside a BEGIN PARALLEL ... END PARALLEL code fragment.

3.1.5 PARALLEL DO

The Directive, PARALLEL DO, directs the compiler to partition candidate DO LOOPs into partitions that will execute in parallel. The PARALLEL DO acts on the next executable FORTRAN statement. Therefore there can only be COMMENTs (including C#MTL Directives) between a PARALLEL DO and the affected DO statement.

FORMAT: C#MTL PARALLEL DO [(switch][, NGRAN=granule_size)]

WHERE: *switch* may be **STATIC** (the following DO Loop is to be parallel processed with partitions scheduled at compiler time), or **SELF-SCHEDULED** (the following DO Loop is to be parallel processed with partitions scheduled at execution time).

granule_size is the maximum set of iterates in the Parallel DO LOOP that an individual Task will work on at one time. This is convenient for performance tuning and load balancing.

3.1.6 END PARALLEL DO

The Directive, END PARALLEL DO, marks the end of a PARALLEL DO structure. This blocking structure resolves ambiguities when there are C#MTL Directives to be executed after a parallel DO LOOP's termination statement but before
the Task exectues the next granule of the same DO LOOP. The only legal FOR-
TRAN statements between the termination statement of the Parallel DO LOOP and
its END PARALLEL DO Directive are COMMENTs (e.g. C#MTL Directives).

FORMAT: C#MTL END PARALLEL DO

3.1.7 SHARE

The Directive, SHARE, informs the compiler of COMMON Blocks that are shared
among tasks within a particular BEGIN PARALLEL ... END PARALLEL Block.
"R" preceding the COMMON Block name signifies its variables are read only
within this scope. Within a BEGIN PARALLEL ... END PARALLEL Block all
FORTRAN variables are assumed to be non-shared unless they appear in a COM-
MON Block listed in the SHARE Directive.

FORMAT: C#MTL SHARE ([R]/common block name/
                        [,[R]/common block name/ ...])

3.1.8 GET

The Directive, GET, tells the compiler to get data from a portion of an array
contained in a SHARED COMMON Block, and put it in a Task's local array of the
same name. There is a subarray notation (in the spirit of FORTRAN 8x) to direct
what portion of the array should be transferred. The Directive's arguments are a
list of symbolic names for array variables that are to be copied from shared space.

A GET of a scalar variable is not allowed. All scalars in SHARED COMMON
Block(s) will be transmitted to all Tasks automatically at the beginning of a BEGIN
PARALLEL ... END PARALLEL Block.

FORMAT: C#MTL GET (array_variable(subarray)[, array_variable(subarray)...])

3.1.9 PUT

The Directive, PUT, directs the compiler to put data from a Task's local array into
a portion of a shared array of the same name. There is a subarray notation (in
the spirit of FORTRAN 8x) to direct what portion of the array should be transferred. The Directive's arguments are a list of symbolic names for array variables
that are to be copied to shared space.

A PUT of a scalar variable is not appropriate because there are multiple local
versions of the same scalar. The choice of which one should be broadcasted is
ambiguous. The BROADCAST Directive (described later) provides four functions
for BROADCASTing scalar quantities.

FORMAT: C#MTL PUT (array_variable(subarray)[, array_variable(subarray) ...])

3.1.9 BARRIER

The Directive, BARRIER, is a global synchronization mark that requires all Tasks to reach this particular point in the BEGIN PARALLEL ... END PARALLEL Block before any and all Tasks can proceed beyond the same point. The END PARAL-LEL Directive has within it an implicit BARRIER.

FORMAT: C#MTL BARRIER

3.1.10 POST

The Directive, POST, marks a position in a BEGIN PARALLEL ... END PARAL-LEL Block where a Task signals a named semaphore when it gets to that point in the code.

FORMAT: C#MTL POST(semaphore name)

3.1.11 WAIT

The Directive, WAIT, marks a position in a BEGIN PARALLEL ... END PARAL-LEL Block where a Task WAITs for one or all Tasks to POST the semaphore with the same name.

FORMAT: C#MTL WAIT(wait option, semaphore name)

WHERE: *wait option* =
  ALL, Task waits for all slave tasks to POST the semaphore with the this name before proceeding,
  PRIOR, Task waits for the Task running the prior granule of Parallel DO Loop iterates to POST the semaphore with this name before proceeding,
  NEXT, Task waits for the Task running the next granule of Parallel DO Loop iterates to POST the semaphore with this name before proceeding,
  integer expression, Task waits for the specified Parallel DO Loop iterate to POST the semaphore with this name before proceeding.

Semaphores that use the integer expression wait option must be declared as a one dimensional array of semaphores in the C#MTL INITIALIZE SEMAPHORE Directive. The size of the array is equal to the MAX(integer expression), and the integer expression must always yield non-negative integers.

3.1.12 BROADCAST

The directive, BROADCAST, instructs the compiler to do a global reduction (either SUM, PRODUCT, MAX, or MIN) of the slave tasks' local copy of a scalar variable and BROADCASTs the final result to all parallel Tasks including the Master Task using that scalar variable. Each Task retrieves the final value of the scalar only after all Tasks have completed their global reduction. BROADCASTed variables need not be contained within a SHARED COMMON Block.

FORMAT: C#MTL BROADCAST (reduction, scalar)

WHERE: *reduction* =
> **SUM**, Sum of all spawned Task copies of scalar,
> **PRODUCT**, Product of all spawned Task copies of scalar,
> **MAX**, Maximum of all spawned Task copies of scalar,
> **MIN**, Minimum of all spawned Task copies of scalar.

3.2 ETA Systems Multitasking Directives Example

The following simple example illustrates the majority of the Directive design summarized in Section 3.1. A larger variety of examples are available from ETA Systems (Arnold 1987).

```
       PROGRAM EXAMPLE
C
       PARAMETER (NTASKS=2, NDX=100,NDY=100,NDZ=100,ND=6)
       COMMON /A/ SHW(NDX,NDY,NDZ,NV),FW(NDX,NDY,NDZ,NV)
       COMMON /B/ VOL(NDX,NDY,NDZ,3), DTL(NDX,NDY,NDZ),CFL,VT,HM,QFIL,VIS2,
                  VIS4,BC,DTMIN,IL,JL,KL,I2,J2,K2,ISTEP,IEND,EPS
C
C#MTL INITIALIZE MAXTASKS (NTASKS)
C#MTL INITIALIZE SHARED ( /A/, /B/ )
C#MTL INITIALIZE BROADCAST ( TRESID )
       CALL START
       DO 100 ISTEP=1,IEND
C#MTL BEGIN PARALLEL
C#MTL SHARE ( /A/, R/B/ )
C#MTL GET ( SHW, VOL, DTL )
       TRESID = 0.0
C#MTL PARALLEL DO
       DO 20 K=2,KL
       CALL DISSIPAT(RESID)
    20 TRESID = TRESID + RESID
C#MTL PUT ( SHW(#LOWER:#UPPER,:,:,:) )
C#MLT END PARALLEL DO
C#MTL BROADCAST (SUM, TRESID)
C#MTL END PARALLEL
       CALL PRINT(ISTEP,TRESID)
       IF ( TRESID .LT. EPS ) ISTEP = IEND
   100 CONTINUE
       STOP
       END
```

Note the syntax in the GET and PUT Directives. When the subarray is not specified the entire array is moved: e.g. C#MTL GET (SHW, VOL, DTL) .

The ":" implies the full extent of the referenced dimension: e.g. C#MTL GET (SHW(:,:,:,:)) would be equivalent to C#MTL GET (SHW).

The #LOWER and #UPPER refer to the local extent of a PARALLEL DO. Each Task sees a different (local) range for the DO 20 Loop, i.e. its lower and upper bound. The #LOWER and #UPPER refer to this range. If there were two Tasks executing the PARALLEL DO Loop, then #LOWER:#UPPER for one task would refer to the first half of the range (K=2,KL/2), and for the other Task would refer to the second half of the range. Note that #LOWER-1:#UPPER+1 is a legal subarray, and is an example of a range with boundary elements beyond the Task's local DO Loop range. When data overlaps between Tasks of this type occur, the Semaphore Directives are usually needed for Task Synchronization.

4. SUMMARY

Management strategies of shared address space in a multitasking application depends greatly on the memory architectures. FORTRAN in its traditional style has a natural match with shared memory architectures, but less so with multi–memory architectures. Since FORTRAN does not preserve data typing for the lifetime of variables, it is quite difficult for the compiler to automatically recognize the memory management issues at a macroscopic level. For these reasons FORTRAN is difficult to extend for parallel processing without depending on a specific architecture. Such dependence betrays one of the major requirements for an effective, widely used language.

A generic programming model for Parallel FORTRAN can be provided via a set of compiler directives. This allows the user to program large grain, macroscopic parallelism without formal modifications to the FORTRAN language. Addressing this high level parallelism using traditional FORTRAN77 is beyond the scope of current compiler techniques (Kennedy 1987).

The set of directives presented in this paper are not sensitive to system architecture. A program so written can run on a shared memory architecture (Cray) as well as on a local memory architecture (hypercube) or a hybrid memory architecture (ETA10). Array oriented constructs are provided that allow the user to state the explicit mapping between local and shared address space. This also allows a history of all access to shared space to be traced and analyzed for debugging purposes.

This opportunity for portable parallel FORTRAN has encouraged us to implement the Directives software product in portable standard FORTRAN. Porting the product to another system architecture would require replacing calls to our proprietary Multitasking Library with those appropriate of another system.

5. ACKNOWLEDGMENTS

In addition to Pacific Sierra Research, Bob Sur (of ETA Systems) contributed greatly to the software implementation of these Directives, for which we thank him greatly. Many thanks also to William Satzer for helpful comments during the preparation of the manuscript.

6. REFERENCES

Alliant Computer Systems Co., 1986, *FX/FORTRAN Language Manual*, Vol 1., Section 4.3, Acton, Mass.

Arnold, C.N. 1987, *Programming Methods for Multitasking Large Problems on the ETA10*, ETA Systems Technical Note, St. Paul, Mn.

Cray Research, 1986, *Cray Microtasking Users Guide*, Minneapolis, Mn.

Dongarra, J.J. and Sorensen, D.C., SCHEDULE: Tools for Developing and Analyzing Parallel Fortran Programs, in *The Characteristics of Parallel Algorithms*, (ed. by Jamieson, Gannon, and Douglass), The MIT Press, Cambridge, Mass.

ETA Systems, 1988, *Multitasking Library User's Guide & Reference*, Pub–1120, St. Paul, Mn.

Fredrickson, Jones, and Smith, 1985, Synchronization and Control of Parallel Algorithms, *Parallel Computing*, Vol. 3, No. 4, North Holland, Amsterdam, The Netherlands.

Jordan, H.F., 1987, The Force, in *The Characteristics of Parallel Algorithms*, (ed. by Jamieson, Gannon, and Douglass), The MIT Press, Cambridge, Mass.

Kennedy, K. and Allen, 1986, Private Communication.

Kennedy, K., 1987, *Automatic Decomposition of Fortran Programs for Execution on Multiprocessors* (invited lecture), Third SIAM Conference on Parallel Processing for Scientific Computing, Los Angeles, Ca.

Leasure, B. and Wolfe, M., 1985, Private Communication.

Lusk, E., Boyle, J, Butler, R., Disz, T., Glickfeld, B., Overbeek, R., Patterson, J., Stevens, R., 1987, *Portable Programs for Parallel Processors*, Holt, Rinegart and Winston Inc., New York.

Montry, G., 1985, *A FORTRAN Multitasking Library for Use on the ELXSI 6400 and CRAY XMP*, Sandia National Laboratory Technical Note SAND–85–1378, Albuquerque, NM.

Osterhaug, A., 1986, *Guide to Parallel Programming on Sequent Computer Systems*, Sequent Computer Systems Inc., Beverton Oregon.

Parallel Computing Forum, 1988, *PCF FORTRAN*, distributed at 1988 International Conference on Parallel Processing, available from B. Leasure, Kuck and Associates, Champaign, Il.

Snelling, 1986, *A Portable Multitasking Library for the Cray XMP, ETA10, IBM3090, and FPS T–Series*, European Centre for Mid–Range Weather Forcasting Technical Note, Reading, England.

Parallel iterative methods for solving large sparse sets of linear equations

L. C. W. Dixon   September 1988

The Numerical Optimisation Centre, Hatfield Polytechnic, Hatfield, England.

ABSTRACT: In this paper we will consider the automatic construction of preconditioners for solving large sparse sets of linear equations by iterative techniques on parallel processing machines. The discussion will concentrate on preconditioners for Jacobi and Conjugate Gradient methods for general sparse systems, but will refer to some specialised preconditioners already proposed and adopted for particular sparse systems as well as suggesting an automatic approach.

1. INTRODUCTION

In this paper we will be concerned with the solution of large sparse sets of linear equations

$$Ax = b \tag{1}$$

by iterative methods.

Most iterative methods for solving (1) are developments of one of two basic ideas, namely Jacobi's method and the conjugate gradient algorithm. Experience on sequential machines has demonstrated that to be effective both classes of algorithms need to include a preconditioning matrix. Experience has also shown that the inclusion in implementations on parallel computers of preconditioners that have been very successful on sequential machines can often be detrimental. It is therefore appropriate to reconsider the design and construction of preconditioners for use on parallel processing computers. The main aim of this paper is to propose a parallel method for constructing preconditioners of general sparse systems. The relationship of this approach with well known preconditioners proposed for specific systems will also be discussed.

2. THE JACOBI METHOD AND ITS EXTENSIONS
2.1 The Basic Method

The well-known Jacobi method for solving a set of equations

$$Ax = b$$

is iterative, and can be written

$$x^{(k+1)} = x^{(k)} - Ax^{(k)} + b \tag{2}$$

It is well known that if x* is the solution of (1) and the error $e^{(k)}$ is defined by

$$e^{(k)} = x^{(k)} - x*$$ (3)

then

$$e^{(k+1)} = (I - A) e^{(k)}$$ (4)

so the method converges if

$$||I - A|| < 1$$ (5)

The method can of course only be applied to systems that satisfy (5), and then is only useful if

$$||I - A|| \leq p < 1$$ (6)

Given (6) an upper limit can be calculated on the number of iterations needed to go from an estimate $x^{(0)}$ with error $||e^{(0)}||$ to a value $x^{(k)}$ with error $||e^{(k)}|| < \varepsilon_0$. As

$$||e^{(k)}|| < p^k ||e^{(0)}||$$ (7)

then the final value of k must satisfy

$$p^k ||e^0|| < \varepsilon_0$$ (8)

The method is therefore very effective when

$$||I - A|| < \frac{1}{2}$$ (9)

Let us consider this algorithm in more detail. The matrix A only appears in the product $Ax^{(k)}$, the sparse matrix A can therefore be stored by simple row linkage. The algorithm requires no additional storage and if the computation is being undertaken on P processors, the computation of Ax and the subsequent vector additions can be divided in rows between the processors and each row of A need only be stored on the processor handling that row. At the end of an iteration the current vector $x^{(k)}$ is broadcast to each processor and the next iteration can commence.

The method is therefore very effective on a parallel processor when condition (6) applies, but this condition is of course a major restriction. In standard texts describing iterative methods on a sequential machine, the Gauss-Seidel method is often introduced next as it can be a considerable improvement on such machines.

2.2 The Gauss Seidel Method;
The Gauss Seidel method can be written

$$x_i^{(k+1)} = x_i^{(k)} - \sum_{j=1}^{i-1} A_{ij} x_j^{(k+1)} - \sum_{j=1}^{n} A_{ij} x_j^{(k)} + b_i$$ (10)

Its performance can be analysed by splitting A into three parts

$$A = L + D + U$$ (11)

where L is lower triangular, U upper triangular and D diagonal. Then the iteration (10) can be rewritten

$$(L + I) \ x^{(k+1)} = (I-D-U) \ x^{(k)} + b \qquad (12)$$

This now implies that

$$||e^{(k+1)}|| < ||(L+I)^{-1}(I-D-U)|| \ ||e^{(k)}|| \qquad (13)$$

so the iteration is very effective if

$$||(L+I)^{-1}(I-D-U)|| < \tfrac{1}{2} \qquad (14)$$

If as is usual the matrix is prescaled so D=I this becomes simply

$$||(L+I)^{-1}(U)|| < \tfrac{1}{2} \qquad (15)$$

The Gauss Seidel method (10) is not however effective on most parallel systems as the appearance of the terms $x_j^{(k+1)}$, j=1 ... i-1 in the formula for $x_i^{(k+1)}$ implies that these cannot be computed in parallel. A compromise is possible and has been suggested, namely to divide the rows into P sets S_q where if i ε S_q, row i is handled on processor q, and, then if i ε S_q^q, row i and $S_q \stackrel{q}{=} (q;r)$, x_i is updated by the formula

$$x_i^{(k+1)} = x_i^{(k)} - \sum_{j=q}^{i-1} A_{ij} \ x_j^{(k+1)} - \sum_{j=i}^{r-1} A_{ij} \ x_j^{(k)}$$

$$- \sum_{j \notin S_q} A_{ij} \ x_j^{(R)} + b_i \qquad (16)$$

where now only the new values of x^{k+1} updated on that processor already are used.

2.3 The Splitting Method
The Gauss Seidel algorithm is an example of a general <u>splitting</u> method [1], let

$$A = N + M \qquad (17)$$

then the iteration becomes for a selected C

$$(N+C)x^{(k+1)} = (C-M)x^{(k)} + b \qquad (18)$$

and the equivalent condition to (9) is simply

$$||(N+C)^{-1}(C-M)|| < \tfrac{1}{2} \qquad (29)$$

In contrast to the previous three iterations (2), (10), (16) where the split is predetermined and the matrix either satisfies (9), (15) or (19) or does not, we may now pose a problem

PROBLEM 1; Select a splitting combination (N,M,C) which satisfies (19), and for which (18) can be solved easily on a parallel computer.

This splitting method is only one way of extending the Jacobi approach, there are at least two others, preconditioning and transformation.

2.4 The Preconditioning Method
In the preconditioning method the set of equations (1) is premultiplied

by a sparse matrix R [2] so instead of solving (1) we solve

$$RAx = Rb \tag{20}$$

If the Jacobi method is applied to this problem it will converge rapidly if

$$||I - RA|| < \tfrac{1}{2} \tag{21}$$

as $||x^{(K+1)}-x*|| < \tfrac{1}{2} ||x^{(K)}-x*||$ is then still satisfied.

Definition: A matrix R satisfying (21) is termed an approximate sparse inverse.

Now let N = $||I - RA||$ then if R = 0, N = $||I||$ whilst if R = A^{-1}, N = $||0||$. These results are of course true for any norm. So as we introduce additional elements into R we should be able to ensure that N decreases.

We may therefore pose a second problem.

PROBLEM 2: To determine a sparse approximate inverse R.

A parallel automatic method for solving this problem will be outlined in the final section of the paper.

2.5 The Transformation Method
Instead of preconditioning the matrix we could choose to transform the variables,

solving $ASy = b$ where $x = Sy$ \tag{22}

If we apply the iteration

$$y^{(k+1)} = (I-AS)y^{(k)} + b \tag{23}$$

this converges rapidly if

$$||I-AS|| < \tfrac{1}{2} \tag{24}$$

as $||y^{k+1}-y*|| < (\tfrac{1}{2})^{k} ||y^{(1)}-y*|| \tag{25}$

This of course implies

$$||x^{(k+1)}-x*|| < (\tfrac{1}{2})^{k} ||S|| \ ||y^{(1)}-y*||$$
$$< (\tfrac{1}{2})^{k} ||S|| \ ||S^{-1}|| \ ||x^{(1)}-x*|| \tag{26}$$

so considerably more iterations may be required to obtain the accurate value of x.

PROBLEM 3: Find a sparse transformation S so that $||I-AS|| < \tfrac{1}{2}$.

2.6 The Combined Method
It is natural to combine the concepts of preconditioning and transformation giving

$$RASy = Rb \qquad x = Sy \tag{27}$$

$$y^{(k+1)} = (I-RAS)y^{(k)} +Rb \tag{28}$$

This iteration will converge rapidly if R and S are constructed so

$$||I{-}RAS|| < \tfrac{1}{2} \tag{29}$$

The iteration is still efficient on a parallel processor as it consists of 4 sparse matrix * vector products, each of which can be divided into appropriate row blocks.

PROBLEM 4: Determine sparse matrices R & S such that $||I{-}RAS|| < \tfrac{1}{2}$.

3. CONJUGATE GRADIENTS

3.1 The preconditioning problem
The conjugate gradient algorithm can be expressed as ten steps:-

Step 1   choose $x^{(1)}$, ε_0, $k_{max} > n$, $k=1$

Step 2   set $t = -g^{(1)} = Ax^{(1)}-b$

Step 3   stop if $||g|| < \varepsilon_0$ or $k > k_{max}$

Step 4 $z = At$

Step 5 $\alpha = -g^T t/t^T z$

Step 6 $x^{(k+1)} = x^{(k)} + \alpha t$

Step 7 $g^{(k+1)} = g^{(k)} + \alpha z$

Step 8 $\beta = g^{(k+1)T} g^{(k+1)}/g^{(k)T} g^{(k)}$

Step 9 $t = -g^{(k+1)} + \beta t$

Step 10 $k = k+1$ goto Step 3

We note that the matrix A again only appears in the form of a sparse matrix * vector product in step 4, so this and the 3 vector updates, steps 6, 7, 9, can be divided in blocks between the processors. The only data transfers needing broadcasting are t at step 4 and α and β from steps 5 and 8.

It is therefore again an ideal algorithm for parallel computation, but for the fact that is is both unstable against round off error and limited in this form to positive definite symmetric matrices.

It is therefore usual to precondition the conjugate gradient method by introducing a matrix R and solving

$$RAR^T(R^{-T}x) = Rb \tag{30}$$

i.e. $\tilde{A}y = \tilde{b}$

where $\tilde{A} = RAR^T$, $y - R^{-T}x$, $\tilde{b} = Rb$

We note that the preconditioning RAR^T is simply a special case of the combined method introduced in section 2.6 and is the natural restriction for symmetric matrices.

The stability of the conjugate gradient method is normally discussed in terms of the condition ñumber of A and we note that if

$$||I - \tilde{A}||_2 < \tfrac{1}{2} \tag{31}$$

then $\qquad\qquad K(\tilde{A}) < 3 \qquad\qquad$ (32)

For such a well conditioned matrix the conjugate gradient method does not suffer due to round off error and indeed we might argue that the bound $\tfrac{1}{2}$ is too restrictive in this case. It will however be retained.

PROBLEM 5: Find a preconditioning matrix R such that $||I-RAR^T|| < \tfrac{1}{2}$.

We note that given such a matrix R, then two additional matrix vector products are needed at each iteration at step 4 to form

$$z = RAR^T t \tag{33}$$

and an initial matrix product at step 2 to obtain

$$\tilde{b} = Rb \tag{34}$$

and a final matrix product to obtain

$$x* = R^T y* \tag{35}$$

The matrix R need never be inverted.

3.2 The Incomplete Choleski Methods

Given a positive semi definite matrix A a popular direct method of solution would be to obtain its Choleski Decomposition and then solve two triangular systems to solve (1) i.e. find L such

$$LL^T = A \tag{31}$$

then solve $\qquad LL^T x = b \tag{32}$

in two stages $\quad Ly = b, \; L^T x = y \tag{33}$

The well-known disadvantage of this method for a sparse matrix is that the matrix L may be less sparse than A.

One way of computing the elements of L may be written

FOR $\qquad\qquad\qquad$ i=1 to n $\qquad\qquad\qquad\qquad$ (34)

$\qquad$ FOR $\qquad\quad$ j=1 to i-1 $\qquad\qquad\qquad\qquad$ (35)

$$L_{ij} = (A_{ij} - \sum_{k=1}^{j-1} L_{ik}L_{jk})/L_{jj} \tag{36}$$

$$L^2_{ii} = A_{ii} - \sum_{k=1}^{i-1} L^2_{k} \tag{37}$$

This top/down approach evaluates the elements of L sequentially one at a time.

A popular method of preconditioning the conjugate gradient method is to use the incomplete Choleski decomposition, [3], [4], [5]. In its simplest form this prescribes the sparsity pattern of L to be the same as A. If we define the set S as containing the non zero values of A then (35) becomes

$$\text{FOR } j=1 \text{ to } i-1 \text{ if } (i,j) \, \varepsilon \, S \qquad (35)$$

with $L(i,j)$ not existing i.e. being taken as zero in (36) and (37) if $(i,j) \notin S$.

The above choice of S is not necessary. For particular problems many authors have discussed alternatives, for instance Mulligan [6] discusses the case where

$$A = C^T + B^T + D + B + C \qquad (38)$$

where B corresponds to the first upper diagonal and C to the Nth upper diagonal.

For this problem

$$S = \{(i, j) \, ; \, i-j \, \varepsilon \, (0,1,N)\} \qquad (39)$$

but he also investigates using

$$S = \{(i,j) \, ; \, i-j \, \varepsilon \, (0,1,N-1,N)\}$$

and $\quad S = \{(i,j) \, ; \, i-j \, \varepsilon \, (0,1,N-2,N-1,N)\}$

which lead to the Meijerink and Van der Vorst [4] preconditioners IC(1,1), IC(1,2) and IC(1,3) respectively.

The modified incomplete Choleski decompositions were introduced by Gustafsson [5]. If we modify the incomplete Choleski decomposition to LDL^T where the diagonal elements of L are unity then we can avoid the need for square roots and modify (37) to ensure that the row sums of LDL^T equal the row sums of A

i.e. $\quad \displaystyle\sum_j \sum_k L_{ik} L_{jk} D_k = \sum_j A_{ij} \qquad (40)$

For this modified algorithm and for particular problems derived from partial differential equations, Gustafsson showed

$$K(L^{-1} D^{-1} L^{-T} A) = O(h^{-1}) \qquad (41)$$

where h is the mesh size parameter.

Mulligan implemented these preconditioners on an FPS M64/330 superstation and confirmed the superiority of the modified form of the less sparse preconditioners and discusses their parallel implementation.

In the context of this paper we note that the incomplete Choleski method leads to

$$LL^T = A + E \qquad (42)$$

where $E_{i,j} = 0$ if $(i,j) \, \varepsilon \, S$.

No bounds on the size of E are however given. Note that we have however

$$I = L^{-1}AL^{-T} + L^{-1}EL^{-T}$$

So $$||I - L^{-1}AL^{-T}|| = ||L^{-1}EL^{-T}||$$ (43)

and $K(L^{-1}AL^{-T}) < \dfrac{1 + || L^{-1}EL^{-T} ||}{1 - || L^{-1}EL^{T} ||}$ if E is small.   (44)

This analysis indicates that if we wish to relate these results to those obtained in section 2 then we need to pose

PROBLEM 6:   Select a sparsity pattern S in the incomplete Choleski framework so $||L^{-1}EL^{-T}|| < \frac{1}{2}$

While discussing results for the special problem it is worth recalling that while the condition number of A is $O(N) = O(h^{-2})$ where N is the number of unknowns and h is the node spacing and while Gustaffson's preconditioner is $O(h^{-1}) = O(N^{1/2})$, Yserentant [7] has recently derived a preconditioner giving $O(\log^2 N^{1/2}) = O(\log^2 h^{-1})$ which is of course a considerable improvement. Similarly Ong [8] has extended Yserentants result to the three dimensional problem and obtained a preconditioner leading to a condition number of $O(N^{1/3})$, requiring only $O(N)$ operations. Both these preconditioners are sparse and indicate that alternative approaches can lead to great improvements.

The idea of constructing a sparsity pattern S automatically in the incomplete Choleski method was introduced by Jennings et al [9], [10]. In their partial elimination (PEL) method they computed the elements of the Choleski decomposition in a different order. When computing the element L_{ij}, they have computed the values of L_{ik}, L_{jk} for all values of k < min(i,j) and can therefore do the update

$$a_{ij}^{(k+1)} = a_{ij}^{(k)} - L_{ik}L_{jk} \qquad\qquad k = 1,\ldots, j-1$$
$$j \leq i$$

they then test whether

$$(a_{ij}^{(j)})^2 < \psi^2 a_{jj}^{(j)} a_{ii}^{(j)} \tag{45}$$

where the parameter ψ is a tolerance parameter.

If the test is satisfied then

$$a_{ij}^{(j)} = 0 \qquad \text{and } L_{ij} = 0$$

and the diagonal elements are modified to

$$a_{jj} = a_{jj} \left(1 + \frac{|a_{ij}|}{\sqrt{a_{ii}a_{jj}}} \right)$$

$$a_{ii} = a_{ii} \left(1 + \frac{|a_{ij}|}{\sqrt{a_{ii}a_{jj}}} \right) ;$$

otherwise $L_{ij} = a_{ij}^{(j)}/L_{jj}$ j < i

and $L_{ii} = \sqrt{a_{ii}^{(i)}}$ j = i

In this way $LL^T = A + E$ where E is made up of matrices of the form

$$
\begin{array}{c}
\quad j \qquad\quad i \\
\begin{array}{c} j \\ i \end{array}
\left(
\begin{array}{cc}
s \mid a_{ij} \mid, & a_{ij} \\
a_{ij} & , \dfrac{1}{s} \mid a_{ij} \mid
\end{array}
\right)
\end{array}
\qquad\qquad
s = \left(\dfrac{a_{jj}}{a_{ii}} \right)^{1/2}
$$

which are all positive semi definite and small. This partial decomposition can either be used to precondition the conjugate gradient method or as a splitting for the Jacobi method (section 2.3) with $N=LL^T$, $M=E$, $C=0$.

A similar automatic scheme has been proposed by Papadrakakis [11] called (PPR) in this he sets

$$ L = (D + wC) \, D^{-1/2} \tag{46} $$

where D are the diagonal elements of A, C the elements of the lower triangular part of A not set to zero by the test

$$ C_{ij} = 0 \quad \text{if} \quad A_{ij}^{2} < \psi \, A_{ii} \, A_{jj} $$

and w is relaxation the parameter. This is of course simpler to compute and uses even less store than the simplest incomplete Choleski method.

Neither of these methods in any sense attempts to choose S to make $||L^{-1}EL^{-T}||$ small. Following the approach adopted in this paper we would intend to satisfy problem 6.

4. THE NEW APPROACH

In this paper we have proposed six new but related problems, namely.

PROBLEM 1. Select a splitting combination (N,M,C) which satisfies $||(N+C)^{-1}(C-M)|| < \tfrac{1}{2}$ and for which

$$ (N+C) \, x^{(K+1)} = (C-M)x^{(K)} + b $$

can be solved easily on a parallel computer

PROBLEM 2. Determine a sparse matrix R such that $||I-RA|| < \tfrac{1}{2}$.

PROBLEM 3. Determine a sparse matrix S such that $||I-AS|| < \tfrac{1}{2}$.

PROBLEM 4. Determine sparse matrices R and S such that $||I-RAS|| < \tfrac{1}{2}$.

PROBLEM 5. Determine a sparse matrix R such that $||I-RAR^T|| \; \tfrac{1}{2}$.

PROBLEM 6. Select a sparsity pattern S in the incomplete Choleski framework so that $||L^{-1}EL^{-T}|| < \tfrac{1}{2}$.

In all these related problems the value of the RHS i.e. $\tfrac{1}{2}$ is heuristic and could be replaced by any number significantly less than one.

4.2 The Norms
To consider how we might solve these related problems we first have to consider which norm is appropriate.

Three norms are available as possibilities for a nonsymmetric matrix B

(1) $||B||_{\infty}$ $= \underset{i}{\text{Max}} \ \underset{j}{\sum} | B_{ij} |$

(2) $||B||_2$ $= \sqrt{\text{max e.v. of } B^T B}$

(3) $||B||_F$ $= \sqrt{\text{trace } (B^T B)}$ $= \left[\underset{i}{\sum} \ \underset{j}{\sum} | B_{ij} |^2 \right]$

If we take the case of problem 2 as the one to consider in detail in this paper

$$B = I - RA$$

so $B_{ij} = \delta_{ij} - \underset{K}{\sum} R_{iK} A_{Kj}$

4.3 The Infinity Norm
Consider the infinity norm first:-

$$N = ||B_{ij}||_{\infty} = \underset{i}{\text{max}} \ \underset{j}{\sum} | \delta_{ij} - \underset{K}{\sum} R_{iK} A_{Kj} |$$

i.e. $N = \underset{i}{\text{max}} \ N_i$

$$N_i = \underset{j}{\sum} | \delta_{ij} - \underset{K}{\sum} R_{iK} A_{Kj} |$$

As the elements of row R_{iK} only effect N_i we have n independent problems that can be solved in parallel namely

Determine   Reduce $\underset{j}{\sum} | \delta_{ij} - \underset{K}{\sum} R_{iK} A_{Kj} |$
    R_{iK}

This is an l_1 function, and can be converted to a linear programming problem:

$$\underset{(u_j, v_j, R_{iK})}{\text{Min} \ \underset{j}{\sum} u_j + v_j}$$

$$u_j \geq \delta_{ij} - \underset{K}{\sum} R_{iK} A_{Kj}$$

$$v_j \geq - \delta_{ij} + \underset{K}{\sum} R_{iK} A_{Kj}$$

$$u_j \geq 0 \ v_j \geq 0$$

We note that with $R_{iK} = 0$, $N_i = 1$ and if R_{iK} is the ith row of A^{-1} then

$N_i = 0$.

We may therefore expect to be able to start at the origin and steadily increase the non-zero values of R_{iK} until $N_i < \frac{1}{2}$.

4.4 The Frobenius Norm.
If we use the Frobenius Norm F

$$F^2 = \sum_i \sum_j (\delta_{ij} - R_{iK} A_{Kj})^2$$

we notice that if we let $T = F^2$ we can decompose T into a set of independent problems as

$$T = \sum_i T_i \qquad\qquad T_i = \sum_j (\delta_{ij} - R_{iK} A_{Kj})^2$$

and each T_i can also be reduced in parallel as in Section 4.3

Let us now consider T_i in more detail. It is a quadratic function of the unknowns R_{iK} $K=1\ldots n$. When $R_{iK}=0$ all K, $T_i=1$ when R_{iK} is the ith row of A^{-1}, $T_i=0$. As T_i is quadratic we can reduce T_i to zero by finding the minima in ever increasing subspaces. As we introduce an extra variable we reduce T_i. Unfortunately we do not know how far to reduce T_i, there is no simple relationship as there was for N_i. If we decided to reduce each component of T equally we would need to reduce T_i to $0.5/n$. The introduction of the factor n arises because if

$$\left| e_{max}^{(k+1)} \right| < \tfrac{1}{2} \left| e_{max}^{(k)} \right| \quad \text{then} \quad \left\| e^{k+1} \right\|_2^2 < \tfrac{1}{4} n \left| e_{max}^{(k)} \right|^2$$

while $\left\| e^{(k)} \right\|_2$ could be $\left| e_{max}^{(k)} \right|^2$ so we only

have $\left\| e^{(k+1)} \right\|_2^2 < \tfrac{1}{4} n \left\| e^{(k)} \right\|_2^2.$

It is therefore important to determine whether as n increases we are really interested in making $\|e\|_\infty$ or $\|e\|_2$ small. Obviously making $\|e\|_\infty < 10^{-5}$ could be considerably easier than making $\|e\|_2 < 10^{-5}$ if $n=10^5$. If we accept that we are trying to reduce $\|e\|_\infty$ then an alternative method to reducing N_i is to reduce T_i stopping when $N_i < \tfrac{1}{2}$. Regrettably as N_i is non smooth N_i can increase when T_i decreases. For instance let us consider the first iteration of the two methods, and introduce the diagonal R_{ii}.

Minimising N_i gives $R_{ii} = 1/A_{ii}$ if $|A_{ii}| > \sum_{j \neq i} |A_{ij}|$

$$N_i = \sum_{j \neq i} \frac{|A_{ij}|}{|A_{ii}|}$$

or $\qquad R_{ii} = 0$

$$N_i = 1$$

so N_i is only reduced if A is diagonally dominant.

In contrast

Minimising T_i gives $R_{ii} = \dfrac{A_{ii}}{\sum_j A_{ij}^2}$

$$T_i = 1 - \frac{A_{ii}^2}{\sum_j A_{ij}^2}$$

$$N_i = \left(1 - \frac{A_{ii}^2}{\sum_K A_{ij}^2} \right) + \sum_{j \neq i} \left| \frac{A_{ii} A_{ij}}{\sum_K A_{iK}^2} \right|$$

which could be a reduction or an increase even if A is diagonally dominant.

5. CONCLUSIONS

In this paper we have introduced a systematic approach for finding sparse matrices that would enable systems of linear equations that involve other sparse matrices to be solved efficiently on a parallel processor by dividing sparse matrix vector multiplants between the different processors.

Six variants of the fundamental approach have been formulated. The second of these has been examined in detail and it has been shown that determining the sparse approximate inverse can itself be posed as a set of independent problems that could be solved on a parallel processing machine.

It has been shown that in this particular case the problem can be posed as a degenerate linear program or as the minimisation of a quadratic function. In either case variables should be introduced one at a time and the iteration terminated when the norm $N_i \leq \frac{1}{2}$.

6. ACKNOWLEDGEMENTS

This research was funded by US Army Grant No. DAJA45-87-C-0038

7. REFERENCES

1. P. Concus, G. Golub, D. O'Leary, "A Generalised Conjugate Gradient Method for the numerical solution of elliptical partial differential equations" in J. R. Bunch & D. J. Rose eds. Proceedings of the Symposium on Sparse Matrix Computations, Academic Press, pp 309-332. (1975).
2. L. C. W. Dixon, Algorithms for Optimisation: Presented at ISTS Symposium, Los Angeles, 1988; Published in "High Speed Computing", Ed. D.P. Casavent, SPIE, Volume 880, 1988.
3. D. S. Kershaw, "The Incomplete Cholesky - Conjugate Gradient Method for the Iterative Solution of Systems of Linear Equations", J. Comp. Phys. 26, pp 43-65 (1978).
4. J. A. Meijerink and H. A. Van der Vorst, "An Iterative Solution Method for Linear Systems of which the Coefficient Matrix is a Symmetric M-matrix", Math. Comp. 31, No.137, 148-162, (1977).
5. I. Gustafsson, "A Class of First Order Factorisation Methods", BIT 18, pp 142-156 (1978).
6. S. P. Mulligan, "A comparison of Preconditioned Conjugate Gradient Methods for the Solution of a Linearised Two Dimensional Poisson Equation", presented at Loen II, Tromsø (1988).
7. H. Yserentant, "On the Multi Level Splitting of Finite Element Spaces", Numerische Mathematik, Vol.49 p 379-412 (1986).
8. M. E. Ong, "The 3D Linear Hierarchical Basis Preconditions and its Shared Memory Parallel Implementation", presented at Loen II, Tromsø(1988).
9. A. Jennings and G. M. Malik, "Partial Elimination", JIMA, 20, 307-316 (1977).
10. M. A. Aziz and A. Jennings, "A Robust Incomplete Choleski Conjugate Gradient Algorithm". Int. J. Num. Meth. Eng.20 pp 949-66(1984).
11. M. Papadrakakis and C. J. Gantes "Preconditioned Conjugate and Secant Newton Methods for Nonlinear Problems".Int. J. Num. Meth. Eng. to appear.

Parallel algorithms for sparse matrix solution

Iain S Duff

Computer Science and Systems Division, Harwell Laboratory, OXON OX11 0RA.

ABSTRACT: We discuss the solution of sets of sparse linear equations by direct methods on parallel computers. We consider three levels at which parallelism can be exploited. The first partitions the system at a macro level; the second exploits parallelism within a sparse matrix, by allowing simultaneous elimination with different pivots; and the third uses the level 3 BLAS by designing the sparse code to operate on full submatrices. We illustrate our points with a variety of codes developed from Harwell Library Subroutines on a range of machines including an Alliant FX/8, a CRAY-2, and an IBM 3090-400/VF.

1.   INTRODUCTION

We consider a range of techniques for exploiting parallelism in the direct solution of sets of linear equations

$$Ax = b \qquad (1.1)$$

where the coefficient matrix A is sparse. We are concerned both with large scale parallelism where the individual tasks are large and the method is thus appropriate for macrotasking, and with much finer grain parallelism appropriate for shared memory machines and vector supercomputers.

An important issue that we want to emphasize is that there are several levels of parallelism present in large sparse systems; a phenomenon that is also present in much more complex scientific calculations. Thus this study is not only of interest in its own right but also provides useful pointers to the use of parallelism in general. We identify three such levels. The "system level", where the original problem, perhaps not even expressed in matrix form, is partitioned at a macro level, the "matrix level", and the "submatrix level". We discuss these three levels in Sections 2 to 4 respectively.

In Section 2, we examine the exploitation of large grain parallelism at the system level examining both the case of symmetric and unsymmetric matrices. We observe a close similarity to techniques of domain decomposition used in the solution of partial differential equations and illustrate the gains which might be obtained in the general unsymmetric case. We consider an automatic method for obtaining fine grain parallelism at the matrix level in Section 3 and show how computational kernels can be employed to achieve a high degree of vectorization in Section 4. In Section 5, we conclude that it is important to exploit all levels of parallelism if the efficient solution of sparse equations is required.

2.   PARALLELISM AT THE SYSTEM LEVEL

When considering parallelism at the system level, we adopt a partitioning strategy akin to that of domain decomposition. As in that case this partitioning can be performed before the problem is formulated in matrix terms. However, we illustrate the partitioning here by considering the factorization of a large sparse matrix. An example of a useful partitioning in the symmetric case is to order the matrix into doubly bordered block diagonal form

$$\begin{pmatrix} A_{11} & & & & A_{1N} \\ & A_{22} & & & A_{2N} \\ & & A_{33} & & A_{3N} \\ & & & \cdot & \cdot \\ & & & & \cdot & \cdot \\ A_{N1} & A_{N2} & \cdot & \cdot & \cdot & A_{NN} \end{pmatrix}, \tag{2.1}$$

where the blocks A_{ii} are square and ideally of a similar size. The operations on each block A_{ii} (except the last) are completely independent and so the subtasks corresponding to the factorization of each submatrix can be executed in parallel.

The form of (2.1) is exactly that which would be obtained by a dissection strategy on the underlying grid or the associated graph in the case of non-grid problems. The solution of the whole system (1.1) can then be effected in several ways. A common method is to partition x and b in (1.1) according to the partition (2.1) and then to solve the reduced system

$$A_{NN} - \sum_{k=1}^{N-1} A_{Nk} A_{kk}^{-1} A_{kN} x_N = b_N - \sum_{k=1}^{N-1} A_{Nk} A_{kk}^{-1} b_k, \tag{2.2}$$

for x_N, using the parallelism in the N-1 independent solutions of the subproblems involving $A_{kk}, k = 1, N-1$. We then use this value of x_N in the independent solutions of

$$A_{ii} x_i = b_i - A_{iN} x_N, \quad i = 1, ...N-1.$$

If a direct method is used for solving the reduced equations (2.2), then it is seldom possible to take advantage of sparsity when solving (2.2) because the reduced matrix is usually full. Furthermore, even on problems with an underlying simple structure, the size of the matrix A_{NN} is often several times the square root of the order of the overall system so that the work is dominated by the solution of the reduced system.

A popular method for solving (2.2) is to use preconditioned conjugate gradients. This is discussed in work on domain decomposition for the solution of partial differential equations (see for example, Glowinski et al. 1987) and is more than a full field of study in its own right.

We do not discuss the symmetric case further but note that the foregoing discussion is equally valid when A is symmetric in structure only, a common case in linear systems obtained from discretizations of partial differential equations.

We now examine the situation where A is unsymmetric. The unsymmetric analogue of (2.1) is a bordered block triangular fcrm (BBTF)

$$\begin{pmatrix} A_{11} & & & & & A_{1N} \\ \cdot & A_{22} & & & & A_{2N} \\ \cdot & \cdot & A_{33} & & & A_{3N} \\ \cdot & \cdot & \cdot & \cdot & & \cdot \\ \cdot & \cdot & \cdot & \cdot & \cdot & \cdot \\ A_{N1} & \cdot & \cdot & \cdot & \cdot & A_{NN} \end{pmatrix} . \tag{2.3}$$

The most popular algorithm for obtaining permutations to the form (2.3) is due to Hellerman and Rarick (1971), but Arioli and Duff (1988) found that for purposes of stability and parallelism, the sizes of the blocks A_{ii}, $i \neq N$ were too small and the block A_{NN} too large. They experimented with other algorithms for obtaining the form (2.3) and favoured one based on an unsymmetric analogue of some commonly used techniques for bandwidth minimization. The effect of this ordering can be seen clearly in Figures 2.1 and 2.2 which show the original and reordered matrix of dimension 1107 from the Grenoble data set of simulation studies in computing from the collection of sparse matrix test problems by Duff, Grimes, and Lewis (1987).

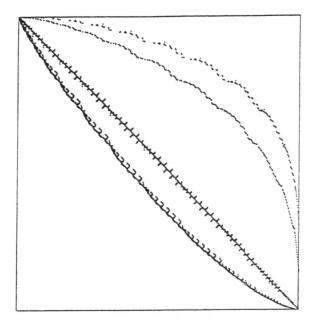

Figure 2.1 Matrix of order 1107 from computer simulation studies.

Arioli and Duff (1988) experimented both with the use of preconditioned biconjugate gradients and the use of direct methods throughout and preferred the latter because of difficulties with convergence and finding a good preconditioner.

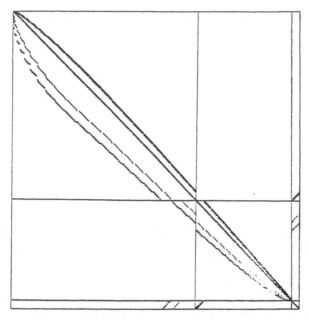

Figure 2.2 Matrix of Figure 2.1 reordered by algorithm of Arioli and Duff.

When using direct methods, they employed the implicit form for the initial factorization. That is, they used the block form

$$\begin{pmatrix} B & C \\ D & E \end{pmatrix}, \tag{2.4}$$

where **B** and **E** are square and the second block column contains all the border columns. Implicit factorization of this block form was used (see, for example, Duff, Erisman, and Reid 1986, p. 61), that is **B** is factorized, but **C** and **D** are stored in their original form without fill-ins. Where **B** has a block structure, the factorization can be explicit or implicit. We choose an implicit factorization for **B** so that no fill-in is held in its off-diagonal blocks.

Since the block **B** is itself block triangular, there is scope for easy use of parallelism both in the factorization of block **B** and the formation of the Schur complement

$$E-DB^{-1}C. \tag{2.5}$$

We make use of the fact that **B** is in block triangular form so that the amount of sequential work needed to factorize it on a parallel machine is just the work required to factorize the largest block on the diagonal of the block triangular form. In (2.5), the Schur complement is formed by solving equations with right-hand sides given by **C**, so potentially the time required on a dedicated parallel machine is simply that of the particular column of **C** requiring most operations. Of course, for that to be the case, the parallelism would have to be high enough to enable all other columns to be processed at the same time. In our comparison in Table 2.1 from Arioli and Duff

(1988), we show the number of operations on the critical path for a 4-processor machine (for example, the CRAY-2) and for one with high enough parallelism to enable this (indicated by ∞ proc in Table 2.1). We give the number of columns in the border in each case.

For the runs in this table, we have included some unsymmetric matrices arising from the solution of partial differential equations in the oil industry. For comparison we use the principal Harwell Library subroutine for sparse unsymmetric equations, MA28 (Duff 1977).

Matrix	Order	MA28	Using BBTF			Border size
			Non-parallel	Parallel		
				4 proc	∞ proc	
GRE115	115	5.6	14	5.4	3.6	12
GRE185	185	63	112	48	32	19
GRE216	216	39	111	48	30	28
GRE216	216	25	112	48	29	28
GRE343	343	119	285	119	71	32
GRE512	512	402	720	301	174	51
GRE1107	1107	1928	3610	1829	1364	30
SAYLR1	238	46	88	34	23	13
SAYLR4	3564	92759	97939	37499	22435	102
STEAM1	240	147	285	118	71	31
ORSIRR1	1030	2589	6429	2831	1782	55
ORSIRR2	886	1626	4767	1829	940	73
ORSREG	2205	11854	34738	15579	9916	84

Table 2.1.   Results of parallel implementation. Figures in middle columns are for thousands of operations in critical path.

We can see from the results in Table 2.1, that on none of these problems is the use of a BBTF better than MA28 when run in sequential mode, but that it has some potential for taking advantage of parallelism.

In all cases, we allow pivoting only within the blocks on the diagonal (using threshold pivoting with the parameter set to 0.1 as for the MA28 runs) and in the factorization of the Schur complement (where partial pivoting is used).

3.   PARALLELISM AT THE MATRIX LEVEL

We now discuss the exploitation of parallelism at the matrix level. We may assume, for example, that some preordering of the kind discussed in the previous section has been performed and we are now considering the factorization of the subproblem represented by A_{ii} from (2.1) or (2.3). Throughout this section we assume that some ordering has already been chosen and consider the exploitation of parallelism for this given ordering. Methods similar to those discussed in the previous section could be used to obtain this ordering, and we note that the ordering chosen has a strong influence on the amount of parallelism that can be obtained.

Of course, full Gaussian elimination exhibits plenty of parallelism. At each major step the updates on each row (or column or individual entry) of the reduced matrix are independent and the main bottleneck to parallelism is in the selection of pivots. In the sparse case, however, this bottleneck is partially avoided in the sense that often several pivots can be selected and used simultaneously. A simple example of this is a tridiagonal matrix, when we can assume that pivoting from the diagonal in any order is numerically stable. If we adopt the conventional strategy of pivoting down the diagonal in order, then no advantage can be taken of parallelism in the sense that the operations corresponding to the pivot in position (i, i) must complete before we can use the pivot in position $(i+1, i+1)$. A very simple degree of parallelism with no extra work can be obtained if we pivot simultaneously from both ends. Far greater parallelism can be achieved, at the cost of about doubling the arithmetic, if an odd-even cyclic reduction (equivalently, nested dissection) ordering is used. Here we first pivot simultaneously on all odd-numbered diagonal entries, then on those numbered $2k$, k odd, then $4k$, k odd etc. In the case of systems of order $2^m - 1$, we perform the factorization in m steps, with 2^{m-k} pivots being chosen at the kth step. For a 15×15 tridiagonal matrix, the factorization can be displayed by the tree shown in Figure 3.1.

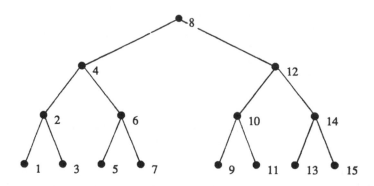

Figure 3.1.   Elimination tree for cyclic reduction on tridiagonal system.

This concept of viewing Gaussian elimination as an elimination tree can be extended to any structurally symmetric system and the elimination tree can be used to determine the parallelism inherent in the sparsity of the matrix, in the sense that any leaf node can be processed immediately and simultaneously and thereafter a node is available for processing as soon as the work at its sons is complete (see, for example, Duff 1986). Trees of the kind illustrated in Figure 3.1 have their number of nodes equal to the order of the system. However, it is often more efficient to coalesce some nodes, for example to reduce a simple chain in the tree to a single node. That way each node may represent several eliminations. If we do this and employ a multifrontal factorization scheme (Duff and Reid 1983), then the work at a node consists in performing several steps of Gaussian elimination on a small full ('frontal') matrix, passing the Schur complement to the father node. That is, we can partition the full frontal matrix as in (2.4) viz.

$$\begin{pmatrix} \mathbf{B} & \mathbf{C} \\ \mathbf{D} & \mathbf{E} \end{pmatrix} , \tag{3.1}$$

and can perform Gaussian elimination choosing pivots from $\mathbf{B}$ and forming the Schur complement $\mathbf{E} - \mathbf{D}\mathbf{B}^{-1}\mathbf{C}$ which is the passed to the father node.

Duff (1988a) considered the implementation of an elimination tree based multifrontal method on the Alliant FX/8 and found the results given in Table 3.1 for a small matrix of order 900.

Number processors	Time	Speed-up
1	2.59	–
2	1.36	1.9
4	0.74	3.5
6	0.57	4.5
8	0.46	5.6

Table 3.1. Results of parallel multifrontal code on the Alliant FX/8 on matrix from discretization of the Laplacian on a 30×30 grid.

More recently, Amestoy and Duff have experimented with a modified version of this code and obtained speed-ups of 2.45 on a three processor IBM 3090/VF and 3.3 on a four processor CRAY-2.

4.   PARALLELISM AT THE SUBMATRIX LEVEL

The final level of parallelism that we wish to consider is at a submatrix level and is achieved through the use of computational kernels, principally the matrix-matrix kernels of the level 3 BLAS (Dongarra, Du Croz, Duff, and Hammarling 1988). The main benefit of using level 3 BLAS is that the ratio of data movement to computation is much reduced, for example the multiplication of two matrices of order n requires $3n^2$ storage hits for $2n^3$ arithmetic operations. This has obvious pay-offs in an environment with a hierarchy of storage as in vector supercomputers with vector registers. We can obtain additional parallelism either within a level 3 BLAS computation (by blocking it) or by designing the algorithm to use several computational kernels (or the same on different data) simultaneously.

Although these kernels are for full matrices they can be used in the solution of sparse systems through the calculation (3.1). Amestoy and Duff (1988) have used such kernels in the solution of sparse systems on vector supercomputers, and we show a summary of their results in Table 4.1 where we can see that some very impressive computational rates can be obtained. This is all the more impressive because the underlying sparse matrix technique is attempting to keep the actual number of floating-point operations as low as possible.

The vectorized version thus reaches about half the maximum rate on both the IBM and the CRAY, and the issue now concerning us is how the method can be parallelized. At the tree level we adopt exactly the procedure discussed in the previous section and within the nodes we use parallel level 3 BLAS. Our results for two of our test matrices are shown in Table 4.2, where the runs were performed on the IBM 3090/VF. We also ran the code successfully on the four processors of the CRAY-2 but the speed-up was only about 2.4, largely because of memory conflicts on that machine. Ironically, as we reported in Section 3, an unvectorized version of our code did achieve good speed-up on the CRAY-2 (3.3 on 4 processors) helped by the

Order	No. entries	No. nodes in tree	No. ops (millions)	Megaflops IBM 3090	CRAY-2
3600	17642	1863	12	13	27
4900	24082	2522	21	15	32
3562	156610	412	70	28	79
3948	117816	1285	441	40	176
8738	591904	1185	2277	49	226

Table 4.1.   Performance of vectorized multifrontal code on one processor of the IBM 3090/VF and one processor of the CRAY-2.

reduction in contention for memory, but the resulting Megaflop rate was far below that of the vectorized uniprocessor runs.

Order	No. entries	Parallelism	No. proc.	Elapsed time (secs)	Mflops	Speed-up
3562	156610		1	2.49	28	1
		Over tree	3	1.27	55	1.96
		Within node also	3	1.05	67	2.37
3948	117816		1	10.88	40	1
		Over tree	3	5.47	81	1.99
		Within node also	3	5.34	82	2.04

Table 4.2.   Performance of parallel multifrontal code on the IBM 3090/VF.

We see from these results that reasonable speed-ups are obtained and that there is an observable although not dramatic effect from utilizing parallelism within the nodes. The reason for this is twofold. First, the frontal matrices are not very large, particularly near the leaf nodes, so our parallel tasks are not large. Second, the operations within each node are highly vectorized so further gains are not reflected in the speed-up of the overall code.

Often in vector computing we are faced with a trade-off between swopping storage for speed, or number of operations for increased speed per operation. We finish this section with a nice illustration of this phenomenon, taken from Duff (1988b). Here we use a highly-vectorized version of a code for the factorization of full systems (not included in the level 3 BLAS).

The reduced matrix becomes steadily denser because of fill-in in sparse Gaussian elimination. Thus, at some stage, it is not worth paying attention to sparsity. At this point, the reduced matrix can be expanded as a full matrix, holding any remaining zero entries explicitly, and a full matrix code can then be used to effect the subsequent decomposition. The result is a hybrid code hopefully combining the advantages of the reduction in operations due to sparsity in the early stages with the high computational rates of a full linear algebra code in the latter. The point at which such a switch is best made depends, of course, both on the vector computer characteristics and the relative efficiency of the sparse and full codes. We report on the performance of such a hybrid code in Table 4.3, from Duff (1988b), where the sparse decomposition is effected by MA28 (with threshold parameter 0.1) and the full decomposition by SGEFA from SCILIB.

Density for switch to full code	Order of "full" matrix	Millions of operations	Time in seconds
No switch	0	7	21.8
1.00	74	7	21.4
0.80	190	8	15.0
0.60	235	11	12.5
0.40	305	21	9.0
0.20	422	50	5.5
0.10	531	100	3.7
0.05	677	207	2.7
0.03	804	346	2.6
0.01	1182	1100	3.9
.005	1420	1908	6.1

Table 4.3   CRAY-2 performance of MA28 with switch to full code. Matrix from five-point discretization of the Laplacian on a 50×50 grid.

Several comments can be made on these results. First the speed-up of over 8 is quite substantial. Also the suggestion of abandoning the use of sparse codes is refuted since it is clear that the increase in number of operations by switching at lower and lower densities of reduced matrix eventually more than compensates the much higher computational rate of the full code. Indeed, for this matrix of order only 2500, it is best to perform more than half the eliminations in sparse mode, and the solution using SGEFA on the whole system required over 30 seconds. Additionally, the example we have used is a particularly bad one for a sparse direct code since fill-in is very high for such regular problems. On a network problem for example, the reduced matrix remains quite sparse until very late in the factorization. Naturally, if we store the zeros of a reduced matrix, we might expect an increase in the storage requirements for the decomposition. Although the luxury of 256 Mwords on the CRAY-2 gives us plenty of scope for allowing such an increase, the increase in storage for floating-point numbers is to some extent compensated by the reduction in storage for the accompanying integer index information. Thus, in the above example, the overall storage requirements only increase from 300,120 words for the entirely sparse code to 327,988 words at a switch over density of 0.6 and 691,153 words at a switch over density of 0.1. Admittedly, at the optimal switch over in terms of speed, about 1.25 million words are required and, for the run in the last row of Table 4.3, over 4 million words of storage were needed.

5.   CONCLUSIONS

We have demonstrated that there are various levels at which parallelism can be exploited in the solution of sparse linear equations. Macro-level partitioning is particularly important if the system to be solved is much larger than appropriate for the computing system in use. In addition, such partitioning schemes can be useful in local or distributed memory environments. The other more fine-grained parallelism can be employed within the blocks of the partition.

We have indicated that parallelism can be obtained from the multifrontal solution scheme and great gains can be obtained from the use of level 3 BLAS computational kernels on vector supercomputers.

6.   REFERENCES

Amestoy, P. R. and Duff, I. S. (1988). Vectorization of a multifrontal code. Report TR 88/3, CERFACS, Toulouse.

Arioli, M. and Duff, I. S. (1988). Experiments in tearing large sparse systems. Report CSS 217, Computer Science and Systems Division, AERE Harwell. To appear in Proceedings of *Advances in Numerical Computation,* held at the NPL in July 1987 in memory of Jim Wilkinson.

Dongarra, J. J., Du Croz, J., Duff, I. S., and Hammarling, S. (1988). A set of level 3 Basic Linear Algebra Subprograms. Report TM 88 (Revision 1), Mathematics and Computer Science Division, Argonne National Laboratory. Report AERE R 13297, Computer Science and Systems Division, AERE Harwell.   Submitted to *ACM Trans. Math. Softw.*

Duff, I. S. (1977). MA28 – a set of Fortran subroutines for sparse unsymmetric linear equations. AERE R8730, HMSO, London.

Duff, I. S. (1981). Full matrix techniques in sparse Gaussian elimination. In *Numerical Analysis Proceedings, Dundee 1981,* Lecture Notes in Mathematics 912, G.A. Watson (ed.), Springer-Verlag, Berlin, 71-84.

Duff, I. S. (1986). Parallel implementation of multifrontal schemes. *Parallel Computing* **3**, 193-204.

Duff, I. S. (1988a). Multiprocessing a sparse matrix code on the Alliant FX/8. Report CSS 210, Computer Science and Systems Division, AERE Harwell. *J. Comput. Appl. Math.* (To appear).

Duff, I. S. (1988b). Experience with the Harwell Subroutine Library on the CRAY-2. Report CSS 227, Computer Science and Systems Division, AERE Harwell.   In *CRAY User Group 1988 Spring Proceedings.* K. Winget (Editor). CUG Inc, 338-341.

Duff, I. S. and Reid, J. K. (1983). The multifrontal solution of indefinite sparse symmetric linear systems. *ACM Trans. Math. Softw.* **9**, 302-325.

Duff, I. S., Erisman, A. M., and Reid, J. K. (1986). *Direct Methods for Sparse Matrices.* Oxford University Press, London.

Duff, I. S., Grimes, R. G., and Lewis, J. G. (1987). Sparse matrix test problems. Report CSS 191, Computer Science and Systems Division, AERE Harwell. *ACM Trans. Math. Softw.* (To appear).

Glowinski, R., Golub, G., Meurant, G., and Periaux, J. (1987). *Proceedings of First International Conference on Domain Decomposition for Partial Differential Equations.* Siam Press, Philadelphia.

Hellerman, E. and Rarick, D. C. (1971). Reinversion with the preassigned pivot procedure. *Math. Programming* **1**, 195-216.

Vectorizing the modified Huang algorithm of the ABS class on the IBM 3090 VF

M Bertocchi and E Spedicato

Dipartimento di Matematica, Statistica, Informatica ed Applicazioni
Istituto Universitario di Bergamo, Via Salvecchio 19, 24100 Bergamo, Italy

ABSTRACT: In this paper we describe various implementations on the IBM 3090 vector computer of the modified Huang algorithm of the ABS class for linear systems. The best performance is obtained using the version of the algorithm where at each step two extra vectors are memorized. The obtained speed in megaflops per second is greater than the speed of the assembler implemented gaussian solver of the ESSL library for n up to about one hundred.

1. INTRODUCTION

The modified Huang algorithm (MHUANG) is a member of the class of direct algorithms for underdetermined or determined linear systems introduced by Abaffy, Broyden and Spedicato (1984) as a generalization of a method proposed by Huang (1975) of which MHUANG is a numerically more stable version.
Define the linear system by

$$(1) \qquad Ax = b \quad x \in R^n \quad , \quad b \in R^m \quad , \quad m \leq n$$

where A is an m x n matrix of rank $q \leq m$, which can be expressed in terms of its rows by

$$(2) \qquad A = (a_1, a_2, \ldots, a_m)^T \quad , \quad a_i \in R^n.$$

Then the algorithm in the standard version is defined by the following procedure (in exact arithmetic):

(A) Initialization phase.

Let $x_1 \in R^n$ be the zero vector, let H_1 be the unit matrix in $R^{n,n}$. Set $i = 1$.

(B) Compatibility phase.

Compute the projected row vector s_i by

$$(3) \qquad s_i = H_i a_i$$

If $s_i \neq 0$ go to (C). If $s_i = 0$ and $a_i^T x_i - b^T e_i = 0$, then if $i = m-1$ stop, x_i is the minimum euclidean norm solution, otherwise set

$$x_{i+1} = x_i \, , \, H_{i+1} = H_i$$

and go to (F), the i-th equation being in this case a linear combination of the previous ones. Otherwise stop, the system is incompatible.

(C) Search vector determination.

Compute the search vector p_i by

(4) $$p_i = H_i^T s_i$$

(D) Update of the solution approximation.

Update the estimate x_i of the solution by

(5) $$x_{i+1} = x_i - \beta_i p_i$$

where the stepsize β_i is given by

(6) $$\beta_i = \frac{(a_i^T x_i - b^T e_i)}{p_i^T p_i}$$

If $i = m$ stop, x_{m+1} is the minimum euclidean norm solution, the unique solution if $m = n$.

(E) Matrix update.

Update the matrix H_i by

(7) $$H_{i+1} = H_i - \frac{p_i p_i^T}{p_i^T p_i}$$

(F) Loop control.

Increment the index i by one and go to (B).

Note that in presence of round - off the tests in the compatibility phase must be substituted by tests of the form

(8) $$||s_i||_2 < \mu_1 ||a_i||_2$$

(9) $$|a_i^T x_i - b^T e_i | < \mu_2 ||b||_2$$

with suitable choice of μ_1 and μ_2. In our code which is written in double precision and runs on the IBM 3090 VF (about 15 decimal digits) we have set

$$\mu_1 = 10^{-16} \, , \quad \mu_2 = 10^{-14}.$$

An alternative implementation of the modified Huang algorithm, see Abaffy and Spedicato (to appear), is obtained by the following formula for the search vector p_i, which requires the storage of $p_1,\ldots,p_{i-1}$ and of the auxiliary vectors $r_1,\ldots,r_i$:

$$(10) \qquad p_i = r_i - \sum_{j=1}^{i-1} \frac{r_j^T r_i}{r_j^T r_j} p_j$$

where

$$(11) \qquad r_i = a_i - \sum_{j=1}^{i-1} \frac{p_j^T a_i}{r_j^T r_j} r_j$$

By defining the $n \times (i-1)$ matrices R_i and P_i by

$$(12) \qquad R_i = (r_1, \ldots, r_{i-1})$$

$$(13) \qquad P_i = (p_1, \ldots, p_{i-1})$$

and the $(i-1) \times (i-1)$ diagonal matrix D_i by

$$(14) \qquad D_i = \text{diag} \left(\frac{1}{r_1^T r_1}, \ldots, \frac{1}{r_{i-1}^T r_{i-1}} \right)$$

the formulas (10) and (11) can be written in the form $p_1 = r_1 = a_1$ and for $i>1$

$$(15) \qquad p_i = r_i - P_{i-1} D_{i-1} R_{i-1}^T r_i$$

$$(16) \qquad r_i = a_i - R_{i-1} D_{i-1} P_{i-1}^T a_i$$

or also

$$(17) \qquad p_i = Z_i r_i$$

$$(18) \qquad r_i = Z_i^T a_i$$

where

$$(19) \qquad Z_i = (I - P_{i-1} D_{i-1} R_{i-1}^T)$$

The standard version of the modified Huang algorithm has a memory requirement of order $n^2 / 2$ positions, while the number of operations, multiplications and additions, (for a system of m equations) is of order $5mn^2$. The corresponding numbers for the version using formulas (10) and (11) are $2mn$ and $4m^2n$. There is thus a saving in memory for $m < n/4$, and a gain in the number of multiplications that is proportional to the ratio n/m.

Among the properties of the modified Huang algorithm we recall the following, see Abaffy and Spedicato (1983, 1984 and to appear) for proofs and extensive discussion:
- The search vectors p_i are orthogonal.
- The symmetric matrices H_i are idempotent, their subspace is spanned by $a_1, \ldots, a_{i-1}$, the optimal conditioning criterion of Spedicato (1987) and the optimal stability criterion of Broyden (1985) are satisfied.
- The vector x_{i+1} is the minimum euclidean norm solution of the first i equations, implying the inequality:

$$(20) \qquad ||x_{i+1}||_2 > ||x_i||_2.$$

If x^+ is the solution, the following stronger inequality is also satisfied:

$$(21) \qquad ||x_{i+1}-x^+||_2 < ||x_i-x^+||_2.$$

2. VECTORIZING THE MODIFIED HUANG ALGORITHM

Since in the various versions of MHUANG the basic operations are matrix vector multiplications or matrix rank one updates, the algorithms are easily vectorizable using the efficient BLAS2 routines.

Concerning the memory representations of the matrices A and H_i, we can make the following considerations:
- Since the algorithm works on the rows of A, storing A^T instead of A allows use of stride one.
- The form of memorisation of H_i does not affect the update phase, but storage of H_i allows again use of stride one in the computation of $H_i a_i$. Note that, since H_i is symmetric, p_i can be computed with relation

$$p_i = H_i s_i$$

instead of $p_i = H_i^T s_i$.

Equivalently, one can store H_i in the usual way and substitute H_i with H_i^T in any product of H_i by a vector (this being allowed, in exact arithmetic, by the simmetry of H_i).

If the matrix H_i is updated not every single step but every k steps, we obtain a rank k formulation of MHUANG. In such a case, the formula for the update of H_i every k steps is:

$$(22) \qquad H_{i+k} = H_i - \sum_{j=0}^{k-1} \frac{p_{i+j}p_{i+j}^T}{p_{i+j}^T p_{i+j}}$$

while for $h = 1,\ldots,k-1$, the search vector p_{i+h} is given by relation:

$$(23) \qquad u_{i+h} = H_i a_{i+h} - \sum_{j=0}^{h-1} \left(\frac{p_{i+j}^T a_{i+h}}{p_{i+j}^T p_{i+j}} \right) p_{i+j}$$

$$(24) \qquad p_{i+h} = H_i u_{i+h} - \sum_{j=0}^{h-1} \left(\frac{p_{i+j}^T u_{i+h}}{p_{i+j}^T p_{i+j}} \right) p_{i+j}$$

In matrix form, formulas (23) and (24) can also be written in the form:

$$(25) \qquad u_{i+h} = H_i a_{i+h} - P_i D_i P_i^T a_{i+h}$$

$$(26) \qquad p_{i+h} = H_i u_{i+h} - P_i D_i P_i^T{}_{i+h}$$

where

$$(27) \qquad P_i = (p_i, \ldots, p_{i+h-1})$$

$$(28) \qquad D_i = \text{diag} \left(\frac{1}{p_i^T p_i}, \ldots, \frac{1}{p_{i+h-1}^T p_{i+h-1}} \right)$$

Every k steps the number of operations required by formulas (25) and (26) is of order $4kn(n+k)$. For the whole cycle the number of operations required is of order $4n^3 + 2n^3 / k$.
The corresponding number required by the standard modified Huang algorithm is, disregarding symmetry, $6kn^2$.
Thus there is a reduction in the overhead for $k < n/2$. If symmetry is taken into account, then the reduction yields for $k < n/4$.
Notice that for $k = n$ the above formulas reduce to the formulas (10) and (11). In such a case there is the additional saving due to the fact that $H_i = H_1$ is the unit matrix.

The idea of using rank k instead of rank one correction has been considered by Robert and Sguazzero (1986) in the context of classical LU factorisation algorithm and found to be helpful in terms of speed, the gain in speed increasing with k.
A similar approach in the context of implicit LU factorisation algorithm in the ABS class has also been considered by Bertocchi and Spedicato (to appear) and found to be useful for a value of k larger than one but not too larger (for instance k = 8).
Notice that in the implementation of the rank k correction formula (22) it is not efficient to use k times the BLAS2 routine for rank one correction, but it is preferable to unroll the loop on the index k.

3. THE NUMERICAL RESULTS

A code has been written in Fortran double precision (about 15 decimal digits) implementing the modified Huang algorithm in various versions. It has been run on the IBM 3090 VF on the well known Dongarra problem with several values of n.

In the Tables the symbol HUA - k indicates the implementation using the matrix H_j with correction of rank k (k = 1, 2, 4, 8, 16), while HUA - n indicates the implementation using the matrices P_j and R_j, say formulas (15), (16); the number of operations involved is indicated under the symbols.

Since the algorithms give similar accuracy on the Dongarra problem, in Table 1 and 2 we only give the required timings.

In Table 1 we compare the performance of the various implementations in a version where the symmetry has been taken into account in the code HUA-k (say only the lower triangular part of H_j has been updated and use has been made of the BLAS2 subroutines DSLMX in the matrix vector product and DSLR1 in the rank one update).

n	HUA-1 $5n^3$	HUA-2 $9n^3/2$	HUA-4 $17n^3/4$	HUA-n $4n^3$
100	.23	.25	.26	.11
300	4.9	5.0	5.0	2.4
500	19.8	20.2	20.2	9.4
700	53.3	54.7	54.3	26.5
900	112.5	114.2	113.5	58.1

Table 1 - Timings with HUA - k using symmetry

In Table 1 we observe the following:
- HUA-n, which has a sequential overhead only 20% lower than HUA-1, performs in the vector version faster than expected, its timings being about half than of HUA-1.
- The expected reduction in timings in the rank k version for k > 1 does not show.

Since it is well known that use of the symmetry requires a memory addressing which conflicts with the vectorisation requirements, a version of code HUA - k has been written where the symmetry condition has been relinquished in the multiplications involving H_j.
Note also that products of the form $H_j v$, with v a vector, have been implemented in the (equivalent in exact arithmetic) form $H_j^T v$, which allows use of stride one.

Table 2 contains the results from this version of code HUA - k and we can draw the following conclusions:
- The two versions with the rank one update perform similarly, the one without symmetry being slightly faster for smaller n, slower for larger n.
- Use of higher rank correction improves the performance, with an optimal performance at k = 8, a result which agrees with that provided by Bertocchi and Spedicato (to appear) in connection with the implicit Gauss-Cholesky algorithm.

Finally in Table 3 and 4 we compare the performance of HUA-1, HUA-8 and HUA-n with that of the gaussian solver in the ESSL library, giving the Mflops and the ratio Ψ of the number of floating point operations per second and the times τ and the ratio Φ in terms of time.

n	HUA-1 $6n^3$	HUA-2 $5n^3$	HUA-4 $9n^3/2$	HUA-8 $17n^3/4$	HUA-16 $33n^3/8$	HUA-n $4n^3$
100	.20	.17	.16	.15	.16	.11
300	4.9	4.0	3.5	3.4	3.3	2.4
500	20.9	17.0	14.9	14.0	14.6	9.4
700	57.8	46.3	40.3	38.2	41.4	26.5
900	120.9	99.2	87.6	87.2	90.1	58.1

Table 2 - Timings with HUA - k not using symmetry

	HUA-1 $6n^3$		HUA-8 $17n^3/4$		HUA-n $4n^3$		ESSL $2n^3/3$
n	Mflops	Ψ	Mflops	Ψ	Mflops	Ψ	Mflops
100	30	89%	28.4	85%	36.4	109%	33.3
500	35.8	57%	38	61%	53.2	85%	62
900	36.2	54%	35.6	53%	50.2	75%	67

Table 3 - Comparisons with gaussian solver ESSL

From Table 3 we see that Ψ decreases with growing n for all Huang algorithms, being smaller that one for HUA-1, and HUA-8 but larger than one for HUA-n for n up to about 100. This result, at first glance surprising, appears to be related to the fact that HUA-n involves matrix vector operations of costant dimension size while ESSL involves matrix vector operations with decreasing dimension size.
Note that in the experiments of Bertocchi and Spedicato (to appear) with the implicit Gauss - Cholesky algorithm Ψ was always smaller than one but increasing with n.

	HUA-1 $6n^3$		HUA-8 $17n^3/4$		HUA-n $4n^3$		ESSL $2n^3/3$
n	τ	Φ	τ	Φ	τ	Φ	τ
100	2.	10%	.15	13%	.11	18%	.02
500	20.9	6%	14.	10%	9.4	14%	1.33
900	120.9	6%	87.2	8%	58.1	13%	7.24

Table 4 - Comparisons with gaussian solver ESSL

From Table 4 we see that Φ decreases with n growing and altough the number of operations of HUA-n is six times greater than that of ESSL, the time is only five times greater, at least for low values of n.

4. FINAL REMARKS AND CONCLUSIONS

The presented numerical experiments have shown that the use of corrections of rank k larger that one improves the performance of MHUANG, the optimal value of k being around 8.
The formulation of MHUANG in terms of formulas (15) and (16) gives the best performance. For values of n up to about 100 the number of floating point multiplications per second reached by HUA-n is greater than that obtained by the gaussian solver in the ESSL library.

5. ACKNOWLEDGEMENTS

Work done in the framework of a research supported by C.N.R.. Thanks are due to IBM for providing use of the facilities at the Rome ECSEC Centre. Useful comments by Dr. Piero Sguazzero and Dr. Giuseppe Radicati of IBM and Prof. Jozsef Abaffy of the University of Economics in Budapest are gratefully acknowledged.

6. REFERENCES

Abaffy J Broyden C and Spedicato E 1984 Num. Math. 45 pp 361-376
Abaffy J and Spedicato E 1983 Rep. Sofmat 7/83 (Bergamo)
Abaffy J and Spedicato E 1984 Boll. UMI 3-B pp 517-522
Abaffy J and Spedicato E 1987 Optim. 18 2 pp 197-212
Abaffy J and Spedicato E to appear The ABS projector algorithm:
    mathematical techniques for linear and non linear systems, Chichester:
    Horwood Ellis
Bertocchi M and Spedicato E to appear Rep. IBM ECSEC (Rome)
Broyden C G 1985 JOTA 47 pp 401-412
Dongarra J J Gustavson F G and Karp A 1984 SIAM Rev. 26 1 pp 91-112
Dongarra J J and Sorensen D C 1986 Rep. ANL 86-2
Huang H Y 1975 JOTA 16 pp 429-445
Robert Y and Sguazzero P 1986 Rep. IBM ECSEC ICE-006 (Rome)
Spedicato E 1986 Rep. Inst. Angew. Math. Un. Wurzburg 203

Householder factorization on distributed architectures

Michel Cosnard and El Mostafa Daoudi

Laboratoire d'Informatique du Parallélisme, Ecole Normale Supérieure de Lyon
46, Allée d'Italie, F-69364 Lyon Cedex 07, FRANCE

ABSTRACT: Several parallel implementations of the Householder factorization for the solution of dense linear systems are analysed and compared on three distributed memory networks: a ring, a hypercube and a linear array of processors. Theoretical analysis of the arithmetic and communication complexity are studied. As concluded by Saad (1986) and Cosnard et al. (1987b) for Gaussian elimination, experimetal results on the hypercube FPS T20 show that the ring is also the best topology for Householder factorization.

1. INTRODUCTION

The problem of solving dense linear system of equations, Ax=b, where A is a regular square matrix of size n and b is a vector of R^n, is one of the most important problems encountered in scientific computing. Many methods have been developed to solve this problem. Among them the so-called "direct methods" as for examples the Gaussian elimination and the QR orthogonal factorization (Golub and Van Loan 1983). These methods are characterized by two steps: the first one consists in reducing the system into a triangular form, the second one consists in solving the resulting triangular system by backsubstitution. In the absence of informations on the matrix A, the orthogonal factorization is often used for its stability and its ability to solve overdetermined systems (least square problems for example).

Several parallel implementations for the QR factorization have been studied and developed for various architectures: Givens method, with or without square root (Cosnard et al. 1986a, 1986b, 1987a, Lord et al. 1983, Pothen et al. 1987) and the Householder factorization (Berry et al. 1986, Carnevali et al. 1987). In this paper we compare and analyse parallel implementations of Householder factorization on three distinct multiprocessor architectures, namely a ring, a hypercube, and a linear array of processors. We assume that the processors are identical and connected to each other by local links (channels) which are used to exchange messages between neighbours. Moreover each processor has its own memory and there is no data transfer via a common memory or a bus.

Regarding the communications, the time necessary to send (or receive) n consecutive data to (from) a neighbour is defined by Saad (1985) as $n\tau_c + \beta_c$ where β_c is the start-up time and τ_c is the bandwith of the channel. It is clear that β_c and τ_c depend heavily on the architecture and in particular on the number of channels of each processor. We shall modelize globally asynchronous algorithms. Local synchronization corresponding to the communications between neighbour processors is obtained through a send/receive protocol: P_i can send a message to P_j if and only if P_i and P_j are neighbours and P_j is ready to receive the message.

Regarding the arithmetic, we assume that each processor possesses a vector unit with an adder/substracter and a multiplier/divider the two vectorial units can be pipelined so that the scalar product of two vectors of length n is performed in $(\beta_a+(n-1)\tau_a)$ where β_a is the start-up time and τ_a the cycle time of the vector unit.

Contrary to the Gaussian elimination (Saad 1986, Ipsen et al. 1985, Cosnard et al. 1987b), which can be implemented by columns or by rows, the Householder reduction can only be implemented by columns, since in order to calculate the transformation or to apply it, a whole column is necessary. We call pivot the column which is used in the computation of the Householder transformation Q_k at the k-th stage. Q_k is completely determined using a vector of length (n-k+1). Hence the strategy consists for the processor which holds it to prepare the pivot column and then to send it to the neighboring processors (in the sense of the network topology).

2. HOUSEHOLDER FACTORIZATION

Let x be an element of R^n, the Householder transformation consists in calculating an orthogonal symmetric square matrix of order n in the form $Q=I-2ww^t$ with the normalized w constructed in order to transform the vector x into a multiple of the first vector of the identity. The following algorithm computes the QR factorization A=QR. The algorithm requires $4n^3/3$ arithmetic operations (+,-,*,/).

Seq k=[1 **For** n-1]
    Seq
        $vect(a):=(a_{k,k},a_{k+1,k},...,a_{n,k})^t$
        $b:=|vect(a)|_2$
        $v:=vect(a)-be_1$
        $n(v):=2b(b-a_{k,k})$ -- (* $n(v):=|v|_2$ *)
        $n(v):=1/n(v)$
        Seq j=[k+1 **For** n-k]
            Seq

$$s := 2n(v) \sum_{i=k}^{n} a_{ij} v_i$$

Seq i=[k **For** n-k]

$$a_{i,j} := a_{i,j} - s v_i$$

Seq, Par, If and **True** are the CSP/OCCAM operators which describe the sequential, parallel or conditional behavior of the processes (Hoare 1985).

Let :   - T_{compQk} be the total time to compute Q_k at step k,

$$T_{compQ_k} = (\beta_a + (n-k)\tau_a)$$

- T_{applQk} be the total time to compute Q_k at step k,

$$T_{applQ_k} = \sum_{j=k+1}^{n} (2\beta_a + 2(n-k)\tau_a)$$

- T_{calseq} be the computation time of the QR Householder factorization using one processor where the addition and the multiplication are pipelined,

$$T_{calseq} = \sum_{k=1}^{n-1} (T_{compQ_k} + T_{applQ_k})$$

$$T_{calseq} = \left[\frac{2}{3}n^3 - \frac{n^2}{2} - \frac{n}{6} \right] \tau_a + n^2 \beta_a = \frac{2}{3}n^3 \tau_a + n^2 \beta_a + o(n^2)$$

Hence as it is well-known, asymptotically the theoretical execution time is divided by two.

3. PARALLEL IMPLEMENTATIONS OF HOUSEHOLDER FACTORIZATION

Various topologies can be embedded in a hypercube topology. We shall select three of them: ring, hypercube and linear array, in order to compare their performances in the solution of a linear system of equations Ax=b where A is a regular square matrix of size n and b is a vector of R^n on a multiprocessor composed of p identical processors. We consider only the step of reducing the system into a triangular form by QR factorization, as for the solution of the triangular system we refer to the algorithms proposed by Ipsen et al. (1985) and Li and Coleman (1986). We subdivide A into p blocks of n/p columns and assign one block per processor. Several ways to subdivide A are possible (Saad 1985, 1986). In sections 3.1 and 3.2 we assign to processor P_i the columns i+kp for k=0 to n/p-1. In section 3.3 we assign to processor P_i the columns i*n/p+k for k=0 to n/p.

Let T_{comp} be the total time of arithmetic and T_{comm} be the total communication time. T_{comm} corresponds to the transmission time T_{tr} plus the delay time T_{dl} (a processor is idle waiting for communication): $T_{comm} = T_{tr} + T_{dl}$. The total execution T_{exec} corresponds to the execution time of processor P_{p-1}(processor holding the last column).

In order to simplify our analysis of complexity, we assume that arithmetics and communication do not overlap. As pointed by Saad (1985), overlapping could only lead to a gain of a factor at most two if the delay time can be neglected.

3.1. QR factorization on a ring

We assume that the processor network is arranged in a ring of p processors numbered from P_0 to P_{p-1} so that $P_{(i-1) \bmod p}$ and $P_{(i+1) \bmod p}$ $i=0,...,(p-1)$ are the neighbours of processor P_i. We assign to processor P_i the columns i+kp for k=0 to n/p-1. The pipelined algorithm has been introduced by Saad (1986) for Gaussian elimination. It could be easily extented for Householder factorization. In order to describe the algorithm, we call proc the position of the processor.

```
Pipeline Ring Algorithm
  Seq k=[0 For n-1]
     If
             (proc=(k mod p ))
                 Seq
                       compute the Householder transformation Qk
                       Par
                             send Qk to processor ( (proc+1) mod p)
                             apply Qk
          True
                 Seq
                       receive the transformation Qk
                       If
                             (proc+1) mod p <> (k mod p)
                                 Par
                                       send Qk to processor (proc+1)  mod p
                                       apply Qk
                             True
                                 apply Qk
```

At each step k, processor P_{p-1} applies the Householder transformation Q_k to the $\lceil (n-k)/p \rceil$ columns that it holds. Moreover processor P_{p-1} computes Q_k when k is a multiple of p.

$$T_{comp} = \sum_{k/k=ip}^{n-1} (\beta_a + (n-k)\tau_a) + \sum_{k=1}^{n-1} \lceil \frac{n-k}{p} \rceil (2\beta_a + 2(n-k)\tau_a)$$

$$= \left[\frac{2}{3}n^3 - n^2 \right] \frac{\tau_a}{p} + [n^2 - n] \frac{\beta_a}{p} + \frac{n^2}{2}\tau_a + n\beta_a$$

which shows then the computation time is equal to the time for computing the transformations Q_k plus the time for updating the corresponding columns divided by p.

Hence the first part of the algorithm is sequential whilst the second could be fully parallelized.

There are four different parts in the communication algorithm:

1) The start-up of the pipeline takes $(p-1)((n+1)\tau_c+\beta_c)$ corresponding to the time to send the first pivot column to processor P_{p-1}.

2) If the pivot column, assumed of length q, belongs to processor P_{p-1}, then it will be sent to all other processors. This is accomplished in $(p-1)((q+1)\tau_c+\beta_c)$.

3) If the pivot column, assumed of length q, does not belong to processor P_{p-1}, then P_{p-1} will receive it from P_{p-2} and send it to P_0. This is accomplished in $2((q+1)\tau_c+\beta_c)$.

4) During the last p steps, processor P_{p-1} receives the pivot column of length q and does not send it, which takes $(q+1)\tau_c+\beta_c$.

1) and 2) represent the delay time which is equal to:

$$T_{dl} = (p-1)((n+1)\tau_c+\beta_c) + (p-1) \sum_{j=1}^{\frac{n}{p}-1} ((n-jp)\tau_c+\beta_c) = \left[1 - \frac{1}{p}\right]\frac{n^2}{2}\tau_c + \left[1 - \frac{1}{p}\right]n\beta_c + o(n)$$

$$T_{tr} = 2 \sum_{j=1}^{n-p-1} ((n-j+1)\tau_c + \beta_c) - 2 \sum_{j=1}^{\frac{n}{p}-1} ((n-jp)\tau_c + \beta_c) + \sum_{j=n-p}^{n-1} ((n-j+1)\tau_c + \beta_c)$$

$$= \left[1 - \frac{1}{p}\right]n^2\tau_c + 2\left[1 - \frac{1}{p}\right]n\beta_c + o(n)$$

Then the total communication time T_{comm} is:

$$T_{comm} = \frac{3}{2}\left[1 - \frac{1}{p}\right]n^2\tau_c + 3\left[1 - \frac{1}{p}\right]n\beta_c + o(n)$$

3.2. QR factorization on the hypercube

For Householder factorization, we use the strategies described by Saad (1985, 1986) and Cosnard et al. (1987b): subdivide A into p blocks of n/p columns and assign one block per processor. To processor P_i we assign the block formed by columns ip+k for k=0 to n/p-1.

Broadcast Algorithm: Processor Pi
If
      pivot column belongs to processor P_i
          Seq
              compute the Householder transformation Q
              Par
                  broadcast Q
                  apply Q
      True

Seq
       receive Q
      Par
           broadcast Q
           apply Q

The computation time is the same as for the pipelined ring algorithm. For computing the communication time we use the technics introduced in Cosnard et al. (1987b).

$$T_{comm} = \sum_{k=1}^{n-1} (\log_2 p)((n-k)\tau_c + \beta_c) = \log_2 p \left(\frac{n(n-1)}{2} \tau_c + (n-1)\beta_c \right)$$

To improve efficiency the data to be broadcasted could be divided into blocks of equal length saad (1986). This will lead to eliminate the log p factor from the preceding formula. However since the theoretical analysis is very complicated, we shall only give an asymptotic estimation (where $1 < \gamma < 2$):

$$T_{comm} = \gamma \frac{n^2}{2} \tau_c$$

3.3. QR factorization on a linear array

We assume that the processor network is arranged in a linear array of p processors interconnected to each other. Each processor has two neighbours except P_0 and P_{p-1}. We subdivide the matrix A into p blocks each of n/p consecutive columns and we assignto processor P_i the block formed by the columns $i*n/p+k$ for k=0 to n/p-1.

Pipelined Linear Array Algorithm: Processor P_i
 Seq k=[0 **For** (i+1)n/p]
     Seq
        If
            k< i*n/p
               Seq
                   receive Q_k from P_{i-1} the
                   Par
                      send Q_k to P_{i+1}
                      applyQ_k
             True
               Seq
                   compute the Householder transformation Q_k
                   Par
                      send Q_k to P_{i+1}
                      apply Q_k

The computation time corresponds to the time needed by processor P_{p-1} since this processor contains the last column. During the first n-n/p steps, processor P_{p-1} receives the transformation Q_k and then applies it to the n/p columns that it holds. This requires:

$$\sum_{k=1}^{n-\frac{n}{p}} \frac{n}{p}(2\beta_a + 2(n-k)\tau_a)$$

During the last (n/p)-1 steps, processor P_{p-1} triangularizes the last submatrix of size n/p, this requires:

$$\left[\frac{2}{3}\left(\frac{n}{p}\right)^3 - \frac{1}{2}\left(\frac{n}{p}\right)^2 - \frac{n}{6p}\right]\tau_a + \left(\frac{n}{p}\right)^2 \beta_a$$

Then the total computation time is:

$$T_{comp} = \left[1 - \frac{1}{3p^2}\right]\frac{n^3}{p}\tau_a + \left[1 - \frac{2}{p}\right]\frac{n^2}{2p}\tau_a + \left[1 - \frac{1}{2p}\right]\frac{2n^2}{p}\beta_a$$

Remark that the ratio between T_{comp} and the corresponding time for the ring is of order 3/2. We will explain this in the next section. For communication, processor P_{p-1} communicates only during the first n-n/p steps. There are two different parts in the communication algorithm:

1) The start-up of the pipeline takes $(p-1)((n+1)\tau_c+\beta_c)$, the time to send the first pivot column to processor P_{p-1}.

2) During the first n-n/p steps processor P_{p-1} receives from P_{p-2} the pivot column (assumed of length q) in time $2(q+1)\tau_c+2\beta_c$.

Then the total communication time is:

$$T_{comm} = \left(1 - \frac{1}{p^2}\right)n^2\tau_c + 2\left(1 - \frac{1}{p}\right)n\beta_c + o(n)$$

In this case the communication time is divided by 3/2 compared to the pipelined ring.

4. COMPARISON AND EXPERIMENTAL RESULTS

The following table recalls the various theoretical results obtained in the preceding analysis. As can be easily seen, theoretically the hypercube topology performs better than the ring if we divide the data to be transmitted into packets of optimal equal length. It is important to notice that the least communication time is obtained for the linear array and that the associated control is very simple. However the computation time is worse (by a factor 1.5). Since the computation is of order n³, asymptotically, the computation time of the linear array will overcome the communication. The differences can be explained in the following ways. The delay time can be neglected on the linear array but represents 2/3 of the total communication time on the ring. Contrary to the ring, the data do not come back to the first processor. Hence the time is divided by a factor close to 3/2. The computation time is worse on the linear array since P_i terminates its computation after $(i+1)n/p$ steps while on the ring all the processors work with full efficiency except during the last p steps.

	T_{comp}	T_{comm}	
Hypercube without division	$\dfrac{2}{3p} n^3 \tau_a$	$(\log_2 p)\dfrac{n^2}{2}\tau_c$	
Hypercube with division	$\dfrac{2}{3p} n^3 \tau_a$	$\gamma \dfrac{n^2}{2}\tau_c$	$1 \le \gamma \le 2$
Ring	$\dfrac{2}{3p} n^3 \tau_a$	$\dfrac{3}{2}(1-\dfrac{1}{p})n^2\tau_c$	
Linear array	$(1-\dfrac{1}{3p^2})\dfrac{n^3}{p}\tau_a$	$(1-\dfrac{1}{p^2})n^2\tau_c$	

We have implemented and compared these algorithms on the Hypercube FPS T20 (Gustafson et al. 1986) composed of 16 nodes. Each node possesses a vector processing unit and 1 Mbytes of memory. On each node we can store a real matrix (64 bits) of size 256, which leads to test real matrices of size 1024.

Table 1 presents the experimental results which have been obtained for a matrix of size 256 and a number of processors from 1 to 16. These results correspond very well to the theoretical analysis of the preceding section. Once again the pipeline ring algorithm is the best for p=2,4,8,16. However for 16 processors the linear array algorithm is very close to the pipeline ring (3.5 versus 3.2 seconds) and better than the broadcast. This is certainly due to the fact that in this case the communications cannot be neglected.

	Pipeline Ring			Broadcast			Linear Array		
P	Time	Sp	Eff	Time	Sp	Eff	Time	Sp	Eff
1	22.48	1.0	1.0	22.48	1.0	1.0	22.48	1.0	1.0
2	12.28	1.83	0.92	12.30	1.83	0.91	16.24	1.38	0.69
4	7.25	3.10	0.78	7.47	3.01	0.75	10.08	2.23	0.56
8	4.57	4.92	0.62	5.14	4.37	0.55	5.84	3.85	0.48
16	3.24	6.93	0.43	4.12	5.46	0.34	3.55	6.33	0.40

Table 1: Experimental results for matrices of order 256

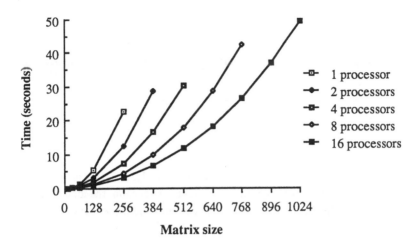

Figure 1: Performances of the pipeline ring algorithm

Table 2 show that for a matrix of size 1024 the performances of the pipeline ring algorithm are very good: it can be executed in 49 seconds against 55 and 65 for the broadcast and linear array algorithms. In this case the megaflops rate is close to 30. Figure 1 depicts the complete results for various matrix sizes of the pipelined ring algorithm. As concluded by [Saa86] for Gaussian elimination, the additional connectivity of the hypercube does not improve efficiency.

5. SPEEDUP EVALUATIONS

The usual way of evaluating the parallelization of an algorithm is to consider a fixed-size problem and to solve it with a variable number of processors. However for distributed processors networks, the amount of available storage increases with the number of processors. Hence it could be interesting to compare the best performances for each number of processors.

Recently, Gustafson (1988) proposed a new method for defining and computing speedups. Gustafson's speedup is obtained by dividing the average time for executing a single arithmetic operation in the solution of the largest problem with p processors by the corresponding average time with a single processor.

Using this new definition, Cosnard et al. (1988) considered Gaussian elimination on the FPS T20 hypercube. They reported experimental results, computed Gustafson's speedups and derived a performance model to analytically explain the results. We use the same technics in order to calculate more precisely the speedups that we could hope to obtain.

From experimental measurements on the hypercube computer, we derive the following numbers:

$$\tau_a = 1.95 \text{ e-7} \qquad \beta_a = 3.1 \text{ e-4} \qquad \tau_c = 1.15 \text{e-5} \qquad \beta_c = 8.0 \text{ e-4}.$$

Following Cosnard et al. (1988), we compute $\tau_{max}(p)$ as the average time needed for one arithmetic operation in the largest size problem. The ratio between $\tau_{max}(p)$ and $\tau_{max}(1)$ gives the Gustafson's speedups. Let M be the size of the memory of each individual processor. It has been shown (Cosnard et al. 1988), that the maximum matrix size is $n_{max}(p) = (pM)^{1/2}$.

The Gustafson's speedups are reported in table 2 for p=1,2,4,8,16.These speedups are considerably higher than the usual one, since they take into account the total potential of the computer. Combining the theoretical analysis of section 3 and these ideas, we could obtain analytical evaluations of $\tau_{max}(p)$.

Pipeline Ring Algorithm : $\tau_{max}(p) = 0.051p^{-0.5} + 0.13p^{-1} + 0.86p^{-1.5} - 0.028p^{-2}$

Broadcast: $\tau_{max} = 0.0003p^{-0.5} + 0.017\log_2 p.p^{-0.5} + 0.1p^{-1} + 0.0091\log_2 p.p^{-1} + 0.91p^{-1.5}$

Linear array : $\tau_{max} = 0.034p^{-0.5} + 0.17p^{-1} + 1.82p^{-1.5} - 0.018p^{-2} - 0.94p^{-2.5} - 0.049p^{-3}$

		pipeline ring			broadcast			linear array		
P	Size	τ_{exp}	τ_{theo}	Sp	τ_{exp}	τ_{theo}	Sp	τ_{exp}	τ_{theo}	Sp
1	256	1.005	1.009	1.0	1.005	1.009	1.0	1.005	1.009	1.0
2	384	0.381	0.396	2.64	0.382	0.388	2.63	0.517	0.571	1.943
4	512	0.169	0.163	5.93	0.172	0.160	5.84	0.248	0.254	4.057
8	768	0.070	0.072	14.32	0.075	0.074	13.43	0.101	0.107	9.949
16	1024	0.034	0.034	29.21	0.039	0.040	25.77	0.046	0.046	22.086

Table 2: Experimental and theoretical speedups

The adequation between the experimental and theoretical values of τ is very good. Hence we can use our theoretical estimates in order to predict the possible speedups for massively parallel architectures. Figure 2 shows the estimated speedups for the pieline ring algorithm and p varying from 32 (Sp=57)to 2048 (Sp=833).

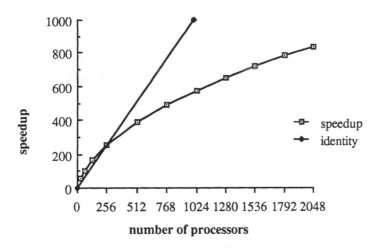

Figure 2: Estimated speedups for the pipeline ring algorithm

6. CONCLUSION

We have analysed various parallel algorithms for computing the QR factorization of a square matrix using Householder reduction. As in the case of Gaussian elimination, a very low connected topology, namely the ring, is sufficient in order to reach very good performances. This is mainly due to the great efficiency of pipelining the data across the channels. Hence communications could be overlapped with computations. Broadcasting through the hypercube is not very powerful. Surprisingly, the linear array topology performs very well with respect to communications. All these variations of a well known algorithm have been analytically modelized. The models fit well with the experimental data available from a FPS T20 hypercube. Using a new way of defining and computing speedups, we could predict that the pipeline ring algorithm could be used with a high efficiency on massively parallel computer assuming a sufficiently large matrix size.

7. REFERENCES

Amdahl G H 1967 *AFIPS Press* pp 483-485

Berry M et al. 1986 *Lect. Notes Comp. Sci.* **237** (Springer Verlag) pp 25-39

Carnevali P et al. 1987 *IBM Preprint ICE-0012* Rome

Cosnard M et al. 1986a *Parallel Algorithms and Architectures* (North-Holland) pp 245-258

Cosnard M, Muller J M and Robert Y 1986b *Numerische Mathematik* **48** pp 239-249

Cosnard M, Daoudi E M and Tourancheau B 1987a *Actes Colloque C3* Angoulème

Cosnard M, Tourancheau B and Villard G 1987b *Lect. Notes Comp. Sci.* **297** pp 611-628

Cosnard M, Robert Y and Tourancheau B 1988 *to appear in Parallel Computing*

Gustafson J L 1988 *ACM 31,5* pp 532-533

Gustafson J L 1988 *International Supercomputing Institut Inc* **vol. I I** pp 130-133

Gustafson J L, Hawkinson S and Scott K1986*Journal Par. Distr. Comp.* **3** pp 297-304

Golub G H and Van Loan C F1983 *Matrix Computations* (The John Hopkins University Press)

Hoare C A R 1985 *Comunicating Sequential Processes* (Prentice Hall)

Ipsen I C F, Saad Y and Schultz M H 1985 *Research Report* **349** (Comp. Sci. Dpt. Yale Univ.)

Li G and Coleman TF 1986 *Tech. Repport*(Comp. Sci. Dpt. Cornell Univ.)

Lord R E, Kowalik J S and Kumar S P 1983 *J. ACM* **30 (1)** pp 103-117

Pothen A, Jha S and Vemulapati U *Hypercube Multiprocessor 87* pp 587-596

Saad Y 1985 *Research Repport* **348** (Comp.Sci. Dpt.Yale Univ.)

Saad Y 1986*Parallel Algorithms and Architectures* (North-Holland) pp 5-18

Saad Y and Schultz MH 1985 *Research Report* **389** (Comp. Sci. Dpt.Yale Univ.)

Vectorized ILU preconditioners for general sparsity patterns

Salvatore Filippone, Giuseppe Radicati di Brozolo

IBM European Center for Scientific and Engineering Computing
Via Giorgione 159
00147 Roma, Italy

Abstract: In this paper we consider vectorization aspects of conjugate gradient-type iterative algorithms for problems with general sparsity patterns. We describe a vectorized implementation of the solution of the two sparse triangular systems that arise when using an ILU preconditioner. We show that on the IBM 3090 VF we can achieve a sustained speed-up of up to 4 over the usual recursive scalar implementation.

1. Introduction

Consider the linear system of equations $Au = b$, where A is a large $m \times m$, sparse, non singular matrix, and b a vector with m components. Conjugate gradient-type methods are efficient and robust iterative algorithms for solving sparse symmetric and unsymmetric linear systems of equations of this kind. A suitable preconditioner is crucial in obtaining a rapid convergence of CG-type methods.

Good preconditioning matrices are obtained by an incomplete LU factorization of the matrix A (Meijerink and van der Vorst, 1977; Gustafsson, 1978; Manteuffel, 1980; Axelsson, 1985). Preconditioners of this kind involve the solution of two sparse triangular linear systems, and this accounts for close to half of the floating-point operations of each iteration.

While most of the kernels of CG-type algorithms are vectorizable and parallelizable, the forward and backsolves in the two sparse triangular systems of the ILU preconditioner are recursive operations that do not vectorize well. In vectorized versions of CG-type codes the scalar preconditioner may account for 80% of the cost of the algorithm, which makes diagonal preconditioning attractive. Many authors have considered alternative types of preconditioners: Dubois, Greenbaum and Rodrigue (1979) consider a truncated Neumann series;

Johnson, Micchelli, and Paul (1983) and Saad (1985) consider polynomial preconditioners; Melhem (1987) reorders the nodes using a multicolor technique; van der Vorst (1982, 1986) and Meurant (1984a) consider a variant of the basic ILU preconditioners; Concus, Golub, and Meurant (1985), and Meurant (1984b) consider a block preconditioner. These techniques are vectorizable, but compared to ILU preconditioners often lead to an increase in the number of iterations, and an increase in the amount of arithmetic operations. Some of these techniques were developed for problems with regularities in the sparsity structures, and are difficult to generalize to problems with more irregular sparsity patterns (e.g. grid refinement, irregular domains), or are not as efficient on 3-D problems as they are on 2-D problems. Therefore these methods are not always competitive with the ILU preconditioners on scalar and vector machines.

Ashcraft and Grimes (1988) and van der Vorst (1987) discuss the vectorization of the ILU preconditioner for problems with regular sparsity patterns arising from the discretization of 2-D and 3-D problems on regular grids in rectangular domains. This technique is referred to as the *hyperplane method*. These vectorized implementations are algebraically equivalent to the standard ILU preconditioners, so that the computational cost is the same.

The problem of parallelizing the solution of the two sparse triangular systems for problems with more general sparsity patterns has been considered by Baxter, Saltz, Schultz, Eisenstat, and Crowley (1988) for the Encore Multimax/320 and the Intel iPSC hypercube, and by Anderson and Saad (1987) for the Alliant FX/8. These techniques are in many respects the generalization of the hyperplane method. They require an additional preprocessing phase before starting the iteration loop to automatically identify at runtime the precedence relation between the unknowns to find sets of equations of a *wavefront* that can be solved concurrently.

This paper describes how the wavefront technique, combined with a rearrangement of the two sparse triangular factors, leads to the an efficient vectorization. This *vectorized wavefront* technique is applicable to problems with very general sparsity patterns. It requires a preprocessing phase to identify and sort the fronts. We describe implementation aspects on the IBM 3090 VF, and discuss the performance of the solution of the two sparse triangular systems. Also the vectorized wavefront approach is algebraically equivalent to the recursive scalar implementation of the ILU preconditioners.

This vectorized wavefront technique is applicable to any problem that involves the solution of a sparse triangular system within an iteration loop, for example SOR and Gauss-Seidel, or CG-methods with SSOR preconditioning.

In section 2 we briefly describe the class of iterative algorithms that we will consider. In section 3 we analyze the computational kernels of these algorithms, and the scope for vectorization; in particular we examine the problem of vectorizing the sparse matrix vector-product. In section 4 we describe the vectorized wavefront method for the solution of a sparse triangular system and present performance data on the IBM 3090 VF. Finally, we present our conclusions in section 6.

2. CG type iterative algorithms

Preconditioned Conjugate Gradient is one of the most efficient iterative algorithms to solve a sparse, symmetric, and positive definite linear system of equations A (Golub and Van Loan, 1983). A suitable preconditioner K is crucial in obtaining a rapid convergence: preconditioning essentially means applying CG to the scaled system $K^{-1}Au = K^{-1}b$. The PCG algorithm is:

- Initialization

    - Compute the preconditioner K;

    - choose u_0, and compute $r_0 = K^{-1}(b - Au_0)$

    - set $p_0 = r_0$, and $\eta_0 = (r_0, r_0)$

- For $i = 0, 1, \ldots$, do until $\dfrac{\|r_i\|_2}{\|u_i\|_2} < \varepsilon$

    - $w = K^{-1}Ap_i$

    - $\alpha_i = \eta_i/(p_i, w)$

    - $u_{i+1} = u_i + \alpha_i p_i$

    - $r_{i+1} = r_i - \alpha_i w$

    - $\eta_{i+1} = (r_{i+1}, r_{i+1});$ $\beta_{i+1} = \eta_{i+1}/\eta_i$

    - $p_{i+1} = r_{i+1} + \beta_{i+1}p_i$

Compared to SOR, Conjugate Gradient has the advantage that it does not require an *a priori* knowledge of the extreme eigenvalues of the matrix for optimal convergence. In CG α_i is chosen so as to minimize $(r_i, A^{-1}r_i)$ in the subspace spanned by $p_0, \ldots, p_{i-1}$, which implies that $(r_{i+1}, r_i) = 0$; each new search direction is chosen so that $(p_{i+1}, Ap_i) = 0$. As a consequence of these choices, the residual at each step is orthogonal to all the previous ones, and the new direction vector is A conjugate to all the previous ones, even though the previous vectors are not involved, and do not need to be stored.

Many generalizations of Conjugate Gradient have been proposed for non-symmetric problems. The simplest methods are based in transforming the non-symmetric problem into a symmetric positive definite one, by either considering AA' or $\begin{pmatrix} 0 & A \\ A' & 0 \end{pmatrix}$ and then using Conjugate Gradient on the transformed system. These methods, respectively the Normal Equations and Biconjugate Gradient, are not always applicable in practice because they may require a large number of iterations to converge; roundoff error may build up rapidly and the methods may actually fail to converge in many cases of practical interest. A derivation of Biconjugate Gradient, Conjugate Gradient Squared (Sonneveld and Wesseling, 1985) converges in many cases of practical interest much faster than Biconjugate Gradient or the Normal Equations, which makes it a very attractive method.

Other iterative algorithms for non symmetric problems are based on generalizations of Conjugate Gradient. Methods of this class are ORTHOMIN, ORTHORES, GMRES (Saad and Schultz, 1986) and many others. Both ORTHOMIN and GMRES compute a new direction vector p in the Krylov subspace spanned by $r_0, \ldots, A^i r_0$, and orthorgonalize it against all the previous ones, which have to be stored. In ORTHOMIN, given a new direction vector, the new solution u_i is computed by solving a one-dimensional minimization problem; in GMRES, several search vectors are computed, and then a global minimization problem is solved.

Preconditioning is used to accelerate the convergence rate. Preconditioners based on Incomplete LU factorization are the most frequently used. ILU basically consists of computing an approximate factorization: $A = LDU - R$. The sparsity structure of the factors L and U is the same as that of the lower and upper triangles of A. A nonzero entry in a factor is accepted if the corresponding entry in A is non zero: $K = LDU$ is then the preconditioner. Variants of the algorithm are based on generating a limited amount of fill in, or on imposing conditions on the row-sum of K. These sort of preconditioners have been successfully used by many authors on positive real matrices (i.e. such that $A + A'$ is positive definite). How to choose good preconditioners for general matrices remains an open research issue.

3. Computational kernels

From an implementation point of view, all the iterative algorithms based on generalizations of Conjugate Gradient share the same structure.   Three computational kernels may be easily identified:

* basic linear algebra: inner products and vector updates of dense vectors. Their vectorization is straightforward.

* sparse matrix-vector product.

* the solution of K^{-1}.

A suitable representation of the nonzero coefficients of a sparse matrix is crucial in vectorizing the sparse matrix vector product efficiently. Using the standard packed row-wise representation the matrix vector product is implemented using the DOT scheme, but it is inefficient because the vectors involved are relatively short.

Other methods for storing sparse matrices so that the sparse matrix vector product vectorizes efficiently have been proposed.   Matrices with a regular sparsity pattern may be stored by diagonals so that the matrix vector product involves contiguous memory locations, and no indirect addressing is necessary. The matrices generated by the discretization of a PDE on a regular grid have a regular sparsity pattern of this sort.

For matrices with more irregular structures, the ITPACK storage scheme is used. The matrix is stored using two matrices, one for the non-zero coefficients, and one for the corresponding column indices. Each row of the first matrix contains the nonzero elements of the corresponding row of the original matrix, and padded with 0 so that all the rows have the same length. Thus the second dimension of the arrays is the largest number of nonzero elements in a row over all the rows of A. Using this representation, the sparse matrix vector product vectorizes with the SAXPY scheme: all the vector operations operate on long vectors, and the contents of vector registers may be reused. On the IBM 3090 VF this method yields a speedup of about 4 over the scalar implementation, and performs at around 20 Mflops. However, the compressed matrix storage fails when some rows contain many more nonzero elements than average. In this case it is necessary to store many zeros to pad the rows, which require extra storage and extra floating point operations proportional to the number of zeros. We are currently considering an alternative data structure to handle this sort of problem.

Preconditioning requires the solution of $Kw = w$ at each iteration step. When an ILU type preconditioner is used this implies the solution of a lower and an upper sparse triangular system:

- $Lw = w$

- $Dw = w$

- $Uw = w$

If no fill in is allowed, the solution of the two sparse triangular systems involves the same number of floating point operations as the sparse matrix vector product.

The relative importance of the three kernels depends on the sparsity structure of the matrix, and the algorithm. In a typical 3D problem, using a 7 point differencing scheme, roughly 20% of the operations are spent in the linear algebra, and 40% each in the sparse matrix vector product and the preconditioner. If a speedup of 4 is achieved in the first two kernels, and nothing in the preconditioner, the global speedup is less than 2. This motivates the need to find an efficient way to vectorize the solution of the two sparse triangular systems.

4. Solving sparse triangular systems on a vector processor

In a dense lower triangular system, equation i cannot be solved until all the previous $i - 1$ equations have been solved. The technique used to vectorize dense systems is based on solving a few equations at each step in scalar mode and substituting into all the remaining ones. This technique is clearly not applicable to sparse triangular systems.

The vectorization and parallelization technique for sparse triangular matrices is based on the observation that to solve equation i only some of the previous $i - 1$ equations are used, and hence only those have to be solved before solving equation i. The solution may be split into *steps*:

- step 1: solve all the equations that do not depend on any other one. Equation 1 is in this class.
- step 2: solve all the equations that only depend on those solved at step 1.
- ...
- step i: solve all the equations that only depend on those solved at steps 1, ... , $i - 1$.

The equations of the system are thus partitioned into sets, *wavefronts*, where all the equations can be solved concurrently. The wavefronts form an ordered set: the equations in front n can all be solved concurrently only after all those of the preceding $n - 1$ fronts have been solved. The dependencies between the equations of a lower (upper) triangular system can be modelled using a digraph, in which each node represents an unknown. The edge (i, j) means that equations i must be solved before equation j. By examining the sparsity pattern, each equation is associated with a wavefront. Equation j is either assigned to front 1 if it does not depend on any other equation, or to front $i + 1$, where i is the last front containing an element referenced by equation j. The equations are then sorted by wavefront. This is similar to the *frontal methods* that are used in direct LU solvers for sparse problems.

In the parallel implementations described by Baxter, Saltz, Schultz, Eisenstat, and Crowley (1988) and by Anderson and Saad (1987) the algorithm is organized in a *parallel event* per wavefront. The elements of a wavefront are distributed across the processors, and solved concurrently. Before processing the next parallel event, all the processors must synchronize. This approach requires only a pointer structure in the vector of unknowns to identify and order the wavefronts. It is not difficult to balance the load among the processors.

On a machine like the IBM 3090 VF it is not feasible to dispatch one wavefront on multiple processors, because the synchronization cost is high relative to the granularity of the algorithm. We considered the potential for vectorization. As with the parallel approach we partition the solve procedure into one *vector event* per wavefront: we vectorize along the number of elements in a wavefront. To do this we sort the equations in a wavefront in decreasing order of backward dependencies, i.e. by decreasing number of nonzero elements in the matrix row. This allows us to handle the case when different rows on the same front have differing lengths, by working with vectors of decreasing length. We then rearrange the arrays that represent the triangular factors so as to access them contiguously with vector operations while processing a wavefront. Using this representation, the solution of the sparse triangular systems vectorizes in a way similar to the matrix vector product, with the addition of a *gather* to collect the equations of a wavefront.

Two equations i and j in the same wavefront may be far apart in the natural ordering. The elements of the vector w involved in the solution of equations i and j are then likely to be far apart, even though they are referred to in the same vector event. On a hierarchical memory machine like the IBM 3090 accessing elements that are far apart causes a noticeable degradation of performance because of cache thrashing. A way around this problem is based on the observation that the equations in a wavefront depend on the equations of only a few of the previous wavefronts. Sorting the vector w so as to store the elements of a wavefront contiguously increases the locality in the access pattern of the vector w and avoids the problem of cache thrashing. In practice this sorting does not need to be performed explicitly: it is sufficient to use two separate vectors, x for the solution and w for the right-hand side, and renumber the column pointers of the triangular factors so that during the loop over the backward dependencies the program gathers the equations that were already solved from x, which is sorted by wavefront.

This renumbering improves the performance quite significantly without adding any overhead in the solution phase. Each triangular factor has to be renumbered according to the order generated by their wavefront structure while they are generated, so that this is inexpensive. With this approach the matrix vector product, and the two sparse triangular systems each produce an output with a different ordering; the information on the ordering is imbedded in the pointer structure of the sparse matrix that uses the output of one of these computational blocks as input. This reordering has to do with the internal representation of the matrix, the triangular factors, and the vectors, but the algorithm yields bit identical results.

In figure 1 we plot the performance in Mflops of the solution of the two sparse triangular systems that arise from the 7 point difference scheme on a 3D cube as the size of the problem increases. The dashed curve in figure 1 represents the Mflop rate using the natural ordering; the performance degrades when the size of the problem becomes large, even though the wavefronts have an increasing average size. The solid curve represents the performance using separate input and output vectors and using the ordering induced by the wavefronts we have just described. The dotted line represents the performance of the scalar code, which is independent of the problem size.

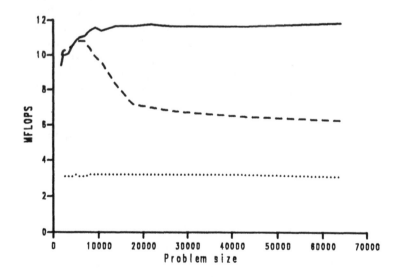

In Table 1 we present performance data for the solution of the two sparse triangular systems that arise from a set of relatively small test problems. The matrices were taken from the Boeing-Harwell sparse matrix collection (Duff,

Grimes, and Lewis, 1987). The matrices were generated by structural analysis and reservoir modelling packages. The last problem in the table, CUBE3D, is obtained from the discretization of an elliptic PDE on a cube using the standard 7 point difference scheme. Column 2 lists the order of the problem, column 3 the average size of the vectors involved in the wavefront approach, column 4 the Mflop rate for the vectorized solver, and column 5 the speedup over the standard scalar implementation.

Description	n	vector length	Mflops	Speed up
STEAM2	600	60	12.9	2.8
ORSIRR_1	1030	25	7.1	2.2
SHERMAN4	1104	23	5.9	2.8
NNC1374	1374	118	10.9	3.5
SAYLR4	3564	60	9.7	3.2
CUBE3D	21982	267	12	4.0

Table 1. Performance of vectorized solver on Boeing-Harwell test matrices.

5. Conclusions

We have described a wavefront technique to vectorize the solution of sparse triangular systems. This technique is applicable to very general sparsity structures, and is not limited to problems arising from the discretization of a PDE on a regular grid. To achieve an efficient vectorization we have to use a special data structure for the sparse triangular factors to store all the coefficients relative to a wavefront contiguously, and we use an internal reordering of the variables to avoid random memory accesses, which degrade the performance noticeably. The preprocessing step that is required to reorganize the two triangular factors is not very expensive, and costs about as much as solving 3 to 5 sparse triangular systems in scalar mode. This phase can probably be optimized further. This overhead makes the vectorized wavefront technique applicable only when the same sparse triangular system has to be solved many times, as in preconditioning of a conjugate gradient-like method. This technique yields identical results to the usual scalar implementation, and a speedup of up to 4 on the IBM 3090 VF even for problems of moderate size.

Both the parallelization and the vectorization technique are economical only if the wavefronts are relatively large. 3D problems are more suited for this sort of approach.   It is easy to see that on a *20 × 20 × 20* grid, using a 7 point differencing scheme, the wavefronts have an average length of 133, which is sufficient to achieve a good vector efficiency. On a *90 × 90* 2D grid, using a 5 point differencing scheme, which generates a sparse problem of roughly the same size, the wavefronts are shorter and have an average length of size 45.   The wavefront structure is present on any regular or irregular grid, and on grids where some nodes are connected by many more edges than the others.   As opposed to multicoloring techniques, which require renumbering of the variables before the incomplete factorization, this technique is a problem dependent scheduling of the solution of the equations by wavefronts.   It gives identical results to the standard sequential algorithm.   It may be interesting to investigate the impact of renumbering the variables according to the order induced by the wavefront structure before the incomplete factorization.

Bibliography

E. Anderson and Y. Saad (1987), **Solving sparse triangular systems on parallel computers,** *preliminary draft.*

C. Ashcraft and R. Grimes (1988), **On vectorizing incomplete factorization and SSOR preconditioners,** *SIAM J. Sci. Stat. Comput.* 9, pp. 122-151.

O. Axelsson (1985), **A survey of preconditioned iterative methods for linear systems of algebraic equations,** *BIT* 25, pp. 166-187.

D. Baxter, J. Saltz, M. Schultz, S. Eisenstat, and K. Crowley (1988), **An experimental Study of Methods for Parallel Preconditioned Krylov Methods,** *Report RR 629, Department of Computer Science, Yale University, New Haven.*

P. Concus, G. Golub, and G. Meurant (1985), **Block preconditioning for the conjugate gradient method,** *SIAM J. Sci. Stat. Comput.* 6, pp. 220-252.

I. Duff, R. Grimes, and J. Lewis (1987), **Sparse Matrix Test Problems,** *Report CSS 191, Computer Science and System Division, Harwell Laboratory, England.*

I. Gustafsson (1978), **A class of first order factorization methods,** *BIT,* 18, pp. 142-156.

M. R. Hestenes and E. Stiefel (1952), **Methods of conjugate-gradients for solving linear systems,** *J. Res. Nat. Bur. Stand.* 49, pp. 409-436.

O. G. Johnson, C. A. Micchelli, and G. Paul (1983), **Polynomial preconditioners for conjugate-gradient calculations,** *SIAM J. Numer. Anal.* 20, pp. 362-376.

T. A. Manteuffel (1980), **An incomplete factorization technique for positive definite linear systems,** *Math. Comp.* 34, pp. 473-497.

J. A. Meijerink and H. A. van der Vorst (1977), **An iterative solution method for linear systems of which the coefficient matrix is a symmetric M-matrix,** *Math. Comp.* 31, pp. 148-162.

R. Melhem (1987), **Toward efficient implementation of preconditioned conjugate gradient on vector supercomputers**, *Int. J. Supercomputer Applications*, 1, pp. 70-98.

G. Meurant (1984a), **Vector preconditioning for the conjugate gradient on CRAY-1 and CDC CYBER 205**, in **Computing methods in Applied Sciences and Engineering, VI**, *R. Glowinski and J.-L. Lions (Ed), Elsevier Science Publishers B.V. (North-Holland), Paris*, pp. 255-271.

G. Meurant (1984b), **The block preconditioned conjugate-gradient method on vector computers**, *BIT*, 24, pp. 623-633.

G. Radicati di Brozolo and M. Vitaletti (1986), **Sparse matrix vector product and storage representations on the IBM 3090 with Vector Facility**, *IBM Technical Report G513-4098, IBM ECSEC, Rome, Italy*.

Y. Saad (1982), **The Lanczos biorthogonalization algorithm and other oblique projection methods for solving large unsymmetric systems**, *SIAM J. Numer. Anal.* 19, pp. 485-506.

Y. Saad (1985), **Practical Use of Polynomial preconditionings for the conjugate gradient method**, *SIAM J. Sci. Stat. Comput.* 6, pp. 865-881.

Y. Saad and M. Schultz (1986), **GMRES: a generalized minimum residual algorithm for solving nonsymmetric linear systems**, *SIAM J. Sci. Stat. Comput.* 7, pp. 856-869.

P. Sonneveld and P. Wesseling (1985), **Multigrid and conjugate gradient methods as convergence acceleration techniques**, in **Multigrid methods for integral and differential equations**, *D. J. Paddon and N. Holbein (Eds), Clarendon press, Oxford, United Kingdom*, pp. 117-167.

H. A. van der Vorst (1982), **A vectorizable variant of some ICCG methods**, *SIAM J. Sci. Stat. Comput.* 3, pp. 350-356.

H. A. van der Vorst (1986), **The performance of FORTRAN implementations for preconditioned conjugate gradients on vector computers**, *Parallel Comput.* 3, pp. 49-58.

H. A. van der Vorst (1988), **ICCG and related methods for 3D problems on vector computers**, *Report A-18, Data processing center, Kyoto University, Kyoto, Japan*.

Complexity of parallel polynomial computations

Dario Bini, Dipartimento di Matematica II Università di Roma, "Tor Vergata".

ABSTRACT. The parallel complexity of the major problems in polynomial computations is reported. The polynomial root-finding (prf-)problem is investigated with more details. Some algorithms for prf are analyzed and implemented in a parallel model of computation proving their polylogarithmic cost. New classes for which prf is in NC are found.

1. Introduction. Polynomial computations are fundamental to the theory and practice of numerical algebraic computations, and the solutions of the related problems are a great part of scientific and engeniering computations on modern computers and constitute an area of active research. Problems as polynomial factorization over finite fields, evaluation of the greatest common divisor (gcd) of two or several polynomials, partial fraction decomposition, just to quote few of them, are very important issues in symbolic computation. Computing discrete Fourier transforms, polynomial products, quotient and remainder of the division of polynomials, computing the values that a polynomial takes at a set of points, polynomial (Lagrange, Newton, Hermite) interpolation, rational interpolation, Padé approximation, continued fraction expansion, solving systems with a Vandermonde, Hankel or (quasi-) Toeplitz matrix, approximating the zeros of a polynomial are all fundamental problems in numerical analysis.

Great progress has been done in the analysis and synthesis of such algorithms in parallel models of computation. The research in this field can be done along two basically different approaches (von zur Gathen 1986). The first is to take a good sequential algorithm and implement it in a parallel environment trying to achieve a near-optimal speed-up. This is appropriate if the number of the available processors is small. The second approach is to reduce the parallel cost as most as possible, allowing an almost arbitrary (polynomial in the input size) number of processors. This second approach is, in principle, theoretical since the intrinsic asymptotic parallel complexity of the problem is investigated. However, a great part of the algorithms obtained through an investigation performed along this line, can be efficiently implemented even with a small number of processors. Our investigation is performed along this second line.

We assume the customary PRAM (parallel random access machine) model, where at each step each processor can perform one operation (compare Quinn 1987). If the operations allowed are arithmetic operations we say that the model is arithmetic, if the operations are Boolean we say that the model is Boolean. We write that an algorithm has a parallel cost $O_A(f(n_1, \ldots, n_m), g(n_1, \ldots, n_m))$ if it computes the result in less than $kf(n_1, \ldots, n_m)$ parallel arithmetic steps, where k is a constant, with $g(n_1, \ldots, n_m)$ processors. Here $n_1, \ldots, n_m$ are the sizes of the problem and f, g are real functions of m variables. Analogously we define the Boolean cost $O_B(f(n_1, \ldots, n_m), g(n_1, \ldots, n_m))$. Moreover we define NC, under the arithmetic (Boolean) model, the class of all the problems which can be solved with a cost $O_A(f(n_1, \ldots, n_m), g(n_1, \ldots, n_m)), (O_B(f(n_1, \ldots, n_m), g(n_1, \ldots, n_m)))$ where the function $f(n_1, \ldots, n_m)$ is a polynomial in $\log n_1, \ldots, \log n_m$ and $g(n_1, \ldots, n_m)$ is a polynomial (*polylogarithmic cost.*)

We observe that, since arithmetic operations between d-digits numbers have Boolean complexity polylogarithmic in d (Savage 1976), in order to prove that a problem belonging to NC in arithmetic sense still belongs to NC in a Boolean sense, it is sufficient to prove that the number $d = d(n_1, \ldots, n_m)$ of digits of arithmetic needed to ensure the correct output is a polynomial function of $n_1, \ldots, n_m$. Observe that this condition is very weak, since it is satisfied by many algorithms which are customarily considered unstable in numerical analysis.

The PRAM models are most popular in the literature on the theory of parallel algorithms, but they are not practical, due to the assumption about the simultaneous access to the shared memory. However many algorithms based on such models are practical; they can be easily rewritten for the more practical models, and the bounds on the numbers of parallel steps and processors slightly change.

The most part of polynomial computations can be dealt in terms of discrete Fourier transforms (DFT) so that the powerful tools of FFT's can be efficiently used. We recall that a DFT at n points can be computed with a cost $O_A(\log n, n)$ with optimum speed-up and with a small overhead constant. The following table contains a list of polynomial computations together with their complexities (Cook 1985, Bini Pan 1988); if not differently specified, n and m are the degrees of the polynomials involved.

Polynomial evaluation at m points	$O_A(\log^2 n, m)$
Polynomial interpolation at $n - 1$ points	$O_A(\log^2 n, n)$
Polynomial multiplication	$O_A(\log n, n)$
Polynomial division	$O_A(\log(m - n), (m - n))$
GCD computation	$O_A(\log^3 n, n^2)$
Partial fraction decomposition	$O_A(\log^3 n, n^2)$
Euclidean algorithm	$O_A(\log^3 n, n^2)$
Composition/decomposition	$O_A(\log^2 n, n)$
(Quasi-)Toeplitz, Hankel systems	$O_A(\log^2 n, n^2)$
(Quasi-)Toeplitz, Hankel determinants	$O_A(\log^2 n, n^2)$

Table 1.

All these problems belong to NC in arithmetical and in Boolean sense. There is another problem in polynomial computations, strongly related to the problems listed in table 1, which has many interesting features, presents some open problems and has a great importance in the applications. Here we restrict our attention to it.

Problem 1. Polynomial root-finding (*prf*-problem). *Given positive integers* n, m, d *compute approximations to all the zeros of the polynomial* $p(z) = \sum_{i=0}^{n} p_i z^i$, *with absolute error* 2^{-d}, *where* p_i *are Gaussian integers such that* $|p_i| \leq 2^{m+1}$.

Without loss of generality we can assume that $p(z)$ is monic, i.e., $p_n = 1$. In the case where $p(z)$ has real zeros it can be proved that the *prf*-problem belongs to NC in both arithmetic and Boolean sense. In the general case the best bound known so far is not polylogarithmic. Pan (1987) has shown an algorithm to solve prf-problem with a cost of $O_A(n \log n \log(n(b+m)), n \log(m+b)/\log(n(m+b)))$ with a polynomial number of digits, based on the geometric construction of Weyl 1924. The major open theoretical problem is wether computing all the zeros of $p(z)$ is in NC.

It is important to point out that, in order to devise a parallel algorithm for polynomial zeros having polylog time, it is not sufficient to construct a good iteration scheme of simultaneous approximation where each iteration has polylogarithmic cost, and then to prove that the convergence of this scheme is global and quadratic. Since this does not generally imply that the number of steps which are sufficient to reach d digits of precision can depend polynomially on $\log n$.

Consider, for instance, Newton's method applied to the equation $z^n - 1 = 0$; choosing as initial point any real $z > n$ the number of iterations needed to get an error bound less than $1/12$ is greater than or equal to n. In order to analyze the complexity of polynomial root-finding it is necessary to give *explicit upper bounds* to the approximation error at any step of the recursion, which hold whatever is the polynomial considered and, therefore, also in the worst case situation. It is not sufficient to use heuristic strategies such as the choice of the starting point, for trying to reduce the number of iterations. It is also important that the numerical scheme can be performed with an arithmetic having a polynomial number of digits, so that a high arithmetic parallelism implies a high Boolean parallelism. Another important issue is that the approximation scheme must be really simultaneous. In fact, it may happen that, in the "simultaneous" approximation process, the slow convergence of a sequence to one zero slows down the convergence of the other sequences to the corresponding zeros. In this case the algorithm delivers approximations of one zero at a time, loosing its parallel features.

In this paper we analyze the prf-problem from a parallel point of view, using algorithms of numerical analysis and polynomial computations. In section 2 we analyze two schemes of simultaneous approximation, which are used for concrete computations: the W-algorithm (Durand 1968, Kerner 1986) and PT-algorithm (Pasquini, Trigiante 1986). Using tools from polynomial computations we prove that both the algorithms can be implemented with a polylogarithmic cost per iteration. But, despite their small parallel cost, such algorithms are not suitable for analizing the intrinsic parallel complexity of the problem. In fact, from one hand, bounds to the number of iterations and to the number of digits of arithmetic are not available, on the other hand the convergence properties are not good enough.

In section 3 we analyze two algorithms, based on Koenig theorem (Householder 1970), which have better parallel properties of simultaneous approximation: Aitken's algorithm and qd-algorithm. We give a parallel implementation of both the algorithms having polylogarithmic cost per iteration and global quadratic convergence.

In section 4 we give a new algorithm based on a generalization of Sebastiao e Silva algorithm (Householder 1971) which has still better convergence properties. Each iteration has a polylogarithmic cost and it is possible to give a polylogarithmic upper bound to the number of iterations sufficient to approximate a factor of the polynomial with error 2^{-b}. The worst case situation has still a cost which is roughly linear in n. But many situations which were considered hard in Schoenhage 1982 and in Pan 1987, can be solved in polylogarithmic time. More classes of polynomials for which prf-problem is in NC are found, and the case of polynomials with real zeros is treated in a simpler way.

3. Two examples. There are two significant examples of methods for the simultaneous approximation of all the zeros of a polynomial, which have a very small parallel cost per iteration but, despite their efficient use in practical computations, are not suitable for analyzing the complexity of prf-problem. They are the W-algorithm given originally by Weierstrass, and Pasquini-Trigiante algorithm, in the following PT-algorithm.

The W-algorithm is based on the following recursion

$$z_i^{(k)} = z_i^{(k-1)} - \frac{p(z_i^{(k-1)})}{\prod_{j=1,n \ j\neq i}(z_i^{(k-1)} - z_j^{(k-1)})}, \quad i = 1, \ldots, n.$$

Many authors conjectured that this scheme converges for almost any initial vector $(z_i^{(0)})$ and no proof of this fact is known. In the case where the polynomial has distinct zeros it is possible to prove that convergence is locally quadratic. The convergence is affected by clustered zeros and in the case of multiple zeros the convergence is linear. However we observe that the parallel cost of each iteration of this method is very small. In fact we can split a single iteration in the following steps

1. Evaluate $p(z_i^{(k-1)})$, $i = 1, \ldots, n$,
2. Compute the coefficients of the polynomial $q(z) = \prod_{j=1,n}(z - z_j^{(k-1)})$,
3. Compute the coefficients of the first derivative $q'(z)$ of $q(z)$,
4. Compute $q'(z_i^{(k-1)}) = \prod_{j=1,n, \ j\neq i}(z_i^{(k-1)} - z_j^{(k-1)})$, $i = 1, \ldots, n$.

Observe that stages 1 and 2 consist in evaluating a polynomial of degree at most n at n different points, so, by table 1, this computation can be performed in $O_A(\log^2 n, n)$. The computation at stage 2 is an interpolation problem, therefore can be solved with the same cost as stage 1. Stage 3 can be perfomed in one step with n processors. Therefore the overall cost of each iteration is just $O_A(\log^2 n, n)$. It is worth pointing out that also the sequential cost of each step of this method i.e. $O(n \log^2 n)$, is very small.

The PT-algorithm is based on the following recursion

$$\mathbf{z}^{(k+1)} = \mathbf{z}^{(k)} - A_k^{-1}\mathbf{w}^{(k)}$$

where $\mathbf{z}^{(k)} = (z_i^{(k)})$, $\mathbf{w}^{(k)} = (p[z_1^{(k)}, \ldots, z_i^{(k)}])$ $A = (a_{i,j})$, $a_{i,j} = 0$ if $i < j$, $a_{i,j} = p[z_1^{(k)}, \ldots, z_j^{(k)}, z_j^{(k)}, \ldots, z_i^{(k)}]$, if $i \geq j$, and $p[v_1, \ldots, v_m]$ are the divided differences of the polynomial $p(z)$ with respect to the points $v_1, \ldots, v_m$ uniquely defined by the relation $p(z) = \sum_{j=1,n} p[v_1, \ldots, v_j] \prod_{i=1,j-1}(z-v_i) + \prod_{i=1,n}(z-v_i)$ where v_i is any set of not necessarily distinct points (Newton representation of $p(z)$). In other words we have that $p[v_1, \ldots, v_j]$ is the leading coefficient of the polynomial $p(z)$ mod $\prod_{i=1,j}(z - v_i)$.

We observe that, assuming n even, if $p(z) = \sum_{j=1}^n \alpha_j \prod_{i=1}^{j-1}(z - v_i) + \prod_{i=1}^n (z - v_i)$ is the Newton representation of $p(z)$ then, denoting $q(z)$ and $r(z)$ the quotient and the remainder of the division of $p(z)$ by $\prod_{i=1,n/2}(z - v_i)$ we have

$$r(z) = \sum_{j=1}^{n/2} \alpha_j \prod_{i=1}^{j-1}(z - v_i), \quad q(z) = \sum_{j=n/2+1}^{n} \alpha_j \prod_{i=n/2+1}^{j-1}(z - v_i) + \prod_{i=n/2+1}^{n}(z - v_i).$$

Therefore it is possible to compute the coefficients α_j given the numbers v_i and the coefficients of $p(z)$, in the following way

1. Compute the coefficients of the polynomial $s(z) = \prod_{i=1,n/2}(z - v_i)$.
2. Compute quotient $q(z)$ and remainder $r(z)$ of the division of $p(z)$ by $s(z)$.
3. Output the leading coefficient $\alpha_{n/2}$ of $r(z)$.
4. Apply recursively this algorithm to $q(z)$ and $r(z)$.

This procedure, applied recursively to the polynomials $q(z)$ and $r(z)$, can be iterated at most $\log n$ times, until all the coefficients α_j have been computed. Since the cost of stage 1 is $O_A(\log^2 n, n)$, beeng essentially an interpolation problem, and the cost of stage 2 is $O_A(\log n, n)$, the overall cost of this algorithm for computing the divided differences is $O_A(\log^3 n, n)$.

One iteration of the PT-method can be performed in the following way

1. For $i = 1, \ldots, n$ compute the coefficients of the matrix A_k as divided differences of $p(z)$ related to the points $z_1^{(k)}, \ldots, z_n^{(k)}, z_i^{(k)}$, and the components of the vector $\mathbf{w}^{(k)}$, which are the divided differences of $p(z)$ related to the points $z_1^{(k)}, \ldots, z_n^{(k)}$.
2. Compute $A_k^{-1}\mathbf{w}^{(k)}$ and update $\mathbf{z}^{(k+1)}$.

Stage 1 of PT-algorithm costs $O_A(\log^3 n, n^2)$, while stage 2 costs $O_A(\log^2 n, n^3)$ (see Borodin, Munro 1975), so the overall cost is $O_A(\log^3 n, n^3)$.

PT-algorithm has some nice properties such as the local quadratic convergence of the arithmetic mean of the approximations to different zeros to the mean of the zeros themselves. Global convergence has been proved in the case of real distinct zeros, but no explicit upper bound to the approximation error is available. Moreover the convergence of $z_i^{(k)}$ is affected by the convergence of the previous components $z_j^{(k)}$, $j < i$ so that the algorithm, despite its parallel formulation, delivers the zeros sequentially.

4. Algorithms based on Koenig theorem.

We analyze two schemes (Aitken and qd-algorithm) of simultaneous approximation, which have good parallel properties and can be used as basic tools for devising asymptotically fast (in some case polylogarithmic) parallel algorithms for the prf-problem. In the sequence of n-ples generated by these algorithms, the convergence of the i-th component to the i-th zero is almost independent of the convergence of the other components. Moreover convergence can be done quadratic and, since at least a factor of the polynomial $p(z)$ is approximated, such methods share the property of PT-algorithm for which the mean of the approximation to a set of zeros converges quadratically to the mean of the zeros. For all these algorithms, which are heavily based on polynomial computations, it is possible to give a priori upper bounds to the approximation error, allowing to estimate the number of iterations needed to reach a given precision (such bounds will be given in the next section in a more general case and can be deduced by setting $h(z) = z$).

First we give the following general result (Householder 1970)

Proposition 1.(Koenig) Let $p(z) = \prod_{i=1,n}(z - z_i)$, be a polynomial having zeros $z_i \neq 0$, $i = 1, \ldots, n$ such that $|z_1| \geq |z_2| \geq \ldots \geq |z_{\mu-1}| > |z_\mu| \geq \ldots \geq |z_n|$, and let $h(z)$ be a polynomial such that $h(z_i) \neq 0$, $i = 1, \ldots, n$. Consider the power series of the function

$$g(z) = \frac{h(z^{-1})}{zp(z^{-1})} = \sum_{i=0,+\infty} c_i z^i$$

and let $h_{\nu,\mu} = \det H_{\nu,\mu}$, $H_{\nu,\mu} = (c_{i+j+\nu-\mu-1})_{i,j=1,\mu}$, be the Hankel determinant (here we assume $h_{\nu,0} = 1$, $h_{\nu,\mu} = c_\nu = 0$ if $\nu < 0$) and $k_{\nu,\mu}(z) = \det A(z)$ the Hankel polynomial, where the matrix $A(z)$ is obtained by replacing the last column of $H_{\nu+1,\mu+1}$ by the vector $(z^\mu, z^{\mu-1}, \ldots, 1)^T$. Then we have

$$\left\| \frac{k_{\nu,\mu}(z)}{h_{\nu,\mu}} - p_{\mu+1,\ldots,n}(z^{-1})z^\mu \right\|_\infty = O(|\frac{z_{\mu+1}}{z_\mu}|^\nu)$$

$$\left| \frac{h_{\nu+1,\mu}}{h_{\nu,\mu}} - z_1 z_2 \ldots z_\mu \right| = O(|\frac{z_{\mu+1}}{z_\mu}|^\nu)$$

$$\left| \frac{h_{\nu+1,\mu}}{h_{\nu,\mu}} \frac{h_{\nu,\mu-1}}{h_{\nu+1,\mu-1}} - z_\mu \right| = O(|\frac{z_\mu}{z_{\mu-1}}|^\nu) + O(|\frac{z_{\mu+1}}{z_\mu}|^\nu),$$

where $p_{\mu+1,\ldots,n}(z) = \prod_{i=1,\mu}(z - z_i)$ and we assume $z_\mu/z_{\mu-1} = 0$ for $\mu = 0$ or $\mu = n+1$.

According to this result, it is possible to approximate a factor of the polynomial $p(z)$, provided that there exists at least a break point in the sequence $|z_1|, |z_2|, \ldots, |z_n|$. Moreover, if two consecutive break points exist, it is possible to approximate also a zero of $p(z)$.

Aitken's method exploit the result of this proposition computing the Hankel determinants according to the following recurrence

$$h_{\nu,\mu-1} h_{\nu,\mu+1} = h_{\nu+1,\mu} h_{\nu-1,\mu} - h_{\nu,\mu}^2.$$

The qd method computes the ratios

$$e_{\nu,\mu} = \frac{h_{\nu+1,\mu+1} h_{\nu,\mu-1}}{h_{\nu,\mu} h_{\nu+1,\mu}}, \quad q_{\nu,\mu} = \frac{h_{\nu+1,\mu} h_{\nu-1,\mu-1}}{h_{\nu,\mu} h_{\nu,\mu-1}},$$

such that $k_{\nu+1,\mu}(z) = k_{\nu,\mu}(z) - z e_{\nu,\mu} k_{\nu,\mu-1}(z)$, $|e_{\nu,\mu}| = O(|z_{\mu+1}/z_\mu|^\nu)$, $q_{\nu,\mu} = z_\mu + O((z_{\mu+1}/z_\mu)^\nu + (z_\mu/z_{\mu-1})^{\nu-1})$, by means of the following recurrence

$$e_{\nu,\mu} q_{\nu,\mu} = e_{\nu-1,\mu} q_{\nu,\mu+1},$$

$$e_{\nu,\mu} + q_{\nu,\mu} = e_{\nu,\mu-1} + q_{\nu+1,\mu}.$$

We observe that both the schemes are intrinsecally sequential and, moreover, the convergence is not quadratic. However it is possible to reach quadratic convergence and a polylogarithmic parallel cost per iteration using the following results.

Proposition 2. Let $\varphi(z) = z^\nu \mod p(z)$, then $c = \varphi(F)T^{-1}h$, where $c = (c_i)_{i=\nu,\nu+n-1}$, $T = (p_{n+j-i})_{i,j=1,n}$, $p_r = 0$ for $r > n$, and $F = (f_{i,j})$ such that $f_{i,i+1} = 1$, $f_{n,j} = -p_{j-1}$, $f_{i,j} = 0$ otherwise, is the Frobenius matrix associated to $p(z)$, and $h = (h_{n-1}, h_{n-2}, \ldots, h_0)^T$ is the coefficient vector associated to the polynomial $h(z)$, i.e. $h(z) = \sum_{i=0,n-1} h_i z^i$.

Proof. Observe that, comparing the coefficients on the two sides of the identity $z^{n-1}h(z^{-1}) = z^n p(z^{-1}) \sum_{i=0,+\infty} c_i z^i$, we get that $\{c_i\}$ satisfies the linear difference equation $c_i p_0 + c_{i+1} p_1 + \ldots + c_{i+n-1} p_n = 0$ with the initial conditions $T(c_1, \ldots, c_n)^T =$ h. Therefore the solution of that equation can be expressed in terms of the Frobenius matrix F as $(c_\nu, \ldots, c_{\nu+n-1})^T = F^\nu T^{-1} \mathbf{h}$. The proof is completed observing that, since $p(F) = 0$, we have $F^\nu = \varphi(F)$.

Proposition 3. We have $F^n = -T^{-1} R$, where $R = (p_{j-i})_{i,j=1,n}$, $p_r = 0$ for $r < 0$. Moreover, if $\mathbf{c} = \varphi(F)\mathbf{v} = \sum_{i=0,n-1} \varphi_i F^i \mathbf{v}$ then $\mathbf{c} = V\mathbf{w}$, $\mathbf{w} = (\varphi_i)_{i=0,n-1}$, $V = (v_{i+j-1})_{i,j=1,n}$, $(v_{n+1}, \ldots, v_{2n})^T = F^n \mathbf{v} = T^{-1} R \mathbf{v}$.

Proof. If $\{c_i\}$ is any solution of the difference equation $\sum_{j=0,n} c_{i+j} p_j = 0$ then we have $R(c_1, \ldots, c_n)^T + T(c_{n+1}, \ldots, c_{2n})^T = 0$, and, since $(c_{n+1}, \ldots, c_{2n})^T = F^n(c_1, \ldots, c_n)^T$, for the arbitrarity of $(c_1, \ldots, c_n)^T$ we have $R + TF^n = 0$. The second relation follows from the fact that the i-th column of V is $F^i \mathbf{v}$.

Now we are ready to give the following algorithm, having quadratic convergence, which can be viewed as a parallel version of Aitken's and qd methods. For simplicity suppose $\nu = 2^k$.

Algorithm 1.

1. Compute $\varphi(z) = z^\nu \bmod p(z)$ by means of repeated squaring modulo $p(z)$.
2. Compute the coefficients $(c_\nu, \ldots c_{\nu+n-1})^T = \varphi(F)\mathbf{v}$, where $\mathbf{v} = T^{-1}\mathbf{h}$.
3. Compute $h_{\nu,\mu}$, $h_{\nu+1,\mu}$, $\mu = 1, \ldots, n$ and $H_{\nu,\mu+1}^{-1}$.
4. Compute the approximation to z_μ given by $\dfrac{h_{\nu+1,\mu}}{h_{\nu,\mu}} \dfrac{h_{\nu\mu-1}}{h_{\nu+1,\mu-1}}$ in the case of Aitken's

   method, or by $q_{\nu,\mu} = \dfrac{h_{\nu+1,\mu} h_{\nu-1,\mu-1}}{h_{\nu,\mu} h_{\nu,\mu-1}}$ in the case of qd-algorithm, and to the

   coefficients of the polynomial $p_{\mu+1,\ldots,n}$ given by the last row of $H_{\nu,\mu+1}^{-1}$.

According to table 1, stage 1 costs $O_A(\log \nu \log n, n)$. Since the product between an $n \times n$ Toeplitz (or Hankel) matrix and a vector can be performed using three DFT's and a system with a triangular Toeplitz matrix can be solved in time $O_A(\log n, n)$ (Bini 1980), the overall cost of stage 2 is $O_A(\log n, n)$. Stage 3 consists in computing determinant and inverse of all the leading principal submatrices of an $n \times n$ Hankel matrix. This can be accomplished with a cost of $O_A(\log^2 n, n^3)$ since the inversion of a Toeplitz or Hankel matrix can be done with a cost of $O_A(\log^2 n, n^2)$.

4. Generalization. The convergence of Aitken and qd-algorithms depends on the ratios $|z_{j+1}/z_j|$, $j = 1, \ldots, n-1$, however, by means of a suitable modification, it is possible to give a more general algorithm whose convergence depends on the ratios $|h(z_{j+1})/h(z_j)|$, where $h(z)$ is almost any polynomial. This algorithm is based on the generalization, given by Householder 1971, of the algorithm of Sebastiao e Silva 1941.

In this section we analyze the generalization of Sebastiao e Silva method, in terms of parallel complexity, number of iterations and number of digits sufficient to reach a given accuracy. Then we show how this method can be used, together with simple geometric considerations, to devise a root-finding algorithm which has a polylogarithmic complexity in a wide set of cases and offers a different tool to prove that the root-finding problem is in NC for polynomials having real zeros.

First we give the following general result

Proposition 4. Let $h(z)$ be any polynomial of degree less than n, and $p(z)$ a monic polynomial of degree n having pairwise different zeros $z_i \neq 0$, $i = 1, \ldots, n$, ordered in such a way that $|h(z_1)| \geq |h(z_2)| \geq \ldots \geq |h(z_n)| > 0$. Consider the polynomial $h^{(\nu)}(z) = h(z)^\nu \bmod p(z)$ and apply the Euclidean algorithm to $s_n(z) = p(z)$, $s_{n-1}(z) = \hat{h}^{(\nu)}(z)$, where $\hat{h}^{(\nu)}(z)$ is the monic polynomial having the same zeros of $h^{(\nu)}(z)$, obtaining

$$s_{n-i+1}(z) = s_{n-i}(z)(z - \alpha_i) - \beta_i s_{n-i-1}(z), \quad i = 1, \ldots, n-1,$$
$$s_1(z) = z - \alpha_n,$$

where we suppose that $\beta_i \neq 0$, $i = 0, \ldots, n-1$, (β_0 is the leading coefficient of $h^{(\nu)}(z)$) and $s_{n-i}(z)$ is a monic polynomial of degree $n - i$, $i = 1, \ldots, n-1$. Here the quantities α_i, β_i, $s_{n-i}(z)$ depend also on ν, i.e. $\alpha_i = \alpha_i^{(\nu)}$, $\beta_i = \beta_i^{(\nu)}$, $s_{n-i} = s_{n-i}^{(\nu)}$. For the sake of simplicity we omit the superscript. Then, setting $\lambda_j = h(z_j)$, we have

$$\|s_{n-i}(z) - p_{1,2,\ldots,i}(z)\|_\infty = O(|\frac{\lambda_j}{\lambda_{j+1}}|^\nu|$$

$$|\alpha_j - z_j| = O(|\frac{\lambda_{j+1}}{\lambda_j}|^\nu + |\frac{\lambda_j}{\lambda_{j-1}}|^\nu) \; j = 2, \ldots, n-1$$

$$|\alpha_1 - z_1| = O(|\frac{\lambda_2}{\lambda_1}|^\nu), \quad |\alpha_n - z_n| = O(|\frac{\lambda_n}{\lambda_{n-1}}|)^\nu$$

It is easy to show that, for almost any polynomial $h(z)$, the polynomial s_{n-i} has degree $n - i$ so that the Euclidean algorithm can be carried out as shown in proposition 4 (Bini, Gemignani 1988). From the above proposition we get the following parallel algorithm having global quadratic convergence.

Algorithm 2.
1. Compute the coefficients of the polynomial $h^{(\nu)}(z) = h(z)^\nu \bmod p(z)$ by means of repeated squaring modulo $p(z)$.
2. Compute the coefficients α_i, β_i and the polynomials s_{n-i} applying the Euclidean algorithm to $p(z)$ and $\hat{h}^{(\nu)}(z)$.

The cost of the algorithm is given by $O_A(\log \nu \log n, n) + O_A(\log^3 n, n^2)$ (compare table 1 for the cost of Euclidean algorithm).

In order to better bound the number of digits of the arithmetic and the number of iterations, we describe now a different implementation of the result given in proposition 4. First we must observe that, since the quantities α_i, β_i, generated by the Euclidean algorithm are the coefficients of the continued fraction decomposition of the function $g(z) = \dfrac{h_\nu(z^{-1})}{z p(z^{-1})}$, from the theory of Padé approximants we have the relations (Householder 1970, page 60-63)

$$\alpha_i = q_i + e_{i-1}, \; \beta_i = q_i e_i, \; i = 1, \ldots, n, \; (e_0 = 0, \; e_n = 0)$$
$$q_i = \frac{h_{i,i} h_{i-2,i-1}}{h_{i-1,i} h_{i-1,i-1}}, \; e_i = \frac{h_{i,i+1} h_{i-1,i-1}}{h_{i-1,i} h_{i,i}} \tag{1}$$
$$z^j k_{i+j,j+1}(z^{-1}) / h_{i+j-1,j} = \det(zI - T_{n-i+1})$$

where T_{n-i+1} is the $(n - i + 1) \times (n - i + 1)$ tridiagonal matrix having diagonal entries $\alpha_1, \ldots, \alpha_{n-i+1}$, superdiagonal entries 1, and underdiagonal entries $\beta_1, \ldots, \beta_{n-i}$, and $h_{i,j}$, $k_{i,j}(z)$ are the Hankel determinant and the Hankel polynomial obtained from the coefficients of the power series $g(z) = \sum_{i=0,+\infty} c_i z^i$. Moreover, if $h^{(\nu)}(z) = \sum_{i=0,n-1} a_i z^i$ so that

$$g(z) = \frac{\sum_{i=0,n-1} a_i z^{n-i-1}}{\sum_{i=0,n} p_i z^{n-i}} = \sum_{i=0,+\infty} c_i z^i,$$

for the Hankel determinants $h_{i,j}$ we have the following formula (Householder 1970, page 55)

$$h_{i,j} = a_{n-1}^{-i-j}(-1)^j \det S_{i,j} \tag{2}$$

$$S_{i,j} = \left. \left(\begin{array}{cccc}
p_n & p_{n-1} & p_{n-2} & \cdots \\
 & p_n & p_{n-1} & \cdots \\
\cdots & \cdots & \cdots & \\
a_{n-1} & a_{n-2} & a_{n-3} & \cdots \\
 & a_{n-1} & a_{n-2} & \cdots \\
\cdots & \cdots & \cdots &
\end{array}\right) \right\} \begin{array}{c} i \\ \\ \\ j \end{array}$$

Algorithm 3.

1. Compute the coefficients of the polynomial $h_\nu(z) = h(z)^\nu \bmod p(z)$ by means of repeated squaring modulo $p(z)$.

2. Compute $h_{\nu,p}$ according to the formula (2).

3. Compute α_i, β_i, according to the formulae (1).

4. Compute the coefficients of the polynomial $t_{n-i+1}(z) = \det(zI - T_{n-i+1})$.

Stage 1 costs $O(\log \nu \log n, n)$, stage 2 costs $O(\log^2 n, n^3)$ since the evaluation of the determinant of a "quasi Toeplitz" matrix can be performed in $O(\log^2 n, n^2)$, moreover, using the same technique as in Pan 1988, it is possible to reduce the number of processors with a light increase of the number of steps, obtaining $O_A(\log^3 n, n^2)$. Stage 4 can be computed with a cost of $O(\log^2, n^2)$ applying a divide and conquer technique by means of the recursion $\det T_n = \det T_q \det \hat{T}_{n-q} - \beta_q \det T_{q-1} \det \hat{T}_{n-q-1}$, which is obtained by expanding $\det T_n$ along the $q+1$-st column, where $\hat{T}_i$ is the $i \times i$ principal submatrix of T_n made up by the last i rows and columns. Therefore the overall cost of algorithm 3 is $O_A(\log \nu \log n, n) + O_A(\log^3 n, n^2)$.

Koenig's theorem as well as proposition 4, give the local quadratic convergence of algorithms 1,2 and 3 but, in order to give an upper bound to the number of iterations sufficient to approximate the result to a given precision, we must make a deeper analysis of the convergence. For this purpose we recall the following result (Bini, Gemignani 1988).

Proposition 5. Let $p(z) = \prod_{i=1,n}(z - z_i)$ be a polynomial satisfying the conditions of problem 1, and proposition 4. Then We have

$$\beta_j < |\frac{\lambda_{j+1}}{\lambda_j}|^\nu 2^B |\frac{(1+\theta_{j-1})(1+\theta_{j+1})}{(1+\theta_j)^2}|, \; j = 1, 2, \ldots, n-1,$$

$$|\alpha_j - z_j| < A_j^{(1)}|\frac{\lambda_{j+1}}{\lambda_j}|^\nu + A_j^{(2)}|\frac{\lambda_j}{\lambda_{j-1}}|^\nu, \; j = 1, 2, \ldots, n;$$

$$||t_j(z) - p_{j+1,\ldots,n}(z)||_\infty \leq |\frac{\lambda_j}{\lambda_{j+1}}|^\nu \frac{2^{2\varphi}}{1+\theta_j}$$

$$A_j^{(1)} = 2^{2\varphi}|\frac{(1+\theta_{j-1})}{(1+\theta'_{j-1})(1+\theta_j)}|, \; A_n^{(1)} = 0,$$

$$A_j^{(2)} = 2^{2\varphi}(|\frac{1}{(1+\theta'_{j-1})(1+\theta_j)}| + |\frac{(1+\theta_{1,j-2})(1+\theta_{0,j})}{(1+\theta'_{j-1})(1+\theta_{j-1})}|), \; A_1^{(2)} = 0,$$

where $\varphi = n^3(m + \log_2 n)/2$, $B = n^2(m + \log n) + m$, $|\theta_j|, |\theta'_j| \leq |\lambda_{j+1}/\lambda_j|2^\varphi$.

Consider the case where $|\frac{\lambda_{j+1}}{\lambda_j}| < 1 - \frac{1}{n^c}$ for some constant c. Then, if $\nu > (\varphi + 1)n^c \log 2$ the denominator of β_j as well as the denominator in the bound to $||t_j(z) - p_{j+1,\ldots,n}(z)||_\infty$ in proposition 5 have modulus greater than $1/2$. Therefore it is possible to give an a priori lower bound to the number $\log \nu$ of the iterations, at stage 1 of algorithm 3, sufficient to output a result within an absolute error 2^{-b}. We have in fact the following

Proposition 8. If $|\frac{\lambda_{j+1}}{\lambda_j}| < 1 - \frac{1}{n^c}$ for some constant c then $\log \nu$ iteration at stage 1 of algorithm 3, where $\nu > n^c(b + 2\varphi) \log 2$, are sufficient to compute the coefficients of the factor $p_{j+1,\ldots,n}(z)$ within b binary digits of absolute precision, that is

$$||t_j(z) - p_{j+1,\ldots,n}(z)||_\infty \leq 2^{-b}.$$

Moreover, if $|\frac{\lambda_j}{\lambda_{j-1}}| < 1 - \frac{1}{n^c}$ holds then an analogous bound on the number of iterations can be obtained for the approximation to z_j.

In other words, the above proposition states that for all the classes $\mathcal{P}(c, h)$ of polynomials such that $p \in \mathcal{P}(c, h)$ implies $h(z_{i+1})/h(z_i) \leq 1 - 1/n^c$, $i = 1, \ldots, n-1$, the root-finding problem is in NC, since ν grows at most polynomially in n, m and b. Actually the above condition can be relaxed in the following way $h(z_{i+1})/h(z_i) \leq 1 - 1/n^{\log^c n}$, $i = 1, \ldots, n-1$.

The above NC property holds also in a Boolean sense, in fact, it is possible to prove that the number of digits of arithmetic, sufficient to assure b correct digits in the result, depends polynomially on n, m and b. This fact can be proved in the following way. First of all suppose for simplicity that $h(z)$ is a monic polynomial with (Gaussian) integer coefficients of modulus at most $2^{m'}$ and observe that the moduli of the coefficients of the polynomial $h^{(\nu)}$ are bounded by $2^{\rho(m,m',n,\nu)}$, where $\rho(m, m', n, \nu)$ is a polynomial. Then observe that q_i and e_i are ratios of (Gaussian) integer numbers which are obtained as determinants of matrices having (Gaussian) integer entries (compare (1) and (2)). Therefore using any Hadamard-like inequality it is possible to get an upper bound to the moduli of $h_{\nu,p}$ as

$$|h_{i,j}| \leq (||S_{i,j}||_\infty)^{i+j} \leq (i+j)2^{\rho(m,m',n,\nu)(i+j)} \leq 2^{2n\rho(m,m',n,\nu)}.$$

That is, using a floating point arithmetic with $f = 2n\rho(m, m', n, \nu)$ binary digits, the computation at stage 1 and 2 of algorithm 3 can be performed with no rounding errors. The result of the computation at stages 3 and 4 is affected by a relative error given by 2^{-f}. Concerning stage 4, observe that instead of computing the monic polynomial $t_j(z) = \det(zI - T_j)$ it is possible to compute the determinant of the scaled matrix $\text{Diag}(h_{j-1,j}^2 h_{j,j+1} h_{j,j})(zI - T_j)$ which is a polynomial with (Gaussian) integer coefficients whose moduli can be bounded again by means of a Hadamard-like inequality. Also in this case a number of binary digits, polynomial in the input sizes m, m', m and b, is sufficient to deliver such coefficients with no rounding errors. The case where $h(z)$ is not monic can be dealt in a similar way.

It is interesting to point out that algorithm 3 yields a tridiagonal matrix T_n such that $p(z) = \det(zI - T_n)$, therefore Gerschgorin theorems on the localization of the eigenvalues of a matrix can be used for a posteriori bounds on the approximation. Another term which is useful to control the approximation error is β_j.

Algorithm 3 can be used as a tool for a more general root-finding algorithm. In fact observe that, if $h(z) = nz - p_{n-1}$ is the linear polynomial having as zero the arithmetic mean g (center of gravity) of the zeros of $p(z)$ then $\lambda_j = z_j - g$. Therefore, fixed a constant c, it is possible to compute some factors if there exists some strong break-point, i.e. a subscript j such that $|\lambda_{j+1}/\lambda_j| < 1 - 1/n^c$. On the other hand, if the latter condition is not satisfied for any j, it means that the zeros are located in an anulus centered in g with relative width $1/n^{c-1}$. In this case it is possible to choose a point u inside the anulus, for instance $u = |p(g)|^{1/n}$, and apply algorithm 3 with $h(z) = z - u$. If also in this case there are no break points then all the zeros are located in the intersection of two anuli which must contain both iu, $-iu$ where $i^2 = -1$. Therefore it is possible to compute the two factors applying a third time the algorithm with $g(z) = z - ip(g)$. So, with at most three applications of algorithm 3 it is possible to split any polynomial $p(z)$ at least into two factors, and it is possible to apply the same procedure to the factors in a recursive way. If at each step of the recursion the factors have degrees proportional to n (for instance between $n/4$ and $3n/4$) then after $O(\log n)$ steps the polynomial is factored into linear factors. In the worst situation, where the degree of a factor is independent of n, the number of application of the algorithm is proportional to n. The cost in this worst situation is $O_A(n \log n \log \nu, n) + O_A(n \log^3 n, n^2)$. One example of this situation, considered hard by Schoenhage 1982, is the case of zeros which are almost in geometric progression, say $z_1 = 1, z_2 = 1 + \epsilon\gamma_1, z_3 = 1 + \epsilon\gamma_1 + \epsilon^2\gamma_2, z_4 = 1 + \epsilon\gamma_1 + \epsilon^2\gamma_2 + \epsilon^3\gamma_3, \ldots$, where ϵ is a small positive number and γ_i, $i = 1, \ldots, n-1$ are complex numbers having almost the same modulus. In this case, only one zero at each application of the algorithm is computed. However this situation is easily solved by choosing $h(z) = p'(z)$, in fact, in this case we have

$$\left|\frac{\lambda_j}{\lambda_i}\right| = \prod_{r=1,n,\ r\neq i,\ r\neq j} \frac{z_r - z_j}{z_r - z_i},$$

so that we have $n - 2$ good break-points, and one application of algorithm 3 yields all the zeros. This choice for $h(z)$ does not work if, for instance, at each application of the algorithm, with the shift in the gravity center, a factor of degree $k < n/4$ with clustered zeros is found. This case can be handled very easily choosing as $h(z)$ the polynomial $p^{(k)}(z)$. See Bini Gemignani 1988 for more details.

In the case of a polynomial having real zeros it is easy to prove that, choosing as

$h(z)$ the polynomial $z - w$, where w is any point such that $n/4 \leq \#\{z_i : z_i < w\} < 3n/4$, we can get factors having degree less than $3n/4$. In fact, if this were not the case, we would find an anulus containing $q \geq 3n/4$ zeros, and a factor $\tilde{p}(z)$ of degree q. Therefore, since $u = |\tilde{p}(g)|^{1/q}$ is inside the anulus, choosing $h(z) = z - u$ allows us to compute the wanted factors.

References.

[1] Ben-Or, M., E. Feig, d. Kozen, p. Tiwari, A fast parallel algorithm for determining all roots of a polynomial with real roots, *SIAM J. on Comput.* (to appear).

[2] Bini D., Parallel solution of certain Toeplitz linear systems, *SIAM J. on Comput.* **13**, pp. 268-276, 1984.

[3] Bini D., Gemignani L., On the parallel complexity of polynomial zeros, II Università di Roma 1988, (to appear in the Proceedings of CNAN, Roma 1988).

[4] Bini D., Pan V., Topics on polynomial and matrix computations, SUNY, Albany 1988.

[5] Bini D., Pan V., Polynomial division and its computational complexity, *Journal of Complexity*, **2**, pp. 179-203, 1986.

[6] Borodin A., Munro I., *Computational Complexity of Algebraic and Numeric Problems*, Elsevier, New York 1975.

[7] Cook S.A., A taxonomy of problems with fast parallel algorithms, *Inform. and Control*, **64**, pp. 2-22, 1985.

[8] Durand E., Solutions numerique des equationes algebriques, Tome 1, Masson, Paris 1968.

[9] von zur Gathen J., Parallel arithmetic computations: a survey, *Lecture Notes in Computer Science*, **233**, pp. 93-112, Springer 1986.

[10] Householder A., S., Generalization of an algorithm of Sebastiao e Silva, *Numerische Math.* **16**, pp. 375-382, 1971.

[11] Householder A., S., *The Numerical Treatment of a Single Nonlinear Equation*, McGraw-Hill, New York 1970.

[12] Kerner I.O., Ein gesamtschrittverfahren zur berechnung der nullstellen von polynomen, *Numerische Math.* **8**, pp.290-294, 1966.

[13] Pan V., Sequential and parallel complexity of approximate evaluation of polynomial zeros, *Computers and Mathematics (with Applications)*, **14**, pp. 591-622, 1987.

[14] Pan V. Fast and efficient parallel evaluation of the zeros of a polynomial having only real zeros, T.R. 88-13, SUNY, Albany, 1988.

[15] Pasquini L., Trigiante D., A globally convergent method for simultaneously finding polynomial roots, *Mathematics of Computations* **44**, pp.135-149, 1985.

[16] Quinn M.J., *Designing Efficient Algorithms for Parallel Computers*, McGraw-Hill, New York 1987.

[17] Savage J.E., *The Complexity of Computing*, Wiley and Sons, New York, 1976.

[18] Schoenhage A., The fundamental theorem of algebra in terms of computational complexity, manuscript, Dept. of Mathematics, University of Tübingen, 1982.

[19] Sebastiao e Silva J., Sur une méthode d'approximation semblable à celle de gràffe, it Portugal. Math., **2**, pp. 271-279, 1941.

[20] Weyl H., Rondbemerkungen zu hautproblemen der mathematik, 2, Fundamentalsatz der Algebra und Grundlagen der Mathematik, Math. Z., **20**, 1924.

Substructure technique for parallel solution of linear systems in finite element analyses

L. Brusa, F. Riccio

CISE Tecnologie Innovative SpA, Via Reggio Emilia, 39 - 20090 Segrate (MI) (I) - Po Box 12081 - 20134 MILANO (I)

ABSTRACT: The paper presents a numerical method for parallel solution of linear systems with positive definite matrices derived from the application of finite element method. The algorithm is based on substructure technique and is designed for shared-memory multiprocessors with vector architecture. Implementation details that can affect the performance are discussed and numerical experimentation on ALLIANT FX/80 is presented.

THE ABOVE DESCRIBED WORK HAS BEEN CARRIED OUT IN THE FRAME OF A 1988 CONTRACT BETWEEN ENEL-DSR AND CISE.

1. INTRODUCTION

The substructure technique has been extensively used for many years in finite element analyses and is still very popular. This method is based on the division of the whole discretized domain into sub-regions so that two classes of variables can be defined, i.e. the internal variables relevant to nodes within substructures, and the interface variables relevant to nodes belonging to two or more substructures. If all the internal variables are numbered before the interface ones, the assembly matrices which describe the discretized problem have a typical block "arrow" structure with decoupled diagonal blocks.
This feature involves many practical advantages widely exploited by the structural engineers. Large problems can be run on computers with small memories while computing time can be saved if few substructures are changed and the global system must be re-analysed. In this case only the matrices relevant to the modified substructures and to the interface variables must be re-processed.
A new merit of substructure technique, recently recognized, is its natural parallelism which can be conveniently exploited for the direct solution of linear systems on multiprocessor computers. The factorization of the matrix can be performed by concurrently computing the rows of the

triangular factors relevant to the internal variables of
each substructure while parallel computations can be
performed at do-loop level in the elimination of the
interface variables. Inherent parallelism can also be
exploited in the execution of forward and backward steps.
This computational scheme is at the basis of the numerical
method reported in this paper which has been applied to the
solution of linear systems with symmetric positive definite
matrices derived from the application of the finite element
method. The algorithm is suited to shared-memory
multiprocessors with vector architecture, which can be used
to concurrently perform Gaussian elimination of the
variables internal to each substructure. Efficiency
therefore strongly depends on the choice of proper vector
algorithms for matrix factorization and for the solution of
forward and backward steps. For these computations a
vectorized version of a frontal technique has been used .
Even if in principle substructuring can provide a high
degree of parallelism (Adams et al. (1984)), Farhat et al.
(1984)) this is not sufficient to guarantee satisfactory
performances that strongly depend on the matching between
numerical method and computer architecture. The performance
of an algorithm in multiprocessing is indeed influenced by
many factors, such as: load balancing among the CPUs, choice
of a proper number of logical tasks and of the granularity
size to limit the weight of the synchronization overhead,
I/O strategies that reduce the interruptions of concurrent
computations as much as possible. These topics are discussed
in the paper and numerical experimentation on ALLIANT FX/80
is presented.

2. DESCRIPTION OF THE ALGORITHM

2.1. The substructure technique

The substructure technique can be used for the solutions of
the linear system:

$$Ax=b \qquad\qquad (1)$$

where matrix A, which will be assumed to be positive
definite, derives from the discretization of partial
differential equations defined in a domain. The method
(Williams (1973), Hitchings et al. (1984), Elwi et al.
(1984)) is based on the division of the discretized region
into a number of smaller pieces, or substructures, by the
introduction of internal boundaries, so that two types of
mesh nodes can be defined: nodes internal to the
substructures and nodes which are common to the substructure
interfaces.

An example of a discretized domain divided into substructures is given in fig. 1 where the solid dots represent internal nodes and the squares represent interface nodes. If system (1) derives from the application of the finite element method, matrix A is obtained as the direct sum of matrices $S^{(j)}(j=1,N)$, relevant to the N substructures of the domain, having the following form:

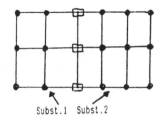

Subst.1 Subst.2

$$S^{(j)} = \begin{vmatrix} A_{II}^{(j)} & A_{IB}^{(j)} \\ \\ A_{IB}^{(j)T} & A_{BB}^{(j)} \end{vmatrix} \quad (2)$$

Fig.1- Example of subdivision into substructures

where $A_{II}^{(j)}$ and $A_{IB}^{(j)}$ are the matrices connecting the internal variables of the substructure j and these variables to the global interface variables, respectively, while matrix $A_{BB}^{(j)}$ is the coupling matrix of the interface variables derived from the only contributions of substructure j. All these matrices have the typical sparse structure due to the application of the finite element method. If the internal variables are numbered first and the interface variables are numbered last, system (1) assumes the form:

$$PAP^T(Px) = Pb \quad (3)$$

where $\underline{P}$ is a permutation matrix and:

$$A=PAP^T= \begin{vmatrix} A_{II}^{(1)} & & & A_{IB}^{(1)} \\ & A_{II}^{(j)} & & A_{IB}^{(j)} \\ & & A_{II}^{(N)} A_{IB}^{(N)} \\ A_{IB}^{(1)T}\cdots A_{IB}^{(j)T}\cdots & A_{IB}^{(N)}(\sum_{j=1}^{N} A_{BB}^{(j)}) \end{vmatrix} \quad Px= \begin{vmatrix} (Px)^{(1)} \\ (Px)^{(j)} \\ (Px)^{(N)} \\ (Px)^{(B)} \end{vmatrix} \quad Pb= \begin{vmatrix} (Pb)^{(1)} \\ (Pb)^{(j)} \\ (Pb)^{(N)} \\ (Pb)^{(B)} \end{vmatrix} \quad (4)$$

The components of vectors $(Px)^{(j)}$ and $(Px)^{(B)}$ are the internal variables of substructure j and the variables relevant to the global interface nodes, respectively. A similar notation is used for the components of vector Pb. The solution of system (3) is obtained by means of Gaussian

elimination according to the following steps.
a) Cholesky decomposition of matrix $\tilde{A}$:
$$\tilde{A}=PAP^T = R^TR \tag{5}$$
It must be noticed that if matrix A is symmetric positive definite, no pivoting is required to ensure numerical stability.
b) Solution of forward step:
$$R^Ty = Pb \tag{6}$$
c) Solution of backward step:
$$R(Px) = y \tag{7}$$
As a consequence of the "arrow pattern" of matrix $\tilde{A}$ with decoupled diagonal blocks, matrix R has the following form:

$$R= \begin{vmatrix} R_{11} & & R_{1,N+1} \\ & R_{jj} & R_{j,N+1} \\ & R_{NN} & R_{N,N+1} \\ & & R_{N+1,N+1} \end{vmatrix} \tag{8}$$

where:

$$A_{II}^{(j)}=R_{jj}^T R_{jj}; \quad R_{j,N+1}=R_{jj}^{-T}A_{IB}^{(j)} \qquad (j=1,N) \tag{9.a}$$
$$M^{(j)} = A_{BB}^{(j)}-A_{IB}^{(j)T}A_{II}^{(j)-1}A_{IB}^{(j)} \qquad (j=1,N) \tag{9.b}$$
$$R_{N+1,N+1}^T R_{N+1,N+1}=\sum_{j=1}^{N}M^{(j)} \tag{9.c}$$

With matrix (8), the following computations are required for the solution of forward and backward steps:
Forward step:
$$R_{jj}^T y_j=(Pb)^{(j)} \quad (j=1,N) \tag{10.a}$$
$$W_j = R_{j,N+1}^T y_j \quad (j=1,N)$$
$$R_{N+1,N+1}^T y_{N+1}=(Pb)^{(B)}-\sum_{j=1}^{N} W_j \tag{10.b}$$

Backward step:
$$R_{N+1,N+1}(Px)^{(B)}=y_{N+1} \tag{11.a}$$
$$R_{jj}(Px)^{(j)}=y_j-R_{j,N+1}(Px)^{(B)} \qquad (j=1,N) \tag{11.b}$$

From examination of eqs. (9), (10), (11), the following remarks can be made .
i)   Matrices $R_{jj},R_{j,N+1},M^{(j)}$ can be obtained by partial decomposition of matrices $S^{(j)}$ relevant to the N substructures. In fact, the Cholesky decomposition of matrix $S^{(j)}$ stopped after the elimination of the internal variables of substructure j produces the following result:

$$\begin{vmatrix} R_{jj}^{-T} & 0 \\ -A_{IB}^{(j)T}A_{II}^{(j)-1} & I \end{vmatrix} \begin{vmatrix} A_{II}^{(j)} & A_{IB}^{(j)} \\ A_{IB}^{(j)T} & A_{BB}^{(j)} \end{vmatrix} = \begin{vmatrix} R_{jj} & R_{j,N+1} \\ 0 & M^{(j)} \end{vmatrix} \tag{12}$$

Therefore the computation of the first N blocks of rows of matrix R (eqs.(9a)) and of the Schur complements

$M^{(j)}$ of matrices $S^{(j)}$ (eqs. (9b)) are independent logical tasks that can be performed concurrently on different processors.
ii) Matrices $M^{(j)}$ can be considered as "superelement matrices", relevant to the interface variables of substructure j, which can be assembled to form the matrix of the global interface variables following the usual procedure of the finite element method. This matrix is then factorized to obtain the triangular factor $R_{N+1,N+1}$.
iii) Eqs (10.a) and (11.b) are independent logical tasks that can be run concurrently on different processors.
iv) An advantage of the substructure technique is the possibility of saving computing time if the original problem must be re-analysed with few substructures changed or added or eliminated from the domain considered. In these cases only the matrices relevant to the modified or new substructures and to the interface variables must be reprocessed.

2.2. The Gaussian elimination algorithm

The independent logical tasks which can be concurrently performed in the application of the substructure technique have a sufficiently complex structure to make this method well fitted to implementation on shared-memory multiprocessors with vector architecture. The performance of the method, therefore, strongly depends on the choice of efficient vector algorithms for the matrix factorization and for the solution of linear systems with lower and upper triangular matrices. The numerical scheme considered is Irons frontal technique (Irons (1970), Abbas (1980)) that can be used for the solution of linear systems of the form (1) where matrix A, as it occurs in the finite element method, is the sum of several contributions from different elements.
The element matrices are assembled one by one and whenever a row and column of matrix A are fully summed, the corresponding variable is eliminated. Eq. (1) is therefore solved by means of Gaussian elimination with symmetric row-column pivoting, where the interchange strategy is determined by the ordering of the elements.
The main steps of the algorithm are:
- definition of the elimination order and other information related to the matrix sparseness;
- execution of steps of forms a), b), c) in sect 2.1. where P is a permutation matrix defined by the elimination order and matrix $\tilde{A}$ is assembled and factorized at the same time.
Following Irons definitions, during the element-by-element assembly process a variable becomes "active" on its first appearance and is eliminated after the last one, that is when it is not present in anyone of the subsequent elements. The subset of active variables continually changes

and at the k-th elimination step, the computer main memory
should only contain the elements of the partially decomposed
matrix relevant to the variables which are active at that
stage. The matrix formed by these elements is termed
"virtual matrix". When a variable is eliminated, the main
memory locations reserved to its row and column in the
virtual matrix are replaced by the contributions of a new
active variable. Each variable is therefore characterized by
two indices which define its position in the elimination
order and in the virtual matrix. The factorization algorithm
is based on the following scheme, shown here below for dense
matrices of order n:

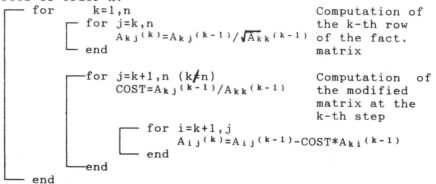

where $A_{ij}^{(o)}$ and $A_{ij}^{(n)}$ are the elements of the original and
of the factorized matrix, respectively.
The standard frontal method performs the previous
computations for the elements of the virtual matrix only,
following the elimination order.
Therefore, the method, like many algorithms for sparse
matrices, is implemented with extensive use of indirect
addressing which scarcely benefits from vectorization. To
overcome this drawback, a vectorized version of the frontal
technique has been set up which allows the use of vectors
with stride one in the modification of the virtual matrix.
This algorithm, described in Brusa et al. (1988), prove to
be highly efficient in spite of the number of computations
involved which are larger than those relevant to the
standard method. The numerical experimentation has shown
that speed-ups ranging form 10 to 30 can be obtained.
The vectorized version of the frontal method has been used
both for the incomplete factorization of substructure
matrices $S^{(j)}$, performed on different processors, and for
the factorization of the matrix relevant to the global
interface variables which is a sequential step of the
solution algorithm. In this last case parallel computations
can be performed by assigning to different processors the
updating of the virtual matrix colummns which can be
evaluated independently one from the other.

The solution of linear systems of form:

$$R^T y = b \qquad (14)$$
$$R x = y \qquad (15)$$

where R is an upper triangular matrix, is performed by means of the following numerical schemes, shown here below for a matrix of order n.
Solution of eq.(14):

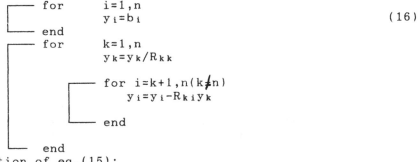

$$
\begin{aligned}
&\text{for} \quad i=1,n \\
&\qquad y_i = b_i \qquad\qquad\qquad\qquad\qquad\qquad (16)\\
&\text{end} \\
&\text{for} \quad k=1,n \\
&\qquad y_k = y_k / R_{kk} \\
&\qquad\qquad \text{for } i=k+1,n\,(k \neq n) \\
&\qquad\qquad\qquad y_i = y_i - R_{ki} y_k \\
&\qquad\qquad \text{end} \\
&\text{end}
\end{aligned}
$$

Solution of eq.(15):

$$
\begin{aligned}
&\text{for} \quad k=n,1 \\
&\qquad H=0 \\
&\qquad \text{for} \quad i=k+1,n\ (k \neq n) \\
&\qquad\qquad H=H+R_{ki} x_i \qquad\qquad\qquad\qquad (17)\\
&\qquad \text{end} \\
&\qquad x_k=(y_k-H)/R_{kk} \\
&\text{end}
\end{aligned}
$$

These algorithms are used for the solution of the linear systems in eqs. (10) and (11), and computations are performed only for the non-zero elements of the k-th row of the upper triangular matrix R.
For the implementation of the schemes (16), (17) use has been made of routines of the BLAS library and of assembler-coded routines for searching operations on integer arrays to define the column indices of the non-zero elements of matrix R rows.
Numerical experimentation has shown that this last type of computations often represents the most time consuming part of the global forward and backward steps. For this reason, it is more convenient to perform a sequential solution of both eqs. (10.b), (11.a) and eqs (10.a), (11.b) with concurrent execution of all the searching operations.

3. IMPLEMENTATION

The algorithm has been implemented on ALLIANT FX/80.
The FX/80 is a shared-memory multiprocessor with up to 8 computational elements (CEs) and up to 12 interactive

processors (IPs). Each CE has vector processing ability with
8 vector registers containing 32 64-bit words each.
The IPs perform interactive user jobs, operating system
tasks and I/O.
The access to memory by the CEs is through a crossbar switch
connected with one or two shared caches containing 32K 64-
bit words each. The chaches in turns are connected with
a main memory containing up to 32M 64-bit words. The IPs
access memory through up to 4 caches containing 4K 64-bit
words each. Loops can be executed in several modes. Vector
mode uses vector registers and arithmetic units on one CE.
Vector-concurrent mode divides iterations into blocks of up
to 32 words each and assignes them to individual CEs where
they run in vector mode simultaneously. Nested loops can run
in concurrent outer/vector inner mode where the inner loop
executes in vector mode and the outer loop in concurrent
mode. Scalar concurrent mode is also available for the
simultaneous execution of independent scalar computations on
different CEs. Concurrent computations are performed on the
"computational complex" that groups up to 8 CEs into one
entity that is treated by the operating system as a single
resource.
The computations presented in the paper have been performed
on the configuration of the system installed at CISE which
has 4 CEs, 1 cache connecting the CEs with a 8M 64-bit words
main memory, 5 IPs with 2 IPs'caches.
The program is written in FORTRAN 77 and compiler directives
are used to concurrently run subroutines performing
independent tasks. When I/O instructions are present in
concurrent tasks, system routines are used to synchronize
the access to the I/O system resources.
The independent logical tasks described in sect. 2.1. refer
to computations relevant to substructures whose number can
be larger than the available CEs. The substructures can be
gathered into NCE groups, where NCE is the number of
processors which can be concurrently used .
In this way the user can balance the load among the CEs by
forming groups with approximately the same computation
volume. The concurrent tasks relevant to each substructure
of a group are executed on one CE in vector mode. The input
data relevant to the substructures (element matrices and
sparseness information) are stored on files. The element
matrices and the relevant sparseness information are
computed in a buffer array REL whose content is discharged
on a file when the array is full. Each record of the input
files contains, therefore, approximately the same number of
information which may refer to more than one element,
according to the buffer length. The factorization step is
consequently performed by reading the input data of a block
of elements and by computing in a buffer array RMAT the rows
of the factorized matrix relevant to the variables which can
be eliminated. When buffer RMAT is full, its content is
discharged on a file which supplies the input data for the

forward and backward steps. The lengths of the buffer arrays
REL and RMAT can be defined by the user and may influence
the granularity of the tasks, that is, the amount of time
the cooperating tasks execute   concurrently in between
synchronization points (Chen et al. (1984)). In fact, if I/O
is executed in few points of the program each processor can
make   more   calculations   independently,   thus   avoiding
synchronization on intermediate results.

4. NUMERICAL RESULTS

The structure considered is shown in fig. 2 where also the
subdivision into 8 substructures is indicated. The finite
element discretization has been perfomed using 1600 brick
parabolic elements: 320 elements
for substructures 1,2,7,8 and 80
elements for substructures 3,4,5,6.
The following two cases have been
considered:
CASE 1 - each   node   has   three
          variables
CASE 2 - each   node   has   one
          variable
The total number of variables of
cases 1 and 2 are 30402 and 10134,
respectively.
Table 1 reports the maximum front-
width and the number of internal
variables of each substructure for
CASE 1. The same quantities for
CASE 2 can be obtained by dividing
by three the data in table 1.
The   computations   have   been
performed by using 1,2,3,4 CEs and
table 2 shows the substructures
analysed by the CEs for the two
cases.

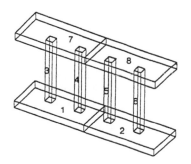

Fig. 2- Substructure subdivision

of the test structure

The solution process has been divided into the following
phases:
- Ordering   step   (definition of the information about
  the matrix sparseness and the elimination order used in
  the application of frontal technique)
- Factorization step (incomplete factorization of the
  substructure matrices and complete factorization of the
  matrix relevant to the interface variables)
- Forward and backward steps.
  The ordering   step is characterized by many
  computations and searching operations on integer arrays
  and few I/O operations. The factorization step produces
  the main contribution to the total I/O operations
  relevant to the reading of the element data in array REL
  and to the writing of the rows of the factorized matrix
  stored in array RMAT. The files containing this last

information are in turn read to supply input data for the execution of forward and backward steps. Concurrent subroutines containing I/O instructions are used only in the factorization and ordering steps.

For each step and for the total solution, the following parameters have been computed:

$$p = \text{degree of parallelism} = t_{PAR}/t_{TOT} \qquad (18)$$
$$S_{MAX}^{(k)} = \text{maximum speed-up} = 1/((p/k)+1-p) \qquad (19)$$

where t_{PAR} is the elapsed time relevant to the portion of the code which can be parallelized, t_{TOT} is the total elapsed time and k is the number of CEs used.

Elapsed times t_{PAR} and t_{TOT} have been evaluated using one CE in vector mode.

The maximum speed-up represents a limit value computed by assuming a perfect load balancing among the processors and by neglecting memory contention and synchronization overhead. The weight of these effects can be estimated by comparing $S_{MAX}^{(k)}$ with the experimental speed-up $S_{ex}^{(k)}$ defined by :

$$S_{ex}^{(k)} = t_1/t_k \qquad (20)$$

where t_k is the elapsed time relevant to the execution on k processors.

To evaluate the influence of I/O on the granularity size, each numerical experiment has been run using two different lengths of the buffer array REL (see sect.3).

No parametrization has been done on the length of array RMAT which has been assumed equal to 1M 64 bit words.

By indicating with NREL the array REL length, the following values have been considered.

CASE 1
a) NREL = 1830
b) NREL = 30000

CASE 2
a) NREL = 210
b) NREL = 30000

The smallest values of NREL permit the storage of the matrix of one element only. Therefore the granularity size is defined by the time spent in the modification of the virtual matrix for the computation of the rows of the factorized matrix relevant to the few variables which can be eliminated after the assembly of each element matrix. When NREL is equal to 30000, blocks of up to 16 elements for CASE 1 and up to 142 elements for CASE 2 can be processed.

Table 3 shows the elapsed times obtained for CASE 1 using different numbers of CEs and the two values of NREL considered. The degree of parallelism, the maximum and the experimental speed-ups are reported for CASE 1 in table 4. The experimental speed-ups are relevant to the elapsed times obtained with NREL = 30000. The same type of results obtained for CASE 2 are shown in tables 5 and 6. As shown in tables 3 and 5, the use of different dimensions NREL of buffer array REL has a small influence on the elapsed times of the factorization step of CASE 1. The reduction of NREL from 30000 to 1830 increases the elapsed time by 15% only when 4 CEs are used. Also for CASE 2 the effect of the buffer REL length becomes significant only when 4 CEs are used, but the increase of the elapsed time due to the reduction of NREL is much greater since it is $\sim$ 55%. The reason for this behaviour is that the front width of CASE 1 is large enough to produce an acceptable granularity size even for an element-by-element solution process, which is the standard coding choice in traditional finite element programs. The number of computations for the updating of the virtual matrix of CASE 2 is much smaller than that relevant to CASE 1. Therefore the synchronization produced by I/O instructions before and after the virtual matrix modification considerably reduces the granularity size. The granularity size can be increased only if the finite elements are processed in blocks. This effect becomes more important when the number of CEs used increases. In this case in fact, the computational load assigned to each CE is reduced with a consequent increase of the I/O relative weight. This weight can be diminished by using few large records. A comparison between the maximum and experimental speed-ups reported in tables 4 and 6 shows that the loss of performance in the ordering and forward-backward steps is about 1% using 2 CEs and below 10% with 3 and 4 CEs, both for CASE 1 and CASE 2. The degradation in the factorization step performance of CASE 1 is $\sim$ 20% with 2 CEs and $\sim$ 40% with 3 and 4 CEs. These figures become 4% and 25% respectively for CASE 2. The higher loss of performance of the factorization step, with reference to the other phases of the solution process, is mainly due to the I/O synchronization overhead which has a more significant weight for CASE 1 then for CASE 2.

In this last case, in fact, the storage of the element matrices requires the use of 1 record for substructures 3,4,5,6 and of 3 records for substructures 1,2,7,8. The number of these records for CASE 1 are 5 and 20, respectively . Owing to the large dimension of array RMAT, the rows of the factorized matrix are stored in few records and therefore the I/O overhead is not very significant in the forward - backward steps.

The effect of the load unbalancing when 3 CEs are used, is evident in the factorization step which has elapsed times nearly equal to those obtained by using 2 CEs. A different subdivision of the domain into substructures could reduce the loss of performance.

As showed by the degrees of parallelism quoted in tables 4 and 6 the substructure method seems to be well suited to be parallelized. The improvement obtained in the global solution using 4 CEs are quite satisfactory with speed-ups of 2.7 and 2.8 for CASE 1 and CASE 2, respectively, and relevant losses of performance by $\sim$ 20% and $\sim$ 10%.

Table 1- Maximum front width and number of internal variables of
the substructures for CASE 1

Substructure	1	2	3	4	5	6	7	8	Interface connect.
Max. front width	432	432	171	171	171	171	432	432	459
n.of internal variables	5634	5634	1737	1737	1737	1737	5634	5634	918

Table 2 - Distribution of the computational load for
CASES 1 and 2.

Nº of CEs used	Substructures analysed by CE n.1	Substructures analysed by CE n.2	Substructures analysed by CE n.3	Substructures analysed by Ce n. 4
1	1,2,3,4,5,6,7,8	=	=	=
2	1,3,4,7	2,5,6,8	=	=
3	1,2	3,4,7	5,6,8	=
4	1,3	4,7	2,5	6,8

Table 3 - Elapsed times in seconds for CASE 1

	NREL = 1830				NREL = 30000			
Nº. of CEs	1	2	3	4	1	2	3	4
Ordering step	1222	622	449	339	1213	620	452	340
Factorizat. step	843	571	561	496	840	569	552	435
Forw.and back. steps	733	418	333	271	734	416	316	257
Total solution	2798	1611	1343	1106	2787	1605	1320	1032

Table 4 - Degrees of parallelism (p), experimental speed-ups (*) (S_{ex}^k), maximum speed-ups $(S_{MAX}^{(k)})$ for CASE1

	P	$S_{ex}^{(2)}$	$S_{ex}^{(3)}$	$S_{ex}^{(4)}$	$S_{MAX}^{(2)}$	$S_{MAX}^{(3)}$	$S_{MAX}^{(4)}$
Ordering step	0.99	1.96	2.68	3.57	1.98	2.94	3.88
Factorizat. step	0.93	1.47	1.52	1.93	1.86	2.63	3.30
Forwar. and back.steps	0.91	1.76	2.32	2.86	1.83	2.54	3.15
Total solution	0.95	1.74	2.11	2.70	1.90	2.72	3.48

(*) $S_{ex}^{(k)}$ are relevant to the elapsed times obtained with NREL = 30 000

Table 5 - Elapsed times in seconds for CASE 2

	NREL = 210				NREL=30000			
Nº. of CEs	1	2	3	4	1	2	3	4
Ordering step	147	75	57	42	148	75	55	42
Factorizat. step	67	45	42	53	61	39	40	34
Forw.and back. steps	85	47	35	30	87	47	35	29
Total solution	299	167	134	125	296	161	130	105

Table 6 - Degrees of parallelism (p), experimental speed-ups (*) (S_{ex}^k), maximum speed-ups $(S_{MAX}^{(k)})$ for CASE2

	P	$S_{ex}^{(2)}$	$S_{ex}^{(3)}$	$S_{ex}^{(4)}$	$S_{MAX}^{(2)}$	$S_{MAX}^{(3)}$	$S_{MAX}^{(4)}$
Ordering step	0.99	1.97	2.69	3.52	1.98	2.88	3.77
Factorizat. step	0.77	1.56	1.52	1.79	1.62	2.05	2.37
Forwar. and back.steps	0.92	1.85	2.48	3.0	1.86	2.5	3.10
Total solution	0.91	1.83	2.27	2.81	1.84	2.54	3.15

(*) $S_{ex}^{(k)}$ are relevant to the elapsed times obtained with NREL = 30 000

CONCLUSIONS

The paper reports an algorithm for the solution of linear systems derived from the application of the finite element method, which is based on the substructure technique. The natural parallelism of this technique and the complex structure of the concurrent tasks make the method well fitted to shared-memory multiprocessors with vector architecture.
The algorithm has been coded for ALLIANT FX/80 and the interest of the study mainly lies in the practical information obtained by experimenting different modalities of implementation which can affect the performance. One of the main problems in setting up efficient parallel codes seems to be the definition of proper input and output data organization on files to reduce I/O synchronization overhead and allow a satisfactory balancing of computational load to be obtained among the processors.
The results obtained are promising and indicate that the elaboration of data in blocks with sufficiently large dimensions can significantly increase the granularity size and consequently the performance.

REFERENCES

Abbas S.F., 1980, "Some novel application of the frontal concept", Int. J. Num. Meth. Eng. Vol. 15, 119-536.
Adams L., Voigt R., 1984, "A Methodology for exploiting parallelism in the finite element process", "High-Speed Computation", Edited by J.S. Kowalik
Brusa L., Riccio F., 1988 "A frontal technique for vector computers". Paper submitted to Int. J. Num. Meth. Eng.
Chen S.S., Dongarra J. J., 1984 "Multiprocessing linear algebra algorithms on the Cray X-MP-2. Experiences with small granularity" J. of Parallel and Distributed Computing, 1,22-31.
Elwi A.E., Murray D.W., 1985, "Skyline algorithms for multilevel substructure analysis", Int. J. Num. Meth. Eng., vol. 21,465-474
Farhat C., Wilson E., 1987, "A new finite element concurrent computer program architecture". Int. J. Num. Meth. Eng., vol.24, 1771-1792
Hitchings D., Balasubramaniam K., 1984, "The Cholesky method in substructuring with an application to fracture mechanics", Computers and Structures, vol. 18, n. 3, 417-424
Irons B.M., 1970, "A frontal solution program for finite element analysis". Int. J. Num, Meth, Engn., vol. 2,5-32.
Williams F.W., 1973, "Comparison between sparse stiffness matrix and substructure methods", Int. J. Num. Meth. Eng. vol. 5, 383-394

CONCLUSIONS

The arithmetic mean method for solving large systems of linear ordinary differential equations on a vector computer

I. Galligani[*], V. Ruggiero[**]

[*] Department of Mathematics, University of Bologna, Bologna, Italy
[**] Department of Mathematics, University of Ferrara, Ferrara, Italy

ABSTRACT: In this paper we consider the *arithmetic mean method*, developed in [1], for solving large systems of linear ordinary differential equations. This method is well suitable for parallel implementation on a multiprocessor system that can execute concurrently different tasks on a few vector processors with shared central memory, such as the CRAY X-MP. The consistency and the stability of the method are analysed and a locally extrapolation technique is applied. The special class of differential equations that arise in solving the diffusion-convection problem by the method of lines is considered: the results of some computational experiments are reported.

1. THE ARITHMETIC MEAN METHOD

We consider linear continuous-time dissipative dynamic systems of the form

$$(1) \qquad \frac{dv(t)}{dt} + Av(t) = b \qquad\qquad 0 < t \leq t^*$$

where $v(0) = g$ is given.

Here, the constant real $n \times n$ matrix A and the real $n \times 1$ vector b are given; the symmetric matrix $A + A^T$ is positive definite. The $n \times 1$ vector $v(t)$ denotes the unknown vector-valued function of the real variable t; t is interpreted as time. Since the eigenvalues of A have positive real part, $v(t)$ is asymptotically stable.

We assume that matrix A is large and sparse with a special sparsity pattern for which it is possible to decompose A in the form

$$(2) \qquad A = A_1 + A_2$$

where A_k or $PA_k P^T$ (k = 1,2) is a matrix of *simple structure* (for example, tridiagonal); P is a permutation matrix.

For a *time step* h>0, equation (1) satisfies the recurrence relation

$$(3) \qquad v(t+h) = e^{-hA}v(t) + e^{-hA} \int_0^h e^{\tau A}b(t+\tau)d\tau$$

with t = 0, h, 2h,...

In order to construct a family of numerical methods for solving the system (1) when A satisfies the condition (2), we consider the recurrence relation (3) and the expression

$$(4) \qquad e^{-hA} = \frac{1}{2} e^{-hA_1} e^{-hA_2} + \frac{1}{2} e^{-hA_2} e^{-hA_1} + O(h^3).$$

Now each matrix e^{-hA_k} in (4) is replaced with a rational function in A_k, R_k (k=1,2), and the integral in (3) is replaced with a quadrature formula. For example, when b is a constant vector, the Euler-MacLaurin summation formula gives:

$$\int_0^h e^{\tau A} b \, d\tau = \frac{h}{2} (I+e^{hA}) b - \frac{h^2}{12} (e^{hA}-I)Ab + \frac{h^4}{720} (e^{hA}-I)A^3b+...$$

I is the identity matrix of order n.

When b is a time-dependent vector, the trapezoidal rule gives:

$$\int_0^h e^{\tau A} b(t+\tau) \, d\tau = \frac{h}{2} (e^{hA}b(t+h) + b(t)) + O(h^3)$$

Thus, we have the following *method of arithmetic mean* [1]

$$w_{m+1}^{(1)} = R_1 R_2 \left(w_m + \frac{h}{2} s_m \right)$$

(5) $$w_{m+1}^{(2)} = R_2 R_1 \left(w_m + \frac{h}{2} s_m \right)$$ $m = 0,1,2,\ldots$

$$w_{m+1} = \frac{h}{2} \left(w_{m+1}^{(1)} + w_{m+1}^{(2)} \right) + \frac{h}{2} z_m$$

where $s_m = (I + \frac{h}{6} A)b$, $z_m = (I - \frac{h}{6} A)b$ when b is a constant vector and $s_m = b(mh) = b_m$, $z_m = s_{m+1} = b((m+1)h) = b_{m+1}$ when b is a time-dependent vector. Starting with the given initial vector $w_0 = g$, one can find the approximation w_m to the solution $v(t)$ of (1) at the time $m \cdot h$ for any time-level $m = 1,2,\ldots$

Widely used expressions of R_k $(k=1,2)$ are:

(6.a) $$R_k = (I + h A_k)^{-1}$$

(6.b) $$R_k = (I + \frac{h}{2} A_k)^{-1} (I - \frac{h}{2} A_k)$$

(6.c) $$R_k = (I + \alpha h A_k)^{-2} (I - \beta h A_k)$$

$$\alpha = \beta/\sqrt{2}, \quad \beta = \sqrt{2} - 1$$

With the forms (6.a)÷(6.c) of R_1 and R_2, the arithmetic mean method (5) is *consistent* with the differential equation (1); besides, it is *first order* accurate in time when we consider the formula (6.a) and *second order* accurate in time when we consider the formulas (6.b) and (6.c). If A_k is a diagonalizable matrix and the real part of each eigenvalue of A_k is positive, the matrices R_k of (6.a) and (6.c) are L-*acceptable* approximations to e^{-hA_k} $(k=1,2)$.

The method (5)-(6.a) may be locally extrapolated with the Richardson technique to generate a method which is *second order* accurate in time. The Richardson technique is defined by

(7) $$w_{m+2} = 2w'_{m+2} - w''_{m+2}$$

where

$$w'_{m+2} = S(h) [S(h)(w_m + \frac{h}{2}s_m) + \frac{h}{2}z_m + \frac{h}{2}s_{m+1}] + \frac{h}{2}z_{m+1}$$

$$w''_{m+2} = S(2h) (w_m + hs_m) + hz_{m+1}$$

and

$$S(h) = \frac{1}{2} [(I+hA_1)^{-1}(I+hA_2)^{-1} + (I+hA_2)^{-1}(I+hA_1)^{-1}]$$

When the symmetric matrices $A_1+A_1^T$ and $A_2+A_2^T$ are positive definite, it is a simple matter to prove that the arithmetic mean method (5)-(6.a) and (5)-(6.b) are *stable* for all h>0. This result is a direct consequence of the following well known

Lemma. Let the symmetric matrix $M+M^T$ be positive definite. Then for every $\alpha \geq \beta \geq 0$, $\|(I+\alpha M)^{-1}(I-\beta M)\| \leq 1$.

Under the same assumption on A_1 and A_2, the arithmetic mean method (5)-(6.c) is stable for all positive h<h*, where

$$h* = \min \{ \frac{1}{\beta} \frac{\lambda_{min}(A_1+ A_1^T)}{\lambda_{max}(A_1^T A_1)}, \frac{1}{\beta} \frac{\lambda_{min}(A_2+ A_2^T)}{\lambda_{max}(A_2^T A_2)} \} .$$

$\lambda_{min}(A_k+A_k^T)$ is the algebrically smallest eigenvalue of $A_k+A_k^T$; $\lambda_{max}(A_k^T A_k)$ is the algebrically largest eigenvalue of $A_k^T A_k$.

Always we can express the matrix A as the matrix sum

(8) $A = L + U$

where L and U are respectively lower and upper triangular matrices with positive diagonal entries. If we make the assumption that b is constant and equal to $b(mh)=b_m$ in the time-subinterval [mh, (m+1)h], formula (1) suggests the following *method of arithmetic mean* ($w_0=g$):

$$(\frac{1}{h}I+L)w_{m+1}^{(1)} = (\frac{1}{h}I-U)w_m + b_m$$

(9) $$(\frac{1}{h}I+U)w_{m+1}^{(2)} = (\frac{1}{h}I-L)w_m + b_m \qquad\qquad m = 0,1,2,...$$

$$w_{m+1} = \frac{1}{2}(w_{m+1}^{(1)} + w_{m+1}^{(2)})$$

that has been considered by V.K. Saul'yev in [4]. A simple consistency analysis indicates that this method has *second order* accuracy in time.

A stability condition for the method (9) is given by the following *Theorem*. Let A be a real $n \times n$ matrix expressed in the form (8), $A = L + U$. Assume that the symmetric matrix $M = A + A^T$ is positive definite. If $h_0 = \min\{\lambda_{min}/|\mu_{min}|, \lambda_{min}/|\mu_{max}|\}$, where λ_{min} is the smallest eigenvalue of M and μ_{min} and μ_{max} are the algebrically smallest and largest eigenvalues of matrix $N = LL^T - UU^T$, then the arithmetic mean method (9) is stable for all positive $h < h_0$.

Proof. Since $0 < \lambda_{min} \leq x^T Mx/x^T x$ and $\mu_{min} \leq x^T Nx/x^T x \leq \mu_{max} \neq 0$, we have for $h > 0$

$$x^T (\tfrac{1}{h} M + N) x \geq (\tfrac{1}{h} \lambda_{min} + \mu_{min}) x^T x$$

$$x^T (\tfrac{1}{h} M - N) x \geq (\tfrac{1}{h} \lambda_{min} - \mu_{max}) x^T x$$

Thus, it is a simple matter to verify that for $h < h_0$ the symmetric matrices $\tfrac{1}{h} M + N$ and $\tfrac{1}{h} M - N$ are positive definite. The matrix $\tfrac{1}{h} M + N$ may be written in the form

$$\tfrac{1}{h}M+N = \tfrac{1}{h}(A+A^T) + LL^T - UU^T = \tfrac{1}{h}(A+A^T) + AL^T - UA^T =$$

$$= \tfrac{1}{h}(A+A^T) + AL^T + LA^T - AA^T = A(L+ \tfrac{1}{h} I)^T + (L + \tfrac{1}{h} I)A^T - AA^T =$$

$$= (L + \tfrac{1}{h} I)W_1 (L + \tfrac{1}{h} I)^T$$

where

$$W_1 = ((L + \tfrac{1}{h} I)^{-1}A) + ((L + \tfrac{1}{h} I)^{-1}A)^T - ((L + \tfrac{1}{h} I)^{-1}A)((L + \tfrac{1}{h} I)^{-1}A)^T$$

In the same way we have

$$\tfrac{1}{h} M - N = (U + \tfrac{1}{h} I) W_2 (U + \tfrac{1}{h} I)^T$$

where

$$W_2 = ((U + \tfrac{1}{h} I)^{-1}A) + ((U + \tfrac{1}{h} I)^{-1}A)^T - ((U + \tfrac{1}{h} I)^{-1}A)((U + \tfrac{1}{h} I)^{-1}A)^T$$

Now, if

$$Q_1 = (\tfrac{1}{h} I + L)^{-1} (\tfrac{1}{h} I - U)$$

and

$$Q_2 = (\tfrac{1}{h} I + U)^{-1} (\tfrac{1}{h} I - L)$$

we have

$$Q_1 Q_1^T = (I - (\tfrac{1}{h} I + L)^{-1} A) (I - (\tfrac{1}{h} I + L)^{-1} A)^T = I - W_1$$

and

$$Q_2 Q_2^T = I - W_2$$

Since the matrices $\tfrac{1}{h} M + N$ and $\tfrac{1}{h} M - N$ are positive definite and, therefore, also the matrices W_1 and W_2 are positive definite, we have $\rho(Q_1 Q_1^T) < 1$ and $\rho(Q_2 Q_2^T) < 1$. Now $Q_1 Q_1^T$ and $Q_1^T Q_1$ have the same eigenvalues. Thus $\|Q_1\|^2 < 1$ and $\|Q_2\|^2 < 1$. By the triangle inequality of matrix norms, we obtain

$$\| Q \| \equiv \| \tfrac{1}{2} Q_1 + \tfrac{1}{2} Q_2 \| \le \tfrac{1}{2} \| Q_1 \| + \tfrac{1}{2} \| Q_2 \| < 1$$

Therefore, since $\rho(Q) \le \|Q\|$, the method (9) is stable for all positive $h < h_0$.

It is interesting to note that the arithmetic mean method, or the extra-polated form, is characterized by having within its overall mathematical structure certain well-defined substructures that can be executed simultaneously, during each time-level. This feature makes the method (5) or (7) or (9) ideally suited for implementation on a multiprocessor system with two or more vector processors.

2. PARALLEL IMPLEMENTATION

We describe an implementation of the arithmetic mean method on a multi-vector system with shared memory, as the CRAY X-MP, when A is a block-tridiagonal matrix where each square block on the diagonal of A is a non singular pxp tridiagonal matrix and each block on the subdiagonal and on the superdiagonal of A is a pxp diagonal matrix. Matrix A is partitioned into qxq blocks; thus n = pxq.

For example, such matrices arise in solving the initial-boundary value problem for the diffusion-convection equation on a rectangular domain Ω ($\phi=\phi(x,y,t)$, $\sigma=\sigma(x,y)$)

(10) $\phi_t = \phi_{xx} + \phi_{yy} - \alpha\phi_x - \beta\phi_y - \gamma\phi + \sigma$

by the method of lines using centered-in space- difference equations. The function $\phi(x,y,t)$ satisfies on the boundary of Ω a Dirichlet or a mixed Dirichlet-Neumann condition and in Ω the initial condition $\phi(x,y,0)$ = $\phi_0(x,y)$.

We consider the two different decompositions (2) and (8) of matrix A; in the decomposition (2), A_1 and PA_2P^T are direct sums of q tridiagonal pxp matrices. Here P is the permutation matrix which reorders the vector u = $(u_{11} u_{12}...u_{1p} u_{21} u_{22}...u_{2p}...u_{q1} u_{q2}...u_{qp})^T$ as Pu = $(u_{11} u_{21}...u_{q1} u_{12} u_{22}....u_{q2}....u_{1p} u_{2p}....u_{qp})^T$.

Formula (9) determines the approximation w_{m+1} to v(t) at the time-level m+1 by solving simultaneously a lower triangular system and an upper triangular system.

These systems are solved with the block forward-elimination algorithm and with the block back-substitution algorithm, respectively. Thus, at each iteration $\ell(\ell=1,2,...,q)$ we have to solve a lower or upper bidiagonal system of order p; for the solution of this system we use the recursive doubling algorithm implemented in the "consistent" version (or cyclic reduction algorithm). On CRAY X-MP, utilizing one processor and an appropriate *data structure* (in order to reduce the memory-bank conflicts), the speed-up of this algorithm is nearly two for p=256 and greater than four for p>8192 [3]. Once the right-hand side terms of (9) have been computed, the total number of vector arithmetic operations for solving each system is $O(q(5 \log_2 p))$ with "degree of parallelism" varying from p/2 to 1 and $O(2q)$ with "degree of parallelism" p.

Formulas (5)-(6.a) determine the approximation w_{m+1} to v(t) at the time-level m+1 by solving simultaneously two sets of two block-diagonal systems

$$(I+h\ PA_2P^T)z_{m+1}^{(1)} = P(w_m + \tfrac{h}{2}\ s_m)$$

(11)

$$(I+hA_1)w_{m+1}^{(1)} = P^Tz_{m+1}^{(1)}$$

and

$$(I+hA_1)z_{m+1}^{(2)} = w_m + \tfrac{h}{2}\ s_m$$

(12)

$$(I+hPA_2P^T)\tilde{w}_{m+1} = Pz_{m+1}^{(2)}$$

$$w_{m+1}^{(2)} = P^T\tilde{w}_{m+1}$$

The matrices $(I+hA_1)$ and $(I+hPA_2P^T)$ of formulas (11)-(12) are direct sums of q tridiagonal pxp matrices; thus each system of (11)-(12) is solved "in parallel" with the usual Gaussian elimination algorithm. The simultaneous solution of q tridiagonal linear systems of size p requires the creation of an appropriate data structure for the coefficients in order to have a "data flow" type algorithm [5].

The extrapolated form of the arithmetic mean method (5)-(6.a) (formula 7)) determines the approximation w_{m+2} to $v(t)$ at the time-level m+2 by solving simultaneously four sets of systems; two sets consist of four block-diagonal systems and two sets consist of two block-diagonal systems. The coefficient-matrix of each block-diagonal system again is the direct sum of q tridiagonal pxp matrices.

Since the linear systems of formulas (9) or (11)-(12) can be solved simultaneously on two different vector processors and the four sets of linear systems of the extrapolated form of (5)-(6.a) can be solved simultaneously on three different vector processors, the arithmetic mean method is ideally suited for implementation on a multiprocessor system that can execute concurrently different tasks on two÷four vector processors (CPUs) with shared central memory, such as the CRAY X-MP. A high-level parallelism among independent tasks is offered by the Cray multitasking.

A Fortran program for a parallel implementation on CRAY X-MP/48 with CMIC\$ microtasking directives of the arithmetic mean method, when A is a block-tridiagonal matrix, has been developed.

Some computational experiments have been carried out with this program on test-problems arising from the application of the method of lines (using centered-in space-difference equations) to the equation (10).

In these experiments particular attention has been reserved for the comparison between the Richardson extrapolation of (5)-(6.a) (formula 7) and the alternating-direction implicit (ADI) method of Peaceman-Rachford defined by

$$(I+\tfrac{h}{2}A_1)w_{m+\tfrac{1}{2}} = (I-\tfrac{h}{2}A_2)w_m + \tfrac{h}{2}((1-\theta)b_m + \theta b_{m+\tfrac{1}{2}})$$

$$(I+\tfrac{h}{2}A_2)w_{m+1} = (I-\tfrac{h}{2}A_1)w_{m+\tfrac{1}{2}} + \tfrac{h}{2}((1-\theta)b_{m+1} + \theta b_{m+\tfrac{1}{2}})$$

with $\theta=0$ or $\tfrac{1}{2}$ or 1. It is worthwhile to remember that the accuracy of the ADI method may depend significantly on the splitting of the source term (see Tables 3 and 4).

Results of these experiments are given in Tables 1-8. In these tables, *error* indicates the maximum-norm of the error at time t=t* and *mean error* indicates the arithmetic average of the absolute values of error at time t=t*. *Time 1, time 2, time 3* indicate the computer-time, expressed in seconds, for solving the problem utilizing one or two or three processors, respectively. The computer-time is subdivided into the computer-time T_f required for the construction of the coefficient matrices as well as for their factorization, the computer-time T_s required for the solution of the linear systems and the computer-time T_t required for the solution of the linear systems and the evaluation of the source term b at different time-levels. (The notation .36(-4), for instance, means 0.36 10^{-4}). The speed-up factor is given in parentheses ().

Test-problem TP1. In (10) $\alpha=\beta=\gamma=0$ and $\sigma=2x(2-x) + 2y(2-y)$; $\phi_0(x,y) = \sin\tfrac{\pi}{2}$ + $x(2-x)y(2-y)$ in Ω and $\phi(x,y,t)=0$ on the boundary of Ω. The domain Ω is the rettangle [0,2]x[0,2] and the net superimposed upon Ω is uniform. This test-problem [2] has a discontinuity between initial and boundary conditions.

Test-problem TP2 [6]. In (10) α,β are constants and $\gamma=\sigma=0$. The domain Ω is the rectangle [0,1]x[0,1]. In Ω, $\phi_0(x,y)=0$. On the boundary of Ω

$$\frac{\partial\phi(1,y,t)}{\partial x} = \frac{\partial\phi(x,1,t)}{\partial y} = 0 \qquad \phi(0,y,t) = u(y,t,\beta), \ \phi(x,0,t) = u(x,t,\alpha).$$

The function $u(x,t,\lambda)$ has the expression of formula (3) in [6]. In this test-problem $\phi(x,y,t) = u(x,t,\alpha) \cdot u(y,t,\beta)$.
The net superimposed upon Ω is uniform.

Test-problem TP3. In (10) α,β are constants, $\gamma=1+2(\alpha^2+\beta^2)$ and $\sigma=0$. The initial and boundary values of $\phi(x,y,t)$ are consistent with $\phi(x,y,t) = e^{-\alpha x} e^{-\beta y} e^{-t}$. The domain Ω is the rectangle $[0,2] \times [0,2]$ and the net superimposed upon Ω is uniform.

The test-problem TP1 illustrates a situation for which the Richardson extrapolation of (5)-(6.a) produces a significantly better numerical solution than the ADI method for the same h. Thus, for the diffusion-convection problem with time-independent boundary values and time-independent source terms, the Richardson extrapolation of the arithmetic mean method appears attractive; it is accurate, economical and L-stable (The ADI method is only A-stable).

The test-problems TP2, TP3 serve to illustrate the effect of the Richardson extrapolation method in the presence of time-dependent boundary values and time-dependent source terms. For all splitting methods these dependencies are known to reduce the accuracy of the time integration. Also, the ADI method suffers from these dependencies, although to a somewhat lesser extent.

In the family of explicit splitting methods (which are second order accurate in time), the method (9) has an inherent parallelism for which the computation can be partitioned into two independent subtasks of the same complexity to be handled by separate vector processors. Tables 3, 4 and 8 show that the arithmetic mean method (9) holds a speed advantage over the ADI method without any appreciable loss of accuracy for those diffusion-convection problems with time-dependent boundary values and time-dependent source terms for which it is required to use a small time-step h in the integration process; for example, this happens for reactor kinetic problems.

Furthermore, looking at the speed-up row of the tables, it can be observed that the performance of the Fortran program is high.

pxq=n	h	Richardson extrapolation		ADI method θ=½	
		error	mean error	error	mean error
64x64	.1(-1)	.24(-2)	.10(-2)	.48(-1)	.19(-2)
	.1(-2)	.16(-3)	.65(-4)	.14(-3)	.41(-4)
	.1(-3)	.14(-3)	.42(-4)	.14(-3)	.42(-4)
128x128	.1(-1)	.23(-2)	.99(-3)	.22	.37(-2)
	.1(-2)	.39(-3)	.40(-4)	.38(-3)	.13(-4)
	.1(-3)	.38(-3)	.15(-4)	.38(-3)	.14(-4)
256x128	.1(-1)	.23(-2)	.98(-3)	.43	.51(-2)
	.1(-2)	.16(-3)	.29(-4)	.66(-4)	.21(-5)
	.1(-3)	.14(-4)	.28(-5)	.68(-5)	.22(-5)
256x256	.1(-1)	.23(-2)	.93(-3)	.43	.51(-2)
	.1(-2)	.16(-3)	.29(-4)	.66(-4)	.28(-5)
	.1(-3)	.14(-4)	.32(-5)	.92(-5)	.26(-5)

Tab. 1. Errors in solving test-problem TP1 at t*=0.1

h	α=β	Formulas (5)-(6.a)		Richardson extrapolation		ADI method	
		error	mean error	error	mean error	error	mean error
.1(-2)	10			.22	.13(-1)	.17(-1)	.19(-2)
	1			.18	.45(-2)	.32(-2)	.54(-3)
	.1			.18	.38(-2)	.23(-2)	.37(-3)
.1(-3)	10	.34	.83(-2)	.41(-1)	.34(-2)	.17(-1)	.19(-2)
	1	.31	.33(-2)	.34(-1)	.11(-2)	.32(-2)	.54(-3)
	.1	.31	.28(-2)	.33(-1)	.88(-3)	.23(-2)	.35(-3)

Tab. 2. Errors in solving test-problem TP2 at t*=0.1; n=pxp=64x64

pxq=n	h	α=β	Richardson extrapolation		ADI method θ=½	
			error	mean error	error	mean error
64x64	.1(-2)	10	.57(-1)	.93(-4)	.13(-2)	.14(-4)
		1	.69(-1)	.16(-2)	.10(-3)	.49(-5)
		.1	.81(-1)	.53(-2)	.12(-3)	.34(-5)
	.1(-3)	10	.33(-2)	.17(-4)	.13(-2)	.14(-4)
		1	.50(-2)	.12(-3)	.10(-4)	.39(-5)
		.1	.55(-2)	.40(-3)	.12(-5)	.36(-7)
128x128	.1(-2)	10	.22	.16(-3)	.36(-3)	.35(-5)
		1	.16	.23(-2)	.43(-3)	.29(-5)
		.1	.18	.79(-2)	.46(-3)	.64(-5)
	.1(-3)	10	.19(-1)	.29(-4)	.34(-3)	.36(-5)
		1	.32(-1)	.34(-3)	.42(-5)	.98(-6)
		.1	.34(-1)	.11(-2)	.46(-5)	.65(-7)
256x128	.1(-1)	10	.63	.76(-3)	.13	.43(-4)
		1	.63	.92(-2)	.18	.27(-3)
		.1	.61	.32(-1)	.18	.80(-3)
	.1(-2)	10	.31	.18(-3)	.13(-2)	.26(-5)
		1	.25	.26(-2)	.18(-2)	.44(-5)
		.1	.29	.89(-2)	.18(-2)	.12(-4)
256x256	.1(-1)	10	.71	.80(-3)	.13	.42(-4)
		1	.71	.95(-2)	.18	.27(-3)
		.1	.70	.33(-1)	.18	.80(-3)
	.1(-2)	10	.45	.21(-3)	.13(-2)	.13(-5)
		1	.39	.29(-2)	.18(-2)	.40(-5)
		.1	.39	.99(-2)	.18(-2)	.12(-4)

Tab. 3. Errors in solving test-problem TP3 at t*=0.1

pxq=n	h	α=β	Explicit method (9) error	mean error	ADI method θ=0 error	mean error
64x64	.1(-2)	10			.12(-2)	.13(-4)
		1			.39(-3)	.57(-4)
		.1			.43(-3)	.21(-3)
	.1(-3)	10	.13(-2)	.14(-4)	.13(-2)	.14(-4)
		1	.42(-4)	.38(-5)	.41(-4)	.43(-5)
		.1	.45(-4)	.19(-4)	.44(-4)	.21(-4)
99x99	.1(-2)	10			.46(-3)	.51(-5)
		1			.40(-3)	.60(-4)
		.1			.44(-3)	.22(-3)
	.1(-3)	10	.55(-3)	.58(-5)	.55(-3)	.58(-5)
		1	.44(-4)	.40(-5)	.42(-4)	.48(-5)
		.1	.46(-4)	.17(-4)	.44(-4)	.22(-4)
128x128	.1(-2)	10			.25(-3)	.27(-5)
		1			.40(-3)	.60(-4)
		.1			.44(-3)	.22(-3)
	.1(-3)	10	.33(-3)	.35(-5)	.33(-3)	.35(-5)
		1	.45(-4)	.43(-5)	.42(-4)	.53(-5)
		.1	.46(-4)	.14(-4)	.45(-4)	.22(-4)

Tab. 4. Errors in solving test-problem TP3 at t*=0.1

pxq=n	h	Richardson extrapolation Time 1 T_f	T_t	Time 3 T_f	T_t	ADI method θ=½ Time 1 T_f	T_t
64x64	.1(-1)	.18(-2)	.48(-1)	.82(-3) (2.20)	.17(-1) (2.82)	.31(-2)	.19(-1)
128x128	.1(-1)	.67(-2)	.15	.29(-2) (2.31)	.56(-1) (2.68)	.11(-1)	.64(-1)
256x128	.1(-1)	.13(-1)	.29	.56(-2) (2.32)	.10 (2.90)	.21(-1)	.12
256x256	.1(-1)	.26(-1)	.55	.11(-1) (2.36)	.20 (2.75)	.41(-1)	.23

Tab. 5. Computer-time for solving test-problem TP1 at t*=0.1

h	Richardson extrapolation Time 1 T_f	T_s	T_t	Time 3 T_f	T_s	T_t	ADI method Time 1 T_f	T_s	T_t
.1(-2)	.18(-2)	.48	.99	.11(-2) (1.64)	.17 (2.82)	.37 (2.68)	.31(-2)	.20	.13(+1)

Tab. 6. Computer-time for solving test-problem TP2 at t*=0.1; n=pxq=64x64

pxq=n	Richardson extrapolation					ADI method θ=½	
	Time 1		Time 3			Time 1	
	T_f	Tt	T_f	Ts	T_t	T_f	Tt
64x64	.18(-2)	.48(-1)	.82(-3) (2.20)	.17(-1) (2.76)	.18(-1) (2.67)	.31(-2)	.21(-1)
99x99	.42(-2)	.89(-1)	.19(-2) (2.21)	.33(-1) (2.67)	.33(-1) (2.70)	.64(-2)	.41(-1)
128x128	.67(-2)	.16	.29(-2) (2.31)	.56(-1) (2.68)	.57(-1) (2.80)	.11(-1)	.70(-1)
256x128	.13(-1)	.29	.56(-2) (2.32)	.11 (2.64)	.11 (2.64)	.21(-1)	.13
256x256	.26(-1)	.55	.11(-1) (2.36)	.20 (2.75)	.20 (2.75)	.41(-1)	.26

Tab. 7. Computer time for solving the test-problem TP3 at t*=0.1; h=.1(-1)

pxq=n	Explicit method (9)					ADI method θ=½	
	Time 1		Time 2			Time 1	
	T_f	Tt	T_f	Ts	T_t	T_f	Tt
64x64	.60(-3)	.21(+1)	.32(-3) (1.88)	.12(+1) (1.75)	.13(+1) (1.62)	.31(-2)	.21(+1)
99x99	.14(-2)	.47(+1)	.74(-3) (1.89)	.26(+1) (1.77)	.27(+1) (1.74)	.64(-2)	.40(+1)
128x128	.24(-2)	.74(+1)	.12(-2) (2)	.42(+1) (1.71)	.43(+1) (1.72)	.11(-1)	.68(+1)

Tab. 8. Computer time for solving the test-problem TP3 at t*=0.1; h=.1(-3)

REFERENCES

[1] I. Galligani, V. Ruggiero: Solving large systems of linear ordinary differential equations on a vector computer. *Parallel Computing* (1988).

[2] J.L. Lawson, J.L. Morris: The extrapolation of first order method for parabolic partial differential equations. *SIAM J. Numer. Anal.* 15,6 (1978), pp. 1212-1244.

[3] V. Ruggiero, F. Durì: Analisi di algoritmi per la risoluzione di sistemi tridiagonali su un calcolatore vettoriale. *Atti Accad. Scienze dell'Istituto di Bologna* XIV, 5 (1988).

[4] K.K. Saul'yev: *Integration of equations of parabolic type by the method of nets.* Pergamon Press, Oxford (1964).

[5] W. Schönauer: *Scientific Computing on Vector Computers.* North-Holland, Amsterdam (1987).

[6] J.L. Siemieniuch, I. Gladwell: Analysis of explicit difference methods for a diffusion-convection equation. *Inter. J. Numer. Meth. Engng.* 12 (1978), pp. 899-916.

This work was supported by the National Research Council of Italy under contract CNR n. 87.00996.01.

Parallelism in a highly accurate algorithm for turbulence simulation

Claudio Canuto,[1,2] Claudio Giberti[2]
[1] Dipartimento di Matematica, Università di Parma, 43100 Parma, Italy
[2] Istituto di Analisi Numerica del C.N.R., Corso C.Alberto, 5 27100 Pavia, Italy

ABSTRACT: A parallel version of a spectral algorithm for the direct simulation of homogeneus, fully developed turbulence has been developed for the four-processor CRAY X-MP/48. We report a detailed performance analysis which enlights the various factors affecting parallel performance.

1. INTRODUCTION

The numerical simulation of fluid motions, particularly at non-laminar regimes, is among the most significant sources of massive computation. The demand for higher and higher resolution power - in order to represent in a faithful way a larger and larger number of complex phenomena - has been satisfied by a two-fold strategy: i) by designing special-purpose methods (e.g., the Vortex Method), or highly-accurate general-purpose methods (e.g., Spectral Methods), which allow the description of the motion by a minimal number of degrees of freedom; ii) by improving the computers' power through vectorization techniques and later concurrent data processing. Nowadays, sophisticated numerical algorithms are going to be implemented on the advanced parallel computers which become available day after day.

The issue of exploiting parallelism in Spectral Methods has been discussed, e.g., by Canuto (1988), where account has also been given of the first existing experiences, mainly on small research machines. The middle- to long-term future in parallel architectures is the development of machines with a very large number of relatively small processors, with local memory and loose connection network (e.g., the Hypercube). The global character of spectral methods may appear to be a severe drawback for their implementation on these architectures, due to heavy communication requirements. However, Canuto (1988) points out that such a problem can be significantly reduced if a specific connection network is available. Indipendently, Pelz (1988) has recently obtained encouraging results on the implementation of a spectral algorithm on a hypercube computer.

On the other hand, in the nearest future, most of the advanced fluid dynamics calculations will take place on the commercially available supercomputers, which have a number of processors in the order of ten, and a large shared memory. Here, the main difficulty is memory contention. This has motivated the present work, which is concerned with the parallel implementation of a spectral algorithm on the four-processor CRAY X-MP/48. We have chosen for our test the Fourier pseudo-spectral algorithm proposed by Orszag (1971) for the direct simulation of fully developed homogeneous turbulence. Indeeed, this algorithm - which is mainly responsible for the early success of spectral methods in turbulence simulation - is conceptually fairly simple, yet it contains the main features of spectral methods as far as parallelism is concerned (incidentally, the same algorithm has been used by Pelz (1988)). Furthermore, the algorithm can find a slightly different application in the systematic investigation of routes to chaos for the truncated Navier-Stokes equations, as the number of retained modes becomes larger and larger(see Franceschini *et al* (1988) and the references therein). The Fourier pseudospectral technique is currently being used in lieu of the conventional Galerkin approach as the number of modes significantly increases.

A repeated application of domain decomposition allows us to exploit the fine-grain parallelism of the Microtasking System of the CRAY X-MP/48 (we refer to Bieterman (1987) for a detailed investigation of the performance of the Cray Microtasking System on general-purpose mathematical software). The main elementary steps which constitute the algorithm are individually analyzed, with the aim of understanding the relative size of the various factors which affect microtasking performance (microtasking overheads, memory bank conflicts, reduced vector lengths, and so on). The efficiency analysis is carried out by defining several different MFLOPS rates, and by computing their values either directly from experiments or through a theoretical law which predicts the wall-clock time growth. Once the "local" speed-ups have been evaluated, the global speed-up is predicted by a generalized Amdhal law, and the value so obtained is compared to the value resulting from experiments.

2. THE SPECTRAL ALGORITHM

Let us briefly recall the main steps of the spectral algorithm we have chosen for our performance analysis. For the sake of simplicity, we use a two-dimensional, non-dealiased version of Orszag's (1971) method, which nonetheless retains all the significant features of the original algorithm.

The Navier-Stokes equations of an incompressible fluid submitted to periodic boundary conditions in the plane are

$$(2.1) \quad \begin{cases} \dfrac{\partial \mathbf{u}}{\partial t} + \mathbf{u} \cdot \nabla \mathbf{u} = -\nabla p + \nu \Delta \mathbf{u} + \mathbf{f}, \\[2mm] \nabla \cdot \mathbf{u} = 0, \\[2mm] \mathbf{u}(\mathbf{x} + 2\pi \hat{\mathbf{e}}, t) = \mathbf{u}(\mathbf{x}, t), \\[2mm] \mathbf{u}(\mathbf{x}, 0) = \mathbf{u}_0(\mathbf{x}), \end{cases}$$

where $\mathbf{u}$ is the fluid velocity, p is the pressure, $\mathbf{f}$ is a density force and ν is the kinematic viscosity. Furthermore, $\mathbf{x} = (x, y) \in R^2$, $\hat{\mathbf{e}}$ denotes the unit versor in the x or y direction, and $t \in R_+$. A Fourier expansion in space yields

$$(2.2) \quad \mathbf{u}(\mathbf{x}, t) = \sum_{\mathbf{k}} \hat{\mathbf{u}}_{\mathbf{k}}(t) e^{i\mathbf{k} \cdot \mathbf{x}}, \quad p(\mathbf{x}, t) = \sum_{\mathbf{k}} \hat{p}_{\mathbf{k}}(t) e^{i\mathbf{k} \cdot \mathbf{x}}, \quad \mathbf{f}(\mathbf{x}, t) = \sum_{\mathbf{k}} \hat{\mathbf{f}}_{\mathbf{k}}(t) e^{i\mathbf{k} \cdot \mathbf{x}},$$

with $\mathbf{k} \in Z^2$. Then, (2.1) in Fourier transform space reads as follows

$$(2.3) \quad \begin{cases} (\dfrac{d}{dt} + \nu |\mathbf{k}|^2)\hat{\mathbf{u}}_{\mathbf{k}} = -i\mathbf{k}\hat{p}_{\mathbf{k}} - (\mathbf{u} \cdot \nabla \mathbf{u})\hat{}_{\mathbf{k}} + \hat{\mathbf{f}}_{\mathbf{k}}, \\[2mm] i\mathbf{k} \cdot \hat{\mathbf{u}}_{\mathbf{k}} = 0, \\[2mm] \hat{\mathbf{u}}_{\mathbf{k}}(0) = \hat{\mathbf{u}}_{0,\mathbf{k}}. \end{cases}$$

The incompressibility constrain allows us to eliminate the pressure, by taking the divergence of the momentum equation. Thus, one gets the equivalent but simplified system

$$(2.4) \quad \begin{cases} (\dfrac{d}{dt} + \nu |\mathbf{k}|^2)\hat{\mathbf{u}}_{\mathbf{k}} = -(\mathbf{u} \cdot \nabla \mathbf{u})\hat{}_{\mathbf{k}} + \mathbf{k}\dfrac{(\mathbf{k} \cdot (\mathbf{u} \cdot \nabla \mathbf{u})\hat{}_{\mathbf{k}})}{|\mathbf{k}|^2} + \hat{\mathbf{f}}_{\mathbf{k}} - \mathbf{k}\dfrac{(\mathbf{k} \cdot \hat{\mathbf{f}}_{\mathbf{k}})}{|\mathbf{k}|^2}, \\[2mm] \hat{\mathbf{u}}_{\mathbf{k}}(0) = \hat{\mathbf{u}}_{0,\mathbf{k}}, \end{cases}$$

again with $\mathbf{k} \in Z^2$ (we assume $i\mathbf{k} \cdot \hat{\mathbf{u}}_{0,\mathbf{k}} = 0$). We now introduce a finite dimensional Fourier- Galerkin approximation, by requiring that the wave-vector $\mathbf{k}$ in (2.4) belong to the set

$$(2.5) \qquad S_N = \{\mathbf{k} = (k_1, k_2)| - N/2 \le k_1, \ k_2 \le N/2 - 1\},$$

where $N/2$ is a suitable truncation parameter. In this manner, (2.4) is transformed into an initial value problem for a system of $2N^2$ complex differential equations. However, the reality of the solution requires

$$(2.6.1) \qquad \hat{\mathbf{u}}_{\mathbf{k}} = \bar{\hat{\mathbf{u}}}_{-\mathbf{k}}$$

for all $\mathbf{k} = (k_1, k_2)$ such that $|k_i| < N/2, (i = 1, 2)$, whereas we set

$$(2.6.2) \qquad \hat{\mathbf{u}}_{(-\frac{N}{2}, k_2)} = \hat{\mathbf{u}}_{(k_1, -\frac{N}{2})} = 0$$

for those modes which do not appear symmetrically in our truncation. In such a way, the size of the sistem to be integrated is halved.

The resulting differential system is advanced in time by a mixed analytical/finite-difference method. First, the right-hand side of (2.4) is evaluated explicitly by the third order Adams-Bashforth scheme, which guarantees conditional stability for differential operators with spectrum on the imaginary axis. The use of an explicit scheme is justified by the fact that the stability limit on the time step Δt is well above the accuracy limit needed to preserve the overall spectral accuracy of the solution. Once the right-hand side of (2.4) has been evaluated, the resulting linear constant-coefficient system is advanced analytically from t to $t + \Delta t$.

During each Adams-Bashforth phase, the convective term $\mathbf{u} \cdot \nabla \mathbf{u}$ is computed from $\mathbf{u}$ by a pseudo-spectral technique. Each component of $\mathbf{u} \cdot \nabla \mathbf{u}$ is a sum of terms of the form $u_i \frac{\partial u_l}{\partial x_m}, (1 \le i, l, m \le 2)$, where u_i, u_l are truncated Furier series. First, the partial derivative is computed in coefficient space. Next, one has to evaluate the product. If the convolution sum formula which expresses the coefficients of $u_i \frac{\partial u_l}{\partial x_m}$ in terms of those of u_i and $\frac{\partial u_l}{\partial x_m}$ is applied in a straightforward manner, the computation requires $O(N^4)$ operations: this becomes exceedingly expensive for large N. On the contrary, the pseudo-spectral technique relies upon the equivalent representation of a truncated Fourier series in physical space through its values at the equally spaced points $\{\mathbf{x}_{\mathbf{j}} = (\frac{2\pi j_1}{N}, \frac{2\pi j_2}{N})| \ 0 \le j_1, j_2 < N\}$. Thus, the gridvalues of u_i and $\frac{\partial u_l}{\partial x_m}$ are computed from their coefficients, pointwise multiplications in physical space is executed, and finally the result is transformed back in coefficient space. If transforms are carried out by FFT's, the total amount of work is only $O(N^2 log N)$ operations. The final result is not the exact expansion of $u_i \frac{\partial u_l}{\partial x_m}$, but rather the expansion of the unique truncated Fourier series which interpolates the product at the gridpoints $\mathbf{x}_{\mathbf{j}}$. The exact values can be recovered by suitable techniques known as dealiasing; they essentially amount to working with an extra shifted grid or with a larger grid. Since the kind of algebra involved in dealiasing is the same as for the aliased calculation, we have not included dealiasing in the present implementation. (For a complete review of spectral method, we refer to Gottlieb and Orszag (1977) and to Canuto et al (1988)).

3. PARALLELISM

There are basically two forms of possible parallelism in a numerical algorithm for solving a boundary value problem. Following the terminology of Canuto (1988), there is a *mathematical parallelism*, which consists of assigning the calculation of different terms in the equations to different processors; and a *numerical parallelism*, in which different portions of the computational domain (in physical or transform space) are assigned to different processors, with the same mathematical task. These two strategies have a counterpart in the CRAY X-MP/48 Multitasking System (Cray 1986). Indeed, the mathematical parallelism corresponds to a "coarse-grain" parallelism, which is more naturally implemented in the *macrotasking mode*: different subprograms (or copies of the same subprogram) are sent to the processors for concurrent execution. Conversely, the numerical parallelism is a "fine-grain" parallelism which is more naturally implemented in *microtasking mode*: tipically the iterations of DO-loops are cyclically distributed among the available processors. The mathematical parallelism has many drawbacks: it requires a perfect balancing of the tasks, whose number has to be a multiple of the processors; moreover, control overheads may become relevant if the computational load is moderate. On the contrary, numerical parallelism occurs in a natural way in spectral methods. Indeed, the tensor product structure of multidimensional spectral methods implies that the elementary transformations (discrete Fourier transforms, differentiation in coefficient space, and so on) which constitute a spectral algorithm can be obtained as a cascade of one dimensional transformations of the same type. Each one can be carried out in parallel over parallel rows or columns of the computational domain (in physical or transform space). It follows that microtasking can be implemented by assigning different "slices" of the computational domain to different processors.

Let us now detail this microtasking strategy for the Orszag algorithm under consideration. At each time step, the largest effort goes into the computation of the convective term $\mathbf{u} \cdot \nabla \mathbf{u}$. If $\mathbf{u} = (v, w)$, the Fourier coefficients of ∇v are given by

$$\left(\frac{\partial v}{\partial x}\right)^{\hat{}}_{\mathbf{k}} = i k_1 \hat{v}_{\mathbf{k}}, \quad \left(\frac{\partial v}{\partial y}\right)^{\hat{}}_{\mathbf{k}} = i k_2 \hat{v}_{\mathbf{k}}, \quad \mathbf{k} = (k_1, k_2),$$

and similarly for ∇w. Thus, they are computed by pointwise products in transform space. Each mode can be assigned to a processor for concurrent differentiation. Note that microtasking this phase leads to parallelism at the expense of vectorization. It is also possible to use a macrotasking strategy in this phase, i.e., different processors compute different partial derivatives. Once the Fourier coefficients of v, w, ∇v, ∇w are avaible, they are transformed into gridpoint values by Fast Fourier Transforms. FFT's on two dimensional array of data are computed by accomplishing a sequence of one-dimensional transforms in one direction, followed by a sequence of transforms in the transpose direction. Thus, each column (in the first sweep) or row (in the second sweep) of the computational domain can be assigned to a processor for concurrent Fourier transforms. A substantial saving in the transform process comes from the reality condition (2.6). Indeed, real transforms can be computed pairwise by a standard complex FFT, thus halving the computational cost.

Next, one gets the gridvalues of $\mathbf{u} \cdot \nabla \mathbf{u}$ by pointwise multiplications and sums in physical space; each gridpoint can be processed independently from all the other ones. After an inverse FFT has returned the coefficients of $\mathbf{u} \cdot \nabla \mathbf{u}$, one is ready for the time advancing phase: the current value of the right-hand side of (2.4) is computed, then added to those at the previous time levels according to the Adams-Bashforth rule, and the new value of $\mathbf{u}$ is computed by an analytic expression. Finally the arrays of right-hand sides are updated for the next time iteration. These phases involve only operations on individual Fourier modes; hence, they are completely amenable to microtasked concurrent processing.

4. PERFORMANCE ANALYSIS

This section is devoted to a detailed investigation of the behavior of the spectral algorithm here considered, from the point of view of its parallel implementation on the CRAY X-MP/48. We first analyze the performances related to microtasking each logically relevant block of the algorithm (differentiation in transform space, Fast Fourier Transforms, time advancing process). In the last subsection we assemble the results for the complete microtasked algorithm. Short comments on the performances related to macrotasking are also given.

All the performance results reported hereafter have been obtained using the machine at CINECA (Italy) in dedicated mode.

4.1 Differentation in Transform Space

We are concerned, here, with the problem of computing the Fourier coefficients of ∇v and ∇w, given the coefficients of v and w. For a fixed truncation parameter $N/2$, the Fourier coefficients of each of the above functions form a two dimensional complex array of order N. Taking into account reality - as discussed in (2.6) -, they are effectively stored columnwise as real vectors of length $N2=N*N$, the real parts being in the first half of each vector of length $NH=N2/2$. Denoting by V, W, the vectors corresponding to v, w, the Fourier coefficients of ∇v and ∇w are computed and stored in DXV, DYV, DXW, DYW by the cycle:

```
            CDIR$ IVDEP
                  DO 10 I=1,NH
                  DXV(I)=-V(I+NH)*OMX(I)
                  DYV(I)=-V(I+NH)*OMY(I)
                  DXW(I)=-W(I+NH)*OMX(I)
                  DYW(I)=-W(I+NH)*OMY(I)
(4.1)             DXV(I+NH)=V(I)*OMX(I)          Work(I)
                  DYV(I+NH)=V(I)*OMY(I)
                  DXW(I+NH)=W(I)*OMX(I)
                  DYW(I+NH)=W(I)*OMY(I)
                  10 CONTINUE
```

Here, OMX, OMY contain respectively the wavenumbers in x and y directions (repeated along the columns to enhance vectorization). Such a cycle is microtasked over NPROC processors (assuming NH to be a multiple of NPROC) as follows ($LC=NH/NPROC$) :

```
            CMIC$ DO GLOBAL
                  DO 1 IP=1,NPROC
                  IND=(IP-1)*LC+1
            CDIR$ IVDEP
(4.2)             DO 10 I=IND,IND+LC-1
                  .
                  Work(I)
                  .
                  10 CONTINUE
                  1 CONTINUE
```

In going from (4.1) to (4.2) we gain parallelism at the expense of vectorization, since the vector length are divided by NPROC. In order to investigate the opposite effects of these features we have first measured the performance in MFLOPS executing 10^4 times the DO-loop (4.1) in uniprocessor mode, as N increases. The results are reported in Table 4.1. Note the high MFLOPS rates due to the particular structure of (4.1).Also, note that NH is a multiple of the vector register length (64). Next, we have measured the performance of the microtasked DO-loop (4.2) in the case $LC=512$ (which corresponds

N	16	32	64	128	256
(NH)	128	512	2048	8192	32768
MFLOPS	123.8	138.1	142.2	143.2	143.6

Table 4.1

to N=64 if NPROC=4). The corresponding MFLOPS - again obtined after 10^4 loops in order to have enough load on each processor - are reported in Table 4.2.

NPROC	1	2	3	4
proc 1	132.7	118.4	108.0	90.4
proc 2	-	118.2	108.1	90.4
proc 3	-	-	108.1	90.4
proc 4	-	-	-	90.4

Table 4.2

We first observe that for a fixed NPROC, all the processors exhibit nearly the same performance, as a conseguence of the perfect load balancing. Furthermore, the performance of each processor working in multitasking mode is always worse than the one of a processor in single-tasking mode (compare with the case NH=512 in Table 4.1), and it decreases as the number of active processors increases. Since all the processors act on vectors of constant length 512 , this degradation has to be ascribed to the following causes: i) overhead due to the microtasking control structures (which are implemented via software on the CRAY X-MP/48), ii) random memory bank conflicts due to interprocessor contention for data in main memory. Following Bieterman (1987), we can attempt to estimate the size of these two factors in the present situation. To this end, we consider the following procedure: obtain the requested processors through the directive GETCPUS, and iterate 10^4 times the call to the microtasked subroutine which contains the structure (4.2). Measuring costs in machine cycles, let us define the overheads for microtasking operations as follows: a cycles for obtaining the cpu's; b cycles for call to a microtasked subroutine; c cycles for the initialization of the DO GLOBAL; d cycles for the control of each DO GLOBAL iteration. Moreover, denote respectively by e and f the overheads for the initialization and the control of each iteration of a non microtasked DO-loop. Finally let z be the total number of cycles needed by each processor to execute the derivative DO-loop (labelled 10) in (4.2). Then, the total wall-clock time w of the procedure under consideration will obey a law of the following kind

$$(4.3) \qquad \frac{w}{\tau} = a + e + 10^4[b + (c + z + NPROC \cdot d) + f]$$

where τ is the cycle time. Average values of the overheads a through f on the CRAY X-MP/48 are (see also Bieterman (1987)): $a \simeq 10^6$; $b \simeq 400$; $c \simeq 370$; $d \simeq 43$; $e \simeq 400$; $f \simeq 13$. Moreover, $\tau = 8.5 \cdot 10^{-9}$ seconds. For NPROC = 4, we have measured $w = 716 \cdot 10^{-3}$s, and an average value for z of $7.18 \cdot 10^3$ cycles. It is easily checked that the two measures match via formula (4.3) within a 2.6% error. Since each derivative DO-loop requires $512 \times 12 = 6144$ floating point operations, the actual MFLOPS rate within each of these loops (neglecting control overheads) equals 100.6. We are now in a position to compare four different performance rates, measured in MFLOPS, related to different implementations of the DO-loop (4.1) in single processor or in parallel form. They are:

$$(4.4) \begin{cases} \mathrm{MF_{sf}} = \text{MFLOPS rate of the single - processor implementation,} \\ \quad \text{acting on full length (e.g., 2048) vectors;} \\ \mathrm{MF_{sc}} = \text{MFLOPS rate of the single - processor implementa-} \\ \quad \text{tion acting on vectors of the same length (e.g., 512 if} \\ \quad \text{NPROC}=4) \text{ as the one of the vectors used in the paral-} \\ \quad \text{lel implementation;} \\ \mathrm{MF_{pa}} = \text{MFLOPS rate of the pure algorithmic part of the mul-} \\ \quad \text{tiprocessor implementation;} \\ \mathrm{MF_{pg}} = \text{global MFLOPS rate of the multiprocessor implemen-} \\ \quad \text{tation.} \end{cases}$$

In the present situation, we have $\mathrm{MF_{sf}} = 142.2$, $\mathrm{MF_{sc}} = 138.1$ (both from Table 4.1), $\mathrm{MF_{pa}} = 100.6$ (from the previous discussion) and $\mathrm{MF_{pg}} = 90.4$ (from Table 4.2). The global loss of efficiency related to the microtasking process is defined as

$$(4.5) \qquad \delta e = \frac{\mathrm{MF_{sf}} - \mathrm{MF_{pg}}}{\mathrm{MF_{sf}}}$$

By noting that $\mathrm{MF_{pg}} \leq \mathrm{MF_{pa}} \leq \mathrm{MF_{sc}} \leq \mathrm{MF_{sf}}$, one can split δe in different parts associated with overheads of different nature, as follows:

$$(4.6) \qquad \delta e = \frac{\mathrm{MF_{sf}} - \mathrm{MF_{sc}}}{\mathrm{MF_{sf}}} + \frac{\mathrm{MF_{sc}} - \mathrm{MF_{pa}}}{\mathrm{MF_{sf}}} + \frac{\mathrm{MF_{pa}} - \mathrm{MF_{pg}}}{\mathrm{MF_{sf}}}$$
$$= \delta e_v + \delta e_b + \delta e_m$$

Here δe_v measures the loss of efficiency due to shorter vectorization, whereas δe_v and δe_m are related to the loss of efficiency respectively due to memory bank conflicts and microtasking overheads. In the current case $\delta e = .364$ and $\delta e_v = .028$, $\delta e_b = .264$, $\delta e_m = .072$. We conclude that the most relevant overhead (73% of the total loss of efficiency) has to be ascribed to the absence of local memories, whereas partitioning vectors over processors has only a minor effect on the overhead (less than 8% of the total). As the vector length increases, the last overhead tends to vanish, leaving the memory bank conflict overhead and the microtasking overhead in a ratio of about 4:1.

Finally, we discuss speed-ups S_p (defined as wall-clock time for the single processor implementation divided by wall-clock time for the p-processor implementation). They are reported in Table 4.3, for different values of N.

processors	2	3	4
N=32	1.48	1.63	1.69
N=64	1.78	2.21	2.54
N=128	1.90	2.53	2.75

Table 4.3

Since the task here considered is fully parallelizable (for p=3 we use the trick of incrementing NH by 1), one could replace - in an idealized situation with no syncronization overheads - wall-clock times by reciprocal of MFLOPS rates. Under this theoretical assumption, in the situation previously discussed (p=4, N=64), one gets in this manner a speed-up of $p(1 - \delta e) = 2.54$, as opposed to 2.45.

Finally, we have also implemented the derivative phase in macrotasking mode: each one of the four processors executes one partial derivatives. The resulting speed-ups, reported in Table 4.4, demonstrate that this strategy is of no use in our situation, since the computational load is too small with respect to the macrotasking overhead.

N	16	32	64
S_4	.12	.34	1.05

Table 4.4

4.2 Fast Fourier Transform

A microtasked implementation (in non-orthodox Fortran!) of a FFT on a two dimensional array of data reads as follows

```
                   CALL INIT
           CMIC$ DO GLOBAL
                   DO 1 I=1,N
                   CALL FFT(A(I,·),N)
                 1 CONTINUE
(4.7)              CALL INIT
           CMIC$ DO GLOBAL
                   DO 2 I=1,N
                   CALL TRANSP
                   CALL FFT(Aᵀ(·,I),N)
                   CALL TRANSP
                 2 CONTINUE
```

Here A is the N × N array of data, INIT initializes constants, FFT performs one complex Fast Fourier Transform on one dimensional data and TRANSP performs transposition of data. Note that one has to repeat the call to the initialization routine before each DO GLOBAL. This is needed because the CRAY FFT routine CFFT2 stores the trigonometric constants in a portion of the work array, which cannot be a global variable. Thus, the microtasked implementation of the Fast Fourier Transform uses a more complex algorithm than the one of the single processor implementation (which needs only one initial call to INIT). This will be properly taken into account in the subsequent performance analysis. We have executed 10^3 times a two dimensional Fast Fourier Transform, both in single processor and in multiprocessor mode. Table 4.5 reports the MFLOPS rates and CPU times using a single processor.

N	32	64	128
Mflops	35.7	56.5	74.8
Seconds	1.2	3.6	12.8

Table 4.5

The CPU growth reflects the $N^2 \log N$ growth of operations and the enhancement of MFLOPS rate due to longer vectorization. Table 4.6 contains MFLOPS rates using NPROC processors, for N=64. Again, we try to investigate the relative weight of the different factors leading to loss of efficiency in the parallelization process. The procedure now used is as follows: we get the CPU's and we iterate 10^3 times the call to a microtasked subroutine which contains the structure (4.7).

NPROC	1	2	3	4
proc 1	56.45	51.42	49.69	47.07
proc 2	-	52.99	48.74	47.36
proc 3	-	-	49.59	47.58
proc 4	-	-	-	47.34

Table 4.6

The dependence of the wall-clock time w on the different steps of the procedure is modelled in the case of four processors by the following law

(4.8)
$$\frac{w}{\tau} = a + e + 10^3 \cdot \{ b + [q + c + N \cdot (\lambda/4 + d)] $$
$$+ [q + c + N \cdot (\mu/4 + \lambda/4 + \mu/4 + d)] + f \}$$

Here the new quantities are q, λ and μ: precisely, the new process requires q for initializations, λ cycles for complex FFT and μ cycles for data transposition. In the current situation (N=64) we have measured $q = 3.0 \cdot 10^3$, $\lambda = 3.62 \cdot 10^3$, $\mu = 2.47 \cdot 10^2$; the wall-clock time is $w = 1.19$ s. These experimental results appear to obey the above law: indeed, inserting the measured values in (4.8), we get $1.40 \cdot 10^8$ on the left-hand side and $1.39 \cdot 10^8$ on the right-hand side.

We discuss now MFLOPS efficiency. Recalling the notation introduced in Sect. 4.1, we have $MF_{sf} = 56.5$ (from Table 4.5) and $MF_{pg} = 47.3$ (from Table 4.6). Note that in the present situation, microtasking is not realized at the expense of vector lengths, as in the previous block: thus, $MF_{sc} = MF_{sf}$, and $\delta e_v = 0$. In the present situation, another, more interesting situation occurs, which is related to the initialization problem mentioned at the beginning of this section. The MFLOPS rate MF_{pg} is affected by the extra computational load connected with the repeated initialization process INIT. In other words, MF_{pg} is not a realistic measure of the performance of each processor on a parallel FFT calculation, since it overstimates the truly "useful" MFLOPS. For this reason, we introduce the MFLOPS rate MF_{pu}, defined as the number of operations executed by each processor in the pure FFT calculations, divided by the corresponding wall-clock time. The previous data yield $MF_{pu} = 42.5$. Finally, the MFLOPS rate on the pure algorithmic part turns out to be $MF_{pa} = 47.9$.
The global loss of MFLOPS efficiency, defined as

(4.9)
$$\delta e = \frac{MF_{sf} - MF_{pu}}{MF_{sf}}$$
$$= \frac{MF_{sf} - MF_{pa}}{MF_{sf}} + \frac{MF_{pa} - MF_{pg}}{MF_{sf}} + \frac{MF_{pg} - MF_{pu}}{MF_{sf}}$$
$$= \delta e_b + \delta e_m + \delta e_i$$

is therefore $\delta e = .248$, with $\delta e_b = .152$, $\delta e_m = .011$, $\delta e_i = .085$. Thus, over 34% of the loss of efficiency is ascribed to the initialization calls, and it should be easily avoided by a different organization of the working areas for the FFT routine. The microtasking control structures are responsible for less than 5% of the degradation; hence, memory bank conflicts are the major cause of performance degradation.

We conclude by considering speed-ups S_p defined as ratio of wall-clock times. They are reported in Table 4.7 for different values of N.

processors	2	3	4
N=32	1.69	2.36	2.84
N=64	1.75	2.41	3.03
N=128	1.78	2.44	2.94

Table 4.7

Again, in the case N=64, p=4 previously discussed, the "MFLOPS" speed-up $p(1 - \delta e)$ =3.0 well agrees with the measured "wall-clock time" speed-up.

4.3 Time advancing

In this subsection we briefly consider the microtasked implementation of the time advancing process. In our program, this phase is accomplished by a single DO-loop in which each Fourier mode is individually advanced. First, we observe that the DO-loop is of length N2, since it is not necessary to distinguish between real and imaginary part of the solution (as it was for the derivative); thus, we expect a lower performance degradation due to shorter vectorization. Table 4.8 reports MFLOPS performed in single-processor mode for different values of LL = N2/NPROC in the case $N2 = 64^2$ and NPROC = 1, 2, 4.

LL	1024	2048	4096
MFLOPS	138.0	138.9	139.3

Table 4.8

Recalling the notation of Sec. 4.1, Table 4.8 gives, for NPROC=4, $MF_{sf} = 139.3$ and $MF_{sc} = 138.0$, i.e., $\delta e_v = 0.1$. This confirms the low influence of vectorization in performance degradation. To evaluate the effects of memory bank conflicts and microtasking overhead we measured (Table 4.9) the performance of the microtasked DO-loop (iterated 10^4 times) in the case LL = 1024 (which corresponds to N = 64 if NPROC = 4).

NPROC	1	2	3	4
proc 1	137.2	133.4	132.3	131.1
proc 2	-	133.5	132.3	131.2
proc 3	-	-	132.3	131.2
proc 4	-	-	-	131.1

Table 4.9

Thus, in going from one to four processors, the loss of efficiency δe (see 4.5) is only 5.9%, whereas, in the case of the derivative, it was 36.4%. Since the measured wall-clock time of the pure algorithmic part of the multiprocessor implementation (with 4 processors) is $t_m = 20.95 \cdot 10^3$ cycles per iteration, and for the single-processor on full length vectors is $t_s = 83.12 \cdot 10^3$ cycles, we have a "local speed-up" $S_4 = t_s/t_m \simeq 3.96$. This value, which rapresents the speed-up of microtasked implementation affected only by shorter vectorization and bank conflicts, is nearly equal to $S_4^* = 4 \cdot MF_{sc}/MF_{sf}$, the speed-up that would be achieved if only vectorization influenced the multi-processor performance; we conclude that no performance degradation is due to bank conflicts; in other words, $MF_{sc} \simeq MF_{pa}$, i.e., $\delta e_b \simeq 0$ and $\delta e_m = 4.9\%$. Unlike differentation, the largest part of the loss of efficiency can be ascribed to microtasking overhead. Speed-ups S_p for different values of N are reported in Table 4.10.

processors	2	3	4
N=32	1.83	2.54	3.07
N=64	1.92	2.78	3.47
N=128	1.99	2.95	3.86

Table 4.10

In the case N=64, p=4 previously discussed, Tables 4.8 and 4.9 yield a "MFLOPS" speed-up of 3.76, as opposed to the measured "wall-clock time" speed-up of 3.47.

4.5 The Complete Algorithm

We finally consider the whole spectral algorithm, aiming at understanding the influence of the different blocks as far as parallel performances are concerned.

Let us define f $(0 \leq f \leq 1)$ to be the fraction of work in the algorithm which can be processed in parallel. We measure it by considering the implementation in single-processor mode and evaluating the fraction of total CPU time spent in executing parallelizable computations. The values of f for several truncation parameters are given in Table 4.11.

N	32	64	128
f	.86	.89	.90

Table 4.11

Next, we split the parallel part of the algorithm into a number K of homogeneous computational blocks, for which we can measure and analize the specific speed-ups, by using the methods described in the previous subsections. Precisely, we have K=5 main structures: 1) differentiation in transform space; 2) Fourier transforms; 3) assembling of the convective term $u \cdot \nabla u$; 4) Adams-Bashforth time advancing; 5) other miscellaneous parallel work. We denote by f_k the fraction of total work corresponding to the k-th structure (k=1,...,K); thus, $f = \sum_{k=1}^{K} f_k$. Moreover, let $S_{p,k}$ be the local speed-up in executing the structure k over p processors (defined as ratio of wall-clock times). Table 4.12 contains the values of $f_k, S_{p,4}$ for N=64.

structure	f_k	$S_{2\,k}$	$S_{3\,k}$	$S_{4\,k}$
1. Derivatives	1.1	1.78	2.21	2.45
2. Fourier Transforms	79.5	1.75	2.41	3.03
3. $u \cdot \nabla u$ assembling	1.7	1.90	2.64	3.17
4. A-B time steps	3.8	1.95	2.84	3.55
5. Others	2.0	1.85	1.96	2.18

Table 4.12

Finally, we predict the global speed-up of the algorithm according to the following law

$$(4.10) \qquad S_{p,\text{global}} = ((1-f) + \sum_{k=1}^{K} f_k S_{p,k}^{-1})^{-1}.$$

With the values of f_k and $S_{p,k}$ given by Table 4.12, this formula yield $S_{2,global} = 1.64$, $S_{3,global} = 2.10$, and $S_{4,global} = 2.49$. The measured values are given in Table 4.13, together with the global speed-ups for other values of N. We conclude that (4.10) is an exceedingly good prediction.

processors	2	3	4
N=32	1.58	2.01	2.32
N=64	1.64	2.14	2.49
N=128	1.69	2.18	2.50

Table 4.13

5. CONCLUSIONS

We have investigated the parallel implementation on the CRAY X-MP/48 of a Fourier pseudo-spectral algorithm for the Navier-Stokes equations. An existing sequential code has been modified with a minimal effort to introduce the Cray Multitasking directives. First, the analysis shows that the macrotasking strategy is not efficient, due to load imbalance and severe control overheads. On the contrary, about 90% of the code is amenable to fine-grain microtasking through domain decomposition. The resulting efficiency is in the range of 60% with four processors. Since about 80% of the parallel work is spent in multidimensional Fast Fourier Transforms, this is the part of the algorithm demanding for a substantial intervention in view of performance improvement. Indeed, a slightly more sophisticated allocation of working arrays for the Cray Library FFT allows a 34% reduction in the loss of efficiency, thus, enhancing the final efficiency to about 65%. A more drastic improvement can come from a reduction of memory bank conflicts in the FFT process. The Cray Library FFT routine has to be replaced by an *ad hoc* version, which allows data processed by different processors to be resident on different memory banks. In this case, the gain in efficiency is contrasted by heavier overheads in pre- and post- FFT data transfers.

ACKNOWLEDGEMENTS

We wish to thank Dr. G. Erbacci of CINECA for his helpful advice on the use of the CRAY X-MP Multitasking System. Support for this reserch has been provided by the Istituto di Analisi Numerica del C.N.R., Pavia. Thanks are also due to the Centro di Calcolo dell' Università di Modena for providing other computer facilities.

REFERENCES

Bieterman M 1987 *Report ETA-TR 68, Boeing Computer Services, Seattle*
Canuto C 1988 *Report IAN-CNR no.609, Pavia,* to appear in *Calcolo*
Canuto C, Hussaini M Y, Quarteroni A, Zang T A 1988 *Spectral Methods in Fluid Dynamics* (New York: Springer Verlag)
Cray Research Inc. 1986 *Multitasking User Guide, Cray Computer System Technical Note, Pub. No. SN-0222* (Mendota Heights, Minnesota)
Franceschini V, Giberti C, Nicolini M 1988 *J. Stat. Phys.* **50** pp 879-896
Gottlieb D, Orszag S A 1977 *Numerical Analysis of Spectral Methods: Theory and Applications* (Philadelphia: SIAM)
Orszag S A 1971 *Stud. Appl. Math.* **50** pp 293-327
Pelz R B 1988 *AIAA Paper 88-3643, 1st Natl. Fluid Dyn. Congress., Cincinnati, OH.*

Vector and parallel implementation of a 2-D fluid-dynamics code for inertial confinement fusion on an IBM 3090-VF vector multiprocessor

S Atzeni

Associazione EURATOM-ENEA sulla Fusione, Centro Ricerche Energia Frascati, C.P. 65 - 00044 Frascati, Rome, Italy

ABSTRACT: As a case study in the parallelization of complex codes for physical research, the implementation of a 2-D laser fusion code on an IBM 3090-VF vector multiprocessor by means of IBM parallel FORTRAN is described. The relationship between physical models, algorithms, and optimization techniques is evidenced (with particular reference to finite difference schemes, sparse linear system solvers and ray-tracing methods). A parallel ICCG solver has also been implemented and tested. Performances of the parallel code are reported for typical, physically significant problems.

1. INTRODUCTION

In this paper we discuss the implementation of DUED, a 2-D fluid code for inertial confinement fusion (ICF), on an IBM 3090-VF vector multiprocessor by means of IBM Parallel FORTRAN. This work may be taken as a case study in the parallelization of complex codes for physical research.

Codes for ICF are huge, embodying many different basic processes, dealt with by means of different algorithms, and severely CPU-intensive. Since the introduction of the first vector super-computers in the mid-seventies, considerable and successful effort has been devoted to the optimal implementation of ICF codes on such advanced computer architectures. A further opportunity for reducing the execution time is now offered by parallelism (see, e.g., Hwang (1987) for a review). In this context, vector multi-processors (i.e., computers with a small number, typically 2-8, of powerful vector CPUs and with a large shared memory) are of particular interest because, in a sense, they can be viewed as "extensions" of the now familiar vector computers. They can be programmed by means of tools (usually provided by the computer manufacturers and essentially hardware-dependent) which add statements for explicitly programming parallel work and/or compiler directives to the standard FORTRAN language and compiler.

Recently, IBM has released Parallel FORTRAN (IBM Corp. 1988) a new multitasking tool for writing and executing parallel programs on the IBM 3090 multiprocessors which has some peculiar features designed to help programmers in reducing the effort needed in parallelizing both existing and new codes. Parallel FORTRAN (PF) is a superset of the IBM VS (vector) FORTRAN (Vers. 2) Language and Compiler. Extensions to the VS FORTRAN language allow for managing explicitly parallel tasks (i.e., for creating them and assigning work to them, for controlling sharing of memory, etc.), and for explicitly programming such constructs as "parallel loops" and "parallel cases". Extensions to the FORTRAN Library Services allow the various tasks to be synchronized as desired and permit control of memory access. Furthermore, in analogy with the well-known vectorizing compilers, the PF compiler can automatically parallelize DO loops, a first step towards the full program automatic parallelization dreamed by many users.

In this paper we show that the availability of such features has made it possible to obtain interesting parallel performances of the DUED code (see Sec. 5) with relatively modest programming and algorithmic work. (Notice that to the best of this author's knowledge, this is the first parallel implementation of a relatively large fusion code).

Since the vector and parallel optimization of a fluid-dynamics code depends on the algorithms employed, which, in turn, depend on the scheme used for the discretization of the partial differential equations modeling the physical system, in Sec. 2 we briefly outline the physical model and the numerical schemes adopted by DUED. The actual vector and parallel implementation is then the object of Sects. 3-5. Some conclusions are drawn in Sec. 6. Further technical details on this work can be found in a recent report (Atzeni 1988a), which also includes a parametric study of the performance of automatically generated parallel DO loops as a function of the granularity of the loops.

2.   THE DUED CODE

2.1 Background on Inertial Confinement Fusion

Inertial Confinement Fusion (ICF) consists in obtaining energy from the thermonuclear (fusion) micro-explosion induced by the irradiation of a small quantity of fusionable material (e.g., a mixture of deuterium and tritium), by very powerful laser beam (or ion-beam) pulses(see e.g., Duderstadt and Moses 1982, Johnson 1984, Atzeni 1987). In a perspective reactor, a small hollow spherical target   (with radius R $\simeq$ 2 mm) is irradiated by converging beams with power P~10^{14} W, for a time Δt ~ 10 ns) and, as a reaction to the ablation of the outer layers (where the incoming beam is absorbed), is imploded at very high velocity ($\geq$ 200 km/s). As the shell collapses the fuel is compressed at high density (~ 100 g/cm^3 in a perspective reactor target) and at the same time heated at temperatures around 10^8 K, thus achieving the conditions for thermonuclear burn. A key issue for the success of ICF and a compelling challenge to the relevant numerical simulation is the understanding and control of fluid and plasma instabilities which could degrade the implosion symmetry, thus hindering the attainment of the needed high compression.

ICF experiments are usually simulated by 2-D codes (3-D codes being too expensive). These take into account a large number of basic processes concerning plasma physics, dense matter physics, equation of state (EOS),radiative transfer,nuclear reactions, magnetic field effects, laser-matter interaction, etc, with space-scales and time-scales varying over many orders of magnitude. Fortunately, most experiments can be studied by means of a fluid model, and neglecting the magnetic fields (for a detailed review as see Atzeni 1987). Elementary processes enter the fluid equation through the EOS, the transport coefficients and the energy and momentum source terms (due to radiation, fast charged particle and neutron transport).

2.2 DUED: Physical Model

DUED is a 2-dimensional, Lagrangian fluid code, implementing a single fluid, 3-temperature model of a nonmagnetized thermonuclear plasma (Atzeni, 1986). Its model is relatively simple, but is nevertheless adequate for the simulation of most aspects of the experiments performed in the so-called "moderate-intensity regime", of the greatest practical interest. Although a few more complex codes exist (see e.g. Ch. 7 of Atzeni (1987)), DUED can reasonably be taken as a reference code for the problems to be dealt with in the numerics and in the program optimization of any ICF fluid code .

Since the relevant fluid equations are most easily written in the Lagrangian frame, i.e., a frame comoving with the fluid (locally moving at the local fluid velocity), it is worth anticipating that the partial differential equations will be solved by finite-difference methods on a matrix-ordered, quadrilateral zone grid (see, e.g., Fig. 1). This is defined by a system of dimensionless Lagrangian coordinates (i,j) such that grid points correspond to integer values of i and j, with $i =1,2,...I_{max}$ and $j=1,2....J_{max}$. In such a Lagrangian system the partial time derivative (i.e., $\partial/\partial t|_{i,j}$), therefore corresponds to the material derivative in an Eulerian system (defined by an R-Z coordinate system); the local Lagrangian-Eulerian transformation is then characterized by the Jacobian $J=\partial(R,Z)/\partial(i,j)$. The fluid equations solved by DUED can then be written, in a cylindrical coordinate system, as

(1)
$$\rho \frac{\partial u}{\partial t} = -\nabla p - \nabla \cdot \Pi^a + \rho g$$

(2)
$$\frac{\partial R}{\partial t} = u$$

(3)
$$\frac{\partial}{\partial t}(\rho J R) = 0$$

(4)
$$C_{vi} \frac{\partial T_i}{\partial t} = -(B_i + p_i)\frac{\partial \rho^{-1}}{\partial t} + \left(\frac{\partial \varepsilon}{\partial t}\right)^a + S_{Fi} + \frac{1}{\rho}\nabla \cdot \chi_i \nabla T_i + C_{ve}\frac{T_e - T_i}{\tau_{ei}},$$

(5)
$$C_{ve} \frac{\partial T_e}{\partial t} = -(B_e + p_e)\frac{\partial \rho^{-1}}{\partial t} + S_{Fe} + S_L + \frac{1}{\rho}\nabla \cdot \chi_e \nabla T_e - C_{ve}\frac{T_e - T_i}{\tau_{ei}} - C_{ve}\frac{T_e - T_r}{\tau_{er}}$$

(6)
$$C_{vr} \frac{\partial T_r}{\partial t} = -(B_r + p_r)\frac{\partial \rho^{-1}}{\partial t} + \frac{1}{\rho}\nabla \cdot \chi_r \nabla T_r + C_{ve}\frac{T_e - T_r}{\tau_{er}}$$

to which appropriate initial and boundary condition are imposed. In Eqs (1-6) ρ is the mass density, u is the fluid velocity, p is the total pressure, Π^a is the artificial stress tensor (Schulz 1964), g is the gravity, $R \equiv (R(i,j), Z(i,j))$ the T_β's are the temperatures (β = e,i,r, for the electrons, ions and radiation, respectively), $C_{v\beta} = (\partial \varepsilon/\partial T_\beta = (\partial \varepsilon_\beta/\partial \rho^{-1})_{T\beta}$, ε_β is the specific energy of the fluid β, p_β is the pressure, S_{Fe} (S_{Fi}) is the fusion specific power delivered to the electrons (ions), S_L is the specific power delivered by the laser to the electrons, $(\partial \varepsilon/\partial t)^a$

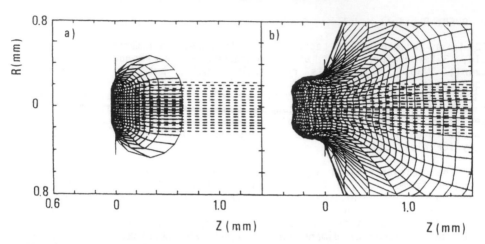

Fig. 1   Simulation of a thin foil target accelerated by a laser pulse.
The mesh (solid lines) and a set of representative rays (dashed lines)
are shown at t = 2 ns (a) and t = 5ns,(b) respectively (after Atzeni,
1988b)

is the specific power dissipated by the artificial stress tensor, the χ's
are the (flux limited) conductivities, and the τ's are the energy exchange
times. The   EOS quantities C_{vi}, C_{ve}, B_i, B_e, p_i and p_e, as well as the
conductivities and the energy exchange times are involved functions of
the density, of the temperatures and of the material properties. In
particular, we compute the EOS quantities by interpolating data stored in
previously generated EOS tables.

The DUED model also includes the nuclear fusion reactions, the equations
for the concentrations of deuterium and tritium, and a diffusive equation
for the transport of the charged fusion products (alpha particles). From
the latter, the terms S_{Fe} and S_{Fi} in Eqs (4) and (5) can be computed.

Laser-plasma interaction is dealt with in the geometric optics
approximation; the trajectories of the laser rays are described by a
simple, second order differential equation (e.g. Atzeni 1986, 1987);
power attenuation along a ray is computed by a certain line integral,
allowing for he computation of the source term S_L in Eq. (5).

Two applications of DUED to the simulation of current experiments are
shown in Figs. 1 and 2; for many other examples see Atzeni (1986, 1987,
1988b).

2.3 DUED: Numerics

Equations (1-6) are solved by a time-marching 2 level scheme, and
discretized in space by finite-differences (f.d.). For the energy
equations (Eqs (4-6)), a time-splitting (or fractional-step) method is
adopted, according to which the temperature increments due to different
classes of physical processes are computed separately. Indeed, we first
solve (splitting I) the fluid equations by a standard explicit scheme
(Schulz 1964), neglecting both the thermal conduction and the energy
exchange terms in Eqs (4-6). Subsequently (splitting II), we compute the

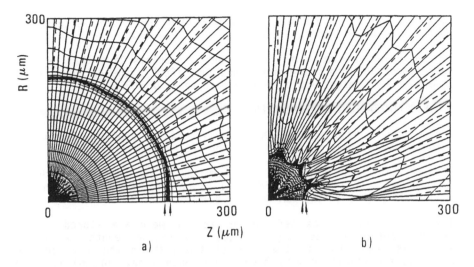

R (μm)

300

0   ⇈   300   0   ⇊   300

Z (μm)

a)   b)

Fig. 2   Implosion of a glass shell, with radius R_0 = 250 μm, and thickness ΔR_0 = 2.5 μm, filled with D-T gas, irradiated by centrally focused laser beams, with both long wavelength (legendre mode ℓ = 12; $\Delta I/\bar{I}$ = 10%) and short wavelength (noice; $\Delta I/\bar{I}$ ~ 1%) azimuthal intensity (I) perturbations. The figures show the Lagrangian mesh (solid) and selected laser rays (dashed) during the implosion   (a) and just before collapse (b). The arrows indicate the boundaries of the solid shell.

temperature increments due to the thermal conduction for each of the three species by using a fully implicit scheme. The arbitrary-quadrilateral shape of the mesh-zones requires the use of a 9-point difference operator (Kershaw 1981). For each specie we then have to solve a linear system of size N = $(I_{max} -1)(J_{max}-1)$; if the unknown temperatures are ordered by columns (of the (i,j) mesh) in a vector T*, we have

$$AT^* = b, \tag{7}$$

where A is a symmetric, block-tridiagonal matrix, each block in turn being tri-diagonal; the half-bandwidth of A is equal to $I_{max}-1$. (Notice that the alpha-particle diffusion equation also is differenced in a similar way). Equation (7) is solved by the well-known ICCG method (Meyerink and van der Vorst 1977, Kershaw 1978). Finally (splitting III), we compute the temperature increments due to the energy exchange between the three species, again by a fully implicit scheme.

As far as laser-matter interaction is concerned, the actual laser beam is divided into NRAY (with NRAY = 10-200) beamlets, each defining an "energy flux tube" and described, at a given time level, by a single ray. The ray is traced through the plasma as if the whole path occurred in a single time step Δt. Tracing the ray consists in first finding its entrance in the simulation domain and then following (through a cumbersome sequence of conditional statements) the sequence of exits from (and entrances into) the various zones it passes through, the path within each zone being given by the solution of the ray equation with the local value of the gradient of the refractive index. The energy deposition of each ray into the mesh is then computed by integrating the energy attenuation equation along the path of ray itself.

Despite the relative simplicity of the model, problems like that of Fig. 2 require about 10^{11} floating-point operations (FLOP); the detailed study of a thermonculear target would require more than 10^{13} FLOP.

3.   CODE OPTIMIZATION: GENERALITIES

DUED is written in standard FORTRAN 77, using **64 bit** storage (**IBM double precision** or CRAY single precision) for the real variables.

It has been compiled with the CFT 1.15 compiler on the CRAY-XMP, with the VS FORTRAN vers. 2.2 on the IBM 3090-VF uniprocessor, and with IBM Parallel FORTRAN (PF) on the IBM 3090-VF multiprocessors.

In DUED all the quantities defined on the 2-D mesh are stored as 2-D arrays (matrices), such as, e.g., A(I,J). The vector length for vector operations is then equal to the size of the mesh in the i direction, which is not necessarily a very high value. Such a data organization is instead particularly suited for automatic parallelization with PF. Indeed matrix updating is performed by nested loops of depth two, with the outer loop being on the index J, and the inner on the index I. If certain conditions, detailed in the PF manual (IBM Corp. 1988), are met, then PF can automatically parallelize the outer loop (with stride equal to the leading dimension of A), and vectorize the inner loop (with unit stride).

In optimizing DUED we have chosen not to alter the basic structure of the code which was designed to insure flexibility of usage, modularity, readability and portability. This means, for instance, that DO loop bounds are usually not known at compile time (because they depend on the selected boundary conditions), and that the size of the loops is not indicated by any compiler directive. Also, given the physics-oriented nature of this work, we have made no effort to optimize cache memory usage on the IBM 3090 or to avoid bank conflicts on the CRAY-XMP.

With regard to vector/parallel implementation, the different algorithms included in DUED can be grouped in three distinct families, each requiring specific treatments (see Table I).

It should be observed that (with the exception of ICCG, for which partially vectorized routines, written e.g. by Anderson and Shestakov (1983), exist in some libraries) the algorithms used by DUED cannot exploit any of the highly optimized scientific routines included in the available mathematical libraries. For instance, no advantage can be taken of the matrix-vector and matrix-matrix operation routines of the IBM ESSL;this means that we cannot expect to achieve a very high vector speed-up, even for long vectors.

Table II shows the relative weight of the different modules of the code in the execution of a few reference simulations concerning, respectively, a) a laser driven implosion with a 2-T, non-nuclear model; b) a purely fluid-dynamics instability, c) the thermonuclear ignition, with a 2-T model and d) a reactor level target with the full model of DUED. It is apparent that it is not possible to individualize a single, time consuming kernel, but that in practice all modules may be important, and it is then necessary to optimize each one.

Table I: Algorithms and optimization

		REMARKS ON	
	Algorithm	**Vectorization**	**Parallelization**
	a) Comput. of coefficients, trivial loops	trivial automatic	automatic parallel loops
I	b) finite-difference explicit c) table interpolation d) as a), with same logic	[careful prog.]	
II	Solution of linear systems (ICCG)	partial [ordering of data]	parallel ICCG
III	ray-tracing	non-vectorizable	parallelized by partitioning

Table II: Modular structure of DUED

			Percentage of total work (scalar)			
Module	Function	Algorithm*	problem+			
			a	b	c	d
A	basic framework	I	10-15	35	15-20	< 5
B	explicit hydro	Ib,Ia	~5	25	10-12	< 5
C	thermal cond**	Ia,Id	6-10	-	10-25	10
D	Eq. of state	Ic	5-8	40	10-20	10
E	radiation loss	Ia,Id	3-5	-	8-10	5
F	ray-tracing	III	20-50	-	-	~30
G	reactions**	Ia,Ib,Id	< 10	-	10-12	5
I	ICCG	II	5-10	-	20-40	30

*   see table I
**   not including the solution of the linear system by ICCG
+   see main text for the definition of the problems

4. VECTORIZATION

For the algorithms of class I (see Table I), vector operation has been
achieved by simply replacing instructions without vector support and some
unnecessary conditional statements. In a few cases, we have also changed
the data structures.As far as the ICCG solver is concerned, taking
advantage of its symmetric block-diagonal structure the matrix A (of Eq.
7) can be stored diagonal-wise in a compact form in an ($N \times 5$) 2-D array.

Such a data ordering leads in a straightforward way to the vectorization of the nonrecursive part of the algorithm (Anderson and Shestakov 1983), while it eliminates the need for indirect addressing in the recursive operations. [For the sake of completeness it should be recalled that ICCG can also be written in a fully vectorizable form (Kershaw 1980). This, however, is rather involved and, above all, is only advantageous for very large matrices and on computers whose vector performances are not degraded much by nonunit stride (which is not the case of the IBM 3090)].

Vectorization of the DUED code has yielded the following results. On the IBM 3090 VF, with scalar performance about 4.5 MFLOPS, fully vectorized modules (modules A-E and G) exhibit vector speed-up VSU $\simeq$ 2-2.7 depending on the mesh size; the ICCG iterations achieve VSU $\simeq$ 1.8, while the ray-tracing cannot vectorize (VSU = 1). The corresponding values for the CRAY XMP (with scalar speed about 11.5 MFLOPS), less sensitive to nonunit stride and to vector length, and without cache problems, are 4-8, 2.7, and 1, respectively). For the execution of the full code, typical values are VSU ~ 1.6-2.2 for the IBM 3090 VF and VSU ~ 1.8-3 for the CRAY-XMP.

5. PARALLELIZATION

We consider the parallel implementation separately for the three classes of algorithms defined in Table I (for more details see Atzeni, 1988a).

The algorithms of class I essentially require the updating of the 2-D arrays, performed by nested loops of depth 2. We have parallelized the loops by using the automatic parallelization option of the PF compiler and introducing, when necessary, appropriate compiler directives.

As expected, the **parallel speed-ups** (i.e., the ratio of the elapsed times measured in a dedicated machine for vector uni-processor execution to that for vector multiprocessor execution) for the modules using algorithms of this family depend on the granularity of the loops. For example, Table III shows that the modules containing small loops (A,B,C) achieve speed-ups of 1.7 on 2 CPUs only for a very large 120×120 mesh, while modules containing big loops (D,E) exhibit speed-ups larger than 1.7 even on a 30×30 mesh.

The ICCG algorithm (class II) contains some recursive operations inhibiting straightforward parallelism, namely, the incomplete Cholesky preconditioning (to be performed only once for each system) and the solution of two triangular systems, to be performed at each ICCG iteration. Such systems arise from the solution, in two subsequent steps, of the system (LDL^T) $q = r$, where D is a diagonal matrix and L is a lower triangular matrix with the same sparsity pattern as A. The other operations are scalar products and sparse-matrix times vector products, which, instead, can rather easily be partitioned by the different CPUs. To achieve parallelism, we have resorted to a parallel variant of the ICCG algorithm (see e.g., Radicati and Robert (1987)) consisting in dividing the matrix A in as many sections as the number of desired parallel tasks, NTASK (in turn usually set equal to the number of available CPUs), and then in computing NTASK "local" parallel preconditioning matrices as schematically shown in Fig. 3a. Each

Table III: Parallel speed-up for several code modules

CODE MODULE	2 CPUs mesh size				4 CPUs mesh size	
	16×30	30×30	60×60	120×120	60×60	120×120
A*		1.26	1.38	1.70		2.02
B*	1.22	1.29	1.51	1.75	2.03	2.62
C*	1.38	1.36	1.40	1.25		
D**	1.67	1.67	1.86	1.92	3.13	3.38
E**	1.79	1.82	1.93	1.98	3.60	3.85
G	1.43		1.57	1.53	2.22	2.50
I+	0.86	1.14	1.87	1.87		3.45

*   small-granularity loops
**large-granularity loops
+   only ICCG iterations (i.e., not considering preconditioning)

conjugate gradient iteration can then be executed in parallel, by **NTASK**

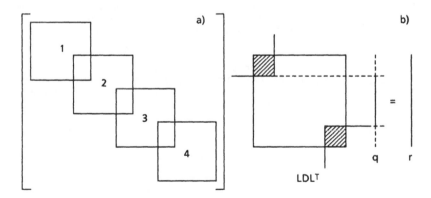

Fig. 3 a)   Schematization of the partition of the coefficient matrix A induced by the local IC preconditioning, with overlapping between adjacent blocks (for 4 CPUs). b) Schematization of the local computation of the system (LDL^T) **q** = **r**, performed by each of the parallel tasks. Notice that each element of **q** within the overlapping regions is computed by two tasks.

tasks, each task computing a sector of the solution by using the local preconditioner computed previously. Information between the tasks is exchanged through the scalar products and the matrix by vector multiply.

The above parallel ICCG in practice seems to converge each time the original, sequential ICCG converges, but often more slowly. Converging is accelerated (and often is as fast as that of the original ICCG) by computing the local preconditioning in partially overlapping sections (Radicati and Robert 1987) (In our case, the optimum overlap is in the range 2-4 x half bandwidth). In the overlapped regions, the elements of $q = (LDL^T)^{-1} r$ are computed by two tasks giving, in general different results. To proceed with the standard ICCG, the average value of the two is taken (see Fig. 3b).

Parallel ICCG has been implemented by scheduling parallel subroutines to parallel tasks and synchronizing them by the use of the synchronization subroutines defining the socalled PARALLEL EVENTS.

As can be seen from the speed up results for module I (see Table III) parallelization of the ICCG iterations for large matrices was very effective. (Parallelization of preconditioning gives even better results, see Atzeni 1988a). The performances of the whole parallel ICCG are, however, difficult to evaluate since this algorithm will, in general, converge in a different number of iterations than the original, serial ICCG.

Parallelization of the ray-tracing (class III algorithm) has been programmed quite easily by exploiting the fact that the NRAY rays to be traced at each time-step are independent of each other. NTASK parallel subroutines are then scheduled, each tracing NRAY/NTASK rays. To balance the work among the tasks, adjacent rays, which are likely to have similar paths) are assigned to different tasks; the mesh data are shared among the tasks. Each task, instead, updates a local energy deposition matrix; subsequently all "local" matrices are added together to yield the actual energy source matrix.

As a result of the large granularity of the tasks and of the good load balancing, very high values of the parallel speed-up are achieved for the ray-tracing, as shown in Table IV. Speed ups larger than 1.9 on 2 CPUs and larger than 3.5 on 4 CPUs are measured for typical problems.

Performances of the whole code vary with the problem, depending on the relative weight of the different modules. Table V shows the speed-ups obtained for the reference problems a),b), and c) (see Sec. 3) as a function of the mesh size. For a 60×60 mesh, a size used in many significant physical studies, parallel speed-ups are in the range 1.5-1.7 on 2 CPUs and in the range 2.1-2.7 on 4 CPUs (Notice that another factor around two has already been gained through vectorization). Such figures compare well with those obtained in the parallelization of other complex codes for scientific and engineering problems.

6.   CONCLUSIONS

In this paper we have discussed some of the problems arising in the implementation of a rather complex research code on a vector multiprocessor. We have employed a new tool for parallelization, the IBM Parallel FORTRAN (PF) Language and Compiler. Its use made the parallelization of the code relatively easy and cheap without requiring any major restructuring of the code.

Table IV - Parallel speed-up for the ray-tracing module

No. of rays*	2 CPUs	3 CPUs	4 CPUs
30	1.88	2.66	3.40
60	1.93	2.81	3.57
120	1.97	2.86	3.66
240	1.97	2.90	3.81

* mesh 60 × 80, with rays crossing about 60 zones

Table V - Parallel speed-up for the whole code

Problem*	2 CPUs			3 CPUs	4 CPUs	
	30 × 30	60 × 60	120 × 120	60 × 60	60 × 60	120 × 120
a		1.66 +		2.19 +	2.70 + ⧧	
b		1.64	1.76		2.34	2.86
c	1.39	1.56	1.61		2.13	2.36

* see main test for the definition of the problems
+ mesh 60×80; 200 rays per step
⧧ theoretical estimate, based on the data reported in tables III and IV

We have also made successful use of a parallel ICCG solver which, in our not too extreme cases, converged very well, but whose theoretical bases are still rather weak.

The performances obtained are more than encouraging in view of the complexity of the code, the non-straightforward parallelization of certain modules, and the novelty of PF. At the same time, they indicate that much work has still to be done to fully exploit the potentials of moderate (not to say massive) parallelism for the solution of many interesting physical problems.

ACKNOWLEDGMENTS

The parallel implementation of the DUED code on the IBM 3090 VF multiprocessor has been performed at IBM-ECSEC, Rome, in the framework of an IBM-ENEA collaboration.

I wish to thank V. Di Chio, G. Radicati, P. Sguazzero, F. Szeleniy and V. Zecca, all of IBM-ECSEC, for their cooperation during the course of this work.

REFERENCES

Anderson D V and Shestakov A I 1983 *Computer Phys. Commun.* **30, 37**

Atzeni S 1986 *Computer Phys. Commun.* **43** 107

Atzeni S 1987 *Plasma Phys. Controll. Fusion* **29** 1535

Atzeni S 1988a *2D Fluid Dynamics Models for Laser Driven Fusion on IBM 3090 Vector Multiprocessors*, Report ENEA-RT-FUS (June 1988), in press

Atzeni S 1988b *2D Numerical Study of the Hydrodynamics of Laser Accelerated Thin Foils*, in preparation

Duderstadt J J and Moses G A 1982 *Inertial Confinement Fusion* (New York: Wiley).

IBM Corp. 1988 *Parallel FORTRAN Language and Library Reference*, IBM order No SC 23-0431-0, Yorktown, NY, USA

Hwang K 1987 *Proc. IEEE* **75** 1349

Johnson T H 1984 *Proc. IEEE* **72** 548

Kershaw D S 1978 *J. Comp. Phys.* **26** 43

Kershaw D S 1980 *Laser Program Annual Report 1979* (Ed. by L W Coleman) Lawrence Livermore National Laboratory, Livermore, California (Rep. UCRL-50021-79)

Kershaw D S 1981 *J. Comp.Phys.* **39** 375

Meyerink J A and van der Vorst H A 1977 *Math. Comp.* **31** 148

Radicati di Brozolo G and Robert Y 1987 *Vector and Parallel CG-like Algorithms for Sparse Non-symmetric Systems*, Informatique et Mathematique Applique de Grenoble, Rep RR 681 M

Schulz W D 1964 *Methods in Computational Physics* (Edited by B Alder et al) Vol 3, p 1 (New York: Academic).

Iteration-by-subdomain algorithms for systems of hyperbolic equations

Alfio Quarteroni
Dipartimento di Matematica, Università Cattolica, Via Trieste 17 - 25121 Brescia and
Istituto di Analisi Numerica del C.N.R., C.so Carlo Alberto 5 - 27100 Pavia, Italy

ABSTRACT: We present a domain decomposition method to be used in connection with numerical approximation of hyperbolic systems by spectral collocations. Its effective realization by a proper iteration-by-subdomain algorithm allows the simultaneous solution of a family of independent subproblems.

INTRODUCTION

Domain decomposition methods for the numerical approximation of partial differential equations lead to a natural exploitation of parallel architectures on modern computers. This is the main reason for their impetuous grown in the last few years.

The research activities carried out in the field until the beginning of 1988 are well documented by the proceedings of the first and second international conference on Domain Decomposition for Partial Differential Equations (see references [1] and [2]).

The contribution of the author, which was mainly focused on the application of domain decomposition techniques to finite element and spectral approximations to elliptic and Navier-Stokes equations, is witnessed by the references [3-11].

In this report we consider a system of hyperbolic equations and discuss a domain decomposition technique to be used in connection with a spectral collocation approximation in the space directions, and a time-marching finite difference scheme. According to this technique, the spatial computational domain, say Ω, is subdivided into a family of dispoint subdomains Ω_k within which the polynomial solution is required to satisfy the differential problem at the internal collocation nodes. At each subdomain interface the various polynomial solutions should satisfy a continuity statement, as well as the compatibility equations, i.e., some suitable characteristic combinations of the original differential equations which represent wave propagation across the interface from one subdomain to its neighbour. This domain decomposition method is capable to face problems which are set in domains of complex geometry. Furthermore, it allows local refinement to resolve internal layers, without loosing the spectral accuracy enjoyed by the single-domain spectral collocation method (see [12], Ch.12]. In order to render our method interesting for calculation within parallel environment, we propose an iteration by subdomain procedure yielding at each step as many independent subproblems as the number of subdomains of the decomposition. The convergence analysis (that is carried out in [13]) shows that convergence is achieved in a number of steps independent of the number of unknowns within each subdomain. This is well documented by the numerical results that we present here.

The details of the method, as well as its application to the case of hyperbolic problems with discontinuous solutions, are presented in [13].

1. THE HYPERBOLIC SYSTEM

We consider systems of conservation laws of the form

$$\frac{\partial u}{\partial t} + div F(u) = f \quad in \ \Omega \times (0, T)$$

which, by the help of the Jacobian matrices $A_j(u) = \frac{\partial F_j(u)}{\partial u}$, can be written in the form

$$(1.1) \qquad \frac{\partial u}{\partial t} + \sum_{j=1}^{m} A_j(u) \frac{\partial u}{\partial x_j} = f \quad in \ \ \Omega \times (0, T)$$

where $m = 1, 2$ or 3, Ω is an open bounded domain of $\mathbb{R}^m$, u and f are two vector functions, $u, f : \Omega \times (0, T) \to \mathbb{R}^p$, with $p \geq 1$, and $A_j(u)$ are $p \times p$ matrices.
The system (1.1) is supplemented by initial conditions of the form:

$$(1.2) \qquad u(x, 0) = \varphi(x) \qquad \forall \, x \in \Omega$$

and by suitable boundary conditions at $(0, T) \times \partial \Omega$.
For any $\xi \in \mathbb{R}^m$ such that $|\xi| \equiv \left(\sum_{j=1}^{m} \xi_j^2 \right)^{1/2} = 1$, let us define the matrix

$$(1.3) \qquad A(\xi) := \sum_{j=1}^{m} A_j(u) \, \xi_j$$

As we assume that the system (1.1) is hyperbolic in time, for any such a ξ $A(\xi)$ has p real eigenvalues and moreover it is diagonalisible. Let us denote by $\{\lambda^k, k = 1, ..., p\}$ the eigenvalues of $A(\xi)$, and by $\{v^k, k = 1, ..., p\}$ the set of the corresponding left eigenvectors, so that

$$(1.4) \qquad v^k A(\xi) = \lambda^k v^k \quad k = 1, ..., p$$

We assume that the eigenvalues are ordered in such a way that the first q of them are positive, and the remaining $p - q$ are negative. If we denote by τ the direction orthogonal to ξ, so that $\tau \cdot \xi = 0, |\tau| = 1$, then

$$(1.5) \qquad v^k \cdot \left(\frac{\partial u}{\partial t} + \lambda^k \frac{\partial u}{\partial \xi} \right) = v^k \cdot \left(f - \sum_{j=1}^{m} A_j(u) \frac{\partial u}{\partial \tau} \tau_j \right) \quad k = 1, ..., p$$

We will refer to (1.5) as to the *compatibility equations* for the problem (1.1).
If Γ denotes a (m-1)-dimensional manifold of $\mathbb{R}^m$, and we denote by ν the unit normal direction to Γ, taking $\xi = \nu$ equations (1.5) restricted to Γ become:

$$(1.6) \qquad v^k \cdot \left(\frac{\partial u}{\partial t} + \lambda^k \frac{\partial u}{\partial \nu} \right) = v^k \cdot \left(f - \sum_{j=1}^{m} A_j(u) \frac{\partial u}{\partial \tau} \tau_j \right) \qquad k = 1, ..., p$$

We note that the left hand side of (1.6) yields a combination (through the components of the eigenvector v^k) of transport equations along a direction which is normal to Γ.

Assume Γ is the boundary of Ω and ν is oriented outward Ω; then for $k = 1, ..., q$, (1.6) yield q transport equations according to which information are propagated from the inside toward the outside of Ω. For such a reason, equations (1.6) for $k = 1, ..., q$ will be called the compatibility equations for the domain Ω.

If we now assume that Ω_1 and Ω_2 are two adjoining subdomains of Ω, and Γ is their common boundary, taking as ν the normal direction to Γ, oriented from Ω_1 to Ω_2, the first q equations of (1.6) are the compatibility equations for Ω_1 (they entail propagation of information from Ω_1 to Ω_2). For the same reason, for $k = q+1, ..., p$, (1.6) provide the compatibility equations for Ω_2.

2. A DOMAIN DECOMPOSITION APPROACH FOR PROBLEM (1.1) USING THE SPECTRAL COLLOCATION METHOD

The reader who is unfamiliar with spectral methods is referred to [12]. In this report we will consider spectral collocation methods using Chebyshev nodes. We assume that Ω is an m-dimensional hypercube. Let Ω_1 and Ω_2 be two open subregions so that $\overline{\Omega} = \overline{\Omega}_1 \cup \overline{\Omega}_2, \overline{\Omega}_1 \cap \overline{\Omega}_2 = \Gamma, \Omega_1 \cap \Omega_2 = \phi$ with Γ normal to one cartesian direction. We assume here that Γ is not a discontinuity surface. The case of solutions that are discontinuous across Γ is faced in [13]. Let N be a given positive integer; we denote by

$$(2.1) \qquad \Sigma := \left\{ x_k = \cos \frac{\pi k}{N} , \ k = (k_1, ..., k_m) , \ 0 \le k_i \le N , \ i = 1, ..., m \right\}$$

the set of Chebyshev-Lobatto points of the reference hypercube $[-1, 1]^m$. Further, we denote by Σ^1 and Σ^2 the corresponding set of points in Ω_1 and Ω_2, respectively. Note that x_k lies on the boundary of the reference hypercube if at least one of the indices k_j is either 0 or N.

A (continuous in time) spectral domain decomposition method for problem (1.1) is defined as follows. At each time $t > 0$ we look for $u_N^i(t) \in (\mathbb{P}_N(\Omega_i))^p$ that satisfies the following set of equations.

(a) At each Chebyshev point internal to Ω_1

$$(2.2) \qquad \frac{\partial u_N^1}{\partial t} + \sum_{j=1}^{m} A_j(u_N^1) \frac{\partial u_N^1}{\partial x_j} = f \ ;$$

(b) at each Chebyshev point internal to Ω_2

$$(2.3) \qquad \frac{\partial u_N^2}{\partial t} + \sum_{j=1}^{m} A_j(u_N^2) \frac{\partial u_N^2}{\partial x_j} = f \ ;$$

(c) at the Chebyshev points belonging to Γ:

$$(2.4) \qquad v^k \cdot \left(\frac{\partial u_N^1}{\partial t} + \lambda^k \frac{\partial u_N^1}{\partial \nu} \right) = v^k \cdot \left(f - \sum_{j=1}^{m} A_j(u_N^1) \frac{\partial u_N^1}{\partial \tau} \tau_j \right) \qquad k = 1, ..., q$$

ν is the outward unit normal direction to Ω_1 on Γ, λ^k and v^k are the eigenvalues and the (left) eigenvectors of the matrix $A(\nu)$, and τ is the tangential direction on Γ.
Moreover we satisfy:

$$(2.5) \qquad v^k \cdot \left(\frac{\partial u_N^2}{\partial t} + \lambda^k \frac{\partial u_N^2}{\partial \nu} \right) = v^k \cdot \left(f - \sum_{j=1}^{m} A_j(u_N^2) \frac{\partial u_N^2}{\partial \tau} \tau_j \right) \qquad k = q+1, ..., p$$

Following the definitions given in section 1, (2.4) are the q compatibility equations for Ω_1 on Γ, while (2.5) are the $p - q$ ones for Ω_2.
Finally, since we have assumed that the solution is continuous across Γ, we require that at each collocation point on Γ

$$(2.6) \qquad\qquad u_N^1 = u_N^2 \quad ;$$

(d) at the Chebyshev points belonging to a "face" Φ of $\partial\Omega_1$ (excluding the interface Γ)

$$(2.7) \qquad v^k \cdot \left(\frac{\partial u_N^1}{\partial t} + \lambda^k \frac{\partial u_N^1}{\partial \nu} \right) = v^k \cdot \left(f - \sum_{j=1}^{m} A_j(u_N^1) \frac{\partial u_N^1}{\partial \tau} \tau_j \right) \qquad k = 1, ..., q$$

where ν is now the outward normal direction to Ω_1 on Φ, τ is the tangential direction on Φ, while λ^k and v^k are the eigenvalues and the (left) eigenvectors of the matrix $A(\nu)$ (note that here q is not necessarily the same as in (2.4)).
The remaining $p - q$ equations that are needed at each collocation point of Φ must be provided by the physical boundary conditions that supplement (1.1) and (1.2).

(e) at the Chebyshev points belonging to a "face" Φ of $\partial\Omega_2$ (excluding the interface Γ) we enforce

$$(2.8) \qquad v^k \cdot \left(\frac{\partial u_N^2}{\partial t} + \lambda^k \frac{\partial u_N^2}{\partial \nu} \right) = v^k \cdot \left(f - \sum_{j=1}^{m} A_j(u_N^2) \frac{\partial u_N^2}{\partial \tau} \tau_j \right) \qquad k = 1, ..., q$$

where ν is the outward normal direction to Ω_2 on Φ, τ the tangential direction on Φ, λ^k and v^k are the eigenvalues and the (left) eigenvectors of the matrix $A(\nu)$.
The remaining $p - q$ equations are prescribed as boundary conditions.

According to our description, the spectral collocation problems in Ω_1 and Ω_2 are coupled throughout the continuity conditions (2.6) at the interface Γ. In order to get rid of such a coupling we propose the following iterative method. Assume the solution is available at the n-th step. Let ν, τ, λ^k and v^k be defined as at the point (c) above (clearly, λ^k and v^k depend on the value of the solution at the points of Γ).

Let $\wedge(\nu)$ and $T(\nu)$ denote respectively the matrix of the eigenvalues of $A(\nu)$ and that of the corresponding (left) eigenvectors, so that:

$$(2.9) \qquad T(\nu)\, A(\nu) = \wedge(\nu)\, T(\nu)$$

Furthermore denote by $T_q(\nu)$ the $q \times p$ matrix given by the first q rows of $T(\nu)$, while $T_{p-q}(\nu)$ will denote the $(p - q) \times q$ matrix given by the remaining $p - q$ rows. The solutions at the new step, say $(u_N^1)^{n+1}$ in Ω_1 and $(u_N^2)^{n+1}$ in Ω_2, can be obtained by solving two independent problems in Ω_1 and in Ω_2, respectively.

Precisely, $(u_N^1)^{n+1}$ satisfies the interior equations (2.2), the interface equations (2.4) together with

$$(2.10) \qquad T_{p-q}(\nu)\, (u_N^1)^{n+1} = T_{p-q}(\nu)\, (u_N^2)^n \quad on\ \Gamma$$

and, finally, the boundary equations given at the point (d) above.

Similarly, $(u_N^2)^{n+1}$ satisfies the interior equations (2.3), the interface equations (2.5) together with

$$(2.11) \qquad T_q(\nu)\, (u_N^2)^{n+1} = T_q(\nu)\, (u_N^1)^n \quad on\ \Gamma$$

and, finally, the boundary equations prescribed at the point (e) above.

The extension of the above iterative process to decompositions with several subdomains is straightforward. At each step, one is left to solve with as many independent subproblems as the number of subdomains. All these subproblems can be solved simultaneously within a parallel computer environment.

3. SOME NUMERICAL RESULTS

In order to show the potential capability of the above domain decomposition method to yield effective solutions of hyperbolic systems, we present some numerical results for a simple problem. Precisely, we consider the special case in which Ω is the one-dimensional interval $(-1,1)$, and $\Omega_1 = (-1, \alpha)$, $\Omega_2 = (\alpha, 1)$ for some $0 < \alpha < 1$. In this case $\Gamma = \{\alpha\}$. The differential system reads as follows

$$(3.1) \qquad \frac{\partial u}{\partial t} + A\, \frac{\partial u}{\partial x} = f \quad in\ \Omega \times (0, T)$$

We take $A = \begin{pmatrix} 1/2 & 1 \\ 1 & 1/2 \end{pmatrix}$, so that (2.9) holds with

$$\wedge = \operatorname{diag}\{\lambda, -\mu\} \text{ with } \lambda = 3/2, \mu = 1/2 \text{ and } T = T^{-1} = \frac{1}{\sqrt{2}} \begin{pmatrix} 1 & 1 \\ 1 & -1 \end{pmatrix}$$

In this case we have therefore

$$p = 1, q = 1, \Lambda_q = (3/2, 0), T_q = \left(\frac{1}{\sqrt{2}}, \frac{1}{\sqrt{2}}\right), \Lambda_{p-q} = (0, -1/2), T_{p-q} = \left(\frac{1}{\sqrt{2}}, -\frac{1}{\sqrt{2}}\right)$$

The hyperbolic system (3.1) needs to be completed by the initial condition

$$(3.2) \qquad\qquad u(x, 0) = \varphi(x) \quad x \in \Omega$$

and by a set of boundary conditions (one equation at the point $x = -1$, and another at the point $x = 1$) that we assume having the form

$$(3.3) \qquad\qquad \begin{aligned} u_1(-1, t) &= \beta(t) \\ u_2(1, t) &= \gamma(t) \end{aligned}$$

Setting $z = Tu$ (characteristic variables), we obtain the following characteristic form of the compatibility equations

$$(3.4) \qquad\qquad \frac{\partial z}{\partial t} + \Lambda \frac{\partial z}{\partial x} = T f$$

We will now apply the multidomain spectral collocation method described in section two to the one dimensional problem (3.1). Let us define

$$x_j^1 = -1 + \frac{\alpha + 1}{2} (t_j + 1), x_j^2 = \alpha + \frac{1 - \alpha}{2} (t_j + 1), j = 0, ..., N \;\; where \;\; t_j = \cos \frac{\pi j}{N}$$

The points t_j are the Chebyshev-Lobatto nodes in the reference interval $[-1,1]$, while x_j^1 and x_j^2 are their images in the subdomains Ω_1 and Ω_2 respectively.
At each time $t > 0$ we look for $u_N^1(t) \in (\mathbb{P}_N(\Omega_1))^p$, $u_N^2(t) \in (\mathbb{P}_N(\Omega_2))^p$ satisfying:

(a) internal equations

$$(3.5) \qquad\qquad \frac{\partial u_N^1}{\partial t} + A \frac{\partial u_N^1}{\partial x} = f \quad at \; x_j^1 \;\; 1 \leq j \leq N - 1$$

$$(3.6) \qquad\qquad \frac{\partial u_N^2}{\partial t} + A \frac{\partial u_N^2}{\partial x} = f \quad at \; x_j^2 \;\; 1 \leq j \leq N - 1$$

(b) interface equations

$$(3.7) \qquad\qquad T_q \frac{\partial u_N^1}{\partial t} + \lambda T_q \frac{\partial u_N^1}{\partial x} = T_q f \quad at \; x = \alpha$$

$$(3.8) \qquad T_{p-q} \frac{\partial u_N^2}{\partial t} - \mu \, T_{p-q} \frac{\partial u_N^2}{\partial x} = T_{p-q} \, f \quad at \; x = \alpha$$

$$(3.9) \qquad u_N^1 = u_N^2 \qquad at \; x = \alpha$$

(c) boundary equations

$$(3.10) \qquad T_q \frac{\partial u_N^2}{\partial t} + \lambda \, T_q \frac{\partial u_N^2}{\partial x} = T_q \, f \quad at \; x = 1$$

$$(3.11) \qquad T_{p-q} \frac{\partial u_N^1}{\partial t} - \mu \, T_{p-q} \frac{\partial u_N^1}{\partial x} = T_{p-q} \, f \quad at \; x = -1$$

$$(3.12) \qquad (u_N^2)_2(1, t) = \gamma(t)$$

$$(3.13) \qquad (u_N^1)_1(-1, t) = \beta(t)$$

Note that (3.7) and (3.11) are the compatibility equations for Ω_1 at the points $x = \alpha$ and $x = -1$, respectively, while (3.8) and (3.10) are those of Ω_2 at the points $x = \alpha$ and $x = 1$, respectively. Finally, (3.12) and (3.13) are the boundary equations.

A fully discrete approximation can now be obtained by using a time marching scheme in (3.5)-(3.13). Whatever scheme (either implicit or explicit) one uses to advance from a known time level t^k to a new one t^{k+1}, the interface condition and the boundary conditions should be imposed at the new time level.

We write now the iteration-by-subdomain method described in section 2 for the solution to the problem (3.5)-(3.13). Assume $(u_N^1)^n$, $(u_N^2)^n$ are available at the n-th step Then in Ω_1 we look for $(u_N^1)^{n+1}(t) \in (\mathbb{P}_N(\Omega_1))^p$ such that

$$(3.14) \qquad \frac{\partial}{\partial t} (u_N^1)^{n+1} + A \frac{\partial}{\partial x} (u_N^1)^{n+1} = f \quad at \; x_j^1 \, , \;\; 1 \leq j \leq N - 1$$

$$(3.15) \qquad T_q \frac{\partial}{\partial l} (u_N^1)^{n+1} + \lambda \, T_q \frac{\partial}{\partial x} (u_N^1)^{n+1} = T_q \, f \quad at \; x = \alpha$$

$$(3.16) \qquad T_{p-q} (u_N^1)^{n+1} = T_{p-q} (u_N^2)^n \quad at \; x = \alpha$$

(3.17) $$T_{p-q} \frac{\partial}{\partial t} (u_N^1)^{n+1} - \mu T_{p-q} \frac{\partial}{\partial x} (u_N^1)^{n+1} = T_{p-q} f \quad at \; x = -1$$

(3.18) $$(u_N^1)_1^{n+1} = \beta(t) \quad at \; x = -1$$

In Ω_2 we solve for $(u_N^2)^{n+1}(t) \in (\mathbb{P}_N(\Omega_2))^p$ that satisfies:

(3.19) $$\frac{\partial}{\partial t} (u_N^2)^{n+1} + A \frac{\partial}{\partial x} (u_N^2)^{n+1} = f \quad at \; x_j^2 \; , \; 1 \le j \le N - 1$$

(3.20) $$T_{p-q} \frac{\partial}{\partial t} (u_N^2)^{n+1} - \mu T_{p-q} \frac{\partial}{\partial x} (u_N^2)^{n+1} = T_{p-q} f \quad at \; x = \alpha$$

(3.21) $$T_q (u_N^2)^{n+1} = T_q (u_N^1)^n \quad at \; x = \alpha$$

(3.22) $$T_q \frac{\partial}{\partial t} (u_N^2)^{n+1} + \lambda T_q \frac{\partial}{\partial x} (u_N^2)^{n+1} = T_q f \quad at \; x = 1$$

(3.23) $$(u_N^2)_2^{n+1} = \gamma(t) \quad at \; x = 1$$

Note that the two problems are independent from each other, and that the method can be obviously extended to the case of a subdivision by M subdomains ($M > 2$), yielding at each step M independent subproblems.

Here above, the iteration-by-subdomain method has been applied to the semidiscrete (continuous in time) problem (3.5)-(3.13). To be effective, the iteration method should be applied at each time-step after that a time marching scheme has been used to get a full space-time discretization of the problem. In this way, at the new time-level t^{k+1}, we can apply the iterative method until the convergence to $u_N^1(t^{k+1})$, $u_N^2(t^{k+1})$ is achieved.

In our numerical results we considered the case of a time discretization based on the second order Crank-Nicolson scheme.

We considered the case of three different sets of initial and boundary data, so that the corresponding exact solutions are:

1st test function: $u(x,t) = e^t(\cos x, \sin x)$

2nd test function: $u(x,t) = e^t(\cos 8x, \sin 8x)$

3rd test function: $u(x,t) = e^t(arctg\ 10x, arctg\ 8(x - 0.5))$

In all cases, we display results obtained at the time $t = 1$ for several values of the time step Δt, the polynomial degree N used inside each subdomain, and the number M of subdomains. In tables 3.1, 3.2 and 3.3 we report the maximum norm of the relative error between the approximate and the exact solutions at the time $t = 1$. The tables respectively refer to the first, second and third case quoted above, for single domain approximations and for approximations with two subdomains.

Δt / N	one domain		two subdomains	
	0.1	0.01	0.1	0.01
4	2.376E-3	2.509E-3	2.852E-4	1.499E-4
12	2.571E-4	2.580E-6	2.563E-4	2.588E-6
20	2.571E-4	2.580E-6	2.563E-4	2.588E-6

Table 3.1 First test function, one and two subdomain approximations

Δt / N	one domain		two subdomains	
	0.1	0.01	0.1	0.01
4	4.392	4.394	1.235	1.224
12	0.1949	0.2049	1.884E-5	2.168E-5
20	6.174E-4	6.302E-6	4.796E-6	4.794E-8

Table 3.2 Second test function, one and two subdomain approximations

Δt	one domain		two subdomains	
N	0.1	0.01	0.1	0.01
4	0.935	0.9447	0.5600	0.5488
12	0.4085	0.4330	9.206E-2	7.002E-2
20	0.1972	0.1830	2.351E-2	2.102E-2

Table 3.3 Third test function, one and two subdomain approximations

As we can see, using two subdomains rather than simply one allows the achievement of a higher precision. Such an achievement is more relevant if the expected solution exhibits important oscillations (and/or variations) within the computational domain. Furthermore, since the matrices associated with the spectral collocation method are full, the use of several subdomains, accompanied with a sound tuning of the polynomial degree within each subdomain, allows the reduction of the overall complexity of the numerical problem.

We report now the results obtained by the iterative procedure presented in section 2 in the resolution of the multidomain problem.

According to the convergence theory presented in [13], at each iteration the error at the subdomain interfaces reduces by a factor which is substantially independent of N and, as N grows up, tends to $k = exp\,(-2/\Delta t\delta)$, where δ is the spectral radius of the matrix $A(\delta = 3/2$ in the current case). Henceforth, convergence is as faster as smaller the time-step Δt is. In the tables below we report the number of iterations that are needed in order to damp the initial error by a factor of 10^{-5}. As usual M denotes the number of subdomains and N the polynomial degree of the discrete solution inside each subdomain.

Table 3.4 shows that the number of iterations is independent of N, while it grows at most linearly with M.

Finally, in the table 3.5 we present the results pertaining to the first test function obtained when $N = 16$ for several values of M and Δt.

M	2	4	8	12
N				
4	2 (2)	5 (4)	8 (5)	12 (5)
12	2 (2)	4 (4)	8 (5)	12 (5)
20	2 (2)	4 (4)	8 (4)	12 (4)

Table 3.4 Number of iterations for the third test function when $\Delta t = 0.1$
(within the brackets are the values for the case $\Delta t = 0.01$)

Δt \ M	2	4	8	12	16
0.1	2	4	8	12	16
0.02	2	4	4	4	5
0.01	2	4	4	4	4

Table 3.5

Acknowledgment. I am grateful to G.Riccobelli for providing the numerical results of this section.

REFERENCES
[1] R.Glowinski et Al., Eds. "Domain Decomposition Methods for PDE's", I, SIAM, Philadelphia, 1988.
[2] T.Chan et Al., Eds. "Domain Decomposition Methods for PDE's", II, SIAM, Philadelphia, 1989 (in press).
[3] A.Quarteroni, "Domain Decomposition Techniques Using Spectral Methods", **Calcolo XXIV** pp.141-178 (1987).
[4] D.Funaro, A.Quarteroni and P.Zanolli, "An iterative procedure with interface relaxation for domain decomposition methods", **SIAM J.Numer. Anal.25** (6), 1988.
[5] L.D.Marini and A.Quarteroni, "A Relaxation Procedure for Domain Decomposition Methods: A Finite Element Approach", pp.129-143 in [1].
[6] L.D.Marini and A.Quarteroni, "A Relaxation Procedure for Domain Decomposition Methods Using Finite Elements", submitted to **Numer. Math.** (1988).
[7] A.Quarteroni and G.Sacchi-Landriani, "Domain Decomposition Preconditioners for the Spectral Collocation Method", to appear in **J. Scientific Comput.** (1988).
[8] A.Quarteroni and G.Sacchi-Landriani, "Parallel Algorithms for the Capacitance Matrix Method in Domain Decompositions", **Calcolo** (1988), to appear.
[9] A.Quarteroni and G.Sacchi-Landriani, Domain decomposition methods in fluid dynamics, Proceedings of the 2nd German-Italian symposium on applications of mathematics in technology, 1988 V.Boffi and H.Neunzert Eds. (to appear).
[10] A.Quarteroni, "Domain Decomposition Algorithms for the Stokes Equations", to appear in [2].
[11] F.Gastaldi and A.Quarteroni, "On the Coupling of Hyperbolic and Parabolic Systems: Analytical and Numerical Approach", to appear in **Applied Numerical Analysis.** (1988).
[12] C.Canuto, M.Y.Hussaini, A.Quarteroni and T.A.Zang, "Spectral Methods in Fluid Dynamics", Springer-Verlag, Berlin and New York, 1988.
[13] A.Quarteroni, "Domain Decomposition Methods for Systems of Conservation Laws: Spectral Collocation Approximations", to appear as ICASE - Report (NASA Langley, Hampton, VA).

A parallel algorithm for a three dimensional inverse acoustic scattering problem

Filippo Aluffi-Pentini

Dipartimento di metodi e modelli matematici per le scienze applicate
Università di Roma "La Sapienza" -00161 Roma- Italy

Emanuele Caglioti*

Istituto Nazionale di Alta Matematica "F. Severi"
Piazzale A. Moro 5 -00185 Roma- Italy

Luciano Misici

Dipartimento di Matematica e Fisica
Università di Camerino -62032 Camerino (MC)- Italy

Francesco Zirilli

Dipartimento di Matematica "G. Castelnuovo"
Università di Roma "La Sapienza" -00185 Roma- Italy

ABSTRACT: A numerical algorithm for a three dimensional inverse acoustic scattering problem is considered. From the knowledge of several far-field patterns of the Helmholtz equation a closed surface ∂D representing the boundary of the unknown obstacle D is reconstructed. The two dimensional surface ∂D is reconstructed by integrating in parallel several initial value problems for ordinary differential equations.

1. INTRODUCTION

Let $\mathbf{R}^3$ be the three dimensional euclidean space, $\underline{x} = (x, y, z) \in \mathbf{R}^3$ be a generic vector, $(\cdot, \cdot)$ will denote the euclidean scalar product and $\| \cdot \|$ the euclidean norm. Let $D \subset \mathbf{R}^3$ be a bounded simply connected domain with smooth boundary ∂D. Let

*   The research of this author has been made possible through the support and sponsorship of Elsag-Elettronica San Giorgio s.p.a.,Genova,to the graduate fellowship program of the Istituto Nazionale di Alta Matematica "F. Severi", Roma.

$u^i(\underline{x})$ be an incoming acoustic plane wave, that is

$$u^i(\underline{x}) = e^{ik(\underline{x},\underline{\alpha})} \tag{1.1}$$

where $k > 0$ is the wave number and $\underline{\alpha} \in \mathbf{R}^3$ is a fixed unit vector. Let us denote with $u^s(\underline{x})$ the acoustic field scattered by the obstacle D and with $u(\underline{x})$ the total acoustic field, that is

$$u(\underline{x}) = u^i(\underline{x}) + u^s(\underline{x}) \tag{1.2}$$

The direct acoustic scattering problem for an acoustically soft obstacle D is the following one:

Problem 1.1: Find $u(\underline{x})$ defined for $\underline{x} \in \mathbf{R}^3 \backslash D$ such that

$$\triangle u + k^2 u = 0 \quad in \ \mathbf{R}^3 \backslash D \tag{1.3}$$

$$u = 0 \quad on \ \partial D \tag{1.4}$$

$$\lim_{r \to \infty} r\{\frac{\partial u^s}{\partial r} - iku^s\} = 0 \tag{1.5}$$

where $\triangle = \frac{\partial^2}{\partial x^2} + \frac{\partial^2}{\partial y^2} + \frac{\partial^2}{\partial z^2}$ is the laplacian and $r = (x^2 + y^2 + z^2)^{1/2}$. We note that (1.5) is the Sommerfeld radiation condition at infinity. It can be shown (Colton and Kress,1983) that the scattered field $u^s(\underline{x})$ when $r \to \infty$ has the following expansion

$$u^s(\underline{x}) = \frac{e^{ikr}}{r} F(\hat{\underline{x}}, k, \underline{\alpha}) + O(\frac{1}{r^2}) \ ; \ r \to \infty \tag{1.6}$$

where $\hat{\underline{x}} = \frac{\underline{x}}{\|\underline{x}\|}$ and $F(\hat{\underline{x}}, k, \underline{\alpha})$ is called far field pattern associated to the scattered field $u^s(\underline{x})$. Let λ_n , $n = 1, 2, \ldots$,be the eigenvalues of the interior Dirichlet problem in D for the Helmholtz equation, $B = \{\underline{x} \in \mathbf{R}^3 \mid \|\underline{x}\| < 1\}$ and $\partial B = \{\underline{x} \in \mathbf{R}^3 \mid \|\underline{x}\| = 1\}$ be the boundary of B. The inverse acoustic scattering for an acoustically soft obstacle D is the following one:

Problem 1.2: Let $k^2 \neq \lambda_n$, $n = 1, 2, \ldots$,and Ω_1 , $\Omega_2 \subseteq \partial B$ be two given subsets of ∂B. From the knowledge of the far field patterns $F(\hat{\underline{x}}, k, \underline{\alpha})$, $\forall \underline{\alpha} \in \Omega_1$, $\forall \hat{\underline{x}} \in \Omega_2$, determine the boundary of the obstacle ∂D.

We observe that Ω_1 is the set of directions of the incoming waves and Ω_2 is the set of directions where the far field generated by the incoming waves is observed.
The inverse Problem 1.2 is of great importance in many applications such as underwater acoustic imaging, medical imaging, and has been recently considered by Colton and Monk (1984,1985,1986,1987) in a series of very interesting papers in the two and three dimensional case . In particular in Colton and Monk (1987) a numerical procedure to solve Poblem 1.2 is proposed.
The method we propose here is a refinement of the one proposed in Colton and Monk (1987) from the point of view of the accuracy and the amount of computation required. Our method is highly parallelizable. In section 2 we illustrate our method, in section 3 some numerical experience obtained with the method proposed in section 2 is shown.

2. THE ALGORITHM

Given D , $k>0$, let $\Omega_1 = \{\underline{\alpha}_i \in \partial B \mid i = 1, 2, ..., N\}$ be the set of directions of the incoming waves and let $\Omega_2 = \partial B$; the data of our problem are the far field patterns $F(\hat{\underline{x}}, k, \underline{\alpha}_i), i = 1, 2, ..., N$.

These far fields are obtained solving numerically the direct Problem 1.1 and we assume that their expression is approximated by a truncated Fourier series, that is

$$F(\hat{\underline{x}}, k, \underline{\alpha}_i) = \sum_{l=0}^{L_{max}} \sum_{m=0}^{l} F_{lm1}^i \gamma_l^m U_{lm}(\hat{\underline{x}}) + \sum_{l=1}^{L_{max}} \sum_{m=1}^{l} F_{lm2}^i \gamma_l^m V_{lm}(\hat{\underline{x}}) \qquad (2.1)$$

where $L_{max} \geq 0$ is given, if (θ, ϕ) are the polar angles, $U_{lm}(\hat{\underline{x}}) = P_l^m(\cos\theta)\cos m\phi$, $V_{lm}(\hat{\underline{x}}) = P_l^m(\cos\theta)\sin m\phi$ are the spherical harmonics, P_l^m are the Legendre polynomials, γ_l^m are normalization factors in $\mathbf{L}^2(\partial B)$ and

$$\hat{\underline{x}}(\theta, \phi) = \frac{\underline{x}}{\|\underline{x}\|} = (\sin\theta\cos\phi, \sin\theta\sin\phi, \cos\theta) \qquad (2.2)$$

The Fourier coefficients of F , $\{F_{lmk}^i\}_{k=1,2}$,are obtained by a method due to Kristensson and Waterman (1982).

From these data our computation proceeds in three steps:

Step 1 From the far field patterns to the Herglotz kernel.

Let $g(\hat{\underline{x}}) \in \mathbf{L}^2(\partial B)$ be the Herglotz kernel associated to the domain D, we have (Colton 1987)

$$\int_{\partial B} F(\hat{\underline{x}}, k, \underline{\alpha})\overline{g(\hat{\underline{x}})} ds(\hat{\underline{x}}) = 1, \ \forall \underline{\alpha} \in \partial B \qquad (2.3)$$

where $ds(\hat{\underline{x}})$ is the surface element of ∂B and $\overline{g}$ the complex conjugate of g. We assume for g the expression of a truncated Fourier expansion

$$g(\hat{\underline{x}}) = \sum_{l=0}^{L_g} \sum_{m=0}^{l} g_{lm1} \gamma_l^m U_{lm}(\hat{\underline{x}}) + \sum_{l=1}^{L_g} \sum_{m=1}^{l} g_{lm2} \gamma_l^m V_{lm}(\hat{\underline{x}}) \qquad (2.4)$$

where $0 \leq L_g \leq L_{max}$. Imposing (2.3) between (2.1) and (2.4) and using the orthogonality properties of the spherical harmonics we have

$$\sum_{l=0}^{L_g} \sum_{m=0}^{l} F_{lm1}^i \overline{g}_{lm1} + \sum_{l=1}^{L_g} \sum_{m=1}^{l} F_{lm2}^i \overline{g}_{lm2} = 1, \ i = 1, 2, ..., N \qquad (2.5)$$

So that the Fourier coefficients $\{g_{lm1}\}, \{g_{lm2}\}$ of g are determined by minimizing the quadratic functional

$$I(g) = \sum_{\{i|\underline{\alpha}_i \in \Omega_1\}} \left| \sum_{l=0}^{L_g} \sum_{m=0}^{l} F_{lm1}^i \overline{g}_{lm1} + \sum_{l=1}^{L_g} \sum_{m=1}^{l} F_{lm2}^i \overline{g}_{lm2} - 1 \right|^2 \qquad (2.6)$$

Step 2 From the Herglotz kernel g to the Herglotz wave function v.

Let $\underline{y} \in \mathbf{R}^3$, the Herglotz wave function $v(k\underline{y})$ is the Fourier transform of the Herglotz kernel $g(\underline{\hat{x}})$, that is

$$v(k\underline{y}) = \int_{\partial B} g(\underline{\hat{x}}) e^{ik(\underline{\hat{x}}, \underline{y})} ds(\underline{\hat{x}}) \tag{2.7}$$

Since $g(\underline{\hat{x}})$ is given by (2.4) we have

$$v(k\underline{y}) = \sum_{l=0}^{L_g} \sum_{m=0}^{l} g_{lm1} \gamma_l^m Q_{lm}(k\underline{y}) + \sum_{l=1}^{L_g} \sum_{m=1}^{l} g_{lm2} \gamma_l^m R_{lm}(k\underline{y}) \tag{2.8}$$

where

$$Q_{lm}(k\underline{y}) = \int_{\partial B} U_{lm}(\underline{\hat{x}}) e^{ik(\underline{\hat{x}}, \underline{y})} ds(\underline{\hat{x}}) \tag{2.9}$$

$$R_{lm}(k\underline{y}) = \int_{\partial B} V_{lm}(\underline{\hat{x}}) e^{ik(\underline{\hat{x}}, \underline{y})} ds(\underline{\hat{x}}) \tag{2.10}$$

The integrals (2.9),(2.10) can be evaluated in terms of spherical Bessel functions of the first kind $j_m(r)$, and their derivatives. We note that the spherical Bessel functions are elementary functions (for exemple $j_0(r) = \frac{\sin r}{r}$). Moreover we note that we have obtained an analytic expression for v and that in a similar way analytic expressions can be obtained for $\frac{\partial v}{\partial r}, \frac{\partial v}{\partial \theta}, \frac{\partial v}{\partial \phi}$ that is the derivatives of v with respect to the polar variables. For later convenience we split v in real and imaginary part and use polar variables

$$v(k\underline{y}) = v^R(kr, \theta, \phi) + iv^I(kr, \theta, \phi) \tag{2.11}$$

<u>Step 3</u>   From the Herglotz wave function v to ∂D. We assume that the origin $O \in D$ and that exists $a > 0, b > 0$ and a function $f(\theta, \phi)$ with $a \leq f \leq b$ such that $\partial D = \{(r, \theta, \phi) \in \mathbf{R}^3 \mid r = f(\theta, \phi), 0 \leq \theta < \pi, 0 \leq \phi < 2\pi\}$. If D is an Herglotz domain we have (Colton and Monk 1987)

$$v(kf, \theta, \phi) + \frac{e^{-ikf}}{kf} = 0, \; 0 \leq \theta < \pi , \; 0 \leq \phi < 2\pi \tag{2.12}$$

Equation (2.12) defines f implicitly as a function of θ and ϕ. We note that the set where (2.12) is satisfied is a rather complicated set that contains ∂D as a subset. From (2.12) differentiating with respect to θ and ϕ we have

$$\left[k\frac{\partial v}{\partial r} - (if + \frac{1}{k})\frac{e^{-ikf}}{f^2} \right] \frac{df}{d\theta} + \frac{\partial v}{\partial \theta} = 0, \; 0 \leq \theta < \pi , \; 0 \leq \phi < 2\pi \tag{2.13}$$

$$\left[k\frac{\partial v}{\partial r} - (if + \frac{1}{k})\frac{e^{-ikf}}{f^2} \right] \frac{df}{d\phi} + \frac{\partial v}{\partial \phi} = 0, \; 0 \leq \theta < \pi , \; 0 \leq \phi < 2\pi \tag{2.14}$$

In order to obtain $f(\theta, \phi)$ we proceed as follows:

(i) for fixed θ and ϕ, let $\theta = \phi = 0$, we solve (2.12), that is we solve

$$v^R(kf, 0, 0) + \frac{\cos kf}{kf} = 0 \tag{2.15}$$

and we verify that the solution found, f_{00}, satisfies

$$v^I(kf_{00}, 0, 0) - \frac{\sin kf_{00}}{kf_{00}} = 0 \qquad (2.16)$$

We note that (2.15) is a non-linear equation in one unknown

(ii) given f_{00} we solve for $0 \leq \theta < \pi$ the differential equation for $\frac{df(\theta, 0)}{d\theta}$ obtained by taking the real part of equation (2.13) with initial condition

$$f(0, 0) = f_{00} \qquad (2.17)$$

Let $f_0(\theta), 0 \leq \theta < \pi$, be the solution found we verify than for $f_0(\theta)$ we have

$$v^I(kf_0(\theta), \theta, 0) - \frac{\sin kf_0(\theta)}{kf_0(\theta)} = 0, \ 0 \leq \theta < \pi \qquad (2.18)$$

(iii) given $f_0(\theta)$ we solve for $0 \leq \phi < 2\pi$ the differential equation for $\frac{df}{d\phi}$ obtained by taking the real part of (2.14) with initial condition

$$f(\theta, 0) = f_0(\theta) \qquad (2.19)$$

and we verify than for $f(\theta, \phi)$ we have

$$v^I(kf, \theta, \phi) - \frac{\sin kf}{kf} = 0, \ 0 \leq \theta < \pi, \ 0 \leq \phi < 2\pi \qquad (2.20)$$

The differential problems considered in (ii),(iii) are initial value problems for a scalar differential equations and are solved numerically via a Runge-Kutta method. The problem considered in (iii) is performed only for a finite number of θ. We note that if the obstacle is cylindrically symmetric with respect to the z-axis,(iii) is not needed and the problem is solved after performing (i),(ii).

Moreover (i),(ii),(iii) are fully parallelizable;in fact: in (i) many roots of (2.15) that satisfy (2.16) can be found independently from different initial guesses. Since the set of zeroes of (2.12) is a complicated set that contains ∂D in proper sense this may be useful. In (ii) the differential equation considered can be integrated independently from the initial conditions obtained in (i). Only the trajectories that exists for $0 \leq \theta < \pi$ must be considered for (iii). Finally in (iii) the differential equation considered can be integrated independently for different values of θ and different initial conditions obtained in (ii). Only the trajectories that generate a closed surface should be considered.

3. NUMERICAL EXPERIENCE

In Fig. 1,2,3,4,5,6,7,8,9,10 are shown the numerical results obtained on some simple geometries with the algorithm described in section 2. The objects considered are all cylindrically symmetric because at this point we are able of generating the far field patterns only of cylindrically symmetric objects. The set Ω_1 is a uniform grid in $(\cos\theta, \phi)$ of 49 points on ∂B together with the north and south poles. All the figures are drawn using 37×37 values of θ and ϕ. In particular in Fig. 1,2,3,4,5,6 is shown the reconstruction of some convex objects.

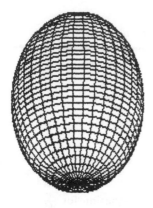

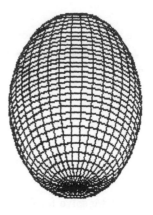

Fig.1   Original
Prolate ellipsoid $x^2 + y^2 + (\frac{2}{3}z)^2 = 1$

Fig.2   Reconstructed
$k = 1, L_{max} = 8, L_g = 6$

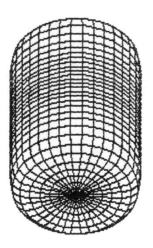

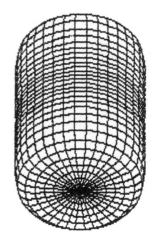

Fig.3   Original
Long cylinder $(x^2 + y^2)^5 + (\frac{2}{3}z)^{10} = 1$

Fig.4   Reconstructed
$k = 3, L_{max} = 8, L_g = 6$

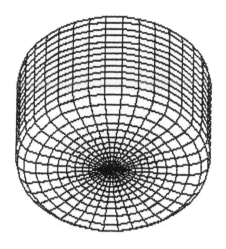

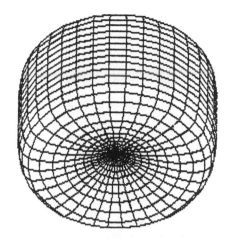

Fig.5   Original
Short cylinder $((\frac{2}{3}x)^2 + (\frac{2}{3}y)^2)^5 + z^{10} = 1$

Fig.6   Reconstructed
$k = 3, L_{max} = 8, L_g = 6$

In Fig. 7,8,9,10 is shown the reconstruction of some non-convex objects. The reconstruction of these objects is not completely satisfactory for $\theta = 0$ and $\theta = \pi$ since the far fields used are not good enough. This may be due to the fact that the objects are non-convex so that the reconstruction is more difficult. To avoid these difficulties we integrate the differential equation (2.13) for $\epsilon \leq \theta \leq \pi - \epsilon$ with $\epsilon = 0.1$ instead of $0 \leq \theta < \pi$.

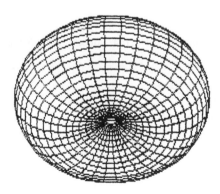

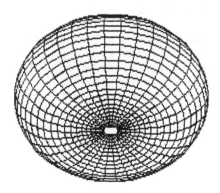

Fig.7   Original
The cushion $r(\theta) = 1 - 0.5\cos 2\theta$

Fig.8   Reconstructed
$k = 3, L_{max} = 8, L_g = 6$

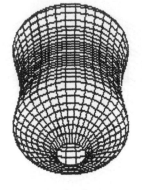

Fig.9   Original   Fig.10   Reconstructed
The peanut $r^2(\theta) = \frac{9}{4}(\cos^2\theta + \frac{1}{4}\sin^2\theta)$ $k = 3, L_{max} = 8, L_g = 6$

The computations are performed on an IBM-3090 with VMS operating system and the figures are drawn using the GRAFMATIC package on a personal computer AT-IBM with ega-color graphic card. The results obtained so far are only preliminary but in our opinion very encouraging.

Acknowledgements

One of us (F.Z.) gratefully acknowledgesthe help of Prof. D. Colton and Prof. P. Monk that have given to him a copy of the computer program used to obtain the numerical experience described in Colton and Monk (1987).

REFERENCES

Colton D., Kress R. 1983,*Integral Equation Methods in Scattering Theory*, New York, J. Wiley & Sons , p.72 .
Colton D.,1984,*SIAM Review*,**26**,323.
Colton D., Monk P.,1985,*SIAM J. Appl. Math.*,**45**,1039.
Colton D., Monk P.,1986,*SIAM J. Appl. Math.*,**46**,506.
Colton D., Monk P.,1987,*SIAM J. Sci. Stat. Comput.*,**8**,278.
Kristensson G., Waterman P.,1982,*J. Acoust. Soc. Amer.*,**72**,1612.

Nonlinear optimization codes for real time solution of large scale problems: a case study on the parallel vector supercomputers CRAY X-MP and IBM 3090/VF

D Conforti, L Grandinetti

Systems Department, University of Calabria, Cosenza, Italy

ABSTRACT : In this paper the implementation of nonlinear programming algorithms on vector supercomputers CRAY X-MP and IBM 3090/VF is taken into consideration. A problem of great practical interest, related to the optimal scheduling of electric power in a network has been chosen as test problem. Analysis of numerical results suggests that the computation performed on vector supercomputers provides a satisfactorily efficient solution of the proposed problem, in spite of its severe computational characteristics.

1. INTRODUCTION

To develop nonlinear programming codes for a vector supercomputing environment is a key issue for solving challenging large size problems, especially when a real-time solution is requested. In fact many important real-life problems, arising from scientific and engineering applications, are intractable with available algorithms on serial processors.

On this basis, a realistic objective to achieve at present is that of an appropriate choice of those existing algorithms whose algebraic and data structure is suitable for vectorization or even for higher forms of parallelism.

The main goal of this paper is, in fact, the selection and testing of a number of nonlinear programming codes which are theoretical very sound and, in addition, possess features conveniently exploitable in a vector processing environment.

The need for these algorithms to compute the partial derivatives of the problem functions (objective function and constraint functions) suggested also the introduction of an automatic differentiation technique. The technique used is based on the Rall scheme, which avoids to code partial derivatives, with a remarkable gain in efficiency and reliability for large problems without any particular structure.

Computational testing of algorithms has been carried out on a large scale, highly nonlinear problem, representing an optimization model of the electric power scheduling in a network.

This computational experience, following a previous study of Grandinetti and Conforti (1988a) on a medium size analogous problem , shows that even on a very difficult large size problem, it is possible to achieve on vector supercomputers satisfactory results.

On the other hand it is given evidence, by comparing performances, that the same problem is intractable on a serial mainframe computer.

Two additional new aspetcs are focused in this paper. First of all a restructured version of one code is presented and discussed, with the aim to show the advantages of designing codes matched to the vector processing capabilities. Secondly, a performance evaluation analysis of two algorithms is presented, based on "a priori" knowledge of the problem structure and of some parameters characterizing the amount of vector and floating-point operations in the algorithm. It is shown that this analysis, although only indicative, may be useful in selecting the best algorithm (in terms of computing time) for solving the given problem on a wide range of machines.

2.   NONLINEAR OPTIMIZATION ALGORITHMS FOR VECTOR PROCESSING

A basic quality for a nonlinear programming algorithm devoted to face large problems and provide solutions in real-time, is that of possessing very sound theoretical properties (e.g. convergence proof) together with the capability to get successful results without any extraoverhead in coding and numerical computing. Several general purpose algorithms suitable to deal with highly nonlinear constraints exist. However the high dimension of the problems to solve and the requirement of its real - time solution, create a "bottle - neck" to the computational efficiency which often makes them intractable on a conventional serial machine. Therefore it is crucial to select algorithms which perform particularly well on commercially available supercomputers.
A class of algorithms possessing both theoretically sound properties and algebraic structure for vector processing is shortly reviewed in the sequel.

2.1 The Recursive Quadratic Programming Method (RQPM)

For solving the following general nonlinear programming problem:

$$\min f(x) , \quad f: \mathbb{R}^n \to \mathbb{R} , \quad f \in C^1 \tag{2.1.1}$$

s.t.

$$c_i(x) = 0, \quad i = 1,\ldots,m'$$
$$c_i(x) \geq 0 , \quad i = m' + 1,\ldots,m, \; c_i : \mathbb{R}^n \to \mathbb{R}, \; c_i \in C^1, \; \forall i,$$

one of the most promising method is the Recursive Quadratic Programming Method (RQPM).
This method is based on the iterative scheme:

$$x_{k+1} = x_k + \alpha_k d_k$$

where:
  x_k current estimate of the solution;
  d_k search direction computed by the solution of a quadratic subprogram;
  α_k steplength parameter for forcing convergence of sequence $\{x_k\}$ to the
     solution x^* .

The general formulation of the quadratic subprogram at the current iteration k is:

$$\min \; Q(d) = f(x_k) + d^T \nabla f(x_k) + \frac{1}{2} d^T B_k d$$

s.t.

$$L_i(d) = 0 , \quad i = 1,\ldots,m'$$

$$L_i(d) \geq 0 , \quad i = m' + 1,\ldots,m,$$

where $L_i(d)$ is a suitable linear approximation of the original constraints. The matrix B_k intendes to approximate in quasi - Newton sense the second derivatives matrix of the Lagrangian function associated to the original problem. It involves the Lagrangian multipliers of the quadratic subprogram; in a sense, they can be viewed as an approximation of those associated to the original problem.

According to the procedure for computing the quadratic subprogram and the steplength parameter, different approaches have been studied.

Han - Powell approach (Han 1977, Powell 1978). The search direction d_k is computed at each iteration, by solving a quadratic subprogram characterized by the following linear approximation of the constraints:

$$L_i(d_k) = c_i(x_k) + d^T \nabla c_i (x_k) = 0 \ , \quad i = 1,\ldots, m'$$

$$L_i(d_k) = c_i(x_k) + d^T \nabla c_i (x_k) \geq 0 \ , \quad i = m' + 1,\ldots, m.$$

The steplength parameter is provided by minimizing the following l_1 penalty function:

$$W_k = f(k) + \sum_{i=1}^{m'} r_i \mid c_i(x) \mid + \sum_{i=m'+1}^{m} r_i \mid \min \left(0, c_i(x)\right) \mid.$$

The non-negative parameters r_i are chosen and revised at each iteration in a proper way to guarantee the descent property of the penalty function along the search direction.

Biggs approach (Biggs 1985). In this version of RQPM, the linear constraints of the quadratic subprogram assume the following structure:

$$L_i(d_k) = c_i(x_k) + d^T \nabla c_i (x_k) = - \frac{1}{2} r_k (\mu_i - \lambda_i), \quad i = 1,\ldots, m'$$

$$L_i(d_k) = c_i(x_k) + d^T \nabla c_i (x_k) \geq - \frac{1}{2} r_k (\mu_i - \lambda_i), \quad i = m' + 1,\ldots, m.$$

In this formulation, μ_i are the Lagrangian multipliers associated to the solution of the current quadratic subprogram and λ_i are a suitable estimate of the multipliers of the original problem. Both these parameters are revised at each iteration. The scalar r_k is a penalty parameter which also plays a role in the line search strategy.

An interesting feature of the Biggs approach is that the search direction is easily computed by solving an appropriate system of linear equations.

The steplength parameter is computed by an approximate minimization of the following augmented Lagrangian function:

$$M_k(\lambda) = f(x) + \frac{1}{r} \left\{ \sum_{i=1}^{m'} \left(c_i(x) - \frac{1}{2} r\lambda_i \right)^2 + \sum_{i=m'+1}^{m} \left[\min\left(0, c_i(x) - \frac{1}{2} r\lambda_i \right) \right]^2 \right\}$$

The penalty parameter r_k is revised at each iteration to guarantee a satisfactory line search.

Schittkowski approach (Schittkowski 1983). The search direction is computed in the same way of the Han - Powell approach. As regard the procedure for computing the steplength parameter, Schittkowski proposed the use of the following augmented Lagrangian function:

$$V_k(x) = f(x) - \sum_{i=1}^{m'}\left[\lambda_i \; c_i(x) - \frac{1}{2} r_i \; c_i^2(x)\right] - \sum_j\left[\lambda_j \; c_j(x) - \frac{1}{2} r_j \; c_j^2(x)\right] -$$

$$\sum_l \left[\frac{1}{2} \frac{\lambda_l^2}{r_l}\right],$$

for any $m' + 1 \le j \le m$ for which $c_j(x) \le \dfrac{\lambda_j}{r_j}$ and for any $m' + 1 \le l \le$ m for which $c_l(x) > \dfrac{\lambda_l}{r_l}$.

The parameters r_i can be selected in a way to guarantee an efficient line search.

The Schittkowski approach has proved very effective expecially in some difficult situations related to highly nonlinear problems (Powell 1984).

The following remarks motivate the choice of the RQPM.
The RQP algorithms are characterized by strong theoretical properties (in fact fast local convergence is proved). In terms of function and gradient evaluation the RQPM is cheaper than other methods. They are suitable to deal with highly nonlinear constraints. Their algebraic structure are appropriate for large scale vector processing implementation. These algorithms have proved to be very effective on the basis of a large amount of experimental computation. Finally, differences among the codes considered may allow to deal with different type of problems.
It is worth noting that the above method is based on gradient computation of both the objective and constraint functions. Therefore it may be very cumbersome and error prone to code the gradient expressions especially when non-structured very large size functions are involved in the problem.
Therefore it is important to compute the numerical value of the partial derivatives automatically, without any explicit coding of their analytic expressions. An implementation based on the Rall scheme (Rall 1981) has been used in conjuction with the algorithms described above.

3. TESTING ON LARGE SIZE ENGINEERING PROBLEMS

It is particularly meaningful to test the RQP algorithms on a very difficult optimization problem which arises from the engineering context and which has proved intractable with standard methods and conventional serial mainframes computers.
The problem considered here is that of computing the optimal power scheduling in a large electric network; in particular we considered the economic dispatching of thermoelectric production .
The specific formulation of the problem is the following:

$$\min \left\{ P_g^T \; AP_g + b^T \; P_g + c\right\} \tag{3.1}$$

s.t.

$$P_g(i) - P_d(i) - V(i) \sum_{j=1}^{q}\left\{ V(j)Y(i,j)\cos\left[\delta(i)-\delta(j)-\Theta(i,j)\right] \right\} = 0$$

$$Q_g(i) - Q_d(i) - V(i) \sum_{j=1}^{q} \left\{ V(j) Y(i,j) \sin \left[\delta(i) - \delta(j) - \Theta(i,j) \right] \right\} = 0, \quad i = 1, \ldots, NN$$

$$S^M(i) - P_g^2(i) - Q_g^2(i) \geq 0 \qquad\qquad\qquad i = 1, \ldots, Ng$$

$$I^M(k) - \left\{ V^2(i) + V^2(j) - 2V(i)V(j)\cos\left[\delta(i) - \delta(j) \right] \right\} Y^2(i,j) \geq 0$$

$$-\delta^M(k) \leq \delta(i) - \delta(j) \leq \delta^M(k) \qquad\qquad\qquad k = 1, \ldots, NL$$

$$P_g^l(i) \leq P_g(i) \leq P_g^u(i) \qquad\qquad\qquad i = 1, \ldots, Ng$$

$$Q_g^l(i) \leq Q_g(i) \leq Q_g^u(i) \qquad\qquad\qquad i = 1, \ldots, Nr$$

$$V^l(i) \leq V(i) \leq V^u(i) \qquad\qquad\qquad i = 1, \ldots, NN$$

$$\delta^l(i) \leq \delta(i) \leq \delta^u(i) \qquad\qquad\qquad i = 1, \ldots, NN$$

The electric network is characterized by the total number of nodes (NN), the number of lines (NL), the number of active generation nodes (Ng) and the number of reactive generation nodes (Nr).

The electric quantities Pg (active power generated), Qg (reactive power generated), V (magnitude of nodal voltage) and δ (phase of nodal voltage) represent the decision variables for the optimization problem. The objective function is a quadratic function approximating the cost of fuel at thermal plants in terms of active power generated. The constraint functions represent energy balance and security and management conditions on the network.

The typical features of the above problem are the following:
- the number of variables and constraints are very large;
- many constraints are inequalities;
- the problem functions are highly nonlinear;
- need for a real - time solution.

Another aspect to point out is that the electrical model taken into consideration is one of the most general and difficult model among those typically formulated for the solution of optimization problems in the electric power systems; more details may be found in the papers by Grandinetti and Conforti (1988a), (1988b) and (1988c).

4. NUMERICAL EXPERIMENTS

The numerical experiments were carried out on the following machines:

AMDAHL 5840 - MVS / JES2 V. 1.3.6 - COMPILER VS FORTRAN 4.1 : serial mainframe, central memory 16 Mbytes, performance 7 MIPS.

CRAY X-MP/48   COS 1.15 - COMPILER CFT 1.15 : multiprocessor machine (four processors of pipeline type), central memory 64 Mbytes, clock cycle 8.5 nsec.

IBM 3090/VF 200 - VM/XA - COMPILER VS FORTRAN VERSION 2 : multiprocessor machine (two processors with vector facility), central memory 16 Mbytes, clock cycle 18.5 nsec.

A medium - size system, the American Electric Power Network 57 - Bus test system (Freris and Sasson 1968), has already been studied by Grandinetti and Conforti (1988b) on the three above machines.

The electric model is characterized by 57 nodes, 78 lines, 4 nodes of active power generation and 7 nodes of reactive power generation. The nonlinear optimization problem based on the model (3.1) is characterized by 124 decision variables and 600 constraints.

The numerical results are reported in Table 1.

TABLE 1

CODE	AMDAHL 5840 Sec	CRAY X-MP			IBM 3090/VF		
		V-ON Sec	V-OF Sec	SPEED UP	V-ON Sec	V-OF Sec	SPEED UP
CODE 1	1459	42.12	152.2	3.61	96.47	124.4	1.29
CODE 2	1264	21.55	130.5	6.05	61.25	117.5	1.92
CODE 3	1274	34.53	125.4	3.63	79.95	105	1.31

The figures represent CPU time in seconds.

CODE 1   : Han - Powell algorithm;

CODE 2   : Biggs algorithm;

CODE 3   : Schittkowski algorithm;

V - ON   : vector mode computation;

V - OFF   : scalar mode computation

SPEED - UP   : CPU times ratio V-OFF/V-ON.

A new large - size test problem has been considered in this paper. The American Electric Power Network 118 - Bus test system (Silvestri 1987) is characterized by 118 nodes, 179 lines, 34 nodes of active generation and 54 nodes of reactive generation.

The nonlinear optimization problem involves 323 decision variables and 1419 constraints.

The numerical results are reported on Table 2. It is important to point out that high accuracy (10^{-7}) on the active constraints and Kuhn - Tucker conditions has been considered in the computation.

TABLE 2

CODE	AMDAHL 5840	CRAY X-MP			IBM 3090/VF		
		V-ON Sec	V-OFF Sec	SPEED UP	V-ON Sec	V-OFF Sec	SPEED UP
CODE 1	18^h	1803	7568	4.2	5466	7080	1.3
CODE 2		869	7579	8.7			

In this case the choice of CODE 1 and CODE 2 is justified by the fact that CODE 1 and CODE 3 have a quite similar behaviour on this type of problem. Moreover the CODE 2 has been used only on the CRAY; in fact, although the Biggs algorithm seems more efficient and more valuable for vector computing, the computation of the search direction may tend to be numerically unstable.

Some remarks about the numerical results. The performance ratio (speed - up) improves for the large size problem, confirming the advantages of vectorization when the dimension of the problem (vector length) increases.

In the case of CRAY, the speed - up ratios confirm that the algebraic structure of the algorithms and the data structures satisfactorily match the vector computing resources.

The behaviour on IBM indicates that a deeper restructuring and optimizing of the program is needed to get higher performances.

Finally the good behaviour of the algorithms is proved by the fact that, in spite of the large scale and high nonlinearity of the problems, the convergence was successfully achieved in any case.

5. A MODIFIED CODE OPTIMIZED FOR VECTOR PROCESSING

With the aim to get better performances on vector processors, we have tried to optimize the CODE 1, based on the Han - Powell algorithm. The numerical experiences were carried out on the CRAY system, using the large - size electric network as a test problem.

The motivation of this choice lies on the fact that the Han - Powell algorithm seems much more robust and reliable than the Biggs algorithm.

An appropriate strategy to maximize the performance of an existing program can be based on the following aspects:

(i)   analysis of the code behaviour , on the basis of program and data organization;

(ii) detecting critical "kernels" in the code, e.g. portion of code which demand a large computational effort;

(iii) restructuring and optimizing these "kernels" on the basis of their features.

In the case of Han - Powell algorithm, the quadratic subprogram highly affects the computation. In fact, for the solution of large - size problem, the partial CPU time devoted to the calculation of the search direction takes the 99% of the whole CPU time. Hence it is worthwhile to restructure and optimize the quadratic subprogram in order to get lower CPU time.

Different tools are available for developing an optimized code which fits the vector features of the machine.

In some cases it is very simple to vectorize a DO LOOP. In fact a suitable "driving" of the vector compiler (e.g. appropriate direttives to the compiler) can force the vectorization, typically in the presence of apparent data dependencies.

Another important aspect is to avoid a large amount of memory reference operations. In fact, keeping temporary results into vector registers save much more time, avoiding start - up delay, bank conflicts, etc..This can be done by suitable unrolling of the DO LOOPS (Dongarra and Hinds 1979).

However a systematic approach in restructuring an existing code can be based on the use of the Basic Linear Algebra Subprograms (BLAS) (Lawson et al 1979), allowing an high degree of optimization of algebraic operations involving vectors and matrices.

Using these kind of tools, new numerical experiments have been carried out on CRAY X-MP, solving the large - size electric problem. The numerical results are reported in Table 3.

TABLE 3

CODE	CRAY X-MP				
	V- ON A Modified Code Sec	V-ON B Original Code Sec	V-OFF C Original Code Sec	SPEED UP B/A	SPEED UP A/B
CODE 1	953	1803	7579	1.9	7.85

The figure in the column marked A represents the CPU time in seconds in the case of vector mode execution of the modified code.

In the columns B and C are reported the CPU times of the original code in vector mode and scalar mode respectively.

The speed - up ratios compare the vector execution of the modified code versus the vector and scalar execution of the original code.

The figures reported prove a remarkable benefits obtained   by   the code restructuring.

6. AN EXAMPLE OF PERFORMANCE EVALUATION TOOL

With the aim to achieve a compact representation of the behaviour of Han - Powell and Biggs algorithms on different vector computing architectures, we used the $n_{1/2}$ - method (Hockney 1988), as a performance evaluation tool.

By the $n_{1/2}$ - method it is possible to determine the relative performances of different algorithms on different models of computer architectures, solving problems with wide range of dimensions.

Following Hockney, a generic algorithm suitable for vector processing environment can be modelled as a sequence of   q   vector operations, each of length n_i , i = 1, ...,q.

On the basis of the relation $t = r_\infty^{-1} (n + n_{1/2})$,   (6.1)

which represents the time to compute a single arithmetic operation on a vector of length n, the total time to compute the q vector operations can be found by the relation

$$T = \sum_{i=1}^{q} r_{\infty}^{-1}(n_i + n_{1/2}) \tag{6.2}$$

The parameters r_{∞} and $n_{1/2}$ represent, respectively, the maximum performance in Mflops and the vector length required to reach the half of the maximum performance.
The expression (6.2) can be rewritten as

$$T = r_{\infty}^{-1}(s + n_{1/2}\, q) \tag{6.3}$$

where $s = \sum_{i=1}^{q} n_i$ is the total amount of floating point operations.
When two or more algorithms have to be compared, the relation (6.3) must be evaluated. In particular s and q must be identified.
Equalizing the time expressions (6.3) in the case, for instance, of two algorithms A and B, it is possible to obtain the following relation:

$$n_{1/2} = \frac{s_B - s_A}{q_A - q_B} \tag{6.4}$$

The expression (6.4) represents a nonlinear function of the problem size (e.g. order of matrices, number of variables, etc.). In the plane $(n, n_{1/2})$ the (6.4) determines regions in which one of the two or more algorithms has better performance. Since the parameter $n_{1/2}$ represent the architectural model, by this way it is possible to find the best algorithm on a specific architecture, solving the given problem.
In the case of Han - Powell and Biggs algorithms the (6.3) becomes, respectively (see Grandinetti and Conforti 1988c for more details):

$$T_P = r_{\infty}^{-1}\left(115n^2 + 25n + n_{1/2}(33n + 13)\right) \tag{6.5}$$

$$T_B = r_{\infty}^{-1}\left(\frac{1}{2}n^3 + 30n^2 + 52n + n_{1/2}(n^2 + 26)\right) \tag{6.6}$$

Hence the (6.4) becomes:

$$n_{1/2} = \frac{\frac{1}{2}n^3 - 85n^2 + 27n}{-n^2 + 16n - 13} \tag{6.7}$$

which is drawn on the Figure 1.

The curve drawn in Figure 1, divides the plane $(n, n_{1/2})$ in two regions, denoted by P and B . In the P region the Han-Pawell algorithm has better performance, whereas in the B region the Biggs algorithm has better performance. Assuming the average values 52 and 68 for $n_{1/2}$ in the case, respectively, of CRAY X-MP and IBM 3090/VF, we note that Biggs algorithm performes better for solving the two electric problems considered in this paper. As a matter of fact, this is confirmed by numerical results.
However it is important to point out that this performance analysis is quite approximated. Only the vector part of the codes has been considered, neglecting the scalar part. This analysis aims to give an indicative prediction of the behaviour of the algorithms.

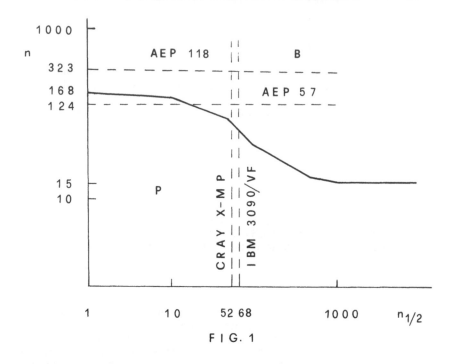

FIG. 1

7. CONCLUDING REMARKS

In this paper we identified nonlinear programming algorithms theoretically very sound and naturally suitable for vector computing. In fact the figures of performance obtained on a large scale, challenging, real - world problem (the optimal management of an electric power system), seem very satisfactory.

This confirms that different kind of engineering problems, in which a real - time solution is a difficult requirement to achieve, can be successfully approached via supercomputing techniques.

In this context the choice of suitable algorithms represent a crucial problem to face. In this paper it has been possible to prove that a code based on Recursive Quadratic Programming algorithm can be successfully optimized for vector computing, with the aim to get better performance. Moreover, the availability of a performance evaluation tool, like the $n_{1/2}$ - method, may be very important for a predective analysis, although approximated, of the behaviour of different algorithms on different architectural models, given a specific problem to solve.

8. REFERENCES

Biggs M C 1985 *Technical Report* **160** Numerical Optimization Centre Hatfield Polytechnic England

Dongarra J J and Hinds A R 1979 *Software-Practice and Experience* **9** 3

Freris L L and Sasson A M 1968 *Proc. of IEE* **115** 10

Grandinetti L and Conforti D 1988a *Mathematical Programming Study* (in printing)

Grandinetti L and Conforti D 1988b *Proc. Int. Conf. on Systems Science and Engineering* ed Cheng Weimin (Beijing: International Academic Publishers) pp 397-401

Grandinetti L Conforti D 1988c *Lecture Notes in Economics and Mathematical Systems* **304** eds Kurzhanski A, Neumann K and Pallaschke D (Berlin: Springer-Verlag) pp 69-85

Grandinetti L and Conforti D 1988d *Proc. of IMACS Symposium on System Modelling and Simulation* eds Tzafestas S, Eisinberg A and Carotenuto L (Amsterdam: Elsevier Science Publishers) (to appear)

Han S P 1977 *Journal of Optimization Theory and Applications* **22** 3

Hockney R W 1988 *Parallel Computers 2* (Bristol: Adam Hilger) pp 439-446

Lawson C, Hanson R, Kincaid D and Krogh F 1979 *ACM Transaction on Mathematical Software* **5** 3

Powell M J D 1978 *Lecture Notes in Mathematics* **630** ed Watson G A (Berlin: Springer-Verlag) pp 144-157

Powell M J D 1984 *Technical Report DAMTP NA6* University of Cambridge England

Rall L B 1981 *Lecture Notes in Computer Science* **120** (Berlin: Springer-Verlag)

Schittkowski K 1983 *Mathematische Operations Forshung und Statistik, Ser. Optimization* **14** 2

Silvestri A 1987 *Private Communication*

Vector and parallel performances of minimization algorithms based on homogeneous models

A. Peretti - C. Sutti

Mathematical Institute - University of Verona - Italy

ABSTRACT: Recent advances in nonlinear optimization evince two priorities, namely to define algorithms reliable for wide classes of objective functions and suitable to supercomputers.
In order to satisfy both requests, we consider minimization methods based on homogeneous models, which are proved convergent for continuous and almost everywhere derivable functions and which present at each iteration many parallelisable tasks. In implementing these procedures, a new parallel matrix factorization has been used.
The vector and parallel resources of the new class of algorithms have been tested on ALLIANT FX/40 and CRAY X-MP/48.

Key words : Unconstrained optimization, nonlinear programming, parallel computing.

1. INTRODUCTION

The class of minimization algorithms that is considered in this paper has been defined keeping in mind some important requirements in mathematical programming and numerical computation: particularly, about optimization, to have robust procedures, that is reliable for a large class of objective functions and, in what concerns computations, to develop application software suitable for the use of parallel computers.
These algorithms have been proved to be convergent for continuous functions, almost everywhere derivable and locally satisfying homogeneous models rather than quadratic.
The analytical aspects of these methods are presented and discussed by Cupello and Sutti [to appear], as well as the characteristics of the objective functions, pointing out that they may have non stationary minima and non convex nor star-shaped at any point level sets.

The idea these algorithms are based on goes back to a paper of Jacobson and Oksman [1972] who proposed a finite procedure which minimizes homogeneous functions with degree more than one, by moving the optimization problem into the solution of a system of linear equations deduced from Eulero's theorem.

By Jacobson et al. [1972,1974] the method is extended to twice continuously differentiable functions with only one stationary minimum. A Householder-like method is first proposed to find the solution of the linear system; this is replaced then by Kowalik and Ramakrishnan [1976] with an LU-like method. In these works for the line search either the Fletcher and Powell's cubic interpolation or the Armijo's rule is used.

By the approach suggested by Jacobson and Oksman [1972], Cupello and Sutti [to appear] define a class of descent, one-step in memory, gradiental, homogeneous models algorithms. These procedures do not require restarts, approximate gradients and neither exact nor inexact line searches. Moreover they appear to be good candidates for parallelism, requiring at each iteration to determine several points and in these points to compute function and gradient and also to solve a system of linear equations, for which algorithms with high level of parallelism exist.

In the below implementation of the minimization procedures, the solution of the system is computed by using a method for matrix factorization recently developped by Cupello and Sutti [1986]; this method, previously tested by Sutti and Peretti [1987], appears to be vector and multivector efficient.

In this paper the vectorial and parallel behaviour of the new class of minimization algorithms is presented and discussed. In particular, in order to produce application software for optimization on parallel systems and since CRAY X-MP/48 and ALLIANT FX/40 are available for us, tests have been done on these machines.

In section 2, after a short description of the new basic minimization procedure and some significant variants of it, the implementing codes are described. Section 3 is dedicated to the subroutine which implements the algorithm for the solution of the linear system: this is an interesting code for linear algebra packages on the mentioned computers.

In section 4 the test objective functions are presented and in section 5 the results from the experiments on the computers used are shown. A comparative analysis between executions of the codes on the CRAY and the ALLIANT is performed.

2.   THE MINIMIZATION PROCEDURES

In this section we first give a short description of the basic scheme of the new minimization procedure and we propose then some different variants of it. The new class of algorithms is based on homogeneous models of the form

$$(1) \qquad F(x) = \alpha + (x-\beta)^T H(x)(x-\beta)/p(p-1) \qquad p>0, p \neq 1$$

Sutti [to appear] shows that any positively homogeneous function F having hessian matrix H, minimum point (β, α) and degree p, necessarily satisfies expression (1), wherever it is differentiable and twice derivable.

Because of the homogeneity, for all x's where F is differentiable, β,p and $\sigma=p\alpha$ satisfy the linear equation

(2) $\beta^T gradF(x)+pF(x)-\sigma=x^T gradF(x)$

By writing the equation (2) for (n+2) points x_i i=1,..,n+2, we obtain a linear system whose solution provides the minimum (β,α) of F. Therefore Cupello and Sutti [to appear] derive iterative procedures to minimize the wide class of functions $f:\mathbb{R}^n -->\mathbb{R}$ mentioned in section 1. At each iteration they build a set of (n+2) points, evaluate f and compute gradient g in these points, and then solve a system of linear equations.
In more details the basic procedure steps look like this:

i)   set j=0,l=0,S=0
ii)   choose $x \in \mathbb{R}^n$ as starting point
iii)   set j=j+1; if j≥M stop, otherwise set $x_1^j=x$
iv)   generate a set of points x_i^j , i=2,..,n+2, in a
        neighbourhood $I=I(x_1^j)$
v)   check for the existence of g_i^j for all i,
        if g_r^j , 1≤r≤n+2 , is not defined, check l, 1≤l≤n such
        that $g(x_r^j)=g(x_r^j+\varepsilon_2 e_l)$ exists, e_l l-th unit vector in $\mathbb{R}^n$
vi)   compute gradient and function values in x_i^j for all i
vii)   solve the linear system

        $(g_i^j)^T\beta^j+f_i^j p^j-\sigma^j=(x_i^j)^T g_i^j$, i=1,..,n+2

        with respect to the (n+2) unknowns $\beta^j,p^j,\sigma^j=p^j\alpha^j$.
        If the determinant of the matrix is zero goto iii)
viii)   find m ,1≤m≤n+2, such that f_m^j =min $f(x_i^j)$
ix)   if either $p^j≤0$ or $p^j=1$ set S=0 and goto xii)
x)   if $f(\beta^j) ≥ f_m^j$ set S=0 and go to xiv),else
        if S=1 then
            if $|\beta^j-\beta^{j-1}|<\varepsilon_2$ and/or $|\alpha^j-\alpha^{j-1}|<\varepsilon_1$ set
            $(x^*,f(x^*))=(\beta^j,\alpha^j)$ and stop
            else set S=0 and goto xi)
xi)   if $|f(\beta^j)-\alpha^j|≥\varepsilon_1$ go to xiii)
        else set S=1 and go to xiii)
xii)   if $f(\beta^j)≥f_m^j$ then go to xiv)
xiii)   set $x=\beta^j$ update the region I to $I=I(\beta^j)$ and goto iii)
xiv)   If m≠1 then set $x=x_m^j$, update the region I to $I=I(x_m^j)$ and
        goto iii)
        otherwise update the region I to $I=I(x_1^j)$ and goto iii)

For all comments on the basic procedure we refer to Cupello and Sutti [to appear].
We now present the variants of the scheme that have been implemented. They differ for the way the points x_i^j,

$i=2,..,n+2, j\geq 1$, are determined, and also for the conditions on the stopping criterium.

More precisely, in what we call first and second variant the points are determined in a random way inside a region around x_i, whose wideness is either prefixed and constant or automatically determined, for every j. In details, in both variants the points satisfy the following relation

$$\tau_1 < |(x_i^j)_k - (x_i^j)_k| < \tau_2 \qquad ,\tau_1,\tau_2 \in R, \quad k=1,..,n, \quad i=2,..,n+2, \quad j\geq 1,$$

where τ_1, τ_2 are either parameters prefixed and constant or such that $\tau_2-\tau_1 \geq || x_1^{j-1} -x_1^j ||$, j>1.

In what we call third and fourth variants points are computed with the following formula

$$x_{i+1}^j = x_i^j + \delta_i^j e_i \qquad ,i=1,..,n$$
$$x_{n+2}^j = x_1^j + k_1^j \delta_1^j e_1$$

where e_i are the unit vectors, δ_i^j are either prefixed or random bounded steps for every i, and k_1^j is a real constant, $0<k_1^j<1$.

Further versions of the procedure are characterized by the different stopping criteria. To stop, some checks on the position and on the value of the minimum are foreseen; the two conditions to be tested may be put together either in a strong manner with an .AND. or in a weak manner with an .OR.. This makes possible to adapt better the algorithm to the problem in exam.

The numerical results in section 5 refer to the second variant where the weak stopping criterium has been chosen.

This version of the procedure turned out to be more convenient in terms of number of iterations and in terms of cpu time, more automatic, by requiring fewer arbitrary parameters to be passed, reliable because it obtains accurate solutions, and suitable for parallel computing with regard to the speeds-up.

For the implementation of the procedure four Fortran subroutines have been written: VRMIN, FGRAD, FVALUE and FCHCK. The first implements the above iterative scheme, the second calculates the coefficient matrix for the linear system, the third calculates the value of the objective function in a given point and the fourth is called when the function has not gradient in some point of its domain so that this point must be replaced by some other point where the gradient exists. More in detail VRMIN receives as parameters the following variables: the dimension N of the problem, IEXIST which is equal to 1 if the function is not everywhere derivable, O otherwise, the starting point X0, the stopping criterium parameters E1 and E2 and the maximum number of allowed iterations ITMAX. Subroutines FGRAD, FCHCK and FVALUE have to be written by the user for each different problem. FGRAD receives the dimension N and a matrix X containing the set of (n+2) points that have been generated; it provides the coefficient matrix FG and the right hand side vector of the linear system. FCHCK receives N and X with the same meaning as before and FVALUE requires N and the point in which we want

the function to be calculated.
In addition the routine LSSRBM, which will be described in
section 3, has been used to solve the linear system at step
vii).

3. THE MATRIX FACTORIZATION

As it has already been pointed out in the introduction, the
solution to the system of linear equations, that is required
by the minimization algorithm, is found by using a method of
matrix factorization recently developped and tested on vector
and multivector computers. In this section we give a short
description of this procedure and some of its performance
results.
As it is shown by Cupello and Sutti [1986], if A is an nxn
matrix, then there exists a factorization of A of the form
$A = L_1 L_2 \ldots L_h D U_k U_{k-1} \ldots U_1$, where L_i and U_i's are elementary
matrices, D is a diagonal matrix and there may be some
permutation matrices among the factors of the product. By
using this factorization to solve the system of linear
equations Ax=b, two phases are to be performed.
The first one calculates the L_i's by operating on the elements
which are under the main diagonal of A and on vector b. In this
phase the elements under the diagonal are annihilated.
In the second phase also the elements above the main diagonal
are annihilated and the U_i's matrices are computed. As it is
impossible now to operate simultaneously on the vector b, the
factorization $(U_k U_{k-1} \ldots U_1)^{-1}$ is saved in memory.
When A is reduced to a diagonal matrix D, the solution to the
system is computed by $x = (U_k U_{k-1} \ldots U_1)^{-1} D^{-1} (L_1 L_2 \ldots L_h)^{-1} b$.
More in details the method works like this:

i) for j=1 to n-1
    if A(j,j)=0 check for the first A(k,j)≠0, j<k≤n, then
    change row j with row k and b(j) with b(k)
    for i=n down to j+1
    find the last A(k,j)≠0 with j≤k<i, then
    for l=j to n

$$\text{compute } A(i,l) = A(i,l) - \frac{A(i,j)}{A(k,j)} A(k,l)$$

    update l

$$\text{then compute } b(i) = b(i) - \frac{A(i,j)}{A(k,j)} b(k)$$

    update i
    update j
ii) for i=1 to n-1
    for j=n down to i+1
    check for the last A(i,k)≠0, with i≤k<j,
    for l=i+1 to k

$$\text{compute } A(l,j) = A(l,j) - \frac{A(i,j)}{A(i,k)} A(l,j)$$

    update l

```
        for l=1 to k-1
```
$$\text{compute } A(j,l)=A(j,l)- \frac{A(i,j)}{A(i,k)} A(k,l)$$
```
        update l
```
$$\text{compute } A(j,l)=A(j,l)- \frac{A(i,j)}{A(i,k)}$$
```
      update j
      update i
iii) for i=1 to n
```
$$\text{compute } b(i)=\frac{b(i)}{A(i,i)}$$
```
      update i
iv)   for j=1 to n
        for i=1 to j-1
          compute b(i)=b(i)+A(j,i)b(j)
        update i
        update j
```

We have written a FORTRAN subroutine to implement this procedure; its name is LSSRBM and it receives the following parameters: N=dimension of the problem, A=coefficient matrix, RHS=right hand side vector, ISING=integer variable which contains 0 if the matrix is non singular and 1 otherwise.

The subroutine is well vectorized by the CRAY FORTRAN compiler in its do loops. Also with the ALLIANT FX/40 we obtained good vectorization and concurrency.

In the next Table 1 we give the speeds-up s_f for the solution of linear systems obtained by running LSSRBM on the CRAY X-MP/48, p=1, and on the ALLIANT FX/40.

The matrices A(NxN) and the vectors RHS(N) are randomly generated

N	s_f(CRAY)	s_f(ALLIANT)
2	<1	<1
4	1.03	<1
8	1.25	1.49
12	1.49	1.78
16	1.71	2.27
24	2.00	3.26
36	2.42	4.64
48	2.67	5.92
64	2.93	7.48
80	2.62	8.89
96	2.70	10.18
112	2.80	11.39
128	2.95	12.56

Table 1

Table 1 is visualized in the following Fig.1, where the dotted line graphs the results from ALLIANT and the full one those from CRAY.

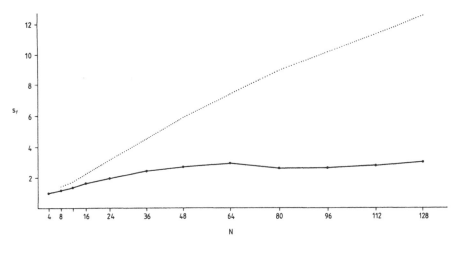

Fig.1

4. THE OBJECTIVE FUNCTIONS

In our numerical experience on the minimization procedure, we utilized objective functions classic in the litterature and other functions prepared on purpose. Particularly the following problems of minimization of homogeneous functions have been tested:

Problem 1) $F(x)=x_1^2+x_2^2$

Problem 2) (Homogeneous quartic)

$$F(x)=[1/2x^TQx+b^Tx+0.25]^2 \quad \text{where}$$

$$Q=\begin{bmatrix} 4.5 & 7 & 3.5 & 3 \\ 7 & 14 & 9 & 8 \\ 3.5 & 9 & 8.5 & 5 \\ 3 & 8 & 5 & 7 \end{bmatrix} \qquad b=\begin{bmatrix} -0.5 \\ -1 \\ -1.5 \\ 0 \end{bmatrix}$$

Problem 3) (Hilbert quadratic form)

$$F(x)=1/2x^THx \quad \text{where} \quad h_{ij}=1/(i+j-1), \quad i,j=1,2,..,n.$$

Problem 4) (Hilbert powered quadratic form)

$$F(x)=[1/2x^THx]^k \quad, \text{ H defined as in 3), } k=2,3,4,5,n=5$$

Problems 3) and 4) lead to a very poorly conditioned system of linear equations, therefore they are significant tests for the stability of the factorization procedure.

Problem 5) (Cupello and Sutti's function 1)

$$F(x)=\begin{cases} (x_1^2+x_2^2)/\cos[\pi/4-|\arctan(x_2/x_1)|] & x_1\neq0 \\ 2^{1/2}x_2^2 & x_1=0 \end{cases}$$

Problem 6) (Cupello and Sutti's function 2)

$$F(x)=\begin{cases}(x_1^2+x_2^2)^{1/4}(\cos[\pi/4-|\mathrm{artan}(x_2/x_1)|])^{3/4} & x_1\neq0\\[2mm]2^{-3/8}(x_2^2)^{1/4} & x_1=0\end{cases}$$

Functions in problems 5) and 6) are not everywhere derivable and have neither convex nor star-shaped at any point level sets. Furthermore they have a non stationary minimum.
We then minimized non homogeneous functions in the following problems:

Problem 7) (Two dimensional Rosenbrock's function)

$$F(x)=100(x_1^2-x_2)^2+(1-x_1)^2$$

Problem 8) (Four dimensional Rosenbrock's function)

$$F(x)=100(x_1^2-x_2)^2+(1-x_1)^2+90(x_3^2-x_4)^2+(1-x_3)^2$$
$$+10.1[(x_2-1)^2+(x_4-1)^2]+19.8(x_2-1)(x_4-1).$$

Problem 9) (Quartic with singular hessian)

$$F(x)=(x_1+10x_2)^2+5(x_3-x_4)^2+(x_2-2x_3)^4+10(x_1-x_4)^4.$$

This last function is very flat in a neighbourhood of the minimum and hence it is a strong test for the stopping criteria.

Problem 10) (Fletcher and Powell's trigonometric function of many variables)

$$F(x)=\sum_{i=1}^{n}[E_i-\sum_{j=1}^{n}(A_{i,j}\sin x_j+B_{i,j}\cos x_j)]^2$$

Moreover we minimized functions with many minima, as:

Problem 11) (Branin's function)

$$F(x)=(x_2-5x_1^2/4\pi^2+5x_1/\pi-6)^2+10(1-1/8\pi)\cos x_1+10$$

This function presents in $\mathbb{R}^2$ an infinity of minima all having value equal to 0.397887.

Problem 12) (Goldstein and Price's function)

$$F(x)=[1+(x_1+x_2+1)^2(19-14x_1+3x_1^2-14x_2+6x_1x_2+3x_2^2]$$
$$[30+(2x_1-3x_2)^2(18-32x_1+12x_1^2+48x_2-36x_1x_2+27x_2^2)]$$
$$D=\{-2\leq x_1\leq2,-2\leq x_2\leq2\}$$

In $D\subset\mathbb{R}^2$, this function has the three local minima $(x_A,f_A)=((-0.6,-0.4),30)$, $(x_B,f_B)=((1.8,0.2),84)$, $(x_C,f_C)=((1.2,0.8),840)$, and the global minimum $(x_G,f_G)=((0,-1),3)$.

5. THE NUMERICAL RESULTS

In this section we present the numerical results which we have obtained for the problems of the previous section, by running VRMIN on CRAY X-MP/48, p=1 (Tables 2,3) and on ALLIANT FX/40 (Table 4).
In Table 2 for each problem the dimension of x, the starting point, the stopping parameters, the number of iterations performed, the difference between the exact and the computed minimum values and the speed-up are listed.

Table 2

P	N	S.P.	ε_1	ε_2	n_{it}	Δf	s_t
1	2	(1,1)	10^{-8}	10^{-8}	1	0	1.021
2	4	(-4,-4,-4,-4)	10^{-8}	10^{-8}	1	0.32E-29	1.066
3	2	(-3,-3)	10^{-8}	10^{-12}	1	0.28E-26	1.070
3	3	(-3,-3,-3)	10^{-8}	10^{-12}	1	0	1.090
3	4	(-3,-3,-3,-3)	10^{-8}	10^{-12}	1	0	1.150
3	5	(-3,....,-3)	10^{-8}	10^{-12}	1	0.11E-21	1.250
3	6	(-3,....,-3)	10^{-8}	10^{-12}	1	0.99E-21	1.380
3	8	(-3,....,-3)	10^{-8}	10^{-8}	1	0	1.580
4	5 (k=2)	(-3,....,-3)	10^{-8}	10^{-12}	2	0	1.175
4	5 (k=3)	(-3,....,-3)	10^{-8}	10^{-12}	2	0.22E-69	1.206
4	5 (k=4)	(-3,....,-3)	10^{-8}	10^{-12}	2	0	1.168
4	5 (k=5)	(-3,....,-3)	10^{-8}	10^{-12}	2	0.48E-113	1.670
5	2	(1,0)	10^{-8}	10^{-8}	1	0.10E-27	1.004
6	2	(1,1)	10^{-6}	10^{-8}	1	0.75E-13	1.009
7	2	(-1.2,1)	10^{-8}	10^{-8}	36	0.13E-9	1.000
8	4	(-3,-1,-3,-1)	10^{-8}	10^{-8}	57	0.85E-11	1.155
9	4	(-3,-1,0,1)	10^{-4}	10^{-8}	44	0.81E-9	1.127
10	2	random	10^{-8}	10^{-8}	12	0.14E13	<1
10	3	"	10^{-8}	10^{-8}	10	0.46E-15	1.101
10	4	"	10^{-8}	10^{-8}	39	0.16E-13	1.188
10	5	"	10^{-8}	10^{-8}	15	0.14E-15	1.423
10	8	"	10^{-8}	10^{-8}	23	0.16E-17	1.993
11	2	(0,10)	10^{-8}	10^{-8}	10	$<10^{-6}$	1.049
11	2	(5,10)	10^{-8}	10^{-8}	11	$<10^{-6}$	1.026
11	2	(10,5)	10^{-8}	10^{-8}	7	$<10^{-6}$	1.061
12	2	(0,-2)	10^{-8}	10^{-8}	10	$<10^{-8}_{G}$	1.063
12	2	(-2,1)	10^{-8}	10^{-8}	10	$<10^{-8}_{A}$	1.013
12	2	(1,1)	10^{-8}	10^{-8}	19	$<10^{-8}_{R}$	1.040
12	2	(1,2)	10^{-8}	10^{-8}	10	$<10^{-8}_{C}$	1.029

From Table 2 the numerical reliability and efficiency of the new minimization method are evinced. In particular, by comparing these results, in terms of number of iterations, with those ones reported by Jacobson et al. [1972,1974] and by Kowalik and Ramakrishnan [1976], our procedure appears very competitive with the minimization algorithms based on homogeneous models. However a drawback of this method is the weak stability of the matrix factorization; because of that, for example Problem 4, where F(x) is homogeneous, requires more than one iteration. A promising approach to overcome this limit of the procedure seems to us to automatically scale the matrix.

The following Tables 3 and 4 present some results about the speeds-up related to problem 3 solved on CRAY and on ALLIANT respectively.

Table 3

N	s_t	s_e	s_f	s_r	σ_1	σ_2
2	1.07	1.15	1.08	1.05	0.45	3.95
3	1.09	1.28	1.13	1.06	0.44	2.63
4	1.15	1.44	1.20	1.06	0.43	1.89
5	1.25	1.61	1.21	1.16	0.41	1.34
6	1.38	1.84	1.37	1.22	0.42	1.08
8	1.58	2.13	1.53	1.34	0.40	0.70
10	1.80	2.49	1.65	1.55	0.40	0.51
20	2.76	3.69	2.38	2.68	0.43	0.17
30	3.64	4.83	3.11	3.61	0.44	0.11
40	4.37	5.78	3.64	5.96	0.45	0.06
60	5.01	6.69	4.15	7.40	0.46	0.04
80	5.95	7.38	5.12	8.67	0.52	0.03

Table 4

N	s_t	s_e	s_f	s_r	σ_1	σ_2
2	1.08	1.61	1.06	1.01	0.55	3.63
3	<1	2.04	1.10	0.58	0.48	5.95
4	<1	2.55	1.16	0.53	0.41	4.82
5	<1	3.53	1.29	0.61	0.33	3.72
6	1.57	4.65	1.37	1.06	0.30	1.47
8	1.98	6.86	1.64	1.15	0.26	1.12
10	2.37	10.06	1.88	1.19	0.21	0.99
20	4.53	22.06	3.21	1.39	0.18	0.61
30	6.55	32.69	4.45	1.45	0.16	0.52
40	8.25	33.55	5.65	1.48	0.23	0.47
60	9.44	40.25	6.76	1.50	0.23	0.45
80	11.56	43.27	7.88	3.02	0.25	0.22

There are listed here: the problem dimension and the speeds-up
of a full iteration, of the tasks of function and gradient
evaluation, of linear system solution and of residual
computation. Two more parameters, σ_1 and σ_2, in the following
defined, are reported.

Tables 3 and 4 show that the procedure is suitable for vector
and parallel computing, regarding to the total speeds-up, and
that all the tasks inside the iteration are well vectorized
and parallelized. Particularly, big advantage is taken from
the task of evaluation of f and g by the parallel system
ALLIANT FX/40 while the task of residual computation performs
better on the vector system CRAY X-MP/48, p=1.

The following Fig.2 visualizes the results of Table 3 (full
lines) and 4 (dotted lines).

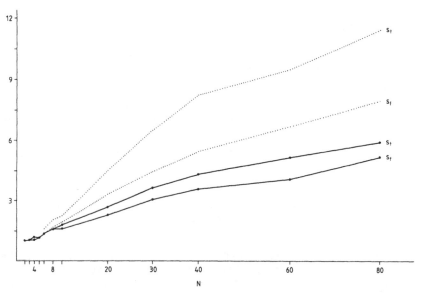

Fig.2

Finally in order to do an a priori analysis of the vector and
parallel performances of the minimization algorithm in object,
we derive the following formula which relates s_t with s_f,
indipendently from problem and system:

$$(3) \qquad s_t \geq \frac{\sigma_1 + \sigma_2 + s_f}{\sigma_1 + \sigma_2 + 1}$$

when $\sigma_1 = \dfrac{t_e}{t_f}$ and $\sigma_2 = \dfrac{t_r}{t_f}$ with t_e, t_r, t_f either vector

or parallel times spent at each iteration to evaluate f and g
in x_i, i=1,...,n+2, to solve the linear system and to perform

all other needed operations.

Formula (3) is deduced on the hypotheses, well verified in the numerical experience, that the total time spent at the j-th iteration is constant for all j, j≥1, and the scalar times spent for f and g evaluation and for residual computation are less than t_e and t_r respectively.

Formula (3) allows to deduce the slope of $s_t(N)$ from $s_f(N)$. Namely it evinces that, if s_f results the term definitely dominant in ratio (3), s_t is definitely bounded below by s_f: that is what the numerical experience confirms.

REFERENCES

Cupello L. and Sutti C. [1986] "A new factorization of matrices" Quad. Istit. Matem. Univ. Verona.

Cupello L. and Sutti C. [to appear] "A parallel minimization algorithm based on a homogeneus model".

Jacobson D.H. and Oksman W. [1972] "An algorithm that minimizes homogeneus functions of n variables in (n+2) iterations and rapidly minimizes general functions" Jour. Math. Anal. Appl., 38.

Jacobson D.H. and Pels L.H. [1974] "A modified homogeneous algorithm for function minimization" Jour. Math. Anal. Appl., 46.

Kowalik J.S. and Ramakrishnan K.G. [1976] "A numerically stable optimization method based on a homogeneous function" Math. Prog., 11.

Sutti C. and Peretti A. [1987] "Sequential and parallel implementations of an algorithm for the factorization of a matrix with rare banded matrices" Tech. Rep. N.O.C. 185, Hatfield Polyt.

Sutti C. [to appear] "On the Eulero's theorem for nonsmooth homogeneous functions".

Vector and parallel processing applications of nonlinear optimization algorithms: design problems, experimental results

Giacomo Patrizi, Cosimo Spera

Dipartimento di Statistica, Probabilità e Statistiche Applicate, Università degli Studi di Roma "La Sapienza"

Dipartimento di Economia, Università degli Studi di Siena.

Abstract: In this paper, two nonlinear optimization codes are tested on many nonconvex, nonlinear optimization problems, by implementing them on two different machines: the Alliant FX/80 parallel and vector processor and the Siemens vector processor VP 200. The results indicate strong synergisms between codes and machines. The memory environment and management choices as well as the algorithmic decisions are shown to be not reducible to automatic compiling and interpreters, at least as conceived at present. Rather special techniques are required to exploit their structures efficiently, which will be discussed.

1. INTRODUCTION :

The ideal of scientific endeavour is generality and synthesis, as indicated by Dieudonné [1977] and Bachelard [1974] and this requirement has been evoked, for the specific field by Lasdon et al. (1988) and by Dongarra & Sorensen (1987). Thus, it would be desirable to dispose of a generalization of a computer language suitable to implement algorithms efficiently both on vector and parallel computers, or to write the algorithms using calls to standard subroutines, which will be implemented on each machine in an efficient way, (much like the way that C is implemented, see Kernighan & Ritchie (1978), or the BLAS routines as proposed by Lawson et al.(1979)).

Most vector processors and parallel and vector processors, called henceforth supercomputers, provide a Fortran compilation facility, extended to accept vectorization or concurrency instructions and which will convert in an automatic (or semi-automatic) fashion Fortran code to make use of the supercomputer facilities. These 'Fortune' facilities could provide a partial answer to the wish evoked above, if they gave rise to efficient code.

Thus, the aim of this paper is to examine the relative merits of two nonlinear optimization codes on two different supercomputers for a wide range of different sized problems. The experimental design is therefore based on three factors and their interactions: problems, machines and codes. The synergisms that will be discovered will point to various design problems, so a subsidiary aim of this paper is to examine these, although no complete solution will be given here.

To fulfill these proposals, in the next section the problems to be solved, the nonlinear optimization algorithms considered and the supercomputers used will be presented. In section 3 and 4 the results of the experiment will be presented by discriminating them by optimization algorithm, while in section 5 the interactions will be analysed. In section 6 the results and the design problems that occur will be discussed for each machine. Conclusions follow in section 7.

2. PROBLEMS, CODES AND MACHINES:

Much experimentation has been effected for different machines concerning linear algebra algorithms, as in Dongarra (1988), so to develop this research, a number of nonlinear, and nonconvex problems were formulated, to prevent the iterative reduction of these problems to well formulated algorithms of linear algebra. In this section the problem types will be presented, then the algorithms used and finally a summary description of the Alliant FX/80 and the Siemens VP 200.

2.1 Problem-types

Three types of problems were considered for various number of variables: the Peano problem, a discrete version of the Peano problem and a modification of a problem suggested by Rosen (1984). For each upto 5 instances were solved from one or more starting points and the parameters were generated randomly.

The Peano problem is derived from his counter-example to the second order sufficiency conditions of Lagrange, see Genocchi & Peano (1884) and discussed by Hancock (1917) and Wilde & Beightler (1969). It may be formulated, when generalised to an arbitrary number of dimensions, as:

$$\text{Min } f(x) = (x_1 - \Sigma_{i=2}^{n} d_{1i} x_i^2)(x_1 - \Sigma_{i=2}^{n} d_{2i} x_i^2) \qquad [2.1]$$
$$\text{s. t.} \qquad \Sigma_{i=1}^{n} x_i^2 \leq n/2 \qquad x_i \geq 0 \qquad [2.2]$$

The problem has a saddle point at the origin and is unbounded from below, unless a suitable constraint is included. The d_{ji} (j = 1,2) are pseudo-random numbers generated by the standard algorithm on the Vax 11/750 vms 4.5, as indicated by Patrizi & Spera (1988a). It is interesting to note that an optimal solution is always given by two variables which assume nonzero values: x_1 & x_i (i $\neq$ 1) so that i = arg. Max ($|d_{1k} - d_{2k}|$). As the numbers are generated pseudo-randomly, this second variable may not be unique and many alternative optima may be present. Further, if a matrix $\{d_{ji}\}$ is generated, for the problem of maximal size, the smaller sized problem can be defined considering a submatrix. It therefore follows that as the problems increase in size, the minimum value will decrease both because of [2.2] and because of an increase in the

probability of finding a better second variable, which
satisfies the condition above. From this random matrix the
other instances are easily generated by considering
apppropriate shuffling procedures, see Patrizi & Spera (1988b)
for details. The problems were solved for a number of
instances for n = 100, 400, 800, 1200. For each instance and
size upto three starting point were used:
x_0^1 = (1, 1, ..., 1); x_0^2 = (1,0,...,0) and
x_0^3 = (1, -1, 1,..., -1), as indicated in the tables.

An important modification is to restrict the problem [2.1]-
[2.2] to integer variables. To impose the integer conditions,
as in Patrizi & Spera (1988a) the following constraints were
added to the problem as given by [2.1]- [2.2]:

$$\cos(2\pi x_i) = 1 \qquad i = 1,2,...,n \qquad [2.3]$$

so that the resulting problem is a continuous nonlinear problem
in n variables and (n + 1) constraints, apart from the
nonnegativity restrictions. As given, the only solution to
these problems could be the origin, so to ensure that the
problems had at least a nonzero integer solution, d_{ii} = 1 was
set for some i, usually 2. The resulting problems were solved
in three instances for n = 100, 200 and a starting points the
origin (x_0^4) and for the VP 200 only, x_0^5 = (2, 2, ..., 2).

The Rosen problems are defined by:

$$\begin{aligned}
\text{Min} \quad & f(x) = c^T x + 0.5\, x^T Q x & [2.4] \\
\text{s.t.} \quad & a_i^T x - b_i + x^T x \exp\{ (-1)^p x_p \} \geq 0 & [2.5] \\
& x_i \geq 0 \qquad i = 1,2,... n/2. & [2.6]
\end{aligned}$$

The matrix Q generated is a pseudo- random symmetric negative
semi-definite matrix of rank n-1, while to generate the other
instances the matrix was modified to be of rank n-3 and n-5.
The vector c, a_i^T for each constraint and the scalar p were
generated pseudo-randomly, while b_i was determined by imposing
a feasible solution of all variables equal to one. Only three
instances of this problem were solved for sizes of n= 100, 200,
400 variables.

The resulting problems are clearly nonconvex, nonlinear and for
one class discrete. Related results for the Vax 11/750 have
been presented before, see Patrizi & Spera (1988a).

2.2 The Codes:

Two nonlinear optimization algorithms are used in this
experimentation. The first one is the very well-known procedure
developed by Murtagh & Saunders (1978,1982), called MINOS,
while the other is called NLGOAL, based on linear
complementarity theory and developed by the first author, see
Patrizi (1985), (1986), (1987), (1988). Both have been
implemented in standard Fortran 77 and were compiled on the
different machines using standard compilers of the vendors,
with all the options and Fortune listings as appropriate, (see
below).

In the Minos routine, the user must supply the problem description and the subroutine to evaluate the gradient. Also a starting point must be furnished and some print specifications, for details see Murtagh & Saunders (1982, 1985). It uses an active set strategy, one of a number of line search procedures and a quasi-newton updating of an estimate of a modified Hessian matrix. It proceeds in an automatic way either performing recursive quadratic programming or adopting an augmented Lagrangian procedure with a penalty parameter which is increased from time to time. A crash procedure is used if the starting point is not feasible.

The NLGOAL procedure requires instead subroutines to define the problem, the gradient the jacobian of the constraints and the Hessian matrix of the objective function. At each iteration point it uses a quadratic approximation to the objective function and a linear approximation to the constraints. Should the problem have equality constraints and/or unsigned variables, simple transformations return at each iteration a quadratic subproblem with linear inequality constraints. This problem is solved by a linear complementarity problem, which may always be processed as Patrizi (1987) has shown, by solving a corresponding linear program with a parametric variation of one cost parameter. Since the approximation may only be appropriate in a given neighbourhood of the iteration point, a trust region is added to the problem by defining a set of linear inequality constraints around the point. Often, these are implemented as box constraints and upto n of the total 2n can be incorporated into the variables by shifting the origin.

This way of considering the trust region avoids a number of problems met in trust regions defined by a single quadratic constraint as formulated by Fletcher (1980 - 1981) or Byrd et al. (1985). It is shown in Patrizi (1988) that if the problem is bounded and has a feasible solution, then the algorithm will converge to a stationary point. Every stationary point of the subproblem will be either inside the trust region or on its boundary and as the trust region is modified to ensure the feasibility of the original problem at the various iterations, it follows that if these points occur inside the trust region, they are stationary points of the original problem. On locating a stationary point others may be located by applying suitable modifications of the trust region. By blocking any stationary point which involves an increase in the objective function, a series of stationary points with nonincreasing objective function values will be obtained. Since the problem is bounded, a local minimum will be reached.

2.3: The Processors:

The Alliant FX/80 consists of 8 concurrent vector processors and 12 interactive processors with a cache size of 512 KB and a main memory of 256 MB. The Concentrix operating System version 1.0, revision C (May 1987) was used, which includes the Unix System 4.2BSD. The FX/Fortran compiler supports: concurrent execution, multiple processors, the vector instruction set and the standard Fortran-77 with a large number of extensions. The vendors indicate 188.8 peak Mflops, while for the coded Linpack (1000 x 1000 linear system in double precision) is 65 Mflops.

The Siemens VP 200 is a pipelined vector computer system with a vector register of 64 KB capacity, two add/logical units pipes, one multifunction pipe and a divide pipe. A mask pipe is also provided for vector operations and the main storage capacity is of 64 MB. For runs which require the vector processor, all the data and the program must reside in the main memory, while for scalar runs, suitable paging facilities are provided. For details see Hwang & Briggs (1985, p. 293 et seq.). The V.S.P. operating system supports the Fortran77/VP version 10.2 level 20. The Fortune listing uses a cost-time estimate, by calculating a weighted total of the operation count for each statement, routine and program. From the respective proportions an estimate of the time taken by the routine can be obtained. The processor is quoted, see Dongarra (1988), with a theoretical peak performance of 533 Mflops and for the coded Linpack (1000 x 1000 linear system in double precision) an actual performance of 422 Mflops.

3. RESULTS FOR THE MINOS ROUTINE:

Of the 116 problems that should have been solved with this routine results can be given for only 25 problems. For all the Rosen problems the Minos routine encountered overflow problems, as it adapted the penalty parameter to obtain a feasible solution. The discrete Peano problems were also not solved because of line search failure or other computing error conditions. These results occured on both machines and they are in sharp contrast with the results for smaller sized problems which were solved satisfactorily by this routine, see Patrizi & Spera (1988a). Undoubtedly, the greater dimensions proved troublesome to the line search routines. These difficulties were also encountered with the VF02AD routine, see Powell (1978), which worked so well on smaller size problems, as reported in Patrizi & Spera (1988a).

Of the remaining 92 problems, the routine was not able to solve any Peano problem from starting points $x_o{}^z$ and $x_o{}^s$ due to line search failure or reaching the limit for the superbasic variables. Occasionally, it converged to the origin as a solution. Instead, from the starting point $x_o{}^1$ the routine converged to an optimal solution in the majority of cases both on the Alliant and on the VP 200 as indicated in table 1, were the time to solve the problems are reported. For the Alliant 13 of the 16 of the continuous Peano problems were solved, while with the VP 200 a satisfactory solution was found only in 3 cases. Again the chief reason for not finding the solution was line search failure. Perhaps, these difficulties are due to the fact that the Alliant operations are carried out with rounding procedures, while the VP 200 a truncation procedure of the nonsignificant digits is effected. Due to the size of the problems only two instances of the Peano 800 were tried and

when in both cases no solution was obtained, the remaining
problems were dropped. In contrast, these were solved
satisfactorily on the Alliant.

All the facilities of automatic vectorization and the
indications of the Fortune listings were used. For the problems
that were solved, a speedup ratio of 2.3 was determined on the
Alliant for the problems of 100 variables, which rose to 3.19
for the larger problems. Instead for the VP 200 a speedup ratio
of 12.0 over the scalar run was determined.

Table 1: Computational results on supercomputers of the Minos
optimization code: (time expressed in seconds)

Problem Type, size and instance		ALLIANT	SIEMENS VP 200
		x_o^1	x_o^1
Peano 100	A	110.7	8.4 *
	B	105.6	8.5 *
	C	103.4	8.8 *
	D	102.4	1.07 *
	E	111.7	9.2 *
Peano 400	A	1515.6	102.9
	B	1662.5	13.4 *
	C	1661.4	133.3
	D	1603.4	40.4 *
	E	..	103.5
Peano 800	A	7406.7	..
	B	7743.0	..
	C	7520.3	..
	D	7012.5	..
Peano 1200	A	..	..

* Line search failure,   .. not completed

The speedup ratio across machines, for the Peano 400 problems,
for the VP 200 versus the FX/80 had an average value of 14.23.
From the final Fortune listings of the runs on the two
supercomputers, a detailed analysis can be effected routine by
routine, see Patrizi & Spera (1988b). These indicate that the
ratios of the times for 1000 calls of the routine on the VP 200
as compared to the FX/80 vary from 27.5 (routine M6RMOD) to
2.62 (DAXPY) to 0.83 (M6RSOL). Although these estimates are not
precise, because of differences in the measurements, they are
useful nevertheless. As MINOS spends over 40% of the time in
this routine for these problems, the vectorization that was
done on the VP 200 is important. The routine is part of the
factorization and updating procedures of the modified Hessian,
so the comments of Ortega (1988) and Ortega & Romine (1988) are
relevant here. In fact, on the Alliant, concurrency of the
outer loop was not achieved, while on the VP 200 vectorization

was obtained. The DAXPY routine is well known so it can be considered parallelized and vectorized efficiently on both machines, while for the other routines a series of considerations apply, which are developed in detail in Patrizi & Spera (1988b).

4. RESULTS FOR THE NLGOAL ROUTINE :

For this routine all 58 problems set were solved on the Alliant. On the VP 200, only 35 of the 58 problems were solved. Firstly, numerical difficulties occured, when starting from the initial point x_0^3. Secondly, on the VP 200 all the problem must reside in main memory. Due to the experimental nature of NLGOAL memory requirements are not optimal and so the larger problems could not fit totally in main memory. Thus the Peano 800 problems and the Peano 1200 problems were not tried. Instead, the Peano integer problems were solved from two initial points instead of one. The total number of problem instances attempted was therefore 99 problems instances. The results are indicated in table 2 and table 3.

The speedup ratio for the VP 200 was 11.12 over the time taken on the scalar runs. For the Alliant FX/80 for the continuous Peano problems the ratio was 3.98 which increased to 4.11 for the integer Peano problems and 5.07 for the Rosen problems. These values correspond well to what can be expected, see Wright (1988).

Table 2: Computational results on supercomputers of the Nlgoal optimization code: (time expressed in seconds)

Problem Type		ALLIANT			SIEMENS VP 200	
		x_0^1	x_0^2	x_0^3	x_0^1	x_0^2
Peano 100	A	140.7	115.7	112.6	27.2	29.2
	B	136.5	110.6	110.8	26.9	28.2
	C	131.2	115.7	113.6	27.0	28.4
	D	130.6	116.6	114.2	26.7	28.0
	E	149.7	120.2	118.7	27.1	28.4
Peano 400	A	5040.2	3900.4	3957.2	826.8	863.0
	B	5289.5	4035.6	4115.3	860.0	894.5
	C	4657.2	3523.2	3721.3	811.4	845.5
	D	4785.6	3665.7	3779.7	850.6	886.7
	E	4923.5	3823.3	3921.3	798.3	835.6
Peano 800	A	10752.3	8008.3	8110.1 **	n.a.	n.a.
	B	9534.7	7423.4	7927.3 **	n.a.	n.a.
	C	9123.1	7512.3	7815.9 **	n.a.	n.a.
	D	9781.6	7625.4	7920.6 **	n.a.	n.a.
Peano 1200	A	13625	n.a.	n.a. **	n.a.	n.a.

** Eigenvalue failure,stationary point located.
n.a. Not attempted.

Table 3: Computational results on supercomputers of the Nlgoal optimization code: (time expressed in seconds)

Problem Type		ALLIANT	SIEMENS VP 200	
		$x_\varnothing^4$	$x_\varnothing^4$	$x_\varnothing^\varnothing$
Peano integer 100	A	316.6	12.5	10.3
	B	296.1	12.5	10.0
	C	225.7	12.5	10.0
Peano integer 200	A	1164.2	60.8	52.3
	B	1057.6	69.9	52.4
	C	1023.9	69.8	52.3
Rosen 100,50	A	88.4	2.3 **	n.a.
	B	85.4	2.6 **	n.a.
	C	80.9	2.3 **	n.a.
Rosen 200,100	A	180.9	19.6 **	n.a.
	B	155.8	38.9 **	n.a.
	C	162.7	38.3 **	n.a.
Rosen 400,200	A	624.4	n.a.	n.a.
	B	1259.1	n.a.	n.a.
	C	1236.1	n.a.	n.a.

** Eigenvalue failure,stationary point located.
n.a. Not attempted.

The largest amount of time is spent in both Supercomputers in the determination of the largest positive eigenvalue and its eigenvector, which always exists as they concern a positive matrix. The eigenvector is required to determine the appropriate objective function for the parametric linear problem which must be solved, see Patrizi (1987). The routine used were supplied by the vendors, while to solve the linear parametric program the routine of Land & Powell (1973), duly modified to permit parallelization and vectorization was used.

The speedup from the VP200 to the FX/80 show a great variability, but in this case the median ratio is about 5 for the Peano and the Rosen problems, with a peak of 20 for the Peano integer problems, as indicated in Patrizi & Spera (1988b). Again, the Fortune runs indicate a great variability in this ratio, but less pronounced than the previous case. For the continuous Peano problems the ratios vary from about 2.67 to 0.329, while no data was obtained for the integer problems.

The eigenvectors routines failed for the 800 and 1200 variables Peano problems on the Alliant. The routine NLGOAL has a default objective function, which was used in these cases, but the optimal solution was not found, but only a stationary point. Numerical difficulties were also encountered with the Siemens VP 200 for the Rosen problems. Considering these problems, this is not surprising as they can be very ill-conditioned.

5.COMPARATIVE RESULTS OF PROBLEMS, CODES AND MACHINES:

MINOS did not yield satisfactory results for the larger problems, nor did the VF02AD routine, so it appears that both routines become erratic with increasing problem size for nonconvex problems. The obvious conclusion is that there occur difficulties in the line search as the problems increase in size and the conditioning becomes worse. As NLGOAL does not suffer from this fall in performance with increasing size and uses no line search routine, there is good evidence that this is the case. An active set strategy is used by the first two procedures, but not by NLGOAL, so also this could be a cause. In fact, this aspect appears important when it is recalled that MINOS failed to solve mainly those problems with many nonlinear constraints.

On comparing results on the two machines a number of important points emerge. Firstly, a rather trivial observation is that as the two machines have quite different operating systems, numerical precision must be considered, since rounding or truncation practices will effect the solutions obtained in these types of problems. More importantly the type of routine and the coding used, seem to greatly affect the potential speedup.

These machines are able to obtain solutions to large problems at high speed, just by automatic or semi-automatic conversion of current routines with a significant speedup and relatively few problems. Thus with standard routines huge problems can be solved. However, much more can be obtained by properly exploiting the machine at hand, as the ratios reported above indicate. These speedup ratios have resulted more by chance than by design, so more detailed experiments and analysis should indicate which type of programming is best suited to which type of supercomputer, as Ortega & Voigt (1985) pointed out.

This would permit to solve really large optimization problems in a very short time and the availability of a robust routine properly programmed for the supercomputer would permit the solution of complex decision problems, which always involve the solution of an optimization problem. There is however another aspect, memory management and resource allocation inside the supercomputer which can give also enormous benefits.

6. SOFTWARE DESIGN PROBLEMS FOR SUPERCOMPUTERS:

The problem of arithmetic precision for different machines, may be troublesome, if particular care is not taken. More serious are the algorithmic limitations of certain routines, when they are extended to general problems. But, even if these aspects are allowed, there seems to be an excessive variability of the implementations between supercomputers. This would tend therefore to confirm the need to develop machine dependent algorithms to exploit fully their power, in contrast with scientific ideals.

However, suppose that the program may be subdivided into segments, or task as Dongarra & Sorensen (1987) indicate and that attached to each task there is a data set A_k which may change dynamically, then the problem of scheduling the processors becomes a well known combinatorial problem.

Let $x_{kpt} = 1$ if the program task P_k ($k = 1,2,\ldots,K$), is processed on p processors ($p = 1,2,\ldots,\pi$), beginning at time t ($t = 1,2,\ldots,T$) and $x_{kpt} = 0$ otherwise. The scheduling problem is:

$$\text{Min} (\Sigma_{t=1}^T \Sigma_{p=1}^\pi \Sigma_{k=1}^K d_{kp} x_{kpt})^2 \qquad [6.1]$$

$$\text{s.t.} \quad \Sigma_p \Sigma_t x_{kpt} = 1 \qquad \forall\ k \qquad [6.2]$$

$$\Sigma_k \Sigma_p A_k x_{kpt} = R_t \qquad \forall\ t \qquad [6.3]$$

$$\Sigma_p \Sigma_k p x_{kpt} \le \pi \qquad \forall\ t \qquad [6.4]$$

$$\Sigma_t \Sigma_p x_{kpt} x_{kpt} = 0 \qquad [6.5]$$

$$\Sigma_t \Sigma_p t x_{kpt} \le \Sigma_t \Sigma_p t x_{kpt} \qquad [6.6]$$

$$x_{kpt} = 0,\ 1. \qquad [6.7]$$

where R_t is the size of the page or other memory structure, d_{kp} is the length of time to process task k on p processors and k,k indicate specific tasks, which must not conflict in [6.5] and which must satisfy a precedence relation in [6.6]. The optimization problem indicated in [6.1] - [6.7] is just a preliminary statement, many more relations and conditions can be introduced, such as conditions, multiple choices, if then relations and so, as it is well known. The result is always a mathematical program in binary integer form to which the results above apply. Much of the data required, like data dependencies and processing times may be generated directly from the compiler and the scalar run, similarly to the suggestions of Dongarra & Sorensen (1987).

Proposition 6.1: The NLGOAL routine solves the scheduling problem [6.1] - [6.7].
Proof: The objective function has a lower bound of zero. A feasible solution is given by running all the tasks on a single processor $p = 1$. Thus an optimal solution or a series of stationary points can be determined from the algorithm, see Patrizi (1988). By adding the linearization of the objective function as part of the trust region, with a suitable bound, a decreasing sequence of stationary points, in terms of objective function values, will be returned.

Proposition 6.2: If an algorithm is fully vectorizable so as to adhere to the Fortran requirements of vectorization, then it can be efficiently parallelizable on applying the scheduling algorithm [6.1] - [6.7].
Proof: The scheduling algorithm will provide an efficient parallelization of the tasks by resolving the data dependencies, the data conflicts and eventual other relations that may be included. Thus, if the algorithm is fully

vectorizable, so that all the inner DO loops have been vectorized, by the scheduling algorithm, they can run concurrently on p processors.

7. CONCLUSIONS

The results presented here indicate the usefulness of the NLGOAL routine which has good solution characteristics both on continuous problems and on integer problems. Thus, the scheduling problems that may arise in parallelization can be practically solved by this routine. Further experimental results are being collected. Of more importance is that the effort of scientific generalization and synthesis can be persued, in line with proposition 6.2. Not only is unity achieved, but also clarity is fostered, since parallelization considered as a scheduling problem is an enlightening way to envisage it.

8: REFERENCES

Bachelard, G., (1974), **La Ragione Scientifica**, Bertani, Verona.

Byrd, R.H., R.B. Schnabel, G.A.Schultz, (1985), A Trust-Region Algorithm for Nonlinearly Constrained Optimization, Working Paper Dept. of Computer Sciences, Univ. of Colorado.

Dieudonnè, J., (1977), **Panorama des Mathématiques pures: le choix bourbachique**, Gauthiers - Villars, Paris.

Dongarra, J.J., (1988), Performance of Various Computers Using Standard Linear Equations Software in a Fortran Environment, Argonne Nat. Laboratory, Math. & Computer Science Division, Technical Memorandum 23.

Dongarra, J.J., D.C. Sorensen, (1987), Schedule: Tools for Developing and Analysing Parallel Fortran Programs, in Jamieson, L.H., D.B. Gannon, R.J. Douglass, (eds.) **The Characteristics of Parallel Algorithms**, The MIT Press, Cambridge, Mass.

Fletcher, R.,(1988),Practical Methods of Optimization, Wiley, New York, (2nd ed.).

Genocchi A., G. Peano, (1884), **Calcolo Differenziale e Principi di Calcolo Integrale**, F.lli Bocca, Torino.

Hancock, H., (1917), **Theory of Maxima and Minima**, Ginn & co., Boston.

Hwang, K., F.A. Briggs, (1985), **Computer Architecture and Paralle Processing**, McGraw-Hill Book Co., New York.

Kernighan, B.W., D.M. Ritchie (1978), **The C Programming Language**, Prentice-Hall, Englewood Cliffs N.J..

Land M., S. Powell, (1973), **Fortran Codes for Mathematical Programming**, Wiley, New York .

Lawson C., R. Hanson, D. Kincaid, F. Krogh, (1979), Basic Linear Algebra Subprograms for Fortran Usage, **ACM Trans. Math. Software,** p. 308 - 371.

Murtagh, B.A., M.A. Saunders, (1978), Large Linearly Constrained Optimization, **Math. Prog.** 14 p. 41 - 72.

Murtagh B.A., M.A. Saunders, (1982), A Projected Lagrangian Algorithm and its Implementation for Sparse Nonlinear Constraints, in (Buckley A.G., J.L.Goffin eds.), **Algorithms** for Constrained Minimization of Smooth Nonlinear Functions, Math. Prog. Study N° 16, North Holland, Amsterdam.

Ortega, J.M., (1988), The ijk Forms of Factorization Methods I. Vector Computers, **Parallel Computing**, 7, p.135 -147.

Ortega, J.M., C.H. Romine, (1988), The ijk Forms of Factorization Methods II. Parallel Systems, **Parallel Computing**, 7, p.149 -162.

Ortega, J.M., R.G. Voigt, (1985), Solution of Partial Differential Equations on Vector and Parallel Computers, **S.I.A.M. Review**, 27, 149 -240.

Patrizi, G., (1985), Risultati Computazionali per Sistemi Lineari di Complementarita`, **Atti delle Giornate di Lavoro A.I.R.O.**, Venezia p. 163 - 177.

Patrizi, G., (1986), Risultati Computazionali di Varianti di un Algoritmo per la soluzione di Problemi generali di ottimizzazione vincolata, in Belli, M., (ed.) **Ricerca Operativa e Informatica**, Franco Angeli, Milano, p. 31 - 44.

Patrizi, G.,(1987), The Equivalence of an LCP to a Parametric Linear Program in a Scalar variable, submitted for publication.

Patrizi, G., (1988), A Complementarity Algorithm for Optimization Problems subject to Nonlinear Constraints, submitted for publication.

Patrizi, G., C. Spera, (1988a), Risultati Computazionali di alcuni algoritmi di ottimizzazione per problemi nonconvessi, nonlineari e vincolati, **Atti delle Giornate di Lavoro A.I.R.O.**, Pisa.

Patrizi G., C. Spera, (1988b), Computational Results of nonlinear algorithms on Supercomputers, working Paper Università degli Studi di Roma 'La Sapienza', Rome.

Plummer, J., L.S. Lasdon, M. Ahmed, (1988), Solving a Large Nonlinear Programming Problem on a Vector Processing Computer, **Annal of O.R.**, 14, p. 291 - 304.

Powell, M.J.D., (1978), A fast Algorithm for Nonlinearly Constrained Optimization Calculations in (Watson, G. ed.), **Numerical Analysis, Dundee 1977**, Lecture Notes in Mathematics 630, Springer-Verlag, Berlin.

Rosen J.B. (1984), Computational Experience with Large-Scale Constrained Global Optimization, C.o.a.l. 10, p.15-22.

Wilde, D.J., C.S. Beightler, (1967), **Foundations of Optimization**, Prentice-Hall, Englewood Cliffs N.J..

Wright, S., (1988), A Fast Algorithm for Equality-Constrained Quadratic Programming on the Alliant FX/8, **Annals of O.R.**, 14, p. 225- 244.

Acknowledgement: The authors are especially grateful to Dr. Winfrid Tschiedel of Siemens for his precious help and guidance in preparing this paper. They would also like to thank the Directors of Siemens A.G. and Alliant Systems (France), for their support and computing facilities while conducting this research. All eventual mistakes, which may be present, must however be considered only the responsability of the authors.

Toeplitz matrices, homothety and least squares approximation

Fridrich Sloboda

Institute of Technical Cybernetics, Slovak Academy of Sciences, 842 37
Bratislava, Dubravska 9, Czechoslovakia

ABSTRACT: Linear operators for digital contour smoothing are described. These operators are defined by circulant Toeplitz matrices and
allow to smooth digital contours in the least squares sense. A family
of these operators defined by the polynomials of the first order generates homothety. A bit level systolic array, which is capable of realizing the proposed smoothing operator, has been suggested. This array is
easily implementable in VLSI and employs the two major principles of parallel processing, namely multiprocessing and pipelining.

1. INTRODUCTION

Toeplitz matrices (Iohvidov 1982, Davis 1979) have become of increasing interest with the rapid growth of signal and image processing. A special type of Toeplitz matrices have the form

$$
C = \begin{bmatrix}
c_0 & c_1 & c_2 & \cdots & & c_{n-1} \\
c_{n-1} & c_0 & c_1 & & & c_{n-2} \\
c_{n-2} & c_{n-1} & c_0 & c_1 \cdots & & c_{n-3} \\
\cdot & & & & & \\
\cdot & & & & & \\
c_2 & c_3 & \cdots & & c_0 & c_1 \\
c_1 & c_2 & \cdots & & c_{n-1} & c_0
\end{bmatrix} . \tag{1}
$$

For these matrices the sum of elements in a row remains constant

$$
\sum_{i=0}^{n-1} c_i = c . \tag{2}
$$

The inverse of a Toeplitz matrix, if it is invertible, can be performed by
Gohberg and Semencul (1972) formula on $O(n^2)$ operations. The inverse of
circulant Toeplitz matrices is required by the restoration of images (Gonzales and Wintz 1982), (Rosenfeld and Kak 1979).Toeplitz systems of linear
equations arise in many scientific and engineering applications and real-
time is often requested. The well known algorithms of Levinson (1947),Dur-
bin (1960), Trench (1964), Zohar (1969), and Bareiss (1969), all require
$O(n^2)$ operations. Recently, Bitmead and Anderson (1980), and Brent et al

(1980) proposed algorithms which require only $O(n \log^2 n)$ operations. An efficient algorithm for the regularization of ill-conditioned least squares problems with triangular Toeplitz matrix has been suggested by Elden (1984). The recent advance in VLSI technology has made it possible to develop VLSI systems utilizing parallelism to attain high efficiency, low cost, and to use highly integrated circuts. Kung and Leiserson (1978) have introduced the notion of systolic arrays, a special kind of highly regular, homogeneous, pipelined processor arrays. They are effectively implementable in VLSI and employ the two major principles of parallel processing, namely multiprocessing and pipelining. Kung and Hu (1981) and Brent and Luk (1983) have suggested parallel algorithms for solving Toeplitz linear systems. Further parallel algorithms for solving Toeplitz linear systems have been suggested by Bini (1984) and Codenotti (1986). Parallel solution of certain Toeplitz least squares problems is described by Bojanczyk and Brent (1986). For real-time applications   one- dimensional systolic array TOPSS-28 has been developed(Nudd 1984). The Hughes Research Laboratories Toeplitz system solver TOPSS-28 allows to perform real-time calculation of splines for digital contour smoothing and to reduce the data required for reference images. A simple algorithm and a pipelined architecture for B-spline interpolation is described by Sankar and Ferrari (1988).

In this paper linear operators for digital contour smoothig are described. These operators are defined by circulant Toeplitz matrices and allow to smooth digital contours in the least squares sense. A family of these operators defined by the polynomials of the first order generates homothety. A bit level systolic array, which is capable of realizing the proposed smoothing operator, has been suggested. This array is easily implementable in VLSI and is devoted for real-time applications.

2. LEAST-SQUARES SMOOTHING

The theory of orthogonal polynomials has made it possible to develop efficient algorithms for smoothing a function of one variable on a equidistant set of points. Let $P_{k,n}(i)$, $k=0,1,2,\ldots,m<n$ be a set of orthogonal polynomials defined on the equidistant set of points $0,1,2,\ldots,n$ and k denotes the degree of the given polynomial. Let us consider that these polynomials have the form (Berezin and Zhidkov 1965)

$$P_{0,n}(i)=1 \quad P_{1,n}(i)=1-\frac{2i}{n} \quad P_{2,n}(i)=1-\frac{6i}{n-1}+\frac{6i^2}{n(n-1)}$$

$$iP_{m,n}(i)=-\frac{(m+1)(n-m)}{2(2m+1)}P_{m+1,n}(i)+\frac{n}{2}P_{m,n}(i)-\frac{m(n+m+1)}{2(2m+1)}P_{m-1,n}(i) \quad (3)$$

Let $f:R_1 \to R_1$ be defined on the set of points $0,1,2,\ldots,n$ and the values of f on these points are f(i), $i=0,1,2,\ldots,n$. Let the approximation function have the form

$$\Phi(i) = P_m(i) = c_0 P_{0,n}(i)+ c_1 P_{1,n}(i)+ \ldots + c_m P_{m,n}(i) \quad (4)$$

and let this function approximate the function f in the least squares sense, i.e.,

$$\sum_{i=0}^{n}[f(i)-\Phi(i)]^2 = \min ! \quad (5)$$

According to the orthogonality of the polynomials, the coefficients c_j are defined by

$$c_j(P_{j,n}, P_{j,n}) = (f, P_{j,n}) \qquad j=0,1,\ldots,m \qquad (6)$$

whereby (Berezin and Zhidkov 1965)

$$c_j = \frac{\sum\limits_{i=0}^{n} f(i) P_{j,n}(i)}{\sum\limits_{i=0}^{n} P_{j,n}^2(i)} = \frac{(2j+1) n^{(j)}}{(j+n+1)^{(j+1)}} \sum\limits_{i=0}^{n} f(i) P_{j,n}(i) \qquad (7)$$

$$j=0,1,\ldots,m$$

and

$$n^{(j)} = n(n-1)\ldots(n-j+1)$$
$$(j+n+1)^{(j+1)} = (j+n+1)(j+n)\ldots(n+1) .$$

Let us consider $N+1$ function values $f(i)$ defined on the equidistant set of points $0,1,2,\ldots,N$, where $N \gg n$. Let the function f be approximated on each subset consisting of $n+1$ points by a polynomial P_m. Let m be odd and let n be even. Let us denote the running subset of $n+1$ points by $i-n/2,\ldots,i-1$, $i,i+1,\ldots,i+n/2$. Then the smoothed value of f in the mid point i is defined by the value of $\Phi(i) = P_m(i)$ as follows (Berezin and Zhidkov 1965)

$$m = 1$$

$n+1=3$: $\Phi(i) = (1/3)(f(i-1)+f(i)+f(i+1))$ $\qquad (8)$

$n+1=5$: $\Phi(i) = (1/5)(f(i-2)+f(i-1)+f(i)+f(i+1)+f(i+2))$ $\qquad (9)$

$n+1=7$: $\Phi(i) = (1/7)(f(i-3)+f(i-2)+f(i-1)+f(i)+f(i+1)+f(i+2)+f(i+3))$ (10)

$$m = 3$$

$n+1=5$: $\Phi(i) = (1/35)(-3f(i-2)+12f(i-1)+17f(i)+12f(i+1)-3f(i-2))$ $\qquad (11)$

$n+1=7$: $\Phi(i) = (1/21)(-2f(i-3)+3f(i-2)+6f(i-1)+7f(i)+6f(i+1)+$
$$+3f(i+2)-2f(i+3)) \qquad (12)$$

$n+1=9$: $\Phi(i) = (1/231)(-21f(i-4)+14f(i-3)+39f(i-2)+54f(i-1)+$
$$+59f(i)+54f(i+1)+39f(i+2)+14f(i+3)-21f(i+4)) . \qquad (13)$$

3. DIGITAL CONTOUR SMOOTHING

Digital contour smoothing belongs to the most important procedures in image processing. This procedure allows to smooth digital contours and so to improve the stability of local and global invariants (Teh and Chin 1986) and to calculate invariants such as curvature which is impossible to calculate without smoothing.

In the next a digital picture Σ is a finite rectangular array whose elements are called points or picture elements. Each point P of Σ is defined then by a pair of Cartesian coordinates (x,y), which we may take to be integer valued. A point $P=(x,y)$ in a digital picture Σ has two types of neighbors :

a/ its four horizontal and vertical neighbors (u,v) such that

$| x-u | + | y-v | = 1$

b/ its diagonal neighbors (u,v) such that

$| x-u | = | y-v | = 1 .$

$$m = 3$$

n+1=5

$$\frac{1}{c}C = \frac{1}{35}\begin{bmatrix} 17 & 12-3 & & & & -3 & 12 \\ 12 & 17 & 12-3 & & & & -3 \\ -3 & 12 & 17 & 12-3 & & & \\ & & -3 & 12 & 17 & 12-3 & \\ -3 & & & -3 & 12 & 17 & 12 \\ 12-3 & & & & -3 & 12 & 17 \end{bmatrix}$$

(18)

n+1=7

$$\frac{1}{c}C = \frac{1}{21}\begin{bmatrix} 7 & 6 & 3-2 & & & -2 & 3 & 6 \\ 6 & 7 & 6 & 3-2 & & & -2 & 3 \\ 3 & 6 & 7 & 6 & 3-2 & & & -2 \\ -2 & 3 & 6 & 7 & 6 & 3-2 & & \\ & & -2 & 3 & 6 & 7 & 6 & 3-2 \\ -2 & & & -2 & 3 & 6 & 7 & 6 & 3 \\ 3-2 & & & & -2 & 3 & 6 & 7 & 6 \\ 6 & 3-2 & & & & -2 & 3 & 6 & 7 \end{bmatrix}$$

(19)

A smoothed contour by operator (19) is shown on Fig.1. A subset of linear operators defined by an NxN circulant Toeplitz matrix C which smooth digital closed contours in the least squares sense is suitable for digital contour approximation and these operators will be called feasible. Let us denote

$$(1/c)CX = X' \qquad (20)$$

where X' has elements x'_i and y'_i. Then a feasible operator is defined as follows[1]:

Definition 1 : A linear operator (1/c)C, where C is an NxN circulant Toeplitz matrix whose elements are defined by (7), is feasible if

$$| x_i - x'_i | < \frac{1}{2} \qquad | y_i - y'_i | < \frac{1}{2} . \qquad (21)$$

According to this definition a feasible operator is defined by the constrained least squares smoothing with box constraints defined by (21) . The following theorem holds :

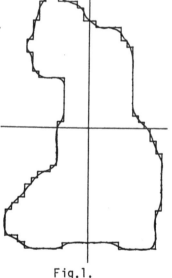

Fig.1.

Theorem 1 : Linear operators defined by (17),(18) and (19) are feasible.

Proof : The proof consists of the analysis of all possibilities of all 4-connected digital arcs of the length of n+1 points on a rectangular array of points. According to this analysis we obtain that for

m=1 and n+1=3

$$| x_i - x'_i | \leq \frac{1}{3} \qquad | y_i - y'_i | \leq \frac{1}{3}$$

m=3 and n+1=5

$$| x_i - x'_i | \leq \frac{12}{35} \qquad | y_i - y'_i | \leq \frac{12}{35}$$

and for m=3 and n+1=7

$$| x_i - x_i' | \le \frac{10}{2T} \qquad | y_i - y_i' | \le \frac{10}{2T}$$

what is the assertion of the theorem.

The above described linear operators allow to smooth simply closed digital curves provided that they are defined by uniformly spaced points. We note that 8-connected digital curves do not have this property. The advantage of these operators is that they do not require the solution of the full system of linear algebraic equations. They are defined by the least squares approximation. The interpolation is sensitive to the accuracy of input values and if they are influenced by noise, which is the case in image processing, the error due to the noise will be introduced also into the interpolation formula. Further advantage is that the smoothed values are defined by the values of the approximation polynomial $P_m(i)$ which allows to calculate the first and the second derivatives $P_m'(i)$, $P_m''(i)$ which are important in order to define the curvature in each point (Sloboda 1988). The original 4-connected digital closed curve does not allow to calculate derivatives. The smoothed values defined by $(1/c)CX$ are directly used for the perimeter length, area an the first and the second order moments calculation (Sloboda 1988).

Digital curve approximation and curve representation have been studied by a number of authors (Freeman 1978), (Freeman and Saghri 1980), (Sklansky et al 1972), (Sklansky 1972), (Toussaint and Davis 1982). The algorithms proposed by them were not thought for curvature calculation.

4. HOMOTHETY

Let X be an Nx2 matrix which represents an array of coordinates of an arbitrary set of N points $P_1=(x_1,y_1)$, $P_2=(x_2,y_2),\ldots$, $P_N=(x_N,y_N)$ in the 2-dimensional Euclidean space R_2. Let us denote by A_N an NxN matrix

$$A_N = \begin{bmatrix} 1 & 1 & 1 & \cdots & 1 \\ 1 & 1 & 1 & \vdots & 1 \\ 1 & 1 & 1 & \cdots & 1 \\ \cdot & & & & \\ \cdot & & & & \\ \cdot & & & & \\ 1 & 1 & 1 & \cdots & 1 \end{bmatrix} \qquad (22)$$

i.e., A_N is an rank-one matrix. Let C be an NxN circulant Toeplitz matrix of the form (1)-(2). It can be easily verified that

$$CA_N = A_N C = c A_N \qquad (23)$$

and

$$A_N A_N = N A_N \ . \qquad (24)$$

This property of circulant matrices enables to prove the theorem on position invariancy :

Theorem 2 : Let X- $(1/N)A_N X$ be an Nx2 matrix and let C be an circulant Toeplitz matrix of the form (1)-(2). Then

$$\frac{1}{N} A_N C (X - \frac{1}{N} A_N X) = 0$$

We shall refer to the neighbors of type a/ as 4-neighbors of P, and to the neighbors of both type, as 8-neighbors (Rosenfeld 1979). The former neighbors are said to be 4-adjacent (4-connected)(Rosenfeld 1979). A path Π of length n from P to Q in Σ is a sequence of points $P=P_0, P_1, \ldots, P_n=Q$ of Σ such that P_i is adjacent to P_{i-1}, $1 \leq i \leq n$. A digital arc is a path $\alpha = P_0$, $P_1, P_2, \ldots, P_n$ such that (Rosenfeld 1979)

a/ $P_i = P_j$ iff i=j, and

b/ P_i is a neighbor of P_j iff $i=j\pm1$.

A simply closed digital curve is a path $\gamma = P_0, P_1, \ldots, P_n$ such that (Rosenfeld 1979)

a/ $P_i = P_j$ iff i=j, and

b/ P_i is a neighbor of P_j iff $i=j\pm1 \pmod{n+1}$.

Let

$$x = x(t) \qquad y = y(t) \tag{14}$$

be a simply closed curve in the 2-dimensional Euclidean space R_2. Let this curve be approximated by a set of N points $P_1 = (x_1, y_1)$, $P_2 = (x_2, y_2), \ldots, P_N = (x_N, y_N)$ which are elements of a finite rectangular array Σ ; and let these points represent a simply closed 4-connected digital curve for which

$$|| P_i - P_{i-1} || = | x_i - x_{i-1} | + | y_i - y_{i-1} | = 1.$$

The discretized parametric equation of this digital closed curve has the form

$$X = \begin{bmatrix} x_1 & y_1 \\ x_2 & y_2 \\ \cdot \\ \cdot \\ \cdot \\ x_N & y_N \end{bmatrix} . \tag{15}$$

The least squares smoothing of a simply closed digital curve, a generalization of the previous section, is then defined by the linear operator $(1/c)C$ which is applied on X

$$(1/c)CX \tag{16}$$

where C is an NxN circulant Toeplitz matrix of the form (1) and c is the sum of all elements in a row. The coefficients of this matrix are defined by (7). For different values of m and n+1 we obtain, for example, the following operators which correspond to (8),(11) and (12) :

$$m = 1$$

n+1=3

$$\frac{1}{c}C = \frac{1}{3} \begin{bmatrix} 1 & 1 & & & & 1 \\ 1 & 1 & 1 & & & \\ & 1 & 1 & 1 & & \\ & & & 1 & 1 & 1 \\ 1 & & & & 1 & 1 \end{bmatrix} \tag{17}$$

where 0 is an Nx2 matrix with zero coefficients.

Proof : At first we show that

$$\frac{1}{N} A_N(X- \frac{1}{N}A_N X) = 0 .$$

According to (23)-(24) we have

$$\frac{1}{N} A_N(X- \frac{1}{N}A_N X) = \frac{1}{N} A_N X - \frac{1}{N}\frac{1}{N} A_N A_N X = (\frac{1}{N} A_N - \frac{1}{N}\frac{1}{N} NA_N)X = (\frac{1}{N} A_N - \frac{1}{N}A_N)X = 0.$$

Similarly, according to (23)-(24) we have

$$\frac{1}{N} A_N C(X- \frac{1}{N}A_N X) = \frac{1}{N} A_N CX - \frac{1}{N}\frac{1}{N} A_N CA_N X = (\frac{1}{N}A_N C - \frac{1}{N}\frac{1}{N}A_N CA_N)X =$$

$$= (\frac{1}{N}CA_N - \frac{1}{N}\frac{1}{N}CA_N A_N)X = (\frac{1}{N}CA_N - \frac{1}{N}\frac{1}{N}CNA_N)X = 0$$

which is the assertion of the theorem.

In the next we shall investigate the following family of circulant Toeplitz matrices. Let A_i, i=1,2,...,N-1 be Nx2 matrices of the form

$$A_1=I, \ A_2=\begin{bmatrix} 1\ 1 & & \\ & 1\ 1 & \\ & & 1\ 1 \\ & & & 1\ 1 \\ 1 & & & 1 \end{bmatrix}, \ \ldots, \ A_{N-1}=\begin{bmatrix} 1\ 1 & \ldots & 1\ 0 \\ 0\ 1\ 1 & \vdots\vdots & 1\ 1 \\ 1\ 0\ 1\ 1 & \ldots & 1\ 1 \\ \vdots & & \\ \vdots & & \\ 1\ 1\ 1 & \ldots & 1\ 0\ 1 \end{bmatrix} \quad (25)$$

where I denotes the identity matrix. Further, let us consider a family of NxN permutation matrices P_i, i=1,2,...,N, which are orthogonal and circulant and have the form

$$P_1=I, \ P_2=\begin{bmatrix} 0\ 1 & & \\ & 0\ 1 & \\ & & 0\ 1 \\ & & & 0\ 1 \\ 1 & & & 0 \end{bmatrix}, \ \ldots, \ P_N=\begin{bmatrix} 0\ 0\ 0 & \ldots & 0\ 1 \\ 1\ 0\ 0 & \ldots & 0\ 0 \\ 0\ 1\ 0 & \ldots & 0\ 0 \\ \vdots & & \\ \vdots & & \\ 0\ 0\ 0 & \ldots & 1\ 0 \end{bmatrix} \quad (26)$$

where $P_i^{-1}= P_i^T$ for i=1,2,...,N. It can be easily verified that for A_{N-k}, k=1,2,...,N-1, defined by (25) it holds that

$$A_{N-k}A_N = A_N A_{N-k} = (N-k)A_N \quad (27)$$

where A_N is defined by (22). Let us denote by A_{N-k}^C the complement of the matrix A_{N-k}

$$A_{N-k}+ A_{N-k}^C = A_N . \quad (28)$$

Because of

$$A_k = P_{k+1}A_{N-k}^C \quad (29)$$

we obtain that

$$A_{N-k}^C = P_{k+1}^{-1}A_k = P_{k+1}^T A_k \quad (30)$$

where P_{k+1} is defined by (26). This property enables to prove the theorem on homothety :

Theorem 3 : Let A_k, k=1,2,...,N-1 be NxN matrices defined by (25) and let P_{k+1} be NxN permutation matrices defined by (26). Then

$$A_{N-k}(X- \tfrac{1}{N}A_N X) = - P_{k+1}^T A_k(X- \tfrac{1}{N}A_N X)$$

i.e., A_{N-k} and A_k generate homothety with the coefficient of homothety $\alpha = -1$.

Proof : According to (27) we have

$$A_{N-k}(X- \tfrac{1}{N}A_N X) = A_{N-k}X- \tfrac{1}{N}A_{N-k}A_N X = A_{N-k}X- \tfrac{1}{N}(N-k)A_N X =$$

$$= \tfrac{1}{N}N A_{N-k}X- \tfrac{1}{N}(N-k)A_N X = \tfrac{1}{N}(NA_{N-k}X- (N-k)A_N X) \ .$$

Because of (28) and (30) we have that

$$A_{N-k} = A_N- P_{k+1}^T A_k \tag{31}$$

so that

$$\tfrac{1}{N}(NA_{N-k}X- (N-k)A_N X) = \tfrac{1}{N}(N(A_N- P_{k+1}^T A_k)-(N-k)A_N)X =$$

$$= \tfrac{1}{N}(NA_N- NP_{k+1}^T A_k- NA_N+ kA_N)X = \tfrac{1}{N}(-NP_{k+1}^T A_k+ kA_N)X \ .$$

Because of

$$kA_N = kP_{k+1}^T A_N = P_{k+1}^T A_k A_N \tag{32}$$

we obtain

$$\tfrac{1}{N}(-NP_{k+1}^T A_k+ kA_N)X = \tfrac{1}{N}(-NP_{k+1}^T A_k+ P_{k+1}^T A_k A_N)X = - P_{k+1}^T A_k(X- \tfrac{1}{N}A_N X)$$

which is the assertion of the theorem.

Let us consider a family of linear operators

$$(1/k)A_k \qquad\qquad k=1,2,...,N-1 \tag{33}$$

where A_k are defined by (25). For these operators it holds the following theorem:

Theorem 4 : Let $(1/k)A_k$, k=1,2,...,N-1 be operators defined by NxN matrices A_k of the form (25), and let P_{k+1} be an NxN permutation matrix defined by (26). Then

$$\tfrac{1}{N-k}A_{N-k}(X- \tfrac{1}{N}A_N X) = - \tfrac{k}{N-k} \tfrac{1}{k}P_{k+1}^T A_k(X- \tfrac{1}{N}A_N X)$$

i.e., operators $(1/k)A_k$ and $(1/(N-k))A_{N-k}$ generate homothety with the coefficient of homothety $\alpha = - k/(N-k)$.

Proof : According to Theorem 3 we have

$$A_{N-k}(X- \tfrac{1}{N}A_N X) = - P_{k+1}^T A_k(X- \tfrac{1}{N}A_N X) \ .$$

By rearrangement we obtain

$$\frac{1}{N-k}A_{N-k}(X - \frac{1}{N}A_N X) = -\frac{k}{N-k}\frac{1}{k}P_{k+1}^T A_k(X - \frac{1}{N}A_N X)$$

which is the assertion of the theorem.

The homothety generated by these operators
is shown on Fig.2. (a) represents the original pattern defined by 10 points, (b) represents pattern obtained by operator $(1/3)A_3$
applied on (a), (c) by $(1/5)A_5$ applied on
(a), (d) by $(1/7)A_7$ applied on (a), (e) by
$(1/9)A_9$ applied on (a). (a) and (e), (b) and
(d) are homothetic. According to Theorem 4
operators $(1/k)A_k$ for $k > N/2$ generate patterns
which are homothetic with the patterns obtained by operators for $k < N/2$.

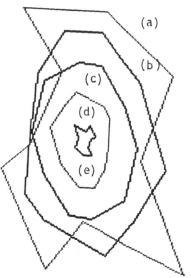

Let A_k be NxN matrices defined by (25), and
let k be odd. Each matrix A_k for k odd has
its symmetric form A_{ks} defined by

$$A_k = P_{(k+1)/2}A_{ks}$$

where $P_{(k+1)/2}$ is an permutation matrix defined by (26). Operators $(1/k)A_{ks}$ for
k odd but are the least squares smoothing   Fig.2.
operators defined by the polynomials of the first order and by k=n+1 points.
For example operator $(1/3)A_{3s}$ is defined by (17). According to Theorem 4 it
subsequently follows that the least squares smoothing by the polynomial of
the first order is limited. The maximal smoothing is obtained by $k = \lfloor N/2 \rfloor$
points where N denotes the total number of points. Theorem 3 and Theorem 4
are valid also for an Nxm matrix X, $2 \leq m \leq N$. Operators $(1/k)A_k$ enable to
generate symmetric patterns. Symmetry plays an important role in mathematics, physics, crystallography and also in art (Hargittai 1986).

5. BIT-LEVEL SYSTOLIC ARRAY

In many scientific, signal and image processing applications high-speed
computation is required which call for novel approaches in computer architectures. Kung and Leiserson (1978) have introduced the notion of systolic
arrays, a special kind of highly regular, homogeneous, pipelined processor
arrays. Some important design considerations for massively parallel VLSI
array processors are discussed in (Kung 1984). For real-time applications
one- dimensional systolic array TOPSS-28 has been developed (Nudd 1984).
This array enables the solution of Toeplitz system of equations.In (Petkov
and Sloboda 1988) a bit-level systolic array for digital contour smoothing
has been suggested. This array is performing the smoothing of digital contours by operator (19).

Let X be an Nx2 matrix which represents a simply closed 4-connected digital
curve. The elements of this matrix are defined by the coordinates of N contour points which are integer values. Let us denote

$$x = (x_1, x_2, \ldots, x_N)^T$$
$$y = (y_1, y_2, \ldots, y_N)^T .$$

The matrix-matrix multiplication CX can be performed by two matrix-vector multiplications Cx and Cy. The bit-level systolic array (Petkov and Sloboda 1988) performs the matrix-vector multiplication

$$u = Cx$$

where C is defined by (19). Let us denote the non-zero elements of C by

$$a_{-3}=-2 \quad a_{-2}= 3 \quad a_{-1}= 6 \quad a_0= 7 \quad a_1= 6 \quad a_2= 3 \quad a_3=-2 \ .$$

The matrix-vector multiplication can be represented by the circulant convolution

$$u_i = \sum_{j=-3}^{3} a_j x_{(i-j)\bmod N} \qquad\qquad i=1,2,\ldots,N \qquad\qquad (34)$$

where u_i is the i-th component of u and $x_0 = x_N$. Let z_i^{in}, $i=1,2,\ldots,N$ denote the initial starting values of the components of the vector z. The word-level systolic array fot the circulant convolution (34) is shown on Fig.3.

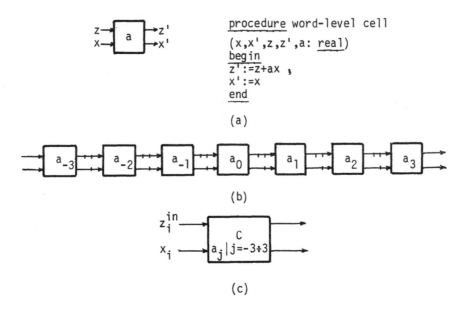

```
procedure word-level cell

(x,x',z,z',a: real)
begin
z':=z+ax ;
x':=x
end
```

(a)

(b)

(c)

Fig.3. The word-level systolic array

The circulant Toeplitz matrix (19) can be represented by the sum of two matrices

$$C = C^{(1)}+ C^{(2)}$$

with the coefficients $a_j^{(1)}$ and $a_j^{(2)}$ for which

$$a_j= a_j^{(1)}+ a_j^{(2)} \qquad\qquad j=-3,-2,\ldots,2,3$$

which are powers of 2, so that the corresponding multiplications can be carried out by shifting the x-data. The coefficients will be represented by the following powers of 2

j	-3	-2	-1	0	1	2	3
a_j	-2	3	6	7	6	3	-2
$a_j^{(1)}$	0	2^0	2^1	-2^0	2^1	2^0	-2^1
$a_j^{(2)}$	-2^1	2^1	2^2	2^3	2^2	2^1	0

The resulting systolic array has the form shown on Fig.4.

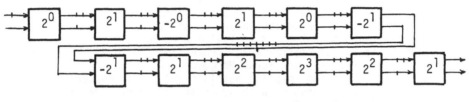

Fig.4.

In the bit-level structure the multiplication by 2^1 is performed by shifting the input x-data upwards by one bit position. The addition is carried out in a curry-ripple array of full adders. For 8-bit input data and according to the sum

$$\sum_{j=-3}^{3} a_j = 21$$

the intermediate results will be represented by $(8 + \lceil \log_2 21 \rceil)$-bit numbers. Hence, one word-level cell, i.e., one column of the bit-level array consits of $(8 + \lceil \log_2 21 \rceil) = 13$ bit-level cells (full adders). The multiplication by -2^0 is performed by converting the input x-words into their 2's complements before addition. This can be done by inverting the corresponding x-inputs of the full adders and adding a 1 via carry input of the LSB full adder. The clock period of this system is controled by the carry-ripple delay from the LSB to the MSB cell, which is estimated by separating the full adders of one column by delay element and thus forming vertical pipelining. The whole array is a regular matrix of full adders arranged in 12 columns and 13 rows. The division by 21 is not considered here and will be performed later as one division, after the local and global invariants have been calculated from the array CX (Sloboda 1988).

6. REFERENCES

Bareiss E H 1969 Numerical solution of linear equations with Toeplitz and
    vector Toeplitz matrices, Numer.Math.13 pp 404-424
Berezin I, Zhidkov N 1965 Computing Methods (Oxford: Pergamon Press)
Bini D 1984 Parallel solution of certain Toeplitz linear systems, SIAM J.
    Comput. 13 pp 268-276
Bitmead R R, Anderson B 1980 Asymptotically fast solution of Toeplitz and
    related systems of linear equations, Lin. Alg. Appl. 34 pp 103-116
Bojanczyk A, Brent R P 1986 Parallel solution of certain Toeplitz least-
    squares problems, Lin. Alg. Appl. 77 pp 43-60
Brent R P, Gustavson F, Yun Y 1980 Fast solution of Toeplitz systems of equa-
    tions and computation of Pade approximants, J. Algorithms 1 pp 259-295

Brent R P, Luk F 1983 a systolic array for the linear-time solution of
  Toeplitz systems of equations, J. VLSI and Comp. Systems 1 pp 1-22
Codenotti B 1986 Error analysis of an APA algorithm for the parallel solu-
  tion of some special Toeplitz linear systems, Calcolo 18 pp 1-11
Davies P 1979 Circulant matrices (New-York: Wiley Interscience)
Durbin J 1960 The fitting of time-series models, Rev. Inst. Int. Statist.
  28 pp 233-244
Elden L 1986 A systolic array for the regularization of ill-conditioned
  least-squares problems with triangular Toeplitz matrix 77 pp 137-147
Freeman H 1978 Application of the generalized chain coding scheme to map
  data processing, Proc. IEEE Comp. Soc. Conf. on Pattern Recognition and
  Image Processing pp 220-226
Freeman H, Saghri J 1980 Comparative analysis of line-drawing modeling
  schemes, Comp. Graphics and Image Processing 12 pp 203-223
Gohberg I, Semencul A 1972 On the inversion of finite Toeplitz matrices
  and their continuous analogs, Mat. Issled 2 pp 201-233
Gonzales R, Wintz P 1987 Digital image processing (Amsterdam: Add.-Wesley)
Hargittai I 1986 Symmetry (New York: Pergamon Press)
Iohvidov I 1982 Hankel and Toeplitz matrices and forms (Boston: Birkhauser)
Kung S Y 1984 On supercomputing with systolic/wavefront array processors,
  Proc. of the IEEE 72 pp 867-884
Kung H T, Leiserson C 1978 Systolic arrays (for VLSI), Sparse matrix Proc.
  ed I S Duff and G W Stewart pp 256-282
Kung S Y, Hu Y 1981 Fast and parallel algorithms for solving Toeplitz sys-
  tems, Proc. Int. Symp. on Micro-computers in Control and Meas. pp 21-33
Levinson N 1947 The Wiener RMS error criterion in filter design and predic-
  tion, J. Math. Phys. 25 pp 261-278
Nudd G R 1984 Concurrent systems for image analysis, VLSI for Pattern Rec.
  and Image processing ed K S Fu (New York: Springer) pp 107-132
Petkov N, Sloboda F 1988 A bit-level systolic array for digital contour
  smoothing, to be published
Rosenfeld A, Kak C 1976 Digital picture processing (New York: AP)
Rosenfeld A 1979 Picture languages (New York: AP)
Sankar P, Ferrari L 1988 Simple algorithms and architectures for B-spline
  interpolation, IEEE Trans. on PAMI 10 pp 271-276
Sklansky J, Chazin R, Hansen B 1972 Minimum-perimeter polygons of digitized
  silhouettes, IEEE Trans. on Comp. 3 pp 260-268
Sklansky J 1972 Measuring concavity on a rectangular mosaic, IEEE Trans.
  on Comp. 21 pp 1355-1364
Sloboda F 1988 Toeplitz matrices,curvature, and least-squares approximation
  to be published
Teh C H, Chin R 1986 On digital approximation of moment invariants, Comp.
  Vision, Graphics, and Image Processing 33 pp 318-325
Toussaint G, Avis D 1982 On a convex hull algorithm for polygons and its
  applications to triangulation problems, Pattern Recog. 15 pp 23-29
Trench W 1964 An algorithm for the inversion of finite Toeplitz matrices,
  J. Soc. Ind. Appl. Math. 12 pp 515-522
Zohar S 1969 Toeplitz matrix inversion: the algorithm of W Trench, J. Ass.
  Comp. Mach. 16 pp 592-601

Parallel processing of programs coupling symbolic and numerical computations

J. S. Kowalik

Boeing Computer Services, P. O. Box 24346 MS 7L-22,Seattle Washington 98124-0346, USA

ABSTRACT: In order to solve complex problems in business, science, and engineering, both numerical and symbolic processing are often needed. Powerful software systems can be built by integrating the explanation and problem-solving capabilities of knowledge-based systems with the precision of traditional numerical computing. We discuss the nature of and parallel approaches to symbolic computation, as well as multiprocessor systems whose architectures may be a step toward parallel computers of the future that process programs coupling symbolic and numerical computation.

1. INTRODUCTION

Traditionally, large-scale numerical computation and artificial intelligence have not had much in common. Large numerical problems such as those encountered in computational fluid dynamics, oil reservoir simulation, or weather simulation have stimulated the design and development of modern supercomputers whose performance has been optimized for floating-point arithmetic operations on arrays and vectors. On the other hand, AI researchers have tackled very different problems related to perception, natural language processing, automated reasoning, learning, etc. – problems that require mainly symbolic computation. Recently AI has attempted to enter the real world of scientific, engineering, and business applications and the ability to couple AI techniques with "conventional" computing, such as statistics, simulation and numerical analysis, has become essential. Examples of problems that require coupling symbolic and numerical computation include:

a.   Visual perception,
b.   Speech recognition combined with natural language understanding,
c.   Robotics integrating sensing, perception, manipulation and reasoning in some task domain,
d.   Knowledge-based systems for engineering design, analysis, or diagnosis.

Each of these applications requires performing accurate arithmetic calculations and processing symbols other than numbers. For example, in order to automate aircraft design the numerical techniques encountered in aerodynamics, structures, weights, and performance computation need to be integrated with symbolic techniques used in data base management, planning, data evaluation, reasoning about earlier designs, heuristic optimization strategies, etc. Solving such complex problems compels us to switch back and forth between formal mathematical models and symbolic models related to qualitative reasoning.

Together with the need for coupled software systems, several new issues will appear: software architecture of coupled programs, development tools and environments, and implementations of coupled programs on high-performance computer systems.

In this paper, we discuss some of the issues related to parallel symbolic/numerical computations and parallel computers whose architecture may be a step toward symbolic/numerical supercomputers of the future.

We focus on computations related to knowledge-based systems. The reader interested in examples of coupled knowledge-based systems is referred to Kowalik (1986), Kowalik and Chalfan (1987), and Kowalik and Kitzmiller (1988).

2. THE NATURE OF SYMBOLIC COMPUTATION

There are two major models for large-scale numerical computation: a continuum model based on near neighbor interactions and a particle model based on discrete point-to-point interactions. Both models have considerable structural regularity, and most of the algorithms appropriate for these models can be expressed as sequences of vector operations. Therefore, we can successfully exploit the pipeline architecture of the fastest vector supercomputers. No such fortunate situation exists for symbolic computation. In part, this is due to a much smaller demand for commercial high-performance symbolic processors. But there are other more fundamental reasons related to the nature of the symbolic computation required in AI. One of them is the wide variety of data structures used to represent and manipulate knowledge: graphs, semantic networks, frames, production rules, sentences, etc. These structures tend to be highly irregular and unpredictable in size and form. They are often created dynamically. Consequently,
a. It is not usually possible to prefetch these data structures to high-speed memories for faster access,
b. We have to deal with time-consuming memory management schemes,
c. The possibility of statically allocating tasks to various processors working in parallel is minimal.

In addition, AI algorithms and programs exhibit behavior that makes it hard to speed them up. The behavior of the typical AI algorithm is highly data dependent and sensitive to data changes. This computational instability and the high degree of logical branching in the code generated for these programs reduces the chances for fine-grained pipelining. Also, in contrast to conventional programs that specify instructions for obtaining the solution, AI programs often provide only a high-level specification of actions to be taken depending upon the system's behavior. This further reduces the program's predictability and the applicability of pipelining. See Rice (1988) for further elaboration.

Given these characteristics of symbolic computation, it is not surprising that we have not progressed with high-speed symbolic processing as far as we have progressed with numerical supercomputing. We are now only beginning to understand what types of computer architectures could be suitable for symbolic processing. Uhr (1987), who explores different multicomputer architectures for AI, predicts that the best hope for computers capable of solving the most demanding AI problems "appears to lie in developing highly parallel multi-computer networks where many different, more or less independent, processors work in parallel." He also stresses the importance of massively parallel algorithms and their role in achieving AI systems that are fast, robust, and flexible enough to deal with the most complex applications. We are in agreement with this assessment and add that future supercomputers will have to deal efficiently with huge coupled software systems.

3. PARALLEL APPROACHES TO SYMBOLIC COMPUTATION

At a low level of primitive operations encountered in AI algorithms, we find such operations as pattern matching, graph searching, sorting, logical operations, and pointer manipulation. Some of these operations allow a high degree of parallelism; e.g., matching. Others at first sight seem to be purely sequential. Consider as an example the task of finding the end of a linked list. Our intuition tells us that this search process is sequential since we cannot proceed from element K to K+1 before traversing all K-1 preceding elements. But the intuition is wrong in this case. It turns out that by using many processors one can solve this problem in a length of time proportional to the logarithm of the number of pointers to be traversed, P. The complexity of this task is O (log P) instead of O (P). The method resembles computing the sum of an array in logarithmic time (see Hillis and

Steele (1986)). This simple example illustrates the point that research into parallel algorithms is of paramount importance and that the active-memory approach, which applies massive parallelism to a large group of identical operations, may have many unexpected applications. Problems with massive identical operations appear often in various AI applications; e.g.: searching, matching, inferencing, etc. Another source of parallelism can be found in AI programming languages: general-purpose such as Lisp and special-purpose such as the Prolog and production system.

Lisp

A version of Lisp called Multilisp, developed at MIT by Halstead (1988), specifies parallel execution using the "future" construct. In Multilisp, a function may return a promissory value instead of an actual value and then attempt to find a processor for performing the actual calculation. The construct "future X" immediately returns a future for the value X and creates a task to concurrently evaluate X, allowing the parallel computation of a value and the use of that value. When the evaluation of X produces the value, that value replaces the future. In some operations the resulting values may be needed immediately before the computation can proceed; e.g., in arithmetic operations. But often operations can be executed without waiting for the specific values involved; e.g. inserting a value into a data structure or transmitting a value from one place to another by assignment.

Multilisp has been implemented on the Concert, a 28-processor shared-memory machine, and the Butterfly. Halstead (1988) presents the performance of Concert Multilisp on two parallel test programs, tree insertion and Quicksort. One of his conclusions is that constructs such as "future" are only part of what is needed to fully exploit different levels of parallelism. In particular, we should have constructs that allow various parts of a program to execute concurrently; that is, we should be able to implement parallelism globally. This in turn requires constructing modular programs. McGehearty and Krall (1988) report results of simulated parallel runs of several Lisp applications that include a program intended to test the efficiency of Lisp implementations in calling recursive functions and an implementation of the inference kernel of the EMYCIN expert system. The tested programs exhibited speed-up ranging from 1 (no speed-up) to 850 times faster. The authors conclude that the "future construct" is of no value or great value to a few programs, and of moderate value to most programs.

Another approach to parallelizing Lisp has been taken by Gabriel and McCarthy (1988). Their version of Lisp, called Qlisp, allows two kinds of parallelism:
a. The parallelism derived from the parallel evaluation of arguments,
b. The unstructured parallelism of process invocation, in which a number of processes are created and messages are passed among them, resulting in concurrent processing.

Prolog

Several attempts have been made to parallelize logic programming, which exhibits a high potential for concurrence. In logic programming there are generally several alternative clauses that can be used to prove a given predicate goal. Each clause in turn has several subgoals requiring the proof. Because any one clause may be used to prove the goal, attempting this proof in parallel is called OR-parallelism. On the other hand, once a particular clause is selected for a proof attempt, all subgoals within this clause must be solved for the clause to succeed. Therefore, executing these subgoals in parallel is called AND-parallelism.

OR-parallelism is easier to implement than AND-parallelism, because to prove a given predicate, separate, independent processors may be activated in parallel, one for each clause that defines the predicate goal. In addition, not all activated processors need to communicate with each other. A major disadvantage of this method is that OR-parallelism attempts to find all solutions to a problem, although only one may be needed. AND-parallelism, on the other hand, attempts to produce the first answer as quickly as possible before trying to find another. However, AND-parallelism involves the parallel execution of goals that are typically highly interdependent, and a significant amount of communication between the processors is required, which increases the cost of the potential parallel speed-up. A version of Prolog that incorporates both AND-parallelism and OR-parallelism has been introduced by Clark and Gregory (1988). DeGroot (1988) advocates a method that restricts the potential AND-parallelism in order to minimize the amount and cost of required communication between processors. In general, both Lisp and Prolog can be parallelized but not as easily as Fortran. In addition, the quality of code produced by their compilers is often unpredictable.

Production Systems

Gupta (1986) investigates parallelism in production systems that consist of a set of data and a set of rules that can act on the data. One of the best known environments for implementation of a production system is OPS5, which provides a natural programming style for if-then rule-based expert systems. The experimental results indicate that at most a speed-up of 10 to 20 times can be expected in typical expert systems. This is rather disappointing but not yet fully understood. A more recent study by Sabharval et al. (1988) examines sources of parallelism in the production system structure and analyzes the potential speed-ups, trade-offs, and architectural implementations. The authors suggest a dedicated n-ary tree machine for parallel execution of rule-based systems. The issue of numerical computing that may be required in the process of inferencing is not discussed.

Other Possibilities

Some specialized AI systems, such as blackboard architectures, also offer a natural possibility for large-grain parallelism. In a blackboard system, there is a global database called the blackboard and logically independent sources of knowledge called knowledge sources which respond to changes on the blackboard. There is no centralized control, and the knowledge sources are self-activating. The principles of blackboard architecture have been used in several complex applications of AI; for example, in intelligent control systems that combine AI, control theory, and operations research to solve real-time problems (Kowalik et al. (1986) and Skillman (1986)). Nii (1986) describes three methods for using multiple processors in the blackboard systems:
1. Partitioning the solution space on the blackboard into separate, loosely coupled regions,
2. Using multi processors to place the blackboard data in a shared memory and distributing the knowledge sources on different processors,
3. Partitioning the problem into independent subproblems and solving each subproblem on a separate processor.

Rice (1988) investigated the potential speed-up of blackboard systems by exploiting parallelism on a simulated distributed memory, message-passing multiprocessor. A series of experiments in the domain of real-time interpretation of passive radar signal data has shown speed-up of roughly one order of magnitude. Rice indicates that it is difficult to implement knowledge parallelism using his approach, since it is an MIMD parallelism.

A promising opportunity for parallel processing in artificial intelligence is offered by the active-memory approach. The central idea in this approach is to identify certain very time-consuming operations that most AI programs have in common and design high-speed parallel systems for executing such operations. For example, one of the most time-consuming operations in AI programs is searching for the stored descriptions that best match a predefined set of features. These matching operations can often be performed using the massive parallelism of SIMD computer architectures with many thousands of processors. Such multiprocessors can be viewed as active-memory systems. The Connection Machine is an implementation of the active-memory concept. Several other examples of massively parallel architectures built to solve AI problems can be found in Fahlman (1988).

4. COMPUTERS FOR SYMBOLIC/NUMERICAL COMPUTATION

We consider first general-purpose computers for symbolic/numerical computation. By a general-purpose computer we mean a system capable of efficient support for wide range of applications involving symbolic and numerical operations. We would call such a system a supercomputer if its numerical performance is roughly equal to the performance of current numerical supercomputers and if it outperforms powerful Lisp workstations (such as the Symbolics 3600) by at least one order of magnitude in symbolic processing. According to this definition, the Cray X-MP is a symbolic/numerical supercomputer. It has been successfully used for coupled symbolic/numerical applications (see, for example, Ragheb and Gvillo (1987)). For applications requiring small amounts of symbolic processing and large amounts of numerical processing, such use of the Cray could be appropriate. For applications that also require large amounts of symbolic processing, the use of the CRAY is not cost effective, since its forte, vector processing capability, would be significantly underused. A major deficiency of the Cray in such applications would be its lack of AI programming tools and facilities. We prefer to regard Cray supercomputers as numerical number crunchers and possibly as components of multicomputer networks in which several specialized computers cooperate.

A system assembled from a collection of specialized components is one of the available options for building symbolic/numerical supercomputers. Kotov et al. (1986) study a system consisting of functionally complete modules, where each module can store and process data, has local control, and can easily transfer data to and from other modules. Any functional module can consist of other specialized modules. We get, in effect, a modular, hierarchical, heterogeneous parallel configuration. Such a configuration may include numerical processors, database processors, operating system processors, symbolic processors, and other specialized high-performance processors.

Another attempt to build a high-performance computing system for symbolic/numerical applications is under way at the University of California, Berkeley, by Despain and coworkers (see Despain and Patt (1987)). The machine, called Aquarius, has the following basic features: (1) it is a MIMD machine made of heterogeneous specialized processing elements, (2) it exploits parallelism at several levels of computation, and (3) it supports logic programming. Initially, there will be at least three types of processors: parallel Prolog processors, floating-point arithmetic processors, and I/O processors. Two significant parallel commercial machines that can handle both numerical and symbolic computation the Connection Machine and the Butterfly, require our special attention. The Connection Machine (CM), which can be regarded as an active-memory extension to the memory of the front-end processor, was initially designed to manipulate semantic networks. It turns out that the machine has much broader applicability, especially with the addition of optional Weitek floating-point processors to the CM-2. This massively parallel computer features 65,536 processors connected by a Boolean N-cube. In the full configuration of CM, there are 4,096 chips, each having 16 processors, connected by a Boolean 12-cube. Each processor is associated with 64K bits of local memory, and 32 processors share one Weitek floating-point processor.
The CM's computing power and versatility stems from:
1. The large number of processors: 64K, 32K, or 16K,
2. The high rate of data access by each processor in its own memory: 5 Mbits per second,
3. The huge total memory: 512 Mbytes in a fully configured machine,
4. The global communication via a mechanism called the router, which allows any processor to communicate with any other processor, and a local communications mechanism called the NEWS grid, which allows fast passing of data according to a regular rectangular pattern; e.g., between nearest neighbor processors,
5. The availability of several programming styles using extensions of familiar languages: Fortran, C, and Lisp.

The machine has been used to solve problems in disparate application areas: machine vision, fluid flow, molecular dynamics, quantum chromodynamics, stellar evolution, seismic analysis, VLSI circuit simulation, machine reasoning, locating information in natural language documents contained in large data bases, and computer graphics. Some indications of its performance for suitable problems and algorithms are impressive. It has been reported that for an engineering problem of predicting airflow around helicopter rotor blades, the CM-2 machine ran 5 to 6 times faster than the CRAY-2 supercomputer. We expect that for many problems that can be simulated by the continuum model or the particle model, the CM-2 machine can be extremely fast.

In the AI domain, the Connection Machine has significant potential applications. It supports well many symbolic operations that include matching, sorting, graph searching, and even parallel manipulation of pointers, mentioned in section 3. It is not clear if and how it can handle conventional rule-based systems, but a promising problem-solving method called memory-based reasoning has been proposed by Stanfill and Waltz (1986). Its basic hypothesis is that certain kinds of reasoning may be supported by searching databases of previously encountered and classified problems for the best match to the new problem. The best matches are retrieved from memory and offered as possible solutions. This memory-based reasoning can be executed on the CM in a length of time proportional to $(\log N)^2$, where N is the number of processors. In general, the CM is suitable for data parallel algorithms whose parallelism is based on simultaneous operations across large sets of data. As illustrated by Hillis and Steele (1986), this style of computing is appropriate for massively parallel architectures with thousands or millions of processors. Furthermore, in many instances we can find parallel algorithms for seemingly sequential computational procedures that solve problems of size N in $O(\log N)$ time using $O(N)$ processors.

Programming the Connection Machine requires new habits. The CM is a SIMD machine and the programmer typically is free from detailed concerns related to hardware and interconnection networks. Synchronization is not needed. Instead, different concerns become important: inventing new data parallel algorithms and reevaluating traditional computing approaches developed for serial computation. Efficient data parallel algorithms maximize the number of processors busy (doing useful work) throughout the computation and minimize the amount of data shifting between the active processors. To accomplish this, it is often necessary to invent suitable data distribution patterns for allocating data to processors.

As mentioned earlier, the Connection Machine can be regarded as an intelligent active memory that extends the capabilities of the front-end processor by performing the execution of data parallel operations. It runs under the programmed control of a front-end processor such as a DEC VAX 8000 computer or a Symbolics 3600 Lisp machine. The role of the front end is to:
1. Support application development and debugging,
2. Run an application and transmit instructions for parallel execution to the CM,
3. Provide utilities for maintenance, diagnosis, and operations.

Use of a VAX front-end computer would be appropriate for numerical computing implemented in Fortran; a Symbolics front-end would be suitable for executing programs implemented in Lisp.

The second machine, the Butterfly, is a shared-memory MIMD multiprocessor whose architecture is a compromise between the bus and the crossbar interconnected architectures. Its key element is the FFT-related Butterfly switch network whose cost grows proportionally to N log N, N being the number of processor nodes. Each node consists of an MC 68020 microprocessor and an MC 68881 floating-point coprocessor with 1 Mbyte of memory, expandable to 4 Mbyte. Up to 256 processors can be assembled to collectively form this shared-memory MIMD multiprocessor. The Mach operating system for the Butterfly GP 1000 provides a Unix environment and supports virtual memory, multiprocessor configuration, and methods for applying parallelism. Fortran and Lisp are available for building coupled systems. In addition to Lisp, there are several AI tools: parallel common Loops, a parallel rule system, and a parallel truth maintenance system.

Programming the Butterfly has not been simple. Two major tasks facing the Butterfly programmer are memory management and parallel execution specification. To achieve good computational performance, it is necessary to manage the shared memory; i.e., allocate program data in shared memory and scatter data frequently accessed by many processors across the machine. The new announced Fortran for the Butterfly will make memory management easier. The second task, specifying parallel execution, is at present left to the Butterfly programmer. The new version of Fortran will allow compiler directives for explicit implementation of parallelism and will support automatic parallelization of DO-loops. The issue of machine scalability and performance for a large number of processors is still open, but see Rettberg and Thomas (1986) and Crowther et al. (1985) for views expressed by manufacturer representatives.

The list of Butterfly applications is long and indicates the versatility of the machine. These applications include parallel combinatorial optimization, functional optimization, discrete event simulation, image understanding, circuit simulation, robot control in real time, use of object-oriented and rule-based programming for fault location and a control optimization planner, continuous speech recognition, and finite element analysis.

5. CONCLUSION

The critical research questions in parallel symbolic/numerical computation can be grouped into three categories: (1) languages and programming tools, (2) software architecture, and (3) computer architecture. In all three areas, we are further along in numerical parallel computation than in the symbolic parallel computation required in AI applications. The subjects of languages, programming tools, and software architecture are discussed in the references provided in section 1. We close with additional comments on computers for symbolic/numerical processing.

Many commercial and experimental multi-processor systems for numerical or symbolic processing have been constructed or proposed. In their recent surveys of computers for symbolic processing, Wah et al. (1987) and Hwang et al. (1987) list or describe more than 30 complete symbolic processing systems. Uhr (1987) identifies 15 major architectural possibilities for the known classes of parallel computers, divided into two distinct categories: systems that simulate a complete graph and those with point-to-point topologies. The majority of these systems have been designed for either numerical or symbolic computing but not for both. Integrating symbolic and numerical processing may be difficult, considering the widely differing requirements and natures of the two types of computing. We believe that in the near future programs coupling numerical and symbolic computation will be implemented mainly on moderately parallel heterogeneous multi-processor systems, such as the Aquarius or Crays networked with symbolic processing workstations. Another possibility is homogeneous multi-processor systems such as the Butterfly that are not specialized for symbolic or numerical computing but can do both.

In the long run, massively parallel systems such as the Connection Machine look very promising. These systems can solve efficiently many important classes of numerical and symbolic problems. In some applications, they may require fast scalar or vector coprocessors to speed up programs that combine fine-grained data parallelism with sequential or vectorized computation. The success of massively parallel computers in symbolic/numerical applications will heavily depend on our ability to construct new data parallel algorithms. Fine-grained data parallel algorithms often will not be reworked familiar sequential algorithms. Moreover, using massively parallel computers may require new ways of thinking about the problems we want to solve and about computational trade-offs.

6. REFERENCES

Clark, K., and S. Gregory, *Parlog: Parallel Programming in Logic,* in *Parallel Computation and Computers for Artificial Intelligence,* ed. J. S. Kowalik, Kluwer

Academic Publishers, Boston, 1988.

Crowther, W., J. Goodhue, E. Starr, R. Thomas, W. Milliken and T. Blackdar, *Performance Measurements on a 128-node Butterfly Parallel Processor*, BBN Report, 1985.

De Groot, D., *Restricted AND–Parallel Execution of Logic Programs, in Parallel Computation and Computers for Artificial Intelligence*, ed. J. S. Kowalik, Kluwer Academic Publishers, Boston, 1988.

Despain, A. M., and Y. N. Patt, *Aquarius–A High Performance Computing System for Symbolic/Numeric Applications*, Spring COMPCON, 1985, IEEE Press.

Fahlman, S. E., *Parallel Processing in Artificial Intelligence, in Parallel Computation and Computers for Artificial Intelligence*, ed. J. S. Kowalik, Kluwer Academic Publishers, Boston, 1988.

Gabriel, R. P., and J. McCarthy, *Qlisp, in Parallel Computation and Computers for Artificial Intelligence*, ed. J. S. Kowalik, Kluwer Academic Publishers, Boston, 1988.

Gupta, A., *Parallelism in Production Systems*, Ph. D. thesis, Dept. of Computer Science, Carnegi -Mellon Univ., March 1986.

Halstead, R. H., *Parallel Computing Using Multilisp, in Parallel Computation and Computers for Artificial Intelligence*, ed. J. S. Kowalik, Kluwer Academic Publishers, Boston, 1988.

Hillis, W. D., and G. L. Steele, *Data Parallel Algorithms*, CACM, vol. 29, no. 12, December 1986

Hwang, K., J. Ghosh and R. Chowkwanyun, *Computer Architectures for Artificial Intelligence Processing, Computer*, Jan. 1987.

Kotov, V. E., A. G. Marchuk and Yu. L. Vishnevsky, MARS - *A Hierarchical Heterogeneous Modular System, in Fifth Generation Architectures*, ed.J. V. Woods, Elsevier Science Publishers, IFIP, 1986.

Kowalik, J. S. *Coupling Symbolic and Numerical Computing in Expert Systems*, North - Holland, 1986.

Kowalik, J. S., K. M. Chalfan, R. I. Marcus and T. L. Skillman, *Composite Software Systems*, unpublished manuscript, 1986.

Kowalik, J. S., and K. M. Chalfan, *High - Speed Computing and Artificial Intelligence Connection, Supercomputer Applications*, vol. 1, no. 1, 1987.

Kowalik, J. S., and C. T. Kitzmiller (ed.), *Coupling Symbolic and Numerical Computing in Expert Systems*, II, North - Holland, 1988.

McGehearty, P. F., and E. J. Krall, *Execution of Common Lisp in a Parallel Environment, in Parallel Computation and Computers for Artificial Intelligence*, ed. J. S. Kowalik, Kluwer Academic Publishers, Boston, 1988.

Nii, H. P., *Blackboard Systems: The Blackboard Model of Problem Solving and the Evolution of Blackboard Architectures, The AI Magazine*, Summer, 1986.

Ragheb, M, and D. Gvillo, *Hybrid Symbolic-Procedural Programming Methodology For Monte-Carlo Particle Transport Stimulations*, Proc. of the Third Science and Engineering Symposium, Minneapolis, MN, Sept. 9-11, 1987.

Rettberg, R., and R. Thomas, *Contention is No Obstacle to Shared-Memory Multiprocessing*, CACM, vol. 29, no. 12, December 1986.

Rice, J. P., *Problems with Problem-solving in Parallel: The Polygon System*, Proceedings of the Third International Conference on Supercomputing, Boston, MA, May 16-20, 1988.

Sabharval, A., S. S. Iyengar, G. de Saussure and C. R. Weisbin, *Parallelism in Rule-Based Systems*, SPIE, vol. 937, *Applications of Artificial Inteligence VI*, 1988.

Skillman, T., *Distributed Cooperating Processes in a Mobile Robot Control System*, Proceedings of the Conference on AI for Space Applications, Huntsville, Alabama, Nov. 13-14, 1986.

Stanfill, C., and D. Waltz, *Toward Memory-Based Reasoning*, CACM, vol. 29, no. 12, December 1986.

Uhr, L, *Multi-computer Architectures for Artificial Intelligence*, John Wiley, NY, 1987.

Wah, B. W., M. B. Lowrie and G.-J. Li, *Computers for Symbolic Processing*, Proceedings of the IEEE, Dec. 1987.

An expert system for numerical optimization: parallel computation

J J McKeown

Department of Engineering Mathematics, The Queen's University of Belfast

ABSTRACT: Nonlinear optimization techniques are highly developed, and
are widely available in the form of computer programs. However, such
programs are often difficult for non-specialists to use without the
help of a numerical analyst or optimizer. A project currently in
progress is described, aimed at developing a program for robust
nonlinear parameter estimation linked to an expert system for diagnosis
of behaviour. This paper discusses the relationship between
robustness, globality and parallelism and describes the approach which
has been adopted, and which involves the use of transputers.

1.   INTRODUCTION

The problem of providing optimization programs in a form in which they can
be used by non-specialists such as engineers and physicists is an
interesting one[1]. The need for such software has become important in the
field of electronics engineering, for example, and this particular need
has provided the focus for the effort being carried out in the Engineering
Faculty at Queens. Electronics engineers, and in particular microwave
engineers, make heavy use of numerical optimization methods in the areas
of nonlinear device modelling, nonlinear circuit analysis and circuit
optimization. Such problems are often ill-conditioned, and are ill-posed
in other respects. For example, many modelling applications make use of
data which, because of measurement difficulties, are barely sufficient for
parameter identification to be carried out. This field of application is
an ideal testing ground for the robust, "intelligent" optimization methods
being developed; it is, however, by no means unique and its distinguishing
feature may well be simply that its practitioners have become more aware
than others of the potential of optimization methods.

The work at Queens has been going on on a fairly informal basis for some
time. Funds have now become available which will allow more resources to
be committed, and the approach to be adopted has recently been under
review. This paper describes some of the experience to date and the plans
for further development.

The work differs from that being carried out elsewhere in two main
respects. First, an aim of the project is to use IKBS techniques to try
to address some of the difficulties which are not suited to automatic
solution. Second, it is accepted that numerical optimization algorithms
can fail for a variety of reasons, and that they will not usually provide
a global solution. The real aim of the optimization is therefore not only

to generate a "solution" but also to provide a measure of the confidence which should be placed in it.

For various reasons, a decision was taken to develop a set of programs in Fortran 77 which would run interactively on a workstation. Rather than attempt to produce a "universal optimizer", it was decided to select one class of optimization problems, that of nonlinear parameter estimation. Problems of this class occur very widely and frequently, both in electronics and in other fields. It is also a well-defined problem class, and usually avoids complications due to constraints. However, it is not a trivial problem; a program which could be guaranteed to achieve a successful solution of most problems in this class, without the intervention of a numerical analyst, would certainly be a significant step forward.

The current state of the work is best described with reference to the pilot program which has already been developed.

2.   THE PILOT PROGRAM

The program currently under development is the second version. The first was a simple piece of software whose main contribution was to demonstrate the need for generality in the basic design. At the same time, it became clear that the interface should allow the maximum of flexibility in the formulation of the problem, and should provide sufficient feedback, in a suitable form, to enable this flexibility to be systematically used.

The form of the program is shown schematically in Figure 1.

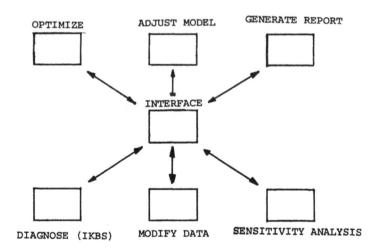

Fig. 1. Layout of the program

The program achieves its aims in three ways.

(1) The interface with the user is designed to allow a high degree of flexibility. The current state of the model can be adjusted by, for example, specifying how many variables are to be determined by the

optimization module, and what their starting values should be. After
returning to the main menu, a report can be requested. This can include a
graphical representation of the fit achieved by these parameter values.
Next, via the main menu, an optimization can be requested based on any one
of a number of possible error norms. If the run is unsuccessful, a
diagnosis can be requested, which will be carried out by the expert system
using a file of data about the run build up automatically by monitoring
procedures. On the basis of this, the user might (depending on the
recommendation of the expert system) terminate the run in order to adjust
the model code, or he might carry out further analyses of the current
model using the sensitivity analysis module. Specified data values can be
ignored or changed.

The program will thus allow a range of possible descriptions of the
problem, with different variables and objective functions; even manual
adjustment of the variables can easily be carried out.

It is expected that this flexibility will aid users to become familiar
with the optimization process, and to tailor it to their own needs, by a
process of "try and see".

(2) The expert system already mentioned, which is here aimed at problem
diagnosis only, should avoid the situation in which a user reaches an
obstacle which he is unable to surmount unless expert help is available.
Experience shows that this is the most common way in which optimization
techniques can fail the nonspecialist.

The expert system currently under development is based on the LEONARDO
shell, which uses a combined backward-forward chaining technique to try to
satisfy a stated goal. It uses a rule base developed during exploratory
projects by students on the MSc course in Engineering Computation.

(3) The robustness of the program, which means essentially the robustness
of the optimization procedures, is the foundation of the design. This
robustness is achieved partly by the methods described below, and arises
partly from the flexibility of the design which allows the user to analyse
any solution so thoroughly that he can have a great deal of confidence in
the soundness of the result. This confidence in, and understanding of,
the solution is regarded as an essential aspect of robustness.

Initial interest in the use of parallel computation in the context of this
program was focussed on the expert system module. However, it has become
clear during the development that the real bottleneck is in the
optimization process; as a result, attention is now concentrated on this
aspect and it will form the basis of the discussion in the following
sections.

3.   PARALLELISM IN THE OPTIMIZER

3.1 Robust optimization

The term "robustness" as applied to a method of optimization can be
defined in various ways. The term has been used by Bandler et al[2], for
example, to describe an algorithm which (for a particular application) is
insensitive to starting point. This is certainly an important aspect of
robustness, and is included in the following definition which will be used
in this paper:

An optimization program is said to be robust if its likelihood of finding an acceptable solution is "high" and if, when it fails to find such a solution, it almost always fails in such a way that the cause of the failure can be deduced, by the program or with its help, from the results generated. A program which is not robust will be said to be fragile.

Inconclusive results can be produced for a number of reasons, including the following:
- noisy function evaluation due, for example, to rounding errors in internal numerical procedures such as integration;
- noisy gradient evaluations due to the same causes, or to discrete representation of internal data;
- ill-conditioning;
- poor choice of step length in numerical differentiation;
- poor choice of convergence criteria;
- actual discontinuities in F;
- actual discontinuities in the gradient of F;
- coding mistakes in the function evaluation routine.

When these factors are considered, it becomes clear that the general object of the computation is not simply to solve a well-defined minimisation problem, but to maximise the probability that an acceptable solution will be found, given a certain amount of computing resource used or time elapsed. It is also clear that certain features of an algorithm can be expected to enhance robustness. For example, a method which makes use of information independently collected from a number of points distributed throughout the search domain is likely to be more robust than one which places high reliance on local information or on a single sequential process which may fail. Confidence might therefore be enhanced by, for example, running a local minimiser from a number of randomly generated starting points in the hope that some may achieve useful results; or using local minimisers based on random searches; or modelling the function as a stochastic process. If such methods fail to generate an acceptable point, it can at least be expected that sufficient information will be generated to allow the sources of difficulty to be diagnosed.

When the problem is viewed in this way the distinction between robust local minimisation of the one hand, and global optimization on the other, becomes blurred to the point of transparency. The similarity between the two classes of problem stems essentially from the need to regard the problem as one of establishing confidence in the solution, rather than of applying a well-defined numerical procedure to a well-behaved function.

The approached suggested above for achieving robustness correspond to the Multistart, Controlled Random search and Bayesian classes of global algorithm respectively.

In the light of these considerations, it has been decided that the programs should be designed to find the global minimum wherever possible, and that algorithms should be selected, and implementations designed, to overcome the inevitable computing burden entailed in this decision. This certainly means, in our case, that parallel methods must be used.

The parallel systems selected for particular attention were transputer networks, because of their prima facie suitability for the task; effort has therefore been applied to the task of analysing the factors affecting the design of suitable algorithms for these machines.

3.2 Parallel robust global optimization on transputer networks

Considerable work has already been done on parallel algorithms for global optimization[3,4,5,6]. These have served to emphasise the importance of matching the parallel algorithm to the architecture of the parallel machine used. In considering the choice of global optimization algorithm to be used, the general criteria to be applied are clearly robustness, efficiency and ease of parallel implementation on a transputer network. Deterministic methods such as grid search can be ruled out by the first of these because of the relative fragility of such sequential processes and also because detailed knowledge of characteristics of the function such as Lipschitz constants cannot be assumed to be available.

In principle, any of the following stochastic methods might be adopted: Multistart methods such as Clustering or Single-Linkage; Trajectory-following; Controlled Random Search; Bayesian algorithms. The final choice between these, and possible other, methods can only be made by experimentation. However, the decision is certainly influenced by the need to use parallel methods, and by the particular characteristics of the parallel systems available.

4. DESIGN OF THE PARALLEL PROGRAMS

This section describes the impressions gained from an initial study of the suitability of transputer networks for use as an optimizing engine, and of the details of writing optimization programs in OCCAM, the language recommended for use on these machines. It may be useful first to describe briefly the Transputer and the OCCAM language.

4.1 Transputer networks

The main features of the transputer from a user point of view are probably the following:
(i) A single transputer of the T800 range is capable of a computing speed greater than one megaflop;
(ii) each has four communications channels for input and output, with a data transfer rate of the order of one Megabyte/sec.;
(iii) a single transputer can run concurrent (though not parallel) processes.
Using these features, OCCAM programs can be designed which implement communications networks appropriate to the application in hand.

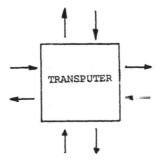

Fig. 2. Transputer communications channels

4.2   The OCCAM language

OCCAM is a high level language for implementing concurrent processes and
has been designed to be the natural language for the transputer. It
departs from other parallel languages, such as the extended Fortran
dialects used with some other parallel systems, in being based on the idea
of communicating processes. From the point of view of a Fortran
programmer, its main feature is perhaps its highly structured form, shown
most clearly in its lack of a statement equivalent to GO TO. This makes
it easy, but essential, to use a top-down style of programming which can
be quite different from that adopted traditionally by optimizers writing
logically complex code in Fortran.

The correctness of parallel and concurrent programs is ensured, within
this structure, by restricting communication between processes. Such
communication may only take place in the form of explicit message-passing
along channels; and a given channel may only connect two processes. These
channels may be mapped onto the hardware channels available for
communication between transputers, and in that case their number is of
course further restricted.

It is possible to specify whether given processes are to be executed
sequentially or concurrently, to specify orders of priority, to make
processes mutually exclusive and to specify the processor on which any
process is to run. Any process can only proceed to completion when data
which it requests are available on its input channels, and when processes
to which it sends data are ready to receive them.

As a preliminary exercise, the author translated an optimization program
(the OPLS program from NOC) from Fortran 66 into OCCAM2. Following
familiarisation with the language, requiring about one week, the task of
translation and testing took about two more weeks. This involved the
complete rewriting of the line search routine because the original Fortran
code proved to be too complex in structure to be easily translated. This
problem arose from the need to express the procedure as a set of
processes, without the use of the GOTO. While for the rest of the program
this proved to be quite easy (though instructive), the line search was so
complex in its logical structure that, without a flow chart for guidance,
the task of translation appeared likely to take more time than was
available. Instead, a cubic line search was written from scratch. This
proved to be a relatively easy task. During the testing process for this,
it was translated into Fortran; this process proved to be extremely
simple, and could almost be done directly at the terminal.

The lessons learned from this exercise were as follows:
(i)   OCCAM 2 is an excellent language in which to express parallelism in
optimization programs;
(ii)   Translation either way between OCCAM 2 and well-structured Fortran
is straightforward; translation from poorly-structured Fortran to OCCAM 2
can be difficult.

These two facts suggest strongly that structured programming, as well as
possessing its well-established advantages, has much to recommend it for
preparing implementations of optimization algorithms which may be run on
parallel machines, even if OCCAM and transputers are not themselves to be
used.

4.3   Selection of an algorithm

It is possible to distinguish at least five main sources of inefficiency
encountered when using a given parallel system to carry out a numerical
task:
(1)   limitations on the fraction of the algorithm which can be
      parallelised;
(2)   time lost due to contention for resources;
(3)   time lost due to synchronisation waits;
(4)   housekeeping necessary to implement parallelism.
Another source of inefficiency, which overlaps with these and in fact
arises from attempts to overcome them, is:
(5)   numerical inefficiency due to choice of an algorithm which would not
      normally be selected if a sequential system were to be used.
At this stage, most attention is being given to the multistart class of
algorithms; this decision was based on the following considerations:
(i)   multistart methods are simple to implement if good local algorithms
are available;
(ii) they promise efficiency even if relatively few repetitions can be
carried out because of time limitations;
(iii) once the communications code is developed for these algorithms, it
should be easy to modify it for the other methods.
It should be made clear, however that other methods are not precluded.
Price et al[3,6] have discussed a transputer implementation of the
Controlled Random Search technique, and have reported good results; we
hope to evaluate this method.

This decision to use multistart methods means that we are interested in
running a number of local optimizations from various starting points, and
combining the results thus obtained in such a way as to maximise the
likelihood of correctly identifying the global minimum. Several
strategies can be applied within this overall scheme; see Rinnooy Kan and
Timmer[7] for an excellent survey of these methods. The following form of
algorithm was selected for the initial analysis.

ALGORITHM

STEP 0   Generate several starting points at random within the search
domain
STEP 1   Run a local minimization algorithm from each starting point and
store the points obtained
STEP 2   Reduce the set of points so obtained, either by clustering and
rejecting a fixed proportion of each cluster, or by a technique such as
single linkage, if necessary generating more random starting points
STEP 3   Check whether a predefined confidence of having generated the
global solution has been achieved
STEP 4   Repeat from step 0.

A transputer version of this algorithm was written as a desk exercise in
order to clarify the issues involved in using the transputer network.

The first question to be answered concerns the level at which the
parallelism is introduced into the global algorithm.

4.4   Alternative parallelisation schemes: horizontal versus vertical

One approach would be to introduce parallelisation at the fine-grain level of matrix operations. This is the normal method used for SIMD and vector machines, but is unattractive for a MIMD network because of the high ratio of time spent in communication rather than numerical computation, and the effect of this on the second of the sources of inefficiency discussed above. Cooper[8] has reported a successful fine-grain application on a transputer network outside the optimization field, but comments on the increasing effect of communication time as networks increase in size. It is clear that for a network whose nodes are themselves fast processors, contention for communication resources will be reduced by designing algorithms which allow these nodes to operate autonomously as far as possible. The decision has been taken therefore to look for medium to large grain parallelism, that is, at the level of single function evaluations or even complete local optimizations.

This leaves two possibilities.

The first is to introduce parallelism into the local optimizer, and to carry out the repetitions in sequence. This can be thought of as a "vertical" scheme of parallelisation.

The advantages of this would appear to be:
(i)   the time needed to carry out one local minimisation is reduced to a minimum; this flexibility may be useful if function evaluations are very expensive.
(ii)   synchronisation losses should be low, especially in the case of least-squares.
The disadvantages are however:
(i)   there may be substantial losses of efficiency from the other sources discussed above;
(ii)   the approach may require a different parallel scheme for each local algorithm and class of objective functions which may be used;
(iii) if failure occurs in one local optimization, the whole process may terminate, reducing the robustness of the system.

The alternative is to allow each processor in the network to carry out complete local optimizations (parallel repetition), and to nominate one processor to combine the results. This might be thought of as a pure horizontal scheme.

The advantages of this approach are:
(i)   simplicity;
(ii)   complete parallelisation;
(iii) no compromise is necessary in the selection of the most efficient local optimizer;
(iv)   high ratio of computation/communication, thus reducing contention;
(v)   can be programmed so that failure in one processor need not affect the others.
The disadvantages foreseeable are:
(i)   the time required for one local optimization is not reduced by the use of parallelism;
(ii)   there may be synchronization losses due to the different times required for local minimization from different starting points.

The second of the two alternatives appears to be more suited to the characteristics of transputers because of the high ratio of uninterrupted computation to communication which it involves, thus allowing the individual transputers to behave as almost autonomous fast computers. The

computing speed available from a single processor should ensure that the
minimum time needed for a single local optimization is not too high for
most purposes.

An attractive approach would be a compromise, with the process normally
carried out by a horizontal technique but with an option to use vertical
parallelism when the cost of function evaluations is very high.

There still remain, however, two approaches to parallel iteration; one is
to divide the search domain and assign one subdomain to each processor;
the other is to allow each processor access to the whole search domain.
Since the first of these options can be viewed as equivalent to the second
with the addition of artificial constraints, it was rejected as a
candidate for early testing as likely to be less efficient. In addition,
such an approach seems likely to be less robust because of the mutually
exclusive search domains; a prematurely ended local minimisation in one
domain would mean that that domain was not searched further. Hence, it
was decided to allow all transputers to search the whole domain.

4.5   Implementation of a multistart algorithm on a transputer network

For the multistart technique, no communication is required between
processors except that between each processor and the central processor
which combines results. However, this communication cannot be carried out
directly because the processor nominated to be the central one cannot be
connected to more than four others. As a result, an arrangement must be
provided whereby each processor not only carries out a local optimization,
but also acts concurrently as part of a communications link between other
processors and the central processor.

There are obviously a number of ways in which this might be arranged; two
natural configurations are the multiplexed network (figure 3) and the
pipeline (figure 4).

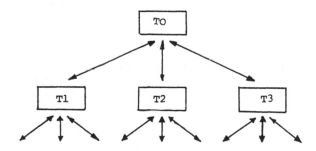

Fig. 3.   Multiplexed network

Fig. 4.   Pipelined network

The multiplexed arrangement provides the shorter data links. However, it is less widely used that the pipeline configuration - perhaps because of its slightly greater complication. Note that no processor need be devoted entirely to communication; this would be wasteful of computing power.

The pipeline configuration has the advantage of simplicity, and appears to be widely accepted by transputer users as an efficient one. This should be particularly true in our case since the effort devoted to communication will be low relative to that spent on other tasks.

The communication processes are coded directly in OCCAM.

4.6 A horizontally parallel algorithm on a transputer

In this section the horizontal algorithm selected for initial testing will be described in sufficient detail to give a flavour of the approach being adopted.

The top-level folds of suitable OCCAM 2 processes which would run in the i'th processor is as follows:

```
PRI PAR
    ---process i,1: communication
    ---process i,2: Minimization -
                Read flag "start"; if true generate a random starting
                point; compute local minimum and write x*,F* to channel
                0
```

This construction will give priority to the communication process, interrupting the minimisation process when communication is required.

The communication process itself might consist of the following processes:

```
ALT
    ---PROCESS i,1,1: read a value of x*,F* either from channel u[i+1] or
                      0(i) and write it to u[i]
    ---PROCESS i,1,2: read "start" from channel d[i] and write either to
                      channel d[i+1] or to I[i]
```

The "either/or" conditions are implemented naturally by OCCAM code; a "read" from a channel will cause the process which executes it to halt until the data are sent by the process addressed, and similarly for "write".

The ALT structure ensures that only one communications process is running at a time - that is, that they may not interrupt each other. The need for this provision is obvious. The array u of channels make up the "up" line, taking information towards the "central" processor. The down line consists of the array d; the array 0 denotes the internal channels carrying data from the minimization processes to the communication processes within the same transputer; and the array I denotes the internal channels in the opposite directions.

The ALT construction is also used within processes 1 and 2 to differentiate between inputs on channels u and 0, and between outputs on channels d or I.

Processor 0 will have different processes running concurrently, such as the following:

```
done:= TRUE
j    := 0
WHILE (NOT done)
  PRI PAR
    ---process 0,1: read x* and F from u[1] and write to process 0,3; set
                    j:=j+1
    ---process 0,2: read start flag from 0,3; send to channel d[1]
    ---process 0,3: update clusters; if converged, set done:=TRUE,
                    start:=FALSE and send start to 0,2
```

A range of multistart algorithms can be accommodated within this scheme.

The graph of this algorithm for a 4-processor network is shown on Figure 6.

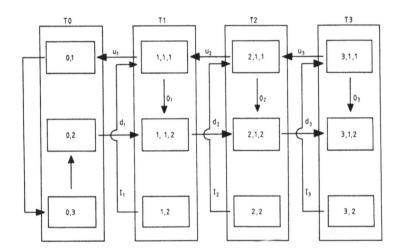

Fig. 5. Graph of horizontal algorithm

It is evident that for the typical problem arising in practice each transputer apart from the zero'th will spend most of its time in the minimization process. At data transfer rates of about one megabyte/second, the time taken for details of local optima to be transmitted to the central node will be of the order of milliseconds while the time needed for a local minimisation itself will normally be of the order of tens of seconds at least. Hence contention losses will be small, and the efficiency of the parallelisation should be close to unity. It can therefore be expected that very little degradation in performance will occur as more transputers are added to the network. Hence, so long as the time taken for one local optimization is acceptable, the number of such local minima which can be generated in the same time is not in effect bounded by the hardware.

This general conclusion is borne out by other workers. For example Woodhams and Price[6] have shown that the Concurrent Controlled Random Search algorithm, which would seem to have a ratio of computation to communication which is inherently lower than the multistart algorithms discussed here, nevertheless has a speed-up very close to 4 on a 4-node network of transputers using the pipeline configuration.

The corresponding graph for a vertical algorithm would be somewhat more complicated, but not essentially different.

5.   CONCLUSIONS

This paper has discussed the current state of a project for the development of a program for robust optimization. The requirement for robustness is very similar to that for global optimization, and both require the use of parallel methods to achieve the performance required on a workstation. The parallel system selected is a transputer network, and it is intended that the optimization code should be implemented in OCCAM 2. We have discussed the considerations which have led to the choices made, and shown how a parallel multistart algorithm can be implemented on a transputer network. It is clear that by programming in OCCAM, a very high degree of control over the execution of the algorithm can be achieved.

ACKNOWLEDGEMENT

Thanks are due to Dr W L Price of the University of East Anglia and Dr R K Cooper of the Aeronautics Department, Queen's University, Belfast for providing pre-publication copies of references 6 and 8 respectively.

REFERENCES

(1) McKeown J J 1986 *An expert systems approach to nonlinear optimization* Flow control of congested networks (eds) A R Odoni, L Bianco, G Szego (eds) NATO ASI series (Springer-Verlag).
(2) Bandler J W, Chen S H, Ye S, Zhang Q J 1988 *Robust model parameter extraction using large-scale optimization concepts* IEEE MTT-S Digest OF-1-4, pp 319-322.
(3) Price W L October 1987 *Global optimization algorithms for a CAD workstation* JOTA, Vol 55, No 1.
(4) McKeown J J 1980 *Aspects of parallel computation in numerical optimization* eds F Archetti and M Cugiani Numerical Techniques for stochastic systems (North Holland).
(5) Dixon L C W 1986 *Optimization on a parallel array processor: a review of the state of the art* NOC TR 187 (Hatfield Polytechnic).
(6) Woodhams F W D and Price W L *An optimizing accelerator for a CAD workstation* (to be published).
(7) Rinnooy Kan A H G and Timmer G T 1987 *Stochastic global optimization methods* Math. Prog. 39, pp 27-78.
(8) Cooper R K 1988 *Successive over-relaxation on a transputer network* COMPAR 88 (Manchester).

Applications of highly parallel processors

Heather M Liddell

Centre for Parallel Computing, Queen Mary College, (University of London), Mile End Road, London E1 4NS

ABSTRACT: Experience at Queen Mary College in parallel computing is based upon successful usage of a 4096 processor DAP since 1980 and more recent 1024 processor "desktop versions". The practical problems involved with algorithm design for such highly parallel systems will be discussed. Examples will be considered from such diverse areas as partial differential equations, image processing and number theory.

1. INTRODUCTION

The AMT DAP 510 is the third generation of Distributed Array Processor which has been in use at Queen Mary College. It was delivered in December 87 as part of an Alvey contract. The original 4096 processor ICL DAP has been used to provide a national, and to some extent an international, service for the academic research community since 1980; this has resulted in a large body of experience in the use of highly parallel computers for a wide range of applications in science and engineering including fluid dynamics, finite and boundary element methods, simulation and modelling of physical systems, computer vision, image and signal processing and number theory. The purpose of this paper is to describe examples of algorithm design and problem mapping for some of these different areas of application.

The original DAP is due to be replaced in the near future by a 4096 processor AMT DAP 610-32. There are many improvements in this latest version of the system, the most obvious from the user point of view is the data visualisation capability and the ability to attach the machine to either a VAX or a SUN host. The QMC DAP 510-8 is attached to a SUN workstation which provides supercomputer power and a high performance graphics workstation environment in one's own office or laboratory. The DAP 500 series (Parkinson, Hunt and MacQueen, 1988 - Figure 1 illustrates the main features of the architecture) are 1024 processor machines, with the single bit processing elements (PEs) arranged as a 32 x 32 array, each with its own memory. The minimum size of the latter is 32K bits per PE, but the architecture supports up to 1 Mbits/PE. Both our 510-8 and the new 610-32 (which will be attached to a VAX host) have 64 Kbits per PE giving total memory sizes of 8 Mbytes and 32 Mbytes respectively. Other improvements over earlier versions are the improved VLSI technology components, and the cycle speed of 10 MHz which is twice as fast as the original 4096 processor DAP. Data visualisation is provided by a fast I/O channel with a transfer rate of 50 Mbytes per second; this can be used to attach a high resolution colour display. It is difficult to do justice to the impact of data visualisation on program development and basic understanding of the problem being modelled; it has been stated that "colour photography has done more for cookery than 1000 years of recipes" - a similar comment could be made about data visualisation with respect to computational recipes (algorithms)!

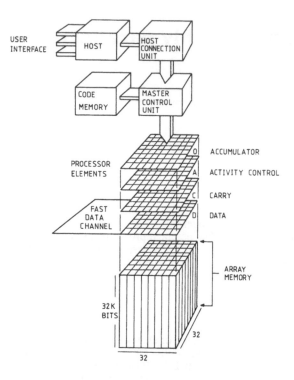

FIG.1. DAP 510 schematic

An important aspect of any multiprocessor system which has to be considered by the algorithm designer is the interprocessor connectivity. The DAP has two systems - connections to nearest neighbours and a bus system for rows and columns which provides rapid data fetch and broadcast facilities. These systems give an excellent communication/computation balance for most applications, with none of the communication bottleneck experienced in some other multiprocessor systems. The DAP is an example of SIMD architecture where all PEs simultaneously execute the same instruction; however, each PE has an activity control register which provides a degree of local autonomy and permits easy simulation of concurrent operations.

Many of the architectural features are reflected in the language FORTRAN-PLUS which is a forerunner of the next FORTRAN standard - 8X. Program development facilities and the run-time environment are provided on the host, data is transferred to the DAP using standard subroutines and computation based on the FORTRAN-PLUS code is done on the DAP. FORTRAN-PLUS provides vector and array extensions to FORTRAN 77, together with other FORTRAN 8X concepts. Other software includes application support libraries, a low level assembler, run-time software and a powerful data routing system called Parallel Data Transforms (Flanders, 1988) which provides underlying support for languages, library and application software.

Reddaway (1987) pointed out that because of the bit-serial but highly word-parallel nature of DAP processing, the user is not constrained to a particular data representation so there are many possible speed/accuracy trade-offs. One result of the bit serial nature of the underlying architecture is that the relative speed of certain functions is unusual; taking the square root of all elements in a matrix takes approximately the same time as matrix addition, and finding the maximum of 1024 (or 4096) numbers is approximately 5 times faster than these operations. Fixed point and short precision calculations are very fast - some examples of various operation speeds are given in Table 1. Note that these times are approximate, since the timing of operations is data dependent. These features are very important for algorithm design in applications such as image and signal processing which only require short precision arithmetic for many calculations. There are in fact a large number of other areas where either short precision or logical (one bit) operations can be used. Examples are random number generators (Smith, Reddaway and Scott, 1985) and Ising model calculations (Pawley,Bowler, Kenway and Wallace, 1985 and Reddaway, Scott and Smith, 1985).

Table 1 : DAP 510 performance on matrix operations
(Approximate values)

Precision	Operation	DAP 510 time
logical	logical	> 1 GOP
8 bit integer	add	420 MOP
	mult (M-M)	60 MOP
	mult (M-constant)	140-280 MOP
32 bit real	add	12 MFLOPS
	mult (M-M)	7 MFLOPS
	square	16 MFLOPS
	square root	11 MFLOPS
	divide	6 MFLOPS
	max of 1024 numbers	60 MFLOPS
24 bit	Floating point-peak	19
32 bit	MFLOPS	13
64 bit		6
logical	Fixed point-peak MOPs	10000
8 bit		400
16 bit		210
32 bit		110

2. ALGORITHMS FOR FINITE ELEMENT CALCULATIONS

The Finite Element method for solving partial differential equations is a typical numerical application; there are various parts of the calculation which illustrate some of the algorithmic techniques which can be used to solve such problems on a parallel computer. A full description of some of these strategies is given in Lai and Liddell (1987), which also includes a mathematical description of the method. The various algorithms developed have been incorporated into a special FE library, which is the DAP equivalent of the

NAG/SERC FE library (Liddell, Parkinson and Wait, 1986) to provide the DAP user community with a framework for solving FE problems on the DAP. The various stages involved in the overall computation are illustrated in Figure 2 (Greenough, Emson and Smith, 1984); much work is currently being done on the pre- and post processing phases of the calculations, but in this paper the emphasis will be on the algorithmic strategies used for the processor stage.

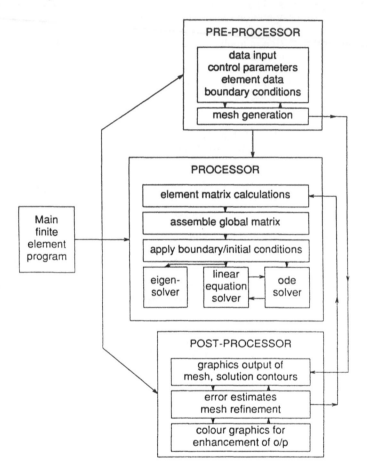

FIG.2. Structure of Finite Element Programs

In the element calculation phase the DAP is treated as a 'long vector', or linear array, rather than a 2D array, with the elements stored consecutively according to the element numbering order. Each element is assigned to one PE with an associated data structure to describe the element topology (shape, number of nodes and a steering vector giving the global nodal numbering of the element) and the element geometry (geometrical location of the element). The long vector method of storage also permits random allocation of elements to processors. The element stiffness matrix calculations can be done in parallel using a serial algorithm in each processor - so overall we have a 'multi-serial' approach which can achieve maximum efficiency since there is no inter-processor communication. A masking strategy can be employed if the number of elements is less than the number of processors.

An FE computation on a parallel processor has a data reassignment and global stiffness matrix assembly phase which has no direct counterpart on a serial computer. This arises because the processor allocation for the global solution phase must be node based rather than element based. The information which gives the element stiffness matrices' contribution to the global system is provided by the steering vectors. If adjacent elements are assembled on different processors, data must be transmitted between processors and this is done using a library utility based on the PDTs mentioned above. Dixon, Ducksbury and Singh (1982) developed a method where the assembly of the global stiffness matrix is not required but Lai and Liddell (1988a) showed that this approach can be more time consuming.

For the solution phase a preconditioned conjugate gradient method is ideally suited to the DAP architecture because the various vector inner products and matrix vector multiply operations can be performed very efficiently, as described by Lai and Liddell (1988a). Since the equations involved tend to be sparse block banded systems a convenient method of storage is by diagonals, and a linear array mapping is again used. This technique is also applied to the solution of the tridiagonal equations that arise in some finite difference methods for solving partial differential equations. Various pre-conditioners have been tested; the incomplete Choleski methods used in serial codes appear not to be very appropriate in a highly parallel environment (this is hardly a surprising result as the best serial algorithms are usually not the best parallel algorithms). Instead either an m-step Jacobi iteration or a multigrid method can be used to precondition the system (Lai and Liddell, 1988a, Wait 1988).

A final example in this section is provided by the elimination of boundary conditions; again the method used on serial computers is not very amenable to parallel computation. Lai and Liddell (1988b) suggested a strategy whereby the boundary conditions are eliminated before rather than after the global assembly phase.

3. MAPPING STRATEGIES FOR LARGE PROBLEMS

One of the major uses of highly parallel computers is for the solution of large problems whose size (n or n^2 or n^3) is much greater than the number of processors, p. In this case a hybrid approach of mixed parallel and serial algorithms is employed, and it is important to choose the best mapping or combination of mappings for the problem, so that interprocessor communication and I/O is minimised as far as possible. As far as the latter is concerned, it is worth noting that in a supercomputer environment it is often less time consuming to recompute than to read data from and write results to disc. A number of different mapping strategies for the DAP have been discussed by Liddell and Parkinson (1988) for computational problems and Reddaway (1987, 1988a) for signal and image processing applications. Two fundamental techniques are 'sliced' and 'crinkled' mapping.

The 'sliced' or 'sheet' mapping technique is illustrated in Figure 3. The overall problem domain is divided into sheets or slices which match the size of the processor array and which are mapped across the array, so that the data for neighbouring matrix elements (or pixels in image processing) are stored in different PEs. This type of mapping is useful for multiplication of large dense matrices, or for examples such as 'blob extraction' in image processing where the processing is restricted to a limited area of the image. Within the sheets a parallel algorithm is employed but the strategy overall is usually a block form of a serial algorithm - i.e. outer serial, inner parallel.

N   N

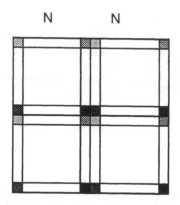

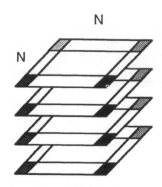

FIG.3. Sliced mapping

The inverse mapping to the above is 'crinkled' mapping (Figure 4) which is a form of domain decomposition applicable to highly parallel systems. In multiprocessor systems with relatively few processors (p), the overall problem domain is split into p sub-domains which are usually overlapping to ease computation of boundary values and each is assigned to a single processor for the calculation phase. On a highly parallel system, such as the DAP, the problem would be split into a large number of sub domains (up to 1024 or 4096) each containing a smaller number of interior points than in the previous case, and neighbouring subdomains are placed on neighbouring processors in the array. A serial algorithm would be employed within each processor's subdomain, but the algorithmic strategy across the domains is parallel so in this case the overall strategy is outer parallel, inner serial. Examples of the types of algorithm used are a serial nested dissection technique applied by Wait (1986) as a preconditioner for the parallel conjugate gradient technique or more simply in forming sums of values where the sum within each processor is formed serially before a parallel version of the SUM function such as that described by Parkinson (1987), is used to form the overall value across the processor array (Reddaway, 1988b). A similar technique can be used for calculating the inner products and matrix vector products within the conjugate gradient method.

2N   N

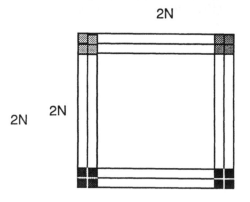

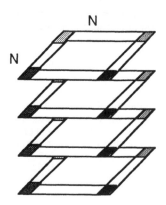

FIG.4. Crinkled mapping

For applications involving nearest neighbours such as the application of the Laplacean operation in the solution of partial differential equations or a smoothing equation in image processing, 'crinkled' mapping is normally best because it minimises the number of data shifts and avoids subimage boundaries. In a comparison of the 'sliced' and 'crinkled' mapping strategies, Liddell and Parkinson (1988) quantified the effect of communication/computation time and showed that although the latter gives only a small gain for numerical applications, where the time for an arithmetic operation is approximately an order of magnitude greater than the time for communication between processors, there is a significant gain for the shorter precision image processing applications - this result is confirmed by the example chosen in the next section.

4. AN IMAGE PROCESSING APPLICATION

Most images have many more pixels than the number of processors on the DAP, so mapping strategies such as those described above are nearly always applied in practice. A typical image size considered is 512 x 512 (8-bit) pixels. If crinkled mapping is used, the image is divided up into 32 x 32 local areas on a 1024 processor DAP, each containing 256 (16 x 16) pixels, which would be stored in one PE, whereas for sheet mapping the area is split into 256 sheets each containing 32 x 32 pixels which are mapped across the processor array. Reddaway (1987) also describes the combination of the two mappings in which (for a 512 x 512 image) the image is divided into 64 x 64 sheets each of which is crinkled into the 32 x 32 array.

With the earlier DAPs the speed of input of data was a major disadvantage but the availability now of data capture equipment which may be attached to the host's VME bus or better still, a fast input device connected directly to the DAP implies that the input of data is virtually 'free' to the processing.

There are many examples of algorithms one could choose from the image processing field for which the DAP is ideally suited because of the bit serial nature of its architecture; for the purposes of this paper the relatively simple Sobel edge detector will be described since this is a good illustration of a nearest neighbour computation for which the various mapping strategies can be compared and which also provides an example of how a parallel approach to simple operations can achieve significant savings in computational time. If $I(i,j)$ represents the image at point (x_i,y_j) the gradient operators I_x and I_y can be used to detect an edge. In order to allow for noise and numerical instability it is advisable to incorporate local averaging or smoothing, which can be represented as a convolution; it is assumed the pixels are arranged in a square lattice, so that each pixel has eight nearest neighbours.

Then

$$I_x = (I(i+1, j+1) + 2*I(i+1,j) + I(i+1,j-1)) - (I(i-1,j+1) + 2*I(i-1,j) + I(i-1,j-1)) \qquad (1)$$

with a similar form for I_y. These can be represented as 3 x 3 convolution operators

-1	0	1		1	2	1
-2	0	2		0	0	0
-1	0	1		-1	-2	-1

$$I_x \qquad\qquad\qquad\qquad I_y$$

Reddaway (1987) pointed out that the evaluation of each (one-way) operator can be speeded up by storing intermediate results (shown in parenthesis in equation (1)) and applying a planar shift function, since all points on the 32 x 32 array are being evaluated in parallel, so that the number of adds per point is 3 (a similar strategy can be applied to the Laplacean operator when solving partial differential equations); If a fully crinkled mapping is used, the overhead for neighbour routing is only 2% and the total time for the evaluation on a DAP 510 (in assembler) is 2 ms (Reddaway, 1988b). For a combined mapping, the extra overhead for data routing and merging causes the time to increase to about 4 ms and for a fully sheet mapping, the time is about 7 ms. Nearest neighbour operations such as (1) are easily expressed in FORTRAN PLUS using the shift functions provided, e.g. for a 32 x 32 image, ignoring boundaries

$$R = I + I(,+)$$
$$R = R + R(,-)$$
$$DIDX = R(+,) - R(-,)$$

where R, I and DIDX have been declared as 32 x 32 matrices.

5. A NUMBER THEORY EXAMPLE

There are many examples in signal processing where the results of number theory can be applied. Prime factors and Winograd transforms are widely used; Number Theoretic Transforms are based on Fermat numbers

$$(2^{2^n} + 1)$$

which allow multiplications to be replaced by add or subtract operations and have the additional advantage of giving exact results. However high precision arithmetic must be used to produce unambiguous results. Another application has been the checking of large Mersenne numbers (of the form $2^p - 1$) to see if they are prime. This involves squaring numbers of p bits precision, where p is very large. These applications are described in Reddaway (1987), who gives a table of results for the Mersenne prime calculation for p around 86000, comparing times on the 4096 processor ICL DAP, the Cray 1 and the Cyber 205 (the DAP checked 16 numbers simultaneously).

The application which will be described here is based on work by Wunderlich (1983) who used the 4096 processor DAP extensively during his sabbatical visit to the Mathematics Department at Queen Mary College. One of the examples he studied was the parallel computation of Legendre symbols of the form (N/p_i) where N is a fixed (possibly large) integer and p_i are distinct primes. The algorithm uses Jacobi reciprocity -

The Jacobi symbol (r,s), where s is odd, and g.c.d. (r,s) = 1, is defined as

$$\prod_{i=1}^{t} (r/p_i)$$

where

$$\prod_{i=1}^{t} p_i = s$$

the p_i are odd primes and (r/p_i) are Legendre symbols.

To compute a Legendre symbol the following three results are applied (Niven and Zuckermann, 1980)

$$(r_1/s) = (r_2/s) \text{ if } r_1 \equiv r_2 \text{ modulo } s$$

$$(2/s) = 1 \text{ if } s \equiv 1 \text{ or } 7 \text{ modulo } 8$$
$$-1 \text{ if } s \equiv 3 \text{ or } 5 \text{ modulo } 8$$

$$(r/s)(s/r) = 1 \text{ if either } r \text{ or } s \equiv 1 \bmod 4$$
$$-1 \text{ if both } r \text{ and } s \equiv 3 \bmod 4$$

The mapping of the problem is very simple - 4096 symbols are computed in parallel using a multi-serial approach; however the methodology is interesting in that considerable use is made of one bit logical variables and the overlay facilities provided by EQUIVALENCE, both being available to the programmer at the DAP FORTRAN (FORTRAN PLUS) level.

A full listing of the program is given in the reference (Wunderlich, 1983); initially the residue R_i of N mod p_i is computed in each processor i, the result being placed in the matrix R; at the second stage the value of R_i/p_i is computed which is placed in the INTEGER *1 matrix LG. Two INTEGER*3 matrix variables are defined to overlay R which allow shifts of 1or 2 to be executed in place of divide instructions. R3, R2, R1 are one bit (logical) variables which determine the residue class of R modulo 8,4,2 (Figure 6), N is an integer which can contain up to 63 decimal digits stored in seven INTEGER*4 locations so that each can hold an integer in the range $0 \le i \le 10^9$.

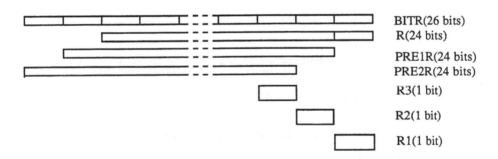

BITR(26 bits)
R(24 bits)

PRE1R(24 bits)
PRE2R(24 bits)

R3(1 bit)

R2(1 bit)

R1(1 bit)

FIG.6 Overlay Structure for residue R in the Legendre symbols computation

The LOGICAL and EQUIVALENCE statements in DAP FORTRAN (FORTRAN PLUS) for this structure are

```
        LOGICAL BITR (,,26), R3(,),R2(,),R1(,)
        EQUIVALENCE (R, BITR(,,3)),
2                   (PRE2R, BITR(,,2)),
3                   (PRE1R, BITR(,,1)),
4                   (R3, BITR(,,24)),
5                   (R2, BITR(,,25)),
6                   (R1, BITR(,,26))
```

R, PRE2R and PRE1R are declared as INTEGER*3 matrix variables.

This particular example illustrates the easy applicability of the FORTRAN PLUS language for this class of problem, and reflects the versatility of the underlying bit-serial architecture. Another example of this type of approach was given by Parkinson and Wunderlich (1984) in the first issue of Parallel Computing,who implemented the continued fraction factoring algorithm on the DAP in order to factor numbers in excess of 60 decimal digits.

CONCLUSIONS

In this paper the advantages of the evolving DAP architecture have been illustrated by studying algorithm design and mapping strategies for three very different applications. This system has now been applied to a wide range of scientific and engineering problems which can be solved efficiently on highly parallel computer architectures. A considerable amount of expertise and experience in the use of such systems has developed as a result of the DAP project which can often be applied to other parallel computers - SIMD, MIMD and mixed architecture systems. There are often many ways of exploiting the parallelism of a particular problem and it is important to take a "top down" parallel approach rather than to attempt to modify algorithms developed for serial machines. However, it has been shown that for large problems it is often advantageous to use a hybrid approach which is a mixture of the best 'parallel' and best 'serial' algorithms.

ACKNOWLEDGEMENTS

Part of the work reported in this paper is supported under SERC and ALVEY grants GR/D/59427, GR/D/59410 and GR/D/20304 (ARCH001). The author also wishes to thank her colleagues Dennis Parkinson, Stewart Reddaway, Marvin Wunderlich and the staff of the Centre for Parallel Computing for their contributions to the work.

REFERENCES

Dixon L.C.W, Ducksbury P. and Singh 1982, *Numerical Optimisation Centre report TR132*

Flanders P.,1988 *ProcJEEE International Specialist Seminar on the Design   and Application of Parallel Digital Processors, IEE Conference Publication 298* pp143-147

Grennough C., Emson C. and Smith I, 1984, *Rutherford Appleton Lab.Report RAL-84-107*

Lai C.H. and Liddell H.M 1987 *Appl.Math.Modelling* 11, pp 330-340

Lai C.H. and Liddell H.M 1988a *Proc. The Mathematics of Finite Elements and Applications VI,Mafelap 1987* ed. J.R.Whiteman (Academic Press:London) pp 145-156

Lai C.H. and Liddell H.M, 1988b, *Parallel Computing*, to be published

Liddell H .M, Parkinson D. and Wait R 1986 *Paper given at 1st Int.Conf. on Vector and Parallel Processing, Loen, Norway*

Liddell H.M and Parkinson D., 1988, *Proc. SIAM 3rd Conference on Parallel Processing,* to be published

Niven I. and Zuckerman H.S 1980 *An Introduction to the Theory of Numbers* (John Wiley and Sons : New York)

Parkinson D. and Wunderlich M., 1984 *Parallel Computing*, 1, pp 65-73

Parkinson D, 1987, *Parallel Computing 5*, pp 75-83

Parkinson D., Hunt D.J and MacQueen K.S. *1988 Proc. 33rd IEEE Computer Society International Conference (IEEE Computer Society Press*, pp 196-199

Pawley G.S., Bowler K., Kenway, R. and Wallace D., 1985, *Comput.Phys.Commun.* 37, pp 251-260

Reddaway S.F. 1987 *Traitement du Signal/Signal Processing, book of Les Houches 1985 Summer School*, ed. J.L.Laconme, T S Durrani and R Stora (Elsevier Science Publishers BV) pp 834-858

Reddaway S.F, Scott D., and Smith K.S, *Comput Phys.Commun.37*, pp 351-356

Reddaway S.F. 1988a, *Parallel Architecture and Computer Vision*, ed. Ian Page (Oxford Science Publications : Oxford) pp 299-314

Reddaway S.F, 1988b, *Paper given at CONPAR 1988*

Smith K., Reddaway S. and Scott D., 1985, *Comput.Phys.Commun. 37,*pp 239-249

Wait R 1986 *Paper given at the 1st Int. Conf. on Vector and Parallel Processing, Loen, Norway*

Wait R, 1988, *Parallel Computing ,* to be published

Wunderlich M. 1983 *Proc. Manitoba Conference on Numerical Mathematics* (Utilitas Mathematica Publ.Inc. Winnipeg)

Supercomputing in industry and research institutions: status and perspectives

J.S. Kowalik & C. Sutti

SUMMARY

The meeting included a Panel Session attended by approximately forty conference participants. The following issues were suggested for discussion:

1.   Key research and technical issues and challenges in supercomputing.
2.   Factors inhibiting the application of supercomputing in science and industry.
3.   Supercomputing education issues.
4.   Italian supercomputing scene (reality) and priorities.
5.   What should be the strategy for promoting supercomputing in Italy?

The Panel Discussion was moderated by Janusz Kowalik who also presented the High Speed Computing program at Boeing as particularly relevant to the broad area of advanced scientific and engineering computation. The following people participated in the panel and contributed their comments which are summarised below: Kowalik, Evans, Patrizi, Wusten, Mathis, Grandinetti, Wayland, Brusa, Atzeni, Schendel and Paruolo.

All speakers agreed that the urgent need for an effective supercomputer education existed. Training potential users and expanding the current expertise of academic community was identified as a pivotal step in promoting the use of supercomputers in industry, government sector and science. New courses in the academic programs would include such topics as: supercomputer hardware, software and programming, parallel algorithms and applications. Another agreed view-point was that a nation-wide communication network linking academic institutions, research establishments and leading industrial centers would be of prime importance to provide access to users.

Several factors inhibiting the use of supercomputing were identified:

1.   Price of supercomputers,
2.   Limited software portability,
3.   Lack of software development tools,
4.   Rapid pace of technology.

Several issues created some controversy:

1.   The anticipated rapid supercomputer technology developments in the near future,

2.   Effective strategies for allocating supercomputer resources in scientific and industrial centers, e.g. minisupercomputers versus shared centralised computing, facilities.

3.   The importance of the hardware/software gap.

The panel participants did not agree on the principal reasons for the existing delay of supercomputer technology in Italy. But the lack of education and the absence of applied orientation in some areas of the Italian sciences were cited as contributing factors. The panelists felt that the current supercomputer technology gap could be overcome by injecting high technology concepts into the leading Italian industries and by modernising university curricula.

Author Index

Aluffi-Pentini F, *193*
Arnold C, *51*
Atzeni S, *169*

Bertocchi M, *83*
Bini D, *115*
Blair J, *51*
Brewer O, *39*
Brode B, *51*
Brusa L, *127*

Caglioti E, *193*
Canuto C, *157*
Conforti D, *201*
Cosnard M, *91*

Daoudi E M, *91*
Dixon L C W, *61*
Dongarra J, *39*
Duff I S, *73*

Evans D J, *1*

Filippone S, *103*

Galligani I, *143*
Giberti C, *157*

Grandinetti L, *201*

Kowalik J S, *249*

Levine D, *39*
Liddell H M, *269*

McKeown J J, *257*
Misici L, *193*

Patrizi G, *225*
Peretti A, *213*

Quarteroni A, *181*

Radicati di Brozolo G, *103*
Riccio F, *127*
Ruggiero V, *143*

Schendel U, *25*
Sloboda F, *237*
Sorensen D, *39*
Spedicato E, *83*
Spera C, *225*
Sutti C, *213*

Zirilli F, *193*

Keyword Index

ABS method, *83*
Acoustic scattering problem, *194*
Active Memory Technology (AMT) DAP, *269*
Adams-Bashforth scheme, *159*
ADI method, *151*
AGE fractional scheme, *20*
Aitken's method, *121*
Alternating Group Explicit (AGE) method, *11*
AMT, *269*
Architecture,
  hypercube, *95*
  linear array, *96*
  ring, *94*
Arithmetic mean method, *144*
Associativity, *30*

Bandwidth minimization, *75*
Biggs method, *203*
BLAS, *46*
BLAS level 3, *79*
Block-Gauss-elimination, *39*
Broadcast, *99*

Cache memory, *46*
Capacity matrix, *37*
Chebyshev nodes, *183*
Cholesky decomposition, *130*
Combined method, *64*
Companion function, *33*
Computational kernel, *107*
Conjugate gradient, *65, 177*
Connection machine, *254*
Constraints, *227*
Crank-Nicolson method, *10, 187*
Cyclic reduction, *4, 149*

DAP, *269*
DFT, *116*
Degree of parallelism, *149*
Dependency graph, *41*
Diffusion-convection equation, *149*
Digital contour smoothing, *239*
Direct methods, *83*
Directives, multitasking, *54*
Dissection strategy, *74*
Divide and conquer, *4*
DO loop, *162, 208*
Domain decomposition, *34, 74, 181*
Douglas-Rachford AGE, *17*

Elimination tree, *78*
Euclidean algorithm, *116*
Expert system, *252, 259*
Explicit methods, *4*

Fan-in algorithm, *5*
FFT, *160, 164*
Finite element analysis, *127, 271*
Flynn classification, *26*
FORTRAN PLUS, *270*
Fractional splitting, *172*

Gaussian elimination, *131*
Gauss-Seidel method, *62*
GCD computation, *116*
Generalised AGE scheme, *12*
Grand leap process, *8*
Graphics tool, *40*
Gustafson speedup, *100*

Han-Powell algorithm, *203*
Helmholtz equation, *193*
Herglotz wave function, *196*

Homogeneous function, *214*
Homothety, *243*
Householder factorization, *92*
Huang algorithm, modified, *83*
Hyperbolic problem, *182*
Hypercube network, *91*

IKBS, *257*
ILU preconditioner, *103*
Incomplete Cholesky method, *66, 89,*
    176
Inertial Confinement Fusion (ICF), *170*
Inverse problem, *193*
Image processing application, *276*
Implicit LU factorization, *87, 103*
Implicit methods, *4*
ITPACK, *107*

Jacobi method, *61*

Koenig theorem, *119*

Lagrangian fluid code, *171*
Laser fusion code, *169*
LDU factorization, *217*
Least-squares smoothing, *238*
Levels of parallelism, *27*
Linear complementarity problem, *228*
Lisp, *251*
Load balancing, *4, 137*
Log-sum-algorithm, *33*
LU decomposition, *46*

Mapping strategies, *273*
Marching problem, *8*
Mathematical parallelism, *160*
Matrix update, *84*
Memory Access Pattern tool, *39*
Method of lines, *150*
Microtasking strategy, *160*
MIMD algorithm, *29*
Minimization algorithm, *213*
MINOS code, *227*
Multidimensional PDE, *17*
Multifrontal method, *79*
Multigrid, *35*

Multiprocessors,
    shared memory, *2, 133, 148*
    loosely coupled, *2*
Multistart algorithm, *265*
Multitasking, *51*

Navier-Stokes equation, *158*
Newton's method, *117*
NGOAL code, *227*
Nonlinear optimization, *202*
Numerical parallelism, *160*
Number theory problem, *276*

Objective function, *219*
OCCAM, *261*
Optimal power flow, *201*
Optimization algorithm, *226*
Ordinary differential equation, *7, 127*

Parabolic equation, *10*
Paracomputer, *26*
Parallel algorithms, *39*
Parallel complexity, *115*
Parallel FORTRAN, *51*
Parallel numerical algorithm, *29*
Parallelism,
    fine grain, *77*
    large grain, *84*
Partial differential equation, *34*
Partial elimination (PEL) method, *68*
Partial fraction decomposition, *116*
Partitioning, *4*
Peaceman-Rachford variant, *11*
Peano problem, *226*
Performance evaluation tool, *208*
PF compiler, *176*
Pipeline, *97*
Poisson-Equation, *35*
Polynomial evaluation, *8, 115*
Polynomial root-finding, *116*
Postprocessing graphics tool, *42*
PRAM model, *115*
Preconditioned biconjugate gradient, *75*
Preconditioned CG method, *35, 74, 105*
Preconditioning method, *63*
Production system, *252*

Prolog, *251*
Pseudo-spectral technique, *159*

QD algorithm, *121*
QR factorization, *92*
Quasi-Newton, *203*

Rank k correction, *87*
Recurrent relations, *31*
Recursive decoupling, *4*
Recursive doubling, *8, 30, 149*
Recursive Quadratic Programming, *202*
Richardson extrapolation technique, *145*
Robust optimization, *259*
Rosen Problems, *227*
Runge-Kutta method, *197*

SAXPY scheme, *107*
SCHEDULE package, *39*
Schittkowski method, *203*
Schur complement, *76*
Schwarz algorithm, *35*
Search vector, *84*
SHARED data management, *52*
Shared variables, *51*
SIMD algorithm, *29*
SOR-method, *35, 105*
Sparse matrix, *73*
Sparse triangular system, *108*
Sparsity pattern, *61*

Spectral collocation, *183*
Spectral method, *158*
Speedup, *100, 163*
Splitting method, *63*
Step by step process, *8*
Substructuring technique, *128*
Supercomputers, *27*
Symbolic computation, *253*
Systolic algorithm, *4, 20*
Systolic array, *23, 245*

Time advancing strategy, *166*
Toeplitz matrix, *237*
Transformation method, *64*
Transputer network, *261*
Tree-height-reduction, *30*
Turbulence simulation, *157*

Ultracomputer, *26*
Unconstrained minimization, *214*
Universal optimizer, *258*

Vectorization, *4, 103, 175*
Vector multiprocessor, *169*
Vector processing, *27, 207*
VLSI, *20*
Vortex method, *157*

Wavefront technique, *104*